David Hackett Souter

David Hackett Souter

Traditional Republican on the Rehnquist Court

TINSLEY E. YARBROUGH

OXFORD
UNIVERSITY PRESS

2005

OXFORD
UNIVERSITY PRESS

Oxford University Press, Inc., publishes works that further
Oxford University's objective of excellence
in research, scholarship, and education.

Oxford   New York
Auckland   Cape Town   Dar es Salaam   Hong Kong   Karachi
Kuala Lumpur   Madrid   Melbourne   Mexico City   Nairobi
New Delhi   Shanghai   Taipei   Toronto
With offices in
Argentina   Austria   Brazil   Chile   Czech Republic   France   Greece
Guatemala   Hungary   Italy   Japan   Poland   Portugal   Singapore
South Korea   Switzerland   Thailand   Turkey   Ukraine   Vietnam

Published by Oxford University Press, Inc.
198 Madison Avenue, New York, New York 10016

www.oup.com

Oxford is a registered trademark of Oxford University Press

Library of Congress Cataloging-in-Publication Data
Yarbrough, Tinsley E., 1941–
David Hackett Souter : traditional Republican on the Rehnquist
court / Tinsley E. Yarbrough.—1st cloth ed.
p.   cm.
Includes bibliographical references and index.
ISBN-13 978-0-19-515933-2
ISBN 0-19-515933-0
1. Souter, David H., 1939–   . 2. Judges—United States—Biography.
3. United States. Supreme Court—Biography. I. Souter, David H., 1939–   .
II. Title.
KF8745.S68Y37   2005
347.73'2634—dc22   2005002395

1 3 5 7 9 8 6 4 2
Printed in the United States of America
on acid-free paper

To

Ben and Jonah

Preface

—————

W HEN THE FIRST PRESIDENT BUSH chose David Hackett Souter to replace Justice William J. Brennan Jr. on the Supreme Court in 1990, commentators (with considerable justification) quickly dubbed the slender New Englander with the dark eyes and shy smile a "stealth candidate," after the Air Force bomber designed to evade even the most sophisticated surveillance technology. The Bush White House did not want a repeat of the 1987 debacle in which President Reagan's nomination of Robert Bork, the acerbic former Yale law professor whose well-documented and highly controversial views on abortion, sexual privacy, and other hot-button issues had provoked a firestorm of opposition, failed miserably. John Sununu, Bush's chief of staff, assured the president that Souter, Sununu's fellow New Hampshirite, would be a reliable addition to the Court's conservative bloc, yet, given his national obscurity, was unlikely to arouse much opposition in the confirmation process.

Souter's nomination did indeed confound the pundits. An undergraduate and law graduate of Harvard as well as a Rhodes scholar, the fifty-year-old nominee clearly possessed superb academic credentials. His professional career to that point, however, had provided him with virtually no national exposure or the controversy that public scrutiny often generates. After two years in private practice in Concord, he had worked for a decade in the New Hampshire attorney general's office, becoming the state's chief legal officer for the last two years of that tenure. He had then served as a state superior court (1978–83) and supreme court (1983–90) justice. His first appointment to a federal bench, a seat on the Court of Appeals for the First Circuit in Boston, had come only a few months before his nomination to the Supreme Court. Nor did he possess the paper trail of legal views that had helped to defeat Bork. Souter's only law review article was a tribute to another jurist, and he had made few speeches; in fact, those seeking off-the-bench reflections of his positions were forced to rely largely on a student thesis he had written years before on the positivism of Justice Oliver Wendell Holmes. The nominee clearly had an extensive public record but not the sort that journalists and potential opponents could easily uncover or exploit.

Souter's New Hampshire record on constitutional and related legal issues had also been generally conservative, yet was sufficiently mixed to create concern among both liberals and conservatives but without really alienating either group. As a hospital board member, for example, he had voted to approve a resolution permitting physicians to perform abortions at the facility. But on the New Hampshire Supreme Court, he expressed sympathy for physicians opposed to performing abortions, suggesting that they could keep faith with their religious and moral scruples by simply referring abortion patients to other doctors. In another case, he concluded that welfare officials violated due process when they placed a man's name on a list of child abusers without notice or opportunity to object. In 1988, however, he spoke for a unanimous court in overturning a rape conviction on the ground that the trial judge erroneously excluded evidence of the victim's sexually provocative public behavior before the incident. He also signed an advisory opinion concluding that the state could constitutionally prevent homosexuals from serving as adoptive or foster parents but objecting to a prohibition against their operating day care centers. While in the state attorney general's office, he had argued that New Hampshire could force residents to display the state motto, "Live Free or Die," on vehicle license plates—a stance the U.S. Supreme Court would later reject. In defending an archconservative New Hampshire governor's lowering of the flag to half-mast on Good Friday, he had reasoned that Jesus was a historical personage as well as a religious symbol. Early in his career as a state's attorney, he signed a brief supporting literacy tests for voters—a requirement Congress later banned nationwide. In a commencement speech, he referred to affirmative action programs as "affirmative discrimination," charging that racial quotas addressed a set of statistics, not an individual.

Souter's lifestyle generated further uncertainty regarding his likely performance as a justice. Liberals feared that the relatively reclusive bachelor and resident of a tiny New Hampshire village, who seemingly preferred books and solitary mountain hikes to people, might be insensitive to the explosive social issues the Court regularly confronted. Spokespersons for conservative groups expressed concern to the White House, on the other hand, that the president's bachelor nominee might conceivably be a homosexual.

In a masterful appearance before the Senate Judiciary Committee, Judge Souter largely disarmed liberals concerned that he might prove to be another Robert Bork. Bork had advanced a jurisprudence of original intent before the committee, rejecting the notion that the Constitution included within its meaning abortion rights or other liberties not mentioned in the document's text or specifically intended by its framers. Souter, by contrast, deftly avoided any appearance of such dogmatism. Although refusing to commit himself on the specific issue of abortion, the nominee assured committee members that his Constitution included room for privacy and other unenumerated rights. At one point, for example, he drew on the Ninth Amendment to the Bill of Rights, asserting that the enumeration of certain rights in the Constitution "was not intended to be in some sense exhaustive and in derogation of other [unlisted] rights retained" by the people. And while embracing "original meaning" as the core to constitutional construction, he made clear that he gave such notions a decidedly more flexible reading than others obviously did. "What I am searching for," he testified, "is the meaning, which in most cases is a principle, intended to be established [by a constitutional provision] as opposed simply to the specific application that the particular provision was meant to have and that was in the minds of those who proposed and framed and adopted it in the first place." In construing a constitutional provision, he asked, "do we ignore, essentially, the development of the law for the last 40, or 200 years? The answer is no; we don't deal with constitutional problems that way." Moreover, he effusively praised Justice Brennan, among the more expansive civil libertarian justices ever to serve on the high bench, predicting that Brennan would be remembered "as one of the most fearlessly principled guardians of the American Constitution that it has ever had and ever will have." When reminded of his criticisms of affirmative action, he expressed the hope that he had been misquoted.

Souter's praise of Brennan may have been somewhat disconcerting to his White House sponsors. But the affinity the nominee displayed for the jurisprudence of the second Justice John Marshall Harlan during the hearings should also have prompted at least some of them to question just what sort of justice their "stealth candidate" might ultimately prove to be. Harlan II, a Republican and Wall Street lawyer when President Eisenhower appointed him in 1955, was a frequent critic of Warren Court decisions that expanded the scope of civil liberties during his sixteen years on the high bench. But Harlan, like Souter, had also been a Rhodes scholar and was imbued with a flexible, evolving, context-based, essentially Anglo-American common law approach to legal issues, including the common law jurist's deep commitment even to those precedents with which he disagreed. Despite his generally conservative reputation on the Court, such a jurisprudence led Harlan, for example, to embrace the concept of an unenumerated right of privacy four years before the Court's recognition of such a guarantee in the *Griswold* case. Harlan also readily joined expansive civil liberties decisions firmly rooted in precedent, as well as the many rulings of the modern Supreme Court, leaving questions about the scope of national regulatory power in the economic field largely to the political arena and the voters rather than to the judiciary. Harlan, in short, was a traditional, northeastern Republican—quite different from the Reagan-Bush I brand of modern Republicanism and its zeal for undoing major Supreme Court precedents that had expanded civil liberties and the scope of national regulatory power over economic affairs and state governments. Souter was of that same stock.

Impressed by the nominee's Senate performance and convinced that Souter might be the best they could hope for from a Bush White House, only a few liberal interest groups and senators opposed his confirmation, which sailed through the Senate by a 90–9 vote. Assured by the White House that President George H. W. Bush had indeed hit a conservative "home run" with his first choice for the high Court, conservatives, with varying degrees of enthusiasm, endorsed the appointment as well.

Justice Souter's largely conservative first-term record on the bench suggested to some that the evolving, flexible, and, in many respects, expansive approach to civil liberties he had embraced before the judiciary committee was largely a pose, the result of extensive administration coaching rather than personal commitment. In subsequent terms, however, the justice established an increasingly liberal voting record, allying much more regularly with Justices Stevens, Ginsburg, and Breyer—the current Court's moderately liberal bloc—than with the chief justice and Justices Scalia and Thomas on the right. He has become, for example, the Court's most ardent defender of precedents requiring church-state separation against those seeking greater government accommodation of religion, while also taking a leading role in efforts to reaffirm and, in some instances, expand the right of privacy, as well as affirmative action precedents in higher education and elections. Arguably, he has also been the most effective critic of the growing body of significant and controversial rulings in which Chief Justice Rehnquist and Justices Scalia and Thomas, joined by Justices O'Connor and Kennedy, have challenged congressional authority over the states, broadly construed the takings clause (the Fifth Amendment guarantee forbidding government taking of private property for a public use without just compensation), embraced expansive notions of state immunity from lawsuits—even those designed to secure enforcement of supreme federal law—and otherwise abandoned long-entrenched precedents. Most important, perhaps, Souter has assumed the mantle of Justice Harlan, becoming the principal Rehnquist Court opponent of the originalist, text-bound Constitution embraced by Robert Bork in the Senate and by Justices Scalia and Thomas, as well as the chief justice to a more limited degree, on the high bench.

This book examines the life, career, and jurisprudence of one of the Rehnquist Court's most intriguing justices—a jurist whose firm regard for precedent, even liberal decisions of the Warren and Burger Court eras with which he may have personally disagreed, has driven him in decidedly different directions from most other Reagan-Bush I appointees to the Supreme Court. During a time of change on the Court, the story of Justice Souter's role and impact seems particularly timely.

This book would not have been possible without the assistance of many individuals and institutions. The East Carolina University Research/Creative Activities Committee provided vital financial support. Many of Justice Souter's friends and others associated with his life and career generously shared their reminiscences in recorded interviews. The staff of the Manuscript Division of the Library of Congress was of invaluable assistance, as were personnel of the New Hampshire State Library, New Hampshire Historical Society, New Hampshire Supreme Court, and Concord Public Library. I am particularly grateful to my superb Oxford editor, Dedi Felman. Whatever this book's ultimate merit, her close reading of the manuscript and excellent suggestions substantially improved its quality. Once again, Cynthia Manning Smith furnished flawless clerical assistance. Cindy retired recently; things will never be the same around here without her encouragement, friendship, skill, and total dedication to East Carolina University. Finally, of course, I am sustained in all my efforts by the love of Mary Alice; our son, Cole, and daughter, Sarah; Sarah's husband, Todd; and the lights of our lives, Ben and Jonah, to whom "Gramps" affectionately dedicates this book.

Contents

David Hackett Souter

I

New England Yankee

D AVID SOUTER WAS expected for lunch at the home of his Concord, New Hampshire, friends Ronald and Mary Ellen Snow. The Supreme Court's fall term had not yet begun, and the justice regularly delayed his return to Washington as long as possible, leaving New Hampshire only a few days before the Court's first conference in late September. But earlier that morning, September 11, 2001, terrorists had launched their horrendous attacks on New York and Washington; Mary Ellen Snow seriously doubted their guest would appear. "Mary Ellen called me at the office that day, assuming that David wouldn't be coming," Ron Snow later recalled with a smile. "And I said, 'You better have lunch ready, because he'll show up.' I went home at a quarter of twelve and at noon David drove into the yard. When we asked him how he got away from the [marshal at his Concord chambers], he said, 'It was simple; I didn't tell them I was going.' He had gone to the florist's and picked up a pot of flowers, and we sat on the side porch of our house. Mary Ellen put up a screen so no one would see him, and we had a long, lovely lunch."[1]

Thus, while much of the nation's officialdom attempted to cope with the 9/11 disaster, anxious about possible further attacks on national institutions and leaders, one member of one of the nation's most powerful bodies eluded the security efforts of his own court staff in order to enjoy a quiet meal with friends. As much as any other, that single incident captures the intensely independent spirit and strong regional attachments that have distinguished Justice Souter and his judicial record.

David Souter's historical roots reflect a mix of nineteenth-century mill and Scottish ancestry and colonial Yankee stock. His great-grandfather James Souter had come from Scotland in the 1850s, part of a large group recruited to work in an Andover, Massachusetts, flax mill. The justice's grandfather Joseph M. Souter and his wife, Lizzie MacLauglan, lived in Melrose, Massachusetts,

3

for many years, where he worked as a blacksmith and foreman for the Boston and Maine Railroad. Both of the justice's mother's parents, however, had an impressive lineage. His mother's ancestors included several *Mayflower* passengers, immigrants of royal descent, and forebears of Presidents Fillmore, Grant, Hoover, Coolidge, Franklin Roosevelt, Nixon, Ford, and Bush. John B. Allen, Souter's great-great-grandfather, played a pivotal role at the 1860 Republican National Convention. A member of the New York delegation, which had voted as a unit for native son William H. Seward, Allen bolted and voted for Abraham Lincoln, beginning his delegation's shift to the Great Emancipator, who would win nomination on the third ballot. Souter's family apparently also had a part in the Underground Railroad movement.[2]

Souter's taciturn, mild-mannered father, Joseph Alexander Souter, was born in Melrose, a small town situated a few miles north of Boston, in 1904. His mother, Helen Adams Hackett, was born in nearby Wakefield in 1908. Her father, Frank Henry Hackett, a Boston native and Wakefield pharmacist whose father and mother were natives of Vermont and Maine, served as chairman of Wakefield's board of selectmen and as local postmaster from 1923 to 1934. A Spanish-American War veteran, he was for ten years also the *Boston Herald's* Wakefield correspondent.[3]

"Aunt Harriett"

But a distant relative whom Souter affectionately refers to as "Aunt Harriett" would exert perhaps the greatest influence on his life. Born in Lowell, Massachusetts, in 1897, Harriett Moulton Bartlett was the daughter of Henry Bartlett, a mechanical engineer and superintendent of the Boston and Maine Railroad (1900–1918), for which Souter's grandfather worked. Raised in a large Cambridge home with two maids, Harriett might have elected a life of leisurely pursuits. Instead, the politically conservative but socially progressive young woman graduated Phi Beta Kappa from Vassar and took a master's degree in sociology from the University of Chicago. A pioneer in medical social work at Boston's Massachusetts General Hospital, she served as a Simmons College professor and director of its medical social work program from 1948 to 1957, devoting much of her energy thereafter to the activities of the National Association of Social Workers. Well before her 1987 death in Cambridge, she had become the recipient of numerous awards for her professional accomplishments.[4]

A tall, strikingly handsome, fiercely independent, and vigorous woman who continued to enjoy swims in Boston's Charles River even late in life, Harriett Bartlett, like Justice Souter, never married. But she invariably became—and insisted on being—the center of attention wherever she happened to be. David Souter "worshipped this woman," according to Melvin Levine, a close friend of Souter's from their time at Oxford together as Rhodes scholars. Bartlett's every activity captured Souter's attention, Levine has recalled. "Aunt Harriett, for example, at the beginning of every winter would have her car put up on blocks. This was a major ritual. He would receive word that Aunt Harriett's car was now up on blocks!"[5]

In October 1961, early in Souter's tenure at Oxford, Bartlett visited England for a professional meeting. One evening she invited Souter, Levine, and two of their friends for sherry and coffee at her hotel. "It was a command performance," Levine recalls. "We all, of course, lined up, and [David] was so excited." Later, while Levine was in medical school at Harvard and Souter was attending law school there, Levine invited David and Bartlett to his apartment. "And I received all kinds of emergency phone calls from [David] about just how we had to get ready for the visit." Because Aunt Harriett, Souter assured his friend, would eat only Goldfish crackers, he insisted they go out and find a package. "When she walked into my apartment, she did not have her coat off before asking, 'Have you "Goldfish" crackers?' . . . And, of course, we had to have sherry, and just her kind of sherry, which we had also prepared for. He wanted Scotch, so I had to pretend to pour him a glass of sherry so Aunt Harriett would think we were drinking sherry. These kinds of manipulations about Aunt Harriett went on all the time!"[6]

Once, on a visit to his friend's home in the village of East Weare, New Hampshire—"the 'Ham,' as [Souter] called it"—Levine met Souter's parents. "His mother was this wonderful woman—exactly the opposite of him [in demeanor]. She was this unpretentious, all-American woman that you would see on a soap opera and in no way bore any resemblance to him. Her speech in no way had his sort of sophisticated lilt to it. She just seemed like someone who would be selling Ivory soap on the radio, just an all-American woman. You just never would have pictured her being his mother. Aunt Harriett [on the other hand] fit the bill."[7]

Levine was convinced that Souter had adopted his speech and mannerisms largely from Aunt Harriett. The future justice even took pride in the fact that Harriett's father, Henry Bartlett, "was one of the first people in New England to lose all his money. [David] always went around boasting that to him the really prestige family was the one that had lost all its money the earliest. I think he wanted more than anything else to represent the true old New England. And I think that sort of symbolized it for him. And it's why [at that point in his life] we had to call him Hackett, because the Souters were not really a very old, well-established family, but the Hacketts were."[8]

Childhood

Harriett Bartlett's professional prominence and social standing undoubtedly impressed David Souter and probably stimulated his own drive to succeed in life. But whatever his fascination with Aunt Harriett, her family, and its social position, or her impact on his personality and life, he was a devoted only child to his parents.

Helen Souter's first marriage, to Harold B. Cheever in 1928, produced no children and ended in divorce. On September 3, 1938, she and Joseph Souter were married in Wakefield. A year later, on September 17, 1939, David was born in Melrose, where Joseph had found employment in a bank. The family would live in Melrose until David was eleven. But at her father's death in 1946, Helen had inherited her parents' farmhouse on Cilley Hill Road in East Weare, New Hampshire, where she had lived for a time in the 1930s between marriages. When Joseph Souter's physician suggested that he seek a more relaxed lifestyle, the family moved to the East Weare house, and Joseph became assistant treasurer of the New Hampshire Savings Bank in nearby Concord.[9]

At the time the Souters moved to East Weare, the village included several dozen homes, a gristmill, and two churches. Quickly accepted by the community as friendly neighbors and good citizens, the Souters maintained a handsome flower garden and a house that was quickly filled with books and antiques. The family faithfully attended services at the village's Holy Cross Episcopal Church, then located in a small wooden building down the hill from their house. Helen Souter was a member of the church's ladies' auxiliary, her husband a vestryman. In the 1950s, the federal government created a flood control district and dam on the Piscataquog River, and much of the village, though not the Souters' house, was displaced. When the flood control project forced the closing of the family's Weare church for many years, the family began attending the St. Andrews congregation in the nearby village of Hopkinton.[10]

David Souter's life growing up in East Weare was in many ways like that of most boys raised in a rural or small-town environment. He reportedly enjoyed swimming and hiking and occasionally dangling garden snakes in the faces of startled female playmates. Like many such schools, the village grammar school he attended had only ten or twelve students to a class. Unlike his classmates, however, David enjoyed talking about antiques with the proprietress of Yesterday's, an antique shop near his home. When he was old enough to drive, he drove her to area auctions. "He always had his nose in a book," more than one neighbor would later remark. Deeply religious, he was not only an altar boy, but also taught a Sunday School class. "We all went to church because our parents made us," a close male friend remembered; "David went because he wanted to. . . . He was very proper. He never swore. We were all trying to be macho; he never seemed to feel that need."[11]

Both in grammar school and at Concord High School, Souter excelled academically, developing close and enduring relationships with a number of his teachers. His Latin teacher Lillian Grossman recalls an exceptional student. At one point while David was in her class, a friend getting a doctorate at a London university asked her to translate a treatise in Latin about London sewers. Grossman assigned the task to Souter and Ruth Ferreira (who now goes by her married name, Houghton), another outstanding student. "My God, you should have seen the job he did! It was as if it were beginning Latin. It was unbelievable!" Souter, Grossman remembers, was "extremely smart. Very quiet, very reflective. He would think before he spoke." Nor would he forget his teachers after graduation. When Lillian Grossman married after his appointment to the Supreme Court, her former student sent her a beautiful silver bowl as a wedding gift, then invited her and her husband for a visit to his chambers in Concord during the Court's summer recess. The justice also nominated a favorite English teacher, Richard O. ("Doc") Blanchard, for a teaching award conferred by Harvard on secondary school teachers. But he also enjoyed sparring with certain teachers. When an English instructor returned one of his papers with the remark that it was "only good for wrapping fish," he promptly assured her that he was "not accustomed to wrapping fish in 20-bond paper, thank you."[12]

Described by more than one classmate as a bookworm who often completed class assignments weeks in advance, Souter obviously relished the classics of literature most students merely endured. Intrigued by a passing comment about the archaeology of ancient Troy, he once produced an unassigned research paper on a German archaeologist. "There was no question about doing a mundane assignment," a teacher remembered at the time of his Supreme Court appointment. "He pursued it to the nth degree." After school each day, he went to the public library to wait for the return trip to Weare with his father, devouring book after book in the library stacks. On at least one occasion, he was apparently asked to leave the nearby New Hampshire State Library for monopolizing a section of the reading room there.[13]

Other students were not entirely certain what to make of their Weare classmate. When David arrived at school carrying a large leather briefcase, several students immediately dubbed him "Suitcase Soutie." He took such good-natured taunts with a smile and was genuinely friendly and popular with most classmates. But he could also be patronizing, especially with female students. "He was apt to call us by our surnames," Ruth Houghton remembers, and often used words "he was pretty sure we wouldn't understand, just to see the look of confusion and confoundment on our faces."[14]

Souter had no romances in high school, and Houghton does not recall seeing him at school mixers. But another classmate, Vicki McLaughlin Maiben, remembers that he had dates for school dances and took a close friend of hers to an important prom. David, Maiben recalls, was "very fun-loving, very warm, a very good, loyal friend." She socialized often with him and a group of friends. Helen Souter was primarily a housewife and gracious hostess for her son's friends, despite her working several years as a salesperson in the dress department of the Harry G. Emmons department store, where at least one summer David worked in the shipping department. Vicki Maiben and several of David's other classmates often met at the Souter home in Weare. "There couldn't have been a more lovely, warm woman than Helen Souter. Mr. Souter was also very, very nice. But mostly he'd be off reading or doing whatever else men do. Mrs. Souter was the one who was with us, and whatever refreshments we had [she provided]. Mostly we talked and joked and laughed. I remember a lot of times talking about literature and books. Good conversation. Whenever you went to David's, you would have good conversation and just a wonderful feeling of comradery and fellowship—he was just fantastic. And laughing—I remember lots of laughing because of his wit and others responding to him."[15]

Souter was very fond of classical music, especially Bach organ compositions. He and Vicki Maiben attended Sunday afternoon organ recitals at St. Paul's School, a private Concord academy. The two enjoyed poetry as well. Souter even penned doggerel of his own. For her eighteenth birthday, Maiben asked David to write a poem in her honor. "For Vicki born in early May," he began, "what fitting tribute can I pay? I speak only of thy beauty, in lines affectionately from 'Soutie.'" When Maiben decided to convert to the Mormon faith and attend Utah's Brigham Young University, David was sympathetic—

although amazed that she would wish to leave New England for the West. Even then, she has remarked, he was "an inveterate Yankee. The woods, the farmland, the countryside—that's where his heart was, and is. He's basically a country boy. That's not right; he's not a country boy. But his heart is in New Hampshire." Souter attempted to persuade Maiben to remain in New England; before she left for what he called the "wild, wild West," he bought her a copy of John Greenleaf Whittier's *Snowbound*.[16]

By his senior year at Concord High School, Souter had compiled not only an impressive academic record but a long list of extracurricular activities as well. Ruth Houghton, who went on to complete a Radcliffe degree in three years, edged out David as valedictorian of the class of 1957. Souter was salutatorian. Coeditor with Houghton of the school yearbook, *The Syb*, he was also a reporter on the student newspaper, president of the National Honor Society chapter, Student Council member, and included in the yearbook superlatives section as the male "most likely to succeed," "most sophisticated," and "most literary." Other entries described him as "Devilish, Honorable, Swell," "degenerate," "witty and in constant demand," as well as someone who "enjoys giving and attending scandalous parties." According to a classmate, he and others had also formed the Sinister Sons of the Somnolent Sagacity, a secret society of school pranksters. Although a serious student, he clearly displayed a wit that would later ingratiate him with his Supreme Court colleagues.[17]

But yearbook photographs picture a slight, studious-appearing Souter sporting a crew cut; his memberships included Concord High's Traffic Squad, recently formed to maintain orderly class changes; and he was described as "dislik[ing] presidents of organizations who don't conduct orderly meetings." As a reporter for the *Crimson Review*, the student newspaper, he had contributed an article entitled "What's My Line?" He wrote, "To prepare us for such a question, the Guidance Department of Concord High School, one of the outstanding schools in the country in the field of guidance and help in vocational choice, has instituted an intensive program affecting each one of us."[18] Asked years later if Souter, however popular he may have been with his classmates, might have been described today as a "nerd," Houghton quickly retorted, "Well, you just look at that picture in the yearbook and you tell me. . . . We did not put our studies first, and it was obvious that he did."[19]

His classmates also considered Souter a person with a high sense of moral rectitude. The 1957 yearbook's prophecy section took the form of a 1975 newspaper issue. An entry on Souter and his close friend James Prowse drew on the future justice's continuing interest in the Episcopal priesthood and

Peyton Place, New Hampshire housewife Grace Metalious's steamy 1956 novel about life in a fictional New England community. "Bishop David H. Souter, high-ranking member of the clergy," the item read, "has announced author John Prowse's recent novel *Waitin' Place* as unfit for good Christians to read." The "novel" had already sold 8 million copies, breaking "all best-seller records . . . and net[ting] author Prowse $700,000 in motion picture royalties." Meanwhile, "Bishop Souter's salary amounts to $4,800 annually."[20]

Harvard

Concord native Harris Berman was a member of Concord High School's 1956 graduating class. Son of the proprietor of a plumbing and heating supply business, Berman attended Harvard as an undergraduate and medical school at Columbia before going on to head a number of HMOs, including the Tufts Health Plan in Massachusetts. Of 180 in Berman's high school class, he has recalled, only thirty attended college; the rest of his classmates "got married and went to work. . . . So the few kids who were intellectual you really got to know." He and David Souter were in different classes and social circles, but Berman knew Souter largely by reputation as "head and shoulders above everybody else in his class." He was hardly surprised when the future justice enrolled at Harvard in the fall of 1957.[21]

In Cambridge, Souter and Berman lived in different houses and again had different friends. But Souter hitched rides to and from college with Berman, who had no doubt that his friend would develop an outstanding academic record. Souter did not disappoint, graduating Phi Beta Kappa and magna cum laude with a major in philosophy. He also joined the Hasty Pudding Club and worked at the Phillips Brooks House, Harvard's oldest and largest public service organization. Every Sunday, he visited his Aunt Harriett and attended services faithfully at the Society of St. John the Evangelist (SSJE) monastery.[22]

While at Harvard, Souter had decided to pursue a career in law rather than theology. In a newspaper interview at the time of his 1976 appointment as New Hampshire's attorney general, he attributed his decision to a Harvard reading assignment, an influential series of lectures on the Bill of Rights by federal appeals court judge Learned Hand. Souter termed the lectures, published the year after his high school graduation, "a beautiful exposition of the importance of classic judicial restraint in the construction of the Bill of Rights." "I read it and reread it," he said, "and from that came my fatal commitment to the law. And with that commitment a philosophy of constitutional constriction on the law." Broad interpretations of written law, he warned, threatened public acceptance of judicial decisions and thus the law's social foundation. "The more we allow language to be debased, the more free-swinging we are in our interpretation of legal language, the greater risk we run of having the public perceive our actions as arbitrary and personal, not grounded in the constitutional process."23

Souter never embraced Hand's extreme deference to political judgments or his conception of the Constitution's provisions as mere admonitions rather than commands. Certainly Souter's record on the U.S. Supreme Court is hardly consistent with Hand's jurisprudence. At Harvard, however, Souter's growing interest in the law appeared to be accompanied by a suspicion of judicial power, especially judicial interpretations founded on moral and ethical precepts or notions of social utility rather than legal language. His senior honors thesis in philosophy examined the legal positivism of Justice Oliver Wendell Holmes, another apostle of judicial self-restraint, albeit one more amenable than Hand would be to judicial intervention on behalf of civil liberties. As is typical of undergraduate students, even those who are unusually gifted, Souter largely discussed debates between positivists and natural lawyers over the relationship of law to morals and related questions without ever assuming a clear position of his own.24

Oxford

In the fall of his junior year, Souter interviewed for the Rhodes scholarship. Concord attorney Malcolm McLane, a former recipient, was then serving as secretary to the New Hampshire Rhodes committee and also sat on the six-state New England regional selection committee. Over the years, McLane and his wife, Susan, were to become Souter's close friends. At that time, however, McLane did not know David, although he knew his father as an official with the New Hampshire Savings Bank. Souter, he recalls, was "a knockout" in the interviews. "He was very self-collected, amiable, relaxed, obviously very intelligent, had been very active—all this from a rather limited background in Weare, New Hampshire." State committees were obliged to pare thirty or forty candidates to two, regional committees from twelve to four. "You arrive [for the regional interviews] knowing nothing about the other applicants other than the two from your state. . . . And we spent Friday—or did in those days—from noon on reviewing the files before we met with [the candidates] briefly for cocktails. . . . We tried not to make any prejudgment. . . .

But when it's over, and the kids are all gone, and they've been told to come back at a certain time, you start to talk like a jury. . . . And, inevitably, one of the techniques of selection is [to ask], 'Is there anybody on your list that everybody agrees has got to be in [his or her] top four?' David came out tops both in the state committee and in the New England committee against some very tough competition."[25]

Souter's Rhodes class of thirty-two Americans left for Oxford in the fall of 1961. In those days, the contingent traveled by ship, with the voyage requiring four or five days. David Wilkinson, son of the president of Brigham Young University, was in that group. "I got on that ship with these other boys who had attended Yale and Harvard and [other] very top prestige schools academically. And I was really out of my element, I could tell. I regarded David and some others as sort of fitting the stereotype image I then had of a New Englander. He certainly was well-mannered—I hate to use the word 'aristocratic.' But to my way of thinking, he and others were in that mold."[26]

Although they were to become very close friends during their days at Oxford, Melvin Levine had a similar initial impression of the future justice. A Long Island native and Brown undergraduate, Levine had met Souter during Rhodes interviews in Boston. "I found him to be rather daunting. When I met him, he was kind of holding forth among a group of other Harvard types, and pontificating. And I was put off by him . . . by his rhetoric and his perhaps overly self-assured demeanor. But that was only a first impression."[27]

At Oxford, Souter was a student in Magdalen College, one of the venerable university's oldest (founded 1458) and most distinguished colleges. Oxford's original medieval buildings surround a cloister quadrangle, but Souter's lodging was in the adjacent, neoclassical New Buildings, first constructed in the eighteenth century. Students occasionally attended lectures but primarily studied with tutors; Magdalen's law tutors included some of the leading British scholars of the day, among them Rupert Cross, John H. C. Morris, and Gunther Treitel. Students typically were assigned one or two tutors each eight-week term. In a first meeting with a tutor, they would be assigned cases, treatises, or other material and told to write a paper based on their reading. The next week they read their paper aloud to their tutors for their comments and criticism. "And you did that," one Magdalen College student remembered, "every week for the eight weeks of the term. . . . It was a wonderful experience, because . . . they were the outstanding scholars of their field. And you had them one-on-one for an hour a week."[28]

Initially, Souter apparently had some difficulty adjusting to Oxford. When

Harriett Bartlett visited there for a professional meeting soon after his arrival, she noted in an October 9 entry of her diary, "David Souter turned up for late tea here at [the] Hotel. . . . A bit blue about [his] situation and living conditions. Hasn't found a tut[or] at Magdalen yet!" The following Saturday, they had spent an entire "lovely" day driving through the countryside. But on a tour of Magdalen the next day, she found his rooms noisy, his fireplace "blocked up [and a] small heater," adding, "He has no teapot yet, but later told me how tea-drinking came natural [there], even with American friends." Several days later, however, she wrote in her diary, "Things [were] going better with [David] now. [He] has seen his tutor and is working hard."[29]

Souter received a first in jurisprudence his two years at Oxford, a mark reserved for a small percentage of students. He also apparently enjoyed an active social life. After an unpromising start, he and Melvin Levine became close friends. Souter was unduly conservative politically for Levine; in fact, deciding that it might be unseemly for someone with a Jewish name to have such a conservative friend, Levine jokingly changed his name to "Ralph Waldo Bronson." "To this day," he remarked years later, "I call him Hackett, and he calls me Bronson." But while Souter made it clear that he had no use for President John F. Kennedy and his administration, he rarely talked about current politics, preferring instead to discuss Justice Holmes and other prominent figures of the past.

Whatever Souter's image with some of his high school classmates, Levine found him "an awful lot of fun to be with. . . . He was the life of the party, and he insisted on being the life of the party. He would hold forth with his little glass of Scotch in one corner and would always attract an audience. . . . He was a very conscientious student, but not what people at the time would have called a 'grind.' He still could relax and have a good time. He loved being witty, and he was incredibly witty—just a marvelous sense of humor."[30]

Just as in high school, however, that hardly meant that Souter was everybody's friend. "He had a way of taking people," Levine soon sensed, "and making them either his close confidants and friends or his worst enemies. And there were not a lot of people in between. So he spent a lot of time avoiding people that he couldn't stand. But if you were in his good graces, he was a wonderful and loyal friend. . . . I don't think he alienated people very much; I think he was alienated by some people. Certain kinds of people turned him off. People he felt were phonies. He really believed in genuineness [and didn't like people who] were insincere or weren't very profound. He loved intellectuals; that was very important to him."[31]

Souter had dated several women during college, law school, and afterward. His principal romantic interest in college was Ann Grant, daughter of a New Hampshire superior court judge, whom he had known since high school. "The whole time we were at Oxford," Melvin Levine has said, "he was talking about Miss Grant—he called her 'Miss Grant.' . . . He was very infatuated with her. . . . He had her pictures all over the place." Souter apparently had not known Grant well in high school, but she and his friend Vicki McLaughlin Maiben played violin in orchestra; perhaps with Maiben's encouragement, Souter and Grant began dating while he was a Harvard undergraduate. The two fell in love, but their relationship eventually ended. "David was always the person," Maiben suggests, for whom "everything had to be in order. He would not consider a marriage or a long-term relationship until things [presumably his education and establishment of a career] were finished. And I think Ann was ready to move on when she graduated and was ready to settle down. That basically, as I recall, was what ended the relationship." "I think it was mutual," Melvin Levine has said. "I think that maybe over time at Oxford [David] so idealized the relationship that no [actual] relationship could ever live up to it." At the time of Souter's Supreme Court nomination, Ann Grant Stanley told a reporter, "I don't recall talking about not seeing each other [any longer]. We just didn't see each other."[32]

To win a Rhodes without some evidence of athletic prowess was quite an accomplishment, yet Souter and Levine "were two of the worst athletes in the history of the scholarships." When they got to Oxford, they quickly realized they "were surrounded with all these American jocks." Feeling not a little intimidated, they decided to take up a sport and chose squash, although neither had the slightest idea what the game involved. Once on the court, neither could hit the ball. Levine is left-handed, but Souter told dubious onlookers that his friend was an American squash champion playing with his left hand simply to reduce his competitive advantage on the court. Finally, Levine recalls, "we decided that we would just hang the rackets above our fireplaces, so that people coming into the rooms would assume that we were athletic."[33]

During one six-week vacation, the two toured Europe by car. Getting the provincial New Englander to make the trip had been a chore in itself, and Levine found the experience both amusing and frustrating. "He had a hard time accepting Europe. When we were in Paris on the Champs-Elysées, he said, 'I just have no idea why people come here when they can go to Commonwealth Avenue [in Boston].' . . . He kept comparing everything to

Boston, and of course nothing could compare to Boston. He was also very concerned that people in Europe didn't speak English. And his major strategy was to talk louder to them. He felt it was really unacceptable that these people were speaking in these foreign tongues! . . . His provincialism about New Hampshire in particular would sometimes be grating when I was trying to admire some of the old European sights. . . . But I think in the long run he certainly had a good time."[34]

The "Stealth" Law Student

After completing a bachelor's degree at Oxford in 1963, Souter returned to his beloved New England for law school at Harvard. He and Levine, who enrolled in Harvard's medical school, saw each other often during their years in Cambridge. "We used each other," Levine has said, "to get away from our peers. I was sick of being with medical students all day, and he was tired of being with law students. We used to have dinner many times a week, and we would spend weekends going to parties or doing other things. . . . [We were part of] a little clique of former Oxonians in Cambridge and Boston for a couple of years. And we would all get together."[35] While at Harvard, Souter dated Ellanor Stengel Fink, a Wheaton College student he met shortly after returning from Oxford.

When the first President Bush nominated Souter for a Supreme Court seat, most of his law classmates, unlike Levine, apparently had little memory of him. Robert L. Brinton, one of the founders of the Lexis-Nexis law database and its general counsel for years, was in Souter's class. When a lawyer at the New York firm of Sullivan and Cromwell contacted Brinton in connection with the American Bar Association's investigation of the nominee's credentials, Brinton was obliged to respond, "I would be delighted to tell you anything that I could report. But . . . I honestly don't remember ever seeing David Souter raise his hand in class."[36] At a class reunion several months later, few of Souter's classmates had any vivid recollections of the new justice. Some even joked that perhaps he had been getting a PhD at Yale while obtaining a law degree at Harvard. Brinton recalls the stark contrast between the extremely reserved Souter and another of their classmates, Laurence Tribe, who was to become a distinguished Harvard professor and prominent member of the Supreme Court bar whose name would regularly appear on short lists of potential justices. "As soon as you would slip in making any kind of recitation, or making any kind of response in class, [Tribe's] hand would shoot up, and he would just be on the edge of his seat to destroy you, if he could. He loved class participation; he loved to hear himself talk. He still does. . . . But David Souter was entirely the opposite. He was very private."[37]

During his second and third years, Souter served as a house proctor and freshman adviser. One of his fellow proctors had a decidedly different recollection of the future justice from most of his contemporaries. At the time of Souter's nomination, R. Eden Martin, a Chicago lawyer and Democrat, shared his memories with the *Chicago Tribune*. Souter and Martin overlapped two years (1964–66) in law school. As proctors, they lived in the freshman residence halls providing personal and academic counseling as well as making certain that college rules were followed. Their rooms were in adjacent entries at Straus Hall, a freshman dormitory at the corner of Harvard Yard. Martin suspected that Souter might not have been well-known among law students because proctors lived and ate in the residence halls. He also disputed press reports of Souter as unduly bookish and antisocial. Martin readily agreed that Souter had "a first-rate mind—and that in addition to law, he is widely read in history, literature and philosophy." But he disputed the notion that "at Harvard he let his legal studies or his intellect interfere with his social life. Souter loved a party, and dated a number of intelligent and attractive women. Also, no one was quicker at the end of the day to put aside the books, start a fire, uncork a bottle of Scotch (usually cheap) and launch a conversation on virtually any subject. No one in the Yard was a better talker and no one had more interesting things to say."[38]

To Martin, a midwesterner, Harvard at that time "seemed disproportionately populated by students from wealthy Eastern families and prep school backgrounds." Souter had a New England background, excellent educational credentials, and, in Martin's judgment, "easy entry to the more rarefied social circles." But the future justice "did not tie himself to any narrow social group. His family was far from wealthy, and he had attended a small public school rather than a prep school." Perhaps for that reason, Souter "had a natural ability to sense when his freshman advisees had problems and a relaxed way of making them comfortable and offering advice." A dean who supervised their section of Harvard Yard, Martin added, had said that Souter showed "compassion and understanding" in his role as proctor.[39]

Souter had remained a devout Episcopalian, attending services regularly at the monastery of the Society of St. John the Evangelist in Cambridge. John L. McCausland, one of the law school classmates Souter invited to attend services with him, would become an Episcopal priest after years of law practice in Chicago and later serve as rector of the Holy Cross Episcopal congregation Souter had attended as a child. But Souter was hardly insular with respect to religion. His closest personal friends among law student proctors were an Irish Catholic and a Jewish student from New York.[40]

Martin also speculated about Souter's failure to make law review at Harvard:

> Personally, I do not doubt that he could have. He was at the top of his class in college and won the Rhodes Scholarship. No one who knows him doubts his unusual intellectual gifts.
>
> I think the answer lies in large part in his values. The law school was full of smart people, competing to get the best grades in order to qualify for clerkships or positions with top firms and companies. In this competitively charged environment, David Souter was less compulsive about grade competition than anyone I know. He had already proved himself academically. . . . Also, he had no interest in working on Wall Street or La Salle Street.
>
> I remember him saying several times, only half in jest, that he intended to go back home, practice law and raise pigs. Money may not have been totally irrelevant, but it ranked pretty low on his personal priority list. Besides, being a grind would have interfered with his social life. So Souter studied what he enjoyed, did very well when he worked at it, and somehow managed to do well enough even when he was not fully engaged by the subject.[41]

Orr and Reno

Souter finished law school in 1966. He had registered for the draft in 1957 but obtained a student deferment during his undergraduate, Oxford, and law school years. Following graduation from law school, he would normally have faced a tour of military duty, especially given the U.S. presence in Southeast Asia. His left leg is slightly shorter than his right, however, so he was reclassified 1-Y in 1966 and exempted from service.[42]

Souter kept his promise to go back home and practice law—if not to raise pigs. In 1965, he served as a summer associate in the Boston firm of Nutter, McLennen and Fish. After his first year of law school, however, he had been a summer associate at Orr and Reno, a Concord firm. The summer in Boston may have helped to convince him that he preferred to pursue a career in the relatively rustic environment of Concord and Weare rather than in New England's largest city. After law school, he became an associate at Orr and Reno.[43]

Although its institutional history dates back to 1847, Orr and Reno's modern roots go back to 1946, when Dudley Orr and Robert Reno returned from World War II to head the firm. In 1952, they were joined by Malcolm McLane, whose father was senior partner of a prominent firm in nearby Manchester and who had served as secretary of New Hampshire's Rhodes selection committee. McLane was not involved in Souter's hiring, which Orr and Reno's senior partners handled. He remembers, however, that "we all gave the green light to David as a genial guy who would fit in."[44]

In those days, the firm numbered fewer than a dozen lawyers. "Concord was then a town of about thirty thousand," McLane recalls. "It was the state capital; it had all the courts from the federal courts down, and the state house and the legislature and all the bureaucracies." But Orr and Reno's practice was then no different from any other small-town practice. "Every new young lawyer was sent out to do the chores, so to speak. To the Registry of Deeds, to the probate court."[45]

The firm did some pro bono work. In fact, in his opening statement at his Senate confirmation hearing, Souter testified that "the first day I ever spent by myself in a courtroom I spent . . . representing a woman whose personal life had become such a shambles that she had lost the custody of her children, and she was trying to get them back." He added, "She was not the last of such clients. I represented clients with domestic relations problems who lived sometimes, it seemed to me, in appalling circumstances. I can remember representing a client who was trying to pull her life together after being evicted because she couldn't pay the rent."[46]

Much of the firm's work consisted of civil matters, including corporate law and taxation, wage and hour issues, and real estate, as well as probate and trust advice and administration. But most of Souter's limited trial experience in the firm was criminal rather than civil. He tried four nonjury cases—two as solo attorney, one as lead counsel, and one as an associate to a senior member of the firm. His first opportunity to try a case solo in a superior court, New Hampshire's major trial division, was an automobile collision case, in which he successfully represented a defendant based on a claim of the plaintiff's contributory negligence. "I had reason, despite my over-preparation," he later wrote, "to be grateful for the court's patience, and with equal thankfulness I remember the opposing counsel, and even the opposing party, for providing that first chance for me to stand up in a courtroom all by myself."[47]

In the most significant litigation with which the young attorney was connected, Souter assisted Ronald Snow, a Yale law graduate who had joined Orr and Reno in 1961. That case, encompassing a number of suits, involved claims against the Franconia Paper Company for pollution of the Pemigewassett River. The federal government had ordered the mill, an Orr and Reno client, to cease dumping untreated waste into the river by a certain date, and firms and residents along the river filed suits against the mill. In one case, plaintiffs sought to recover for damage to house paint caused by atmospheric sulfur dioxide released from river waste. Because at least one other major polluter might have been responsible for the damage, Snow and Souter based their defense on a lack of proof that Franconia was actually responsible for the damage. A verdict for the plaintiffs, Souter later conceded, was "virtually unassailable," and no appeal was taken from the trial court's ruling.[48]

On another front, the Orr and Reno lawyers would be more successful. At that time, there were few sources of water treatment technology. Franconia borrowed what Snow termed "a ton of money" and secured grants to purchase waste treatment equipment from the Copeland Process Corporation, a Chicago concern. Snow and Souter spent much of one summer with engineers on the river, running tests and attempting to come up with strategies for buying time until the Copeland process was in place at the mill. When it failed to work, Franconia was forced to close and file for bankruptcy. On the mill's behalf, Snow and Souter then sued Copeland's parent company. Once convinced the plaintiff was serious, the defendant settled out of court. Franconia's home community, economically devastated by the mill's closing, got a free waste water treatment plant in the deal, and the company's president received enough to pay off creditors. Later, land belonging to the mill became the basis for the Loon Mountain Ski Recreation Area. Thus, within a period of a dozen years, a poor mill town became a thriving resort community.[49]

Souter remained with Orr and Reno for two years, but, as Malcolm McLane put it, he "was [not] cut out to be a country lawyer." Charles Leahy, of Harvard's 1963 law class, was the firm's youngest partner; he and Souter had become rather close. "After David had been here [a while]," Leahy has observed, "I think he [became] just plain bored with private practice. The nature of our practice in those days was pretty much representing individual clients in real estate and trust matters and some business clients. And I think that for David it was in some ways a continuation of school. He had been in school all of his life, and one day he remarked to me that this seemed like just more law school, because of course as a new associate he was doing mostly research and [only] occasionally dealing with clients."[50]

Although he had a slightly different take on his young colleague, Ronald

Snow also sensed Souter's frustration with the sort of private practice his firm and Concord offered. During a day of sailing at Snow's summer house on Lake Winnipesaukee, Snow realized that Souter "was having a difficult time deciding what his career path would be. I think David was always going to be someone who was more suited, in terms of his own happiness, to either a life of public service or teaching the law, as opposed to being a practitioner in the trenches on a day-to-day basis." Snow even remembers telling Souter on that occasion that he envisioned David's becoming a supreme court judge, although at the time he had in mind New Hampshire's, rather than the nation's, highest tribunal. "He was brilliant; that was obvious [even then]. He obviously had a great love of history and read incessantly. He [had] cooked dinner for me and my wife one night at the Weare house, and going into that house and seeing the stacks, literally, of those books five feet high, along with his collection of . . . classical music, made it clear" that Souter would be most satisfied in public service, teaching law, or on the bench. And he told Souter that when out sailing that day.[51]

State's Attorney

In 1968, Souter got an opportunity to make what proved to be a pivotal change in the direction of his career. When an opening for an assistant attorney general became available in the office of George Pappagianis, New Hampshire's attorney general, Pappagianis invited Souter to join his staff. During the decade he was to serve there, of course, Souter would regularly be obliged, as Snow had put it, to go down "into the trenches" on a variety of fronts. But he would find public service decidedly more gratifying than private practice.

Souter was to serve a decade in the attorney general's office—as assistant attorney general, 1968–71; as deputy attorney general, 1971–76; and as the state's chief law enforcement officer, 1976–78. In New Hampshire at the time, the attorney general was appointed for a five-year term by the governor, subject to confirmation by the state's executive council, a five-member body elected, like the governor, for two-year terms and jointly responsible with the governor for administering the state's affairs.

Souter's star really began to rise in state government in 1970, when Governor Walter Peterson named Warren Rudman attorney general and Rudman and Souter quickly became close friends and political allies. Rudman, a Boston native and graduate of Boston College's law school, had practiced law in Nashua, New Hampshire, until Governor Peterson named him to his staff.

Like Peterson, Rudman represented the moderate wing of the New Hampshire Republican Party. In that capacity, they frequently ran afoul of William Loeb, powerful and reactionary publisher of the Manchester *Union Leader*, the state's major newspaper.

In December 1969, President Richard M. Nixon hosted a White House conference on drugs. During a break in the proceedings, Governor Peterson's teenage daughter Meg, a conference participant, told a woman present that she saw nothing wrong with smoking marijuana. The woman turned out to be a wire service reporter, and William Loeb gave the incident full play, beginning the next day with a front-page story headlined, "Governor's Child Thinks Pot's OK, Friends Use It." When officials at Meg Peterson's Petersborough high school disputed her claim that a teacher once arrived at school with a lighted marijuana cigarette, the *Union Leader* exclaimed, "School Head Says Meg Lied."[52]

With Warren Rudman's assistance, Governor Peterson fired off an open letter to Loeb, which was published at the governor's expense on the *Union Leader*'s front page. Conceding that, as governor, he was fair game for the press, Peterson hotly protested the publisher's "despicable tactic of attacking my 15-year-old daughter as a means of getting at me," adding, "I must ask you to stop picking on my 15-year-old daughter."[53]

But the publisher was hardly penitent. The same day, Loeb's paper carried a lengthy rebuttal to Peterson's letter. Denying any personal role in the story's coverage, Loeb wrote that he readily understood "the extent of the governor's anxiety and fright over the political implications of this occurrence." But the state, not the governor, Loeb asserted, was due an apology. "Governor Peterson has embarrassed the entire state of New Hampshire by making it appear, through Meg Peterson's statements as well as his own, that New Hampshire is somehow tolerant of marijuana."[54]

Two days later, the *Union Leader* ran a scolding editorial, reminding members of the governor's family that they lived "in a fish bowl" and were "expected to set an example for other citizens." The editorial concluded, "on the more optimistic side," that "young Meg" now knew that "one must be responsible for what one says" and predicted that the experience would have "incalculable" value for her "personality development." Loeb's widow, Nackey, who took over the paper at his death in 1981, conceded years later that her husband's treatment of the incident may have been "a little strong," but that Loeb "felt strongly it was a bad example for the rest of the young people." Rudman later wrote of Loeb, "There must have been some great anger or frustration that drove him to use his power in such mean-spirited ways."[55]

Rudman was Governor Peterson's counsel during the Loeb affair. Soon he was named attorney general. In the weeks following his appointment, he brought the office's assistant attorneys general in for a chat. When Souter's turn came and Rudman asked him "what his goals were, where he was headed," the future justice replied simply that "he didn't know." But Rudman quickly concluded that Souter "was clearly the most talented person on my staff. He spoke in an utterly concise and direct way. His writings were crisp, and his logic was always well supported by case law."[56]

Bill Cann, the deputy attorney general then in office, wanted to be a judge. Through Governor Peterson, Rudman arranged a judgeship for Cann and Souter's selection as deputy attorney general. That, Rudman later wrote,

> was the beginning of a friendship that still continues. I have worked with many wonderful people, but my friendship with David remains the most re-warding, exciting, fulfilling experience of my professional life. If my six years as attorney general were in many ways more satisfying than my two terms in the Senate, it was largely because of David. He was like a very special younger brother.
>
> People usually separate their professional and personal relationships. David and I, at the office, had a relationship that was both personal and pro-fessional. We worked together closely, for long hours under great pressure, often talking ten or fifteen times a day. We came to share a deep affection, we made each other laugh, and we had complementary talents that kept the office on track no matter how hectic things became.[57]

Dressed almost invariably in a three-piece brown suit, Souter hardly cut a colorful figure as a state's attorney. During his years as Rudman's deputy, and later as attorney general, however, he would be given major credit for recruit-ing a superb staff and inaugurating an unprecedented era of professionalism and nonpartisanship in the office. Staff members consistently developed a re-spect and affection for their boss bordering on adoration.

Souter's first major recruit as Rudman's deputy was Tom Rath, a New Jersey native and Georgetown law graduate. While clerking for a federal judge in New Jersey, Rath sent out a series of letters inquiring about possible positions. One went to the New Hampshire attorney general's office. Several days later, Souter telephoned Rath. The New Hampshire legislature had funded a num-ber of new positions, including one in the office's criminal division. When Rath said that he would like an interview, he quickly learned that Souter moved expeditiously on such matters. He wanted Rath in Concord the next day for a meeting. The day after they talked in New Hampshire, Souter telephoned again, with a job offer, indicating that he wanted an answer by the next day. Largely on the strength of their interview, Rath accepted. "I remember coming out of the interview and telling my wife," he later remarked, "'I don't know whether I got the job or not. But he's about as smart a guy as I've ever met.' He was formal but friendly with a good sense of humor. Very well read. Very creative in his interviewing. Kind of threw a few lines into the water until he found something that you and he were both interested in. And then he would sort of draw you out and get your thinking, not so much agree or disagree, but to see how you thought. It was a good interview. I liked him a lot" from the start.[58]

Rath would succeed Souter first as deputy and then as attorney general before practicing at Orr and Reno for several years and then joining with several other Orr and Reno partners to form a separate firm. Charles Leahy of Orr and Reno recalls Souter, Rudman, and Rath as a very interesting trio: "You had the very aggressive, tough-minded Jewish lawyer, Warren Rudman; the cerebral, very private Yankee, David Souter; and the gregarious Irish politician, Tom Rath." The three complemented each other. Rath "liked to joke," Rudman later wrote, "that his job was 'to go to lunch with Warren and explain what David was saying.' Sometimes it wasn't a joke."[59]

Another Souter addition to the attorney general's office arrived in 1975. A slightly built, scholarly looking, bespectacled University of Chicago law graduate, Wilbur (Bill) Glahn began his career with a Boston firm. Three years later, an acquaintance in the New Hampshire attorney general's office suggested that he contact Souter about a position. "Almost everybody who was interviewed by David Souter can describe that interview. . . . David has a way of asking very interesting questions, and when you hit things off well with David, he always gives you the impression that he's known you a long time and has a great deal of interest in you. He's the first person who ever described for me the notion that the practice of law would be fun." Perhaps a bit apprehensive about how his wife, Hansi, might react to their leaving Boston for Concord, Glahn "went home and said to [his] wife, 'You're not going to understand this, but I just met this guy I want to go work for.' And she did understand, fortunately."[60]

Any effort to pad a résumé could prove embarrassing to a Souter job prospect. Based on a visit to an art gallery in Europe, one applicant had included an interest in Dutch paintings on his vita. "I found out very rapidly in

[my] interview that he knew several times more about Dutch painting than I did." But Souter quickly put the applicant at ease. "He was funny. He said, 'Don't worry about it. We're not hiring an art historian here. We're hiring a lawyer.'"[61]

On rare occasions, a prospect for a position might briefly gain the upper hand in a Souter job interview. Steven A. McAuliffe—husband of teacher-astronaut Christa McAuliffe, killed in 1986's *Challenger* shuttle disaster, and later the first President Bush's federal court appointee—joined Souter's staff in 1977. During their interview, Souter emphasized the office's apolitical character. "'One of the things I do require,'" McAuliffe later remembered Souter's saying, "'is a gentleman's agreement that you will not engage in any type of political activity or partisan politics. I would also ask that your wife not engage in any partisan politics.' . . . Then, he sort of wryly smiled and said, 'Except voting, of course.' And I remember it was the only time I ever felt on an even playing field with David Souter. And I said, 'Seriously?' And he said, 'Absolutely. . . . In fact, I don't want to know what your . . . political registration is for voting.'" The extremely conservative Meldrim Thomson was then New Hampshire's governor. "And I said," McAuliffe continued, "'Well, . . . supposing I were a member of the Socialist Workers Party; wouldn't you want to know that?' And he kind of looked at me—he never cracked a smile—he just looked at me about thirty seconds. And finally he smiled and said, 'Are you?' and I said, 'No.' And we both laughed."[62]

Souter not only subjected staff members to a challenging job interview but he also scrutinized their work closely, helping them to hone their skills as lawyers. He read their briefs closely, monitored letters they had written. "Everything you did of significance," Richard McNamara, who worked in the office's criminal division, told a reporter during the Senate confirmation process, "David Souter reviewed when he was deputy. For your first year at least. I say that in praise of David Souter, because he was a very good teacher." When another assistant wrote his first brief for the state supreme court, Souter presented him with a style manual on legal writing. "He took my brief and tore it apart and helped me put it back together again. I don't know how many times I went back to him."[63]

Affair of the Heart

Two women were among staff members Souter recruited. Souter interviewed Deborah Cooper, then a third-year law student, for a position in 1976, on his first day as attorney general. Prior to an earlier, initial interview with another staff member, Cooper had noted that the office letterhead included no women. When she asked whether there were any women in the office, she was told there had been one, "but she died." Understandably, Cooper found that information distressing. "As you can imagine," she testified during Souter's Senate confirmation hearing, "I faced my second interview with a fair amount of trepidation and substantial reservations about whether this was the office in which I wanted to start my legal career."[64]

Five minutes into the interview, however, her concerns evaporated. "I do not know whether David Souter had his own affirmative action plan. I do not know [his] position on affirmative action. I do know that David treated the women in his office with professional respect and that he gave me and other women equal opportunities. . . . Judge Souter made me believe that my gender was not the reason for my appointment. I know that, to him, my sex was not a factor." Cooper had left her interview with Souter convinced that he "was a man of unquestionable intellect, integrity, and warmth, and with a true devotion to public service. For David Souter, the office of attorney general was governmental, not political. He did not espouse a political philosophy, nor did he ask mine." Cooper thrived in the office. When Tom Rath replaced Souter as attorney general in 1978, she became Rath's deputy.[65]

Souter's second female appointment would attract considerable media attention at the time of his U.S. Supreme Court nomination. The woman with whom he apparently developed the closest attachment during his years after law school was Anne Cagwin, his second female recruit to the attorney general's office. In part perhaps because of Souter's intense regard for his privacy, the time period for their romance remains somewhat obscure. His friends are confident that the affair would not have taken place while Souter was attorney general and Cagwin subject to his supervision. In a C-SPAN interview during the Senate confirmation process, however, the justice's close friend and associate Steven McAuliffe described an incident suggesting that Cagwin and the nominee may have had more than a purely professional relationship while Souter was still attorney general: "When I was in the [New Hampshire] attorney general's office [and] David was just leaving to go on the [superior court] bench, . . . we were all going out to lunch. And he made some comment, and Debbie Cooper . . . and Anne Cagwin were standing there. And I guess [Souter's remark] had a flavor of [male] chauvinism to it. And Anne Cagwin, without missing a beat, and to the shock and horror of everybody who knew David and worked for him, turned around and grabbed him by the tie, and held him up against the wall, and put her face about three inches from his nose, and said, 'What did you say, Souter?' And, of course, David just blanched. [But] she wouldn't let him down until he apologized. . . . I think it would probably take a woman of that kind of force for David to succumb."[66]

Souter's relationship with Anne Cagwin did not last—a turn of events, some of his friends believe, that left him thoroughly devastated. After working with Orr and Reno a couple of years, she married a Concord native and moved to Yarmouth, Maine.

Life in Concord

From the beginning of his professional career, Souter worked seven-day weeks. His social life was centered around his professional associates and their families, with whom he developed extremely close ties and enjoyed tremendous affection and respect. "David inspires unbelievable loyalty in the people who work for him or around him," Bill Glahn has remarked. "And part of it is the way he approaches things. You never feel like David Souter feels he is intellectually superior to you. He is singularly the brightest man I've ever met, yet he [could] carry on a conversation with equal aplomb with my children when they were young, and with me or anyone else. . . . The greatest thing about working with David was, if you screwed up, he told you about it inside the office. But outside the office, you never got blamed for it. And he never took credit for anything. He gave it to you. Everything was a question of helping you. If he was criticizing what you had written, it was clear that there was a good reason for doing so." Glahn introduced Souter, already an inveterate hiker, to mountain climbing in New Hampshire's White Mountains, then saw his friend climb all forty-seven of their peaks before Glahn did.[67]

Like Glahn, Tom Rath became one of Souter's closest friends. "In those days," he has recalled, "the sort of social activity in [Concord], which has always been more a place for married folks than single folks, was principally getting together and having dinner on a Saturday night. And David would do that. We would go out to his house, or he would join us. [At his house,] you kind of have to weave your way through the piles of books and find a place to sit. But we had a lot of fun. He's very funny and a gifted story teller. He's got a great recollection for detail . . . a wonderful sense of humor. [As a chef,] he's very good on lobster; I think that's his specialty. But he also is a wonderful guest, because he'll eat everything. He's a delightful conversationalist; he's just exceptional. Of course, the more at ease he is in a social setting, where he knows people and all, [the more] he really enjoys himself. But he works seven days a week, so he's not going to stay out too late. He's not going to imbibe too much; he's very careful about driving. He's always been very measured in that way."[68]

For the children of his friends, Souter would become a beloved uncle figure. As Bill Glahn put it, "My kids think he walks on water." But Souter was also scrupulously attentive to the needs of elderly relatives and friends, including his Weare neighbors and parishioners at the St. Andrews Episcopal congregation in Hopkinton. At some point after his return to New Hampshire, Souter's parents moved into an apartment on Loudon Road in Concord, while he continued living in the family home at Weare. He proved to be a faithful friend to the village's residents, and they in turn were exceptionally protective of his privacy following his Supreme Court nomination.[69]

Souter did not hesitate to spend lavishly on family and friends. For books, classical music, antiques, and other things that he cherished, he was also quite willing to indulge himself. Occasionally, too, he joined friends for a trip to Boston, dinner, a symphony concert, and a visit to a favorite bookstore. In many ways, however, he fit the stereotype of the tight-fisted New Englander, with Tom Rath only half-joking when he remarked that his friend put "the 'C' in 'Cheap.'" Perhaps as much for financial as health reasons, his typical lunch fare was cottage cheese or yogurt and an apple, which he consumed entirely, including the core and seeds. As a joke, someone cited a study indicating that apple seeds were poisonous. For a time, friends thought the tale had worked. But Souter later insisted that he had done some research of his own, found that apple seeds were dangerous only in large quantities, and returned to his old habit.[70]

The times Souter picked up a restaurant check were sufficiently rare as to invite comment. His Weare house became progressively more dilapidated. Most distressing for his friends, perhaps, was his reluctance to invest in safe transportation. When Warren Rudman was attorney general and Souter his deputy, state officials were given personalized automobile license plates, Rudman's reading "Attorney General 1" and Souter's "Attorney General 2." "One day David picked me up at the airport in his battered fifteen-year-old Chevrolet," Rudman wrote in his 1996 memoir. "One door wouldn't open from the inside. The car was dirty and rusty and missing chrome, a wreck. I hated to ride in it." During the trip from the airport, another motorist spotted the license and began harassing the driver "along the lines of 'You've got to be kidding, Mac! You're the attorney general and you're driving that piece of junk!'" Rudman used the occasion to persuade Souter to buy a clean, used Volkswagen Rabbit. "When he was nominated to the Supreme Court in 1990," Rudman noted, "he was driving a Volkswagen Golf. He's still driving it."[71]

On at least one occasion, Souter's frugality with state funds no doubt enhanced his standing with New Hampshire voters. In 1976, he passed on the opportunity to attend the December annual convention of the National Association of Attorneys General in Honolulu. Souter considered the thousand-dollar estimated cost of the trip "frankly . . . a lot of money." He was also concerned about the impression his trip would create in the public mind. "I figured," he told a reporter, "that there was no way in the world that anyone is ever going to believe that I had gone to Honolulu, Hawaii, in the middle of December, solely for the value of the seminars."[72]

At the same time, he refused to join critics of a Hawaiian convention trip that state public utilities commissioners had recently taken. Although conceding that he was "not a particularly hot conventioneer," he asserted that he had never attended "one in which I did not find the various seminars valuable and come back with some ideas which I wouldn't have had otherwise." He insisted, moreover, that conventions could not be uniformly dismissed as wasteful, tax-paid junkets. "I went to one last time in Texas," he recalled. "Believe me, if you've ever been in San Antonio, Texas, in June, you can believe it wasn't much of a trip."[73]

Souter's decision received mixed reviews in New Hampshire newspapers. The *Portsmouth Herald* thought the experience would have been well worth the expense. Terming "Work" the attorney general's real middle name, the paper was confident that "if he went to Honolulu, the state would find him paying the same devoted attention to the business of the convention as he does to his legalistic labors in Concord." The *Nashua Telegraph* commended the state's attorney general for "his responsive attitude" toward likely public reaction, but emphasized the value of such sessions. The *Telegraph* further noted that the chairman of the state utilities commission and commissioner of agriculture had been named presidents of their respective national organizations, adding, "We look forward to the day when Attorney General Souter is similarly honored."[74]

During his years in the attorney general's office, Souter's functions varied with his position. In New Hampshire, the attorney general was responsible for all criminal prosecutions and appeals. As assistant attorney general, Souter was assigned to the criminal division with trial and appellate duties, although more than half his work, by his later estimate, involved special assignments from the attorney general. As deputy attorney general, he handled cases and projects from the attorney general, oversaw the recruitment and supervision of office staff, advised the state treasurer on the legality of state borrowing practices, and supervised the office's advisory and litigation functions. As attorney general, he was responsible for most of the state's legal affairs and a staff that grew to more than thirty lawyers.[75]

Like attorneys general in most states, New Hampshire's chief law enforcement officer is authorized to render opinions on issues of law to state agencies and officials. The opinions Souter issued suggest that much of his office's work attracted little controversy and often involved relatively technical questions. In 1977, for example, he advised the assistant state treasurer that a classified state employee could legally place a political sticker on his personal vehicle and park it on a public thoroughfare outside his agency, but could not display a political sign in the same manner. Emphasizing that state law was designed to prevent public employees "from participating so deeply in the political process that they make valuable donations to a cause," Souter saw a political sticker as primarily an expression of personal opinion, whereas "a large sign placed on the roof of a classified state employee's car is more in the nature of a political advertisement than a simple act of personal expression. In effect, the owner of an automobile equipped with such a sign is contributing the use of his or her car as an advertising tool and is thereby donating a 'thing of value' [forbidden by state law] to a candidate, party, or measure." On another occasion, he held that a bank "information office" that did not handle deposits or checking but did conduct other activities associated with banking activities was comparable to a branch bank and subject to banking regulations. Other opinions involved, among other things, restrictions on the display of party affiliation by members of state boards and commissions and state insurance regulations. Some of the legal advice Souter dispensed thus involved First Amendment and other constitutional questions, but much of it was far afield of what he would confront as a justice.[76]

On one occasion, Souter also departed from his customary practice of confining his published comments to legal documents. In late December 1976, a jury convicted Gary S. Farrow, a twenty-year-old Concord man, of first-degree murder in the stabbing death of a brain-damaged Laconia youth, based largely on testimony from "street children," as a reporter described them, "scarred by an adolescence of drugs, mindless and violent sexual encounters, suicide attempts and criminal activity." Citing the principle of American justice "that every citizen—even the most vile among us—has the right to a fair trial and the most vigorous defense obtainable," the *Concord Monitor*, in an editorial following the verdict, praised the "spirited, thorough and inquiring" defense Farrow's court-appointed counsel had given their client. But the *Monitor* was hardly generous to police conduct in the case. In a news article, the paper had alluded to the inconsistent testimony of prosecution witnesses and "their admitted deals with police in exchange for testimony." The editorial continued that theme, observing that "both the trial spectators and the jury looked askance at 'trading off' a child molestation charge for testimony at the trial."[77]

In a guest column a week later, Attorney General Souter termed the *Farrow* trial a "model" for both prosecutors and defense lawyers. Like the *Monitor*, Souter praised the "vigor and skill" of the defendant's counsel. He insisted, however, that justice required not only an adequate defense for rich and poor alike, as the paper had stressed, but also "an adequate investigation into the facts and an adequate presentation of the evidence of guilt." Applauding the work of the Concord police and prosecutors in the case, he further asserted, "For weeks through the trial I have had to bite my tongue as one incident in their investigation was misunderstood; the Department was blamed for agreeing to drop an aggravated sexual assault charge against a man in return for his inducing the chief witness against Farrow to talk to the police." The witness in the sex case "had changed her story." If "asked personally" for his opinion, Souter declared, he "would have approved" the county attorney's decision to drop that charge. To the newspaper's reference to the character of the prosecution witnesses, he had a simple rejoinder: "[Police] investigated a case among the only witnesses there were, none of them bishops, scout leaders or professors of logic. The jury believed they had found the truth." He concluded, "The demands of justice are spoken to every one of us, the defense, the prosecution, and the jury. And in the trial of State v. Farrow the demands of justice were well honored." As New Hampshire's chief law enforcement officer, Souter's defense of police and prosecutors in the *Farrow* case was hardly surprising. But his comments also foreshadowed, in a sense, what critics would later characterize as his unduly conservative state judicial record in criminal procedure cases.[78]

No doubt most New Hampshire citizens found little fault with Souter's defense of police and prosecution in the *Farrow* case. Nor was his involvement in suits to protect New Hampshire's proprietary interests likely to arouse protest. Early in his tenure in the attorney general's office, he represented the state when it joined twelve other eastern seaboard states in a dispute against the national government over ownership of the seabed beyond the three-mile marginal sea. When the states refused to acknowledge federal control, the U.S. Justice Department brought an original suit in the Supreme Court, which appointed a special master to oversee the litigation. Most of the states, including New Hampshire, ultimately retained common counsel to handle the suit, but Souter recruited a dozen history graduate students to examine state papers for relevant materials. Despite prodigious research by Souter's staff, a unanimous Supreme Court upheld the federal government's position. Souter also prepared the pleadings and worked with outside counsel in New Hampshire's Supreme Court suit against Maine over the location of the states' common marine boundary, the climax of a two-centuries-old dispute aggravated in the early 1970s by dwindling lobster supplies. Ultimately, a divided Supreme Court accepted a settlement negotiated by the parties.[79]

The Attorney General and the Constitution

Naturally, a number of decisions with which Souter was connected and positions he assumed while in the attorney general's office proved controversial either at the time or when he was nominated to the Supreme Court. Several incidents raised questions in the minds of critics regarding his commitment to racial equality. In 1970 amendments to the 1965 Voting Rights Act, Congress applied nationwide the ban on voter literacy tests that had largely been limited to the southern states under the 1965 statute. Appearing as assistant attorney general before a three-judge federal district court in *United States v. New Hampshire*, Souter filed a memorandum opposing enforcement of the ban in his state. He rested the state's position primarily on *Lassiter v. Northampton Co. Bd. of Elections*, a 1959 case in which the Supreme Court had upheld fairly administered literacy tests against constitutional claims. Because federal officials had cited no evidence that state officials had applied literacy requirements in a racially discriminatory manner, he contended, New Hampshire should be exempted from the 1970 provision.[80]

Souter's memorandum appeared to fly in the face of two 1966 Supreme Court rulings upholding the 1965 Voting Rights Act. In *South Carolina v. Katzenbach*, the Court upheld the statute's ban on literacy tests in states and counties with a history of racial discrimination in voting, while *Katzenbach v. Morgan* affirmed a provision of the law suspending English-language literacy tests for persons who had completed the sixth grade in a language other than English. In both cases, but especially in his opinion for the Court in the *Morgan* case, Justice William J. Brennan made clear that Congress's power under the Fourteenth Amendment to enforce the equal protection clause and the amendment's other provisions through "appropriate legislation" was not limited to judicial constructions of the amendment's scope, such as *Lassiter*. If Congress had a rational basis for concluding that state voting requirements might interfere with Fourteenth Amendment rights, such regulations could be prohibited, whatever the Court's earlier pronouncements.[81]

Souter merely cited *Morgan* without attempting to square Brennan's expansive opinion there with the state's position. Instead, Souter relied on *Lassiter* to make his case, declaring that "allowing illiterates to make a choice in such matters is tantamount to authorizing them to vote at random, utterly without comprehension," and warning that "detriment to the State and its citizens will occur in watering the value of every literate citizen's vote." On October 27, 1970, a unanimous three-judge panel rejected his stance. Less than two months later, the Supreme Court, in an Oregon case, upheld the nationwide literacy test ban.[82]

Souter's Senate confirmation hearings also focused attention on his role in New Hampshire's refusal to comply with 1972 amendments to Title VII of the 1964 Civil Rights Act and Equal Employment Opportunity Commission (EEOC) regulations adopted to enforce the law. The regulations required state and local governments to furnish the EEOC with data regarding the race, national origin, and sex of their employees. State officials refused to provide national origin and racial data in 1973 and furnished none of the required information in 1974—the only state to refuse compliance. Faced with New Hampshire's resistance, the United States brought an enforcement suit in the Concord court of U.S. District Judge Hugh H. Bownes. Although he was Souter's close friend, Judge Bownes frequently ruled against the state on constitutional issues, and this case was no exception. Bownes ruled summarily in favor of federal officials, and the state appealed to a panel of the U.S. Court of Appeals for the First Circuit in Boston.[83]

Souter's involvement in earlier stages of the data dispute is unclear, but he signed the brief the state filed with the appeals court. Contending that they added "nothing essential" to employment discrimination law, the brief charged that the regulations merely "create[d] a gratuitous layer of accountability to the federal government, contrary to constitutional principles limiting federal power." Terming "group statistics . . . not 'relevant'" to an individual's discrimination claim, the brief's author argued that the regulations required states to "become color-conscious rather than color-blind" and could lead to racial quotas; then he declared, "Quotas are an impermissible end. And accordingly so too should be the means to that end." To the extent the regulations rested on Congress's authority to regulate matters affecting interstate commerce, they exceeded congressional power and constituted "evidence of unchecked centralized government."[84]

The brief also raised claims under the Tenth Amendment's reservation to the states of regulatory powers not delegated to the national government under the Constitution, as well as other issues, including violation of the rights of state employees to liberty, privacy, and due process. But all to no avail. On August 5, 1976, a unanimous circuit panel affirmed Judge Bownes, rejecting each of New Hampshire's contentions. Answering the state's claim that the data at issue were irrelevant to effective enforcement of equal employment laws, Judge Edward M. McEntee declared to the contrary that such information was "often highly useful when an agency or court attempts to make the often difficult inference that illegal discrimination is or is not present in a particular factual context." While conceding that "the permissible scope of the use of quotas as a remedy in discrimination cases remains a delicate question," McEntee further observed that "purely hypothetical misuse of data [did] not require the banning of reasonable procedures to acquire such data." The regulations, in the panel's judgment, were clearly within the scope of congressional enforcement authority under the Fourteenth Amendment, particularly in view of the broad scope accorded Congress's power in *Morgan* and other Supreme Court cases. Because the regulations were based on the Fourteenth Amendment, moreover, New Hampshire's claim that they constituted an invalid exercise of the congressional commerce power was "beside the point." The state's other objections, McEntee observed in a footnote, were neither "persuasive [nor] deserving of discussion."[85]

The state continued its attack in the Supreme Court. But Solicitor General Robert Bork filed a three-page memorandum in opposition to New Hampshire's petition for a writ of certiorari ordering the case sent up for review. The high Court denied review.[86]

The state's brief in the EEOC dispute was not Souter's only word on racial quotas. In May before the First Circuit's ruling in August, the attorney general had given the commencement address at the New England Aeronautical Institute and Daniel Webster College, which his mentor Warren Rudman had cofounded and then served as board of trustees chair. According to a *Union*

Leader account entitled "Souter Raps Ethnic Preference," Souter used the occasion to condemn as "affirmative discrimination," as the paper quoted the speaker, policies "whereby a person achieves eligibility for some service strictly by virtue of his ethnic background." As an example, he cited "federal guidelines which require an employer to give preference to a particular ethnic or racial group until a certain percentage requirement is fulfilled." According to the *Nashua Telegraph*, Souter "insisted," in the paper's words, that "such practices do not address individual cases, only percentages." "There are some things government cannot do," he maintained, "and our whole Constitutional history is a history of restraining power."[87]

Despite the attention they would later attract in his Senate confirmation proceedings, Souter's public statements and position on affirmative action programs, literacy tests, and related policies were hardly evidence that he was racially prejudiced. After all, the Supreme Court had not yet issued its first decision on affirmative action, which many people of goodwill consider an offensive kind of reverse discrimination. Given the Court's willingness to uphold a fairly administered literacy test in the *Lassiter* case, Souter's support of such a voter requirement in a state with almost no history of racial bias in voting and elections could not be equated with racial bias either. And a federal requirement that a state without a history of racial bias maintain racial data on its employees might smack more of a prelude to racial quota regulations than a safeguard against discrimination.

Decisions in which Souter participated following *Roe v. Wade*, the Supreme Court's 1973 abortion rights ruling, projected mixed signals regarding his likely position on that controversial issue and later drew fire from both pro-choice and anti-abortion forces during the Senate confirmation process. Despite his relatively reserved personality, the future justice was a member not only of the usual legal and court-related associations but also a host of organizations reflecting his interests in nature and conservation, hiking and mountain climbing, his university experiences, the arts, and historic preservation. Souter devoted much of his time, energy, and interest, however, to serving on the board of the Concord Hospital (1971–85), including six years each as its president and secretary, and as an overseer of the Dartmouth Medical School (1981–87).[88]

In February 1973, shortly after the *Roe* decision, the Concord Hospital board approved a resolution permitting physicians to perform abortions in the hospital. No record was kept of the vote, but Souter later acknowledged voting to approve the proposal and necessary changes in hospital regulations the vote entailed. By contrast, the year before *Roe* was decided, while Souter was deputy attorney general, New Hampshire had defended the prosecution of Joyce Millette, a physician whose patient died as a result of a botched abortion. In a brief filed with the New Hampshire Supreme Court, the state argued that "the maintenance of an unborn child's right to birth is a compelling interest which outweighs any rights of a mother to an abortion, except when necessary to preserve her life."[89]

After *Roe*, the attorney general's office announced that the decision had effectively voided New Hampshire's criminal abortion statutes. But in 1975, the state prohibited use of Medicaid funds for "medically unnecessary" abortions. Several pregnant women brought a suit challenging that regulation before Judge Bownes, who ruled for the plaintiffs on the ground that their abortions were medically necessary and thus covered by the state's statute. But the state appealed Bownes's injunction to the First Circuit, declaring in briefs filed with the appeals panel that "many thousands of New Hampshire residents find the use of tax revenues to finance the killing of unborn children morally repugnant" and that Congress had not adopted the Medicaid program "to aid in the destruction of fetuses." The U.S. Supreme Court later ruled in other cases that the Constitution did not guarantee indigent women a right to government-funded abortions.[90]

Howard B. Myers, the assistant attorney general who wrote the briefs and argued the 1972 case before the New Hampshire Supreme Court, said at the time of Souter's Supreme Court nomination that he did not recall ever discussing the merits of the case with his colleague. Richard V. Weibusch, the Souter assistant who signed the briefs in the abortion-funding case, said, "The language in the briefs is all mine; I don't remember having any discussions with David about the case."[91]

In May 1977, however, Souter voiced his opposition to a bill related to the abortion issue that had been adopted by the state house of representatives. Supporters characterized the twenty-three-page bill as a housekeeping measure designed to clarify inconsistencies and errors in various state laws. But Souter was concerned that it would have the effect of repealing all the state's abortion regulations, even those the *Roe* decision did not forbid. "Quite apart from the fact that I don't think unlimited abortions ought to be allowed," the attorney general told a *Union Leader* reporter, "I presume we would become the abortion mill of the United States." Souter shared his concerns with the state senate's judiciary committee, where the bill died. New Hampshire's restrictive anti-abortion laws, first enacted in 1848, remained in effect when he was nominated to the Supreme Court. As a U.S. Supreme Court justice in 1992, Souter would help to draft a joint plurality opinion reaffirming the essence of *Roe* and emphasizing its long standing as precedent, but also recognizing broader state power to regulate abortions than *Roe* had permitted. Given his comments as New Hampshire's attorney general, he might well have dissented, at least partly, in *Roe* had he been on the high Court when that case was first decided.[92]

Whatever the ambiguity of his position on the abortion issue, Souter clearly endorsed the death penalty as New Hampshire's chief law enforcement officer. In 1976, the U.S. Supreme Court upheld capital punishment in first-degree murder cases under statutes with safeguards designed to prevent arbitrary executions. While the New Hampshire house of representatives was considering reinstatement of the death penalty for certain murder cases in the wake of the high Court's ruling, Souter testified before the house judiciary committee in favor of the proposed legislation. "For a certain, limited class of crime," he told committee members, "I do not believe life imprisonment is sufficient penalty." Capital punishment as a deterrent, he claimed, had "a lot more subtle effect" on society than simply giving someone second thoughts about committing a capital crime. "The very values the criminal, in growing up, is absorbing—are the very values society gives to the crime." Reducing the punishment for a crime, he said, in the long run resulted in lessening the inhibitions of people to commit that crime. Monsignor Philip Kenney of the Manchester Roman Catholic diocese used Souter's logic, however, to oppose the bill, contending that by promoting a permissive attitude toward violence, the death penalty could actually promote, rather than discourage, violence. Emphasizing that capital punishment was reserved primarily for the poor, Kenney further observed, "While it's difficult to get a rich man into heaven, it's even harder to get him into the hangman's noose." New Hampshire ultimately reinstated the death penalty, but the debate over capital punishment and questions about Souter's position on the issue were largely academic; the state's last execution to date occurred in 1939.[93]

During Souter's confirmation proceedings, women's groups, among others, would cite the nominee's involvement in one case while he was in the New Hampshire attorney general's office as evidence that he might be insufficiently sensitive to gender bias claims brought before the Supreme Court. In 1974, Thomas E. Meloon had been convicted of statutory rape in a New Hampshire court under a law that applied only to males, not females. After unsuccessfully appealing his conviction in the state's supreme court, Meloon filed a petition for a writ of habeas corpus before Judge Hugh Bownes, claiming that the law under which he had been convicted discriminated against male defendants in violation of the Fourteenth Amendment's guarantee to equal protection of the laws.

Traditionally, government had enjoyed broad discretion to draw sex distinctions in its laws. In *Craig v. Boren* (1976), however, the Supreme Court had concluded that gender classifications, though not as presumptively invalid as racial discrimination, were "quasi-suspect" and thus to be upheld only if found substantially related to important governmental interests. Applying this "heightened scrutiny" standard, Judge Bownes declared New Hampshire's "males-only" statutory rape statute unconstitutional. When a First Circuit appeals panel affirmed, emphasizing the "special sensitivity" to which discrimination claims were entitled in criminal cases, David Souter petitioned the Supreme Court for review.[94]

For years, the Supreme Court had followed a two-tiered approach in equal protection cases. Laws discriminating on the basis of race, color, or national origin were deemed "inherently suspect" and subjected to strict judicial scrutiny. Courts struck them down unless they were found necessary to promote a compelling state interest that could not be furthered through nondiscriminatory means. All other classifications were presumably examined under a lenient, rational-basis review formula that effectively meant little, if any, scrutiny at all. *Craig* and other recent Supreme Court cases, however, had begun applying a "middle-tier" approach, subjecting gender classifications to a standard of review more rigorous than the rationality test yet less so than the compelling interest formula. Judge Bownes and the First Circuit had applied this heightened review standard to New Hampshire's "males-only" statutory rape law.

In his certiorari petition to the Supreme Court requesting review in the *Meloon* case, Souter scored the *Craig* approach as "amorphous," quoting with approval Justice William H. Rehnquist's assertion in a *Craig* dissent that its substantial relation standard was "so diaphanous and elastic as to invite subjective judicial preferences or prejudices relating to particular types of legislation." While striking down New Hampshire's statutory rape law, the *Meloon* court of appeals panel had also found the new test troubling. Drawing on the First Circuit's concerns and Rehnquist's *Craig* dissent, Souter lamented the Supreme Court's "creat[ion of] a new equal protection test which resides somewhere in the 'twilight zone' between the rational basis and strict scrutiny tests. This new standard lacks definition, shape, or precise limits." The *Meloon* case, he argued, "presents the opportunity for the Court to correct a situation which invites subjective judicial judgments and possible abuse." During his confirmation proceedings, Senator Edward Kennedy of Massachusetts would probe Souter closely about his stance in the *Meloon* case, specifically whether he favored meaningful judicial review of gender discrimination. In his response, the nominee emphasized that, as attorney general, he was serving as the state's advocate, not as a defender of his personal views. He also reiterated, however, his concern that the standard the Supreme Court had begun applying to gender classifications in the *Craig* case was so flexible that it conferred undue discretion on judges who review gender claims.[95]

The Supreme Court denied review in the case. In 1981, however, the Court, speaking through Justice Rehnquist, upheld a California statutory rape law comparable to New Hampshire's males-only statute. The statute, Rehnquist concluded, satisfied *Craig*'s heightened scrutiny standard. Even so, one could understand Souter's concern that the Court's creation of various heightened scrutiny standards for review of gender and certain other nonracial classifications was unduly broadening the scope of judicial discretion in a variety of discrimination contexts.[96]

Governor Thomson

In New Hampshire, as well as years later during his confirmation hearings, a number of the most controversial issues relating to Souter's tenure in the state attorney general's office involved Meldrim Thomson, the plump, jowly political reactionary elected governor in 1972. Born in Pennsylvania in 1912, Thomson was reared in Georgia and Florida, acquiring there not only a permanent southern lilt to his voice but a penchant for colorful and at times outlandish politics characteristic of the South. In 1954, he moved his lawbook publishing business from New York State to Orford, New Hampshire, where he also acquired a maple sugar orchard. Thomson first gained political notoriety when, as a member of the local school board, he persuaded board members to refuse federal funds for remedial reading programs. He lost contests for a U.S. House of Representatives seat in 1964 and the Republican gubernatorial nomination in 1968 and 1970, then ran—again unsuccessfully—in the 1970 general election as a candidate from segregationist Alabama governor George C. Wallace's American Party. Campaigning with the slogan "Ax the Tax," he finally defeated Governor Walter Peterson in the 1972 gubernatorial race.

Thomson would serve three boisterous, at times outrageous, two-year terms as New Hampshire's governor. Speaking in 1978 to a Los Angeles meeting of the ultraconservative John Birch Society, he charged that the nation had "allowed public abortions, hedonistic indecency and queer sexual behavior to be protected by a noble Constitution that has been perverted, tortured and distorted by a nasty minority who in the pursuit of their own self-gratification would destroy America." President Jimmy Carter, he warned his audience in a play on the Twenty-third Psalm, "would lead us beside the communist path to national suicide. He would restore to us the likes of [Henry] Kissinger and [Nelson] Rockefeller. Surely, . . . he will lead us into the shadows of the Kremlin forever." The next month, the *Concord Monitor*, in an editorial entitled "Another Thomson Zany Week," found it "sometimes . . . hard to believe New Hampshire is a part of the United States."97

David Souter's mentor Warren Rudman was attorney general when Thomson became governor. The two had a rocky start to their relationship. When Thomson was making his unsuccessful 1970 gubernatorial bid against Walter Peterson, he had attacked Rudman for failing to prevent an appearance by the "Chicago Three"—controversial opponents of the Vietnam War—at the University of New Hampshire. Rudman promptly retorted that Thomson, as a relative newcomer to the state, "evidently believes that New Hampshire people can be easily duped [by visiting speakers]." Thomson charged in the same campaign that Governor Peterson had no effective drug control policy and that a "wild fire of drug abuse [had] swept across our state, burning and destroying the physical and moral fiber of our young people" during Peterson's administration. As the state's chief law enforcement officer, Rudman no doubt considered Thomson's rhetoric not only a slap at his record but also a thinly veiled reference to the recent marijuana incident involving the governor's daughter, which *Union Leader* publisher and Thomson ally William Loeb had effectively exploited the previous year.98

Walter Peterson's loss to Thomson in 1972 was a consequence largely of his refusal to rule out new state taxes—no match that year for Thomson's "Ax the Tax" platform. Rudman debated Thomson in that campaign, making his contempt for Peterson's opponent, as Rudman later wrote in his memoir, "abundantly clear." But when Thomson was elected, Rudman decided to continue as attorney general, and in time the two developed what Rudman termed "a decent working relationship." After Thomson became governor, Tom Rath remembers, Rudman, "to his great credit," told staff members in the attorney general's office, "I know a lot of you may have different political likes and dislikes about Thomson. But he's the governor, and we're going to serve him the right way. You let me fight the political battles; I want you to provide the governor with the kind of service that [he] ought to be provided." Souter had an excellent talent for mimicry, including a dead-on impression of Thomson. No doubt, he also shared some of Rudman's misgivings about the governor. But as Rudman's deputy, he was largely responsible for assuring that the policy was followed.[99]

When Rudman returned to private practice in 1976, he helped persuade Thomson to appoint Souter as his replacement. Why the reactionary governor would have chosen Souter is a question of some note. Charles Leahy, Souter's friend from Orr and Reno, has speculated that Thomson developed a deep respect for "David's talents and the disinterested and objective way he performed his duties." Thomson, Leahy has remarked, was also "a real southern gentleman." When Henry Waldo, the principal woodsman for a paper company Orr and Reno represented, died, "we all went up to this little town up north . . . for a country funeral . . . and back to the Waldo home. And there was a gentleman running around there with an apron on, waiting on everyone; and it was none other than Mel Thomson. . . . A very human guy." Tom Rath substantially agreed: "Thomson was a courtly man for all [his] . . . fulminations and [the] colorful controversy he got into. . . . He was extraordinarily mannered. And he found in David someone who shared a lot of [his] personal characteristics—very moral, honest. He was impressed with David's classically conservative mind." Rath has also stressed, however, that Thomson had little influence with New Hampshire's executive council, the body empowered to confirm gubernatorial appointments. "So there was always going to be an element of compromise, and it was clear that the executive council wanted David Souter. . . . I think the *Union Leader* would have preferred somebody else, but [Thomson] said, ' . . . I can live with this guy.'"[100]

Whatever the motivation, Thomson nominated Souter to be attorney general in late December 1975 and the executive council unanimously approved the governor's choice on January 7, 1976. Describing his friend as "very much a conservative," a "lawyer's lawyer," and "a very able guy," Warren Rudman also had kind words for the governor. "They can say what they want about Meldrim Thomson, but he has my praise for this appointment. He could have made it a political one but he didn't. He went to a professional."[101]

For his part, Souter warned against unduly broad interpretations of written law and the threat they posed for public acceptance of legal decisions.

Although calling himself a political conservative, he stressed that politics had no bearing on his professional life and that "the legal issues I feel most strongly about are not political ones." While declaring that "it would be irresponsible for the attorney general to support any state agency if he felt what they were doing was clearly wrong," he also emphasized the "lawyer's responsibility—to give his client the best defense he can" and promised that he would defend the positions of state officials in any case in which the law was open to interpretation.102

As Charles Leahy has remarked, Souter probably "respected Mel Thomson as a fundamentally decent human being, even though he didn't agree with him politically, so he could work with him." But Souter and the governor clashed at times over issues facing the state. Thomson and William Loeb pushed hard to bring government-run casino gambling into the state as a means of bolstering New Hampshire's economy. Souter, aided by Rudman, who formed a Citizens Alliance Against Casinos, led a successful 1977 campaign against the venture. In a *Concord Monitor* column, Souter warned that casinos would attract organized crime elements and a host of criminal activities, including large-scale loan-sharking and prostitution. "Casino gambling in any form," he predicted, "would create law enforcement problems that would be intolerable under any circumstances." Testifying during a four-hour evening state legislative committee hearing on a proposal for a voter referendum on the issue, he argued that New Hampshire police, although "honest and dedicated," were "not large nor sophisticated enough to deal with the organized crime problem" casinos would pose. Citing the "exorbitant salaries" commanded by private casino managers, he also dismissed as "ridiculous" the notion of state-run casinos. "You can't run casinos with stupid managers," he exclaimed, "because you will go broke. And you can't buy a smart one for what you pay the chief justice and the governor of this state."103

While Souter was appearing before the legislature, Governor Thomson told members of the state fair association that he was "very much appalled" by such scare tactics. Emphasizing that he would not favor casino gambling unless "there was a clear need for the money," Thomson pointed out to his audience that the same arguments had been raised against legalized dog racing, yet those tracks, he claimed, had not attracted "the mafia, the underworld or anything else like that."104

Souter quickly disputed the governor's claim, insisting that organized crime interests had already attempted to infiltrate the state's dog racing industry. New Hampshire officials, he asserted, had "cleared a man for a greyhound license and it was only by sheer good luck and the grace of God we found out before the license was granted that he was a banker for organized crime." The attorney general was also extremely skeptical that casino gambling would produce the economic benefits for the state that Governor Thomson predicted. "You're going to have to offer something pretty good to get a bunch of New Yorkers to come here when they could drive in an hour or two to Atlantic City." New York, in fact, would soon have casinos itself, he added, and if New Hampshire approved them, neighboring Massachusetts was certain to follow, just to keep its money at home.[105]

Seabrook

Construction of a highly controversial nuclear power plant at Seabrook, New Hampshire, at times put the governor and Souter at odds as well. When environmentalist protesters concerned about the plant's potential impact on marine life, forming the Clamshell Alliance, staged a sit-in at the construction site, 1,414 demonstrators were arrested and confined at National Guard armories in Concord and elsewhere around the state. Although clearly a lover of nature, Souter had little patience with the protesters, whose sit-in was conducted on private property generally excluded from First Amendment protection. Lapsing into political hyperbole rare for the future justice, he termed the sit-in "one of the most well-planned acts of criminal conduct in the state or the nation, for that matter." When a judge in Hampton gave a fifteen-day suspended sentence to the first protester to go to trial, the attorney general rushed personally to court, complaining that "the imposition of a 15-day suspended sentence is for all practical purposes the imposition of nothing." Souter recommended fifteen days in jail and a $200 fine for each demonstrator and told the judge that information gathered by police monitoring of citizens' band radios indicated that the protesters planned to reoccupy the Seabrook site after their release from custody. Lawyers for the Clamshell Alliance denied such plans, but the judge sentenced protesters in the courtroom to fifteen days and a $100 fine.[106]

As a show of solidarity, most of the remaining demonstrators declined to post bond while awaiting trial. The protesters also filed a suit in Judge Bownes's court, challenging the conditions of their confinement in the armories. A Wall Street lawyer telephoned Orr and Reno with instructions to get his daughter released. Charles Leahy had no sympathy for the demonstrators. "It's intolerable to have that type of civil disorder, no matter how well-intentioned the people are. They wanted to get arrested as protesters do; they were trying to make their point. . . . [The arrests were] a matter of restoring civil order, and it was obvious that if [police] simply dispersed the crowd, they'd all be back the next morning." In the armories, Leahy said, "these young people had a good time for a while. But then, of course, after a day or two without a bath or [other amenities]," their attitudes began to change. By the time Leahy arrived at the Manchester armory to obtain his client's release, "her position had changed from wanting to go back and scale the fence and get arrested again to, 'If I get out of here, does it mean I can get a hot shower and clean clothes?'" Leahy was equally certain, though, that conditions in the armory he visited "were perfectly civilized. The jailers . . . were these young National Guard troopers who were the same age as these kids. It was like a party." The federal suit, in his judgment, was "absolute nonsense." Souter clearly shared his sentiments. Judge Bownes apparently agreed as well. The protesters' complaint was dismissed.107

The previous year, Governor Thomson had told a reporter that any state employee wanting to speak out against nuclear power should resign. He later said that comment had been made "on the run" and assured state workers they were free "to speak out on any issue as private citizens." But Thomson obviously shared the sentiments of Souter and other critics regarding the Seabrook protesters, whom he scorned as "a mob whose stated purpose was to illegally occupy the private property of others." Based on Souter's estimate that the protesters' incarceration and trials could cost the state $1 million, the governor sought a grant from the federal Law Enforcement Assistance Administration (LEAA) to cover police expenses and the cost of holding the demonstrators in the armories. After two Washington State nuclear plant workers began soliciting funds to assist New Hampshire, he also made a nationwide appeal for donations. Characteristically, when the LEAA declined assistance, Thomson condemned the agency as "one of the worst of the bureaucratic boondoggles."108

Earlier, Souter himself had drawn the governor's ire. In July 1976, the attorney general, along with his Massachusetts counterpart, filed legal objections to the immediate construction of the Seabrook facility, which had recently won tentative approval from the Nuclear Regulatory Commission (NRC). Stressing that he did not oppose the plant's construction, Souter said that he could not accept the NRC's assumption of final authority to approve the plant's cooling facility—a power reserved to the Environmental Protection Agency—or the absence of a Seabrook-area evacuation plan in the event of a meltdown or some other plant crisis.[109]

Governor Thomson was not happy with what he characterized as Souter's "giving comfort" to the plant's opponents. "It is understandable that the environmentalists would file appeals," Thomson observed in a press release. "Also, it was not hard to guess that Massachusetts, which is in the political grip of environmentalists, would do its utmost to stop . . . construction." But he found it "difficult to comprehend" why Souter would add "weight to the contentions of the nuclear obstructionists." While acknowledging that the matter was entirely in Souter's "hands under the statutes and out of the control of the Governor," Thomson said his own counsel might enter the case in support of Seabrook if "such action would in any way help to assure early construction of the plant."[110]

In an editorial headlined "Just What's Souter's Game?" the *Union Leader's* William Loeb soon entered the fray. Over the past three decades, the publisher asserted, he had observed "certain Attorneys General of New Hampshire who have done a few foolish things." For Loeb, however, Souter had "set the record." The publisher realized that "anti–nuclear power kooks" would try to block development of the "so badly needed" plant. But for Souter to try to block the facility after its opponents "were defeated and the permit granted," Loeb found "incredible."[111]

Another newspaper condemned Souter's action as "intolerable and inexplicable" given the extensive scrutiny and debate to which the project had been subjected. "From what dark and sound-proofed cave did our Attorney General just emerge?" asked Joseph McQuaid, managing editor of the *New Hampshire Sunday News.* "Doesn't he know there have been a full four years of hearings on . . . every . . . issue imaginable concerning the Seabrook proposal?" The NRC, wrote McQuaid, had done "ample foot-dragging" of its own before finally granting a permit. "Even now, after all this time and all these delays," he added, anticipating the coming year's Clamshell Alliance protests, "one group of kooks says it may stage a 'nonviolent confrontation' and 'live' at the site in an attempt to block construction." By sticking "his nose into the act, Mr. Souter, whether or not he intended to do so, has done nothing less than to give aid and comfort to a minority which had been properly turned away at every other door." Loeb reprinted McQuaid's entire editorial "in the hopes that it will bring Attorney General David Souter to his senses."[112]

Reacting to such criticism, as well as a television newsman's suggestion that he had joined forces with Seabrook opponents, Souter sought to clear up what he termed "misunderstandings" in the media regarding his stance on the issue. The objections he had filed with the NRC, he said, "in no way were intended to halt construction" or delay opening of the station. His goal was simply to ensure the safety of the projects. Any implication that he had allied with plant critics, he added, was "simply not so."[113]

In 1978, Souter and Thomson parted company again when the Clamshell Alliance sought to rent the Portsmouth armory for a dance celebrating its 1977 protest at the Seabrook site. Souter told John Blatsos, adjutant general of the National Guard, that the state had "no reasonable grounds for refusal of the request," and the Alliance signed a contract with the Guard to rent the facility, inviting the guardsmen as well as protesters to attend. Thomson, as commander in chief of the National Guard, rescinded the contract, prompting an Alliance leader to remark, "I bet if the John Birch Society wanted to use the armory, Thomson would be rolling out the red carpet." But in a suit brought by the Alliance, the New Hampshire Supreme Court rebuffed the governor and the state's contention that the group be required to post a $10,000 bond for use of the facility. As attorney general, Souter had a legal obligation to defend any of the governor's positions that he found at all legally defensible. But he refused to take a stance merely to accommodate Thomson's political agenda.[114]

Whether serving as the governor's legal advocate or representing legal positions he personally favored, Souter and his staff often defended the eccentric Thomson in court as well as other arenas. The press complained when the governor, executive council, and state prison board of trustees held a closed-door session over growing problems in New Hampshire's state prison, amid demands by Thomson that the trustees either fire Warden Raymond A. Helgemoe or resign themselves. Souter defended the closed-door meeting under an exception to the state's right-to-know statute authorizing executive sessions for discussion of any matter that "would be likely to adversely affect the reputation of any person, other than a member of the body [involved] itself." Under another provision of the law, Helgemoe had a right to demand an open proceeding if the session discussed his personnel status; Souter told reporters before the proceeding that he had advised the governor that the session should be opened if the discussion turned to Helgemoe or criticism of his administration. After the meeting, he said that the session had stayed within the bounds of the exception to the right-to-know statute. But he was hardly happy with the law's language. Asked by a reporter if the "reputation" section of the law could not be used to exclude the public from almost any session, he conceded that the exception "could be stretched so far as to swallow the law entirely." As a whole, he added, in language hardly characteristic of the future justice's typically cautious public rhetoric, the law was a piece of "vague and lousy legislative drafting. [It] stinks."[115]

Not surprisingly, elements of the state press strenuously objected to the closed session. Citing the state's $7.5 million biennial investment in the prison, the *Concord Monitor* editorialized that the people had a right to open sessions on prison conditions, "if only to clarify the state of affairs" in the facility. The paper focused particular attention on Souter's use of the "reputation" exception to the open meetings law. After all, if Warden Helgemoe's name came up, he had a right to be present. Furthermore, Governor Thomson, "in a windstorm of critical news releases, already [had] so sullied Warden Helgemoe's reputation that little could be said in a public session to damage it further." The *Monitor*'s conclusion: "Closing the joint meeting was a sham, a cover-up and an evasion of the law. The public was denied its right to know the truth about the Prison."[116]

Souter, the Governor, and the Constitution

As the state's advocates, Souter and his staff also represented Thomson in two First Amendment religion cases. Although he ultimately asked to file an amicus curiae, or friend-of-court, brief, the attorney general refused to intervene otherwise in a dispute over the recitation of the Lord's Prayer in Rochester, New Hampshire, schools. The governor had said that his office's legal counsel was prepared to defend any challenges to the ritual, authorized under a 1975 statute, and assumed that the attorney general also would "be prepared to assist" the school system. But Souter said his office would not represent Rochester in a suit brought by the New Hampshire Civil Liberties Union. His office, he announced, would defend only the state law allowing such programs, not individual local exercises. Of Thomson's assumption that the attorney general would intervene in Rochester's behalf, Souter testily remarked, "I don't know what's on his mind. I've told him it's not within our jurisdiction." Calling the Rochester program a "patently unconstitutional" violation of the First Amendment guarantee against laws respecting an establishment of religion, a right made binding on the states through the Supreme Court's interpretation of the Fourteenth Amendment, Judge Bownes issued an injunction against the school system, and the city dropped initial plans for an appeal.[117]

Souter did defend the state, however, in a religious liberty and free speech case growing out of a Thomson-initiated change in the inscription on New Hampshire automobile license plates. Earlier, state plates advertised "Scenic" New Hampshire. That was too tame for Thomson, who had the state motto, "Live Free or Die"—adopted from the 1809 toast of New Hampshire Revolutionary War hero John Stark to a former comrade—added to state licenses. George and Maxine Maynard, a Jehovah's Witness couple, considered display of the motto, which Meldrim Thomson would later use as the title to a published collection of his gubernatorial addresses, an affront to their religious beliefs. After they began taping over the motto on the plates of their two automobiles, George Maynard was arrested three times for violating a state law making it a misdemeanor knowingly to obscure figures or letters on state licenses. When he refused to pay fines imposed for the infraction, he was ordered committed to jail. The Maynards then filed a federal suit seeking a ruling that the prosecutions were unconstitutional and an injunction from the court requiring the state to issue them plates without the offensive motto.

According to several friends, Souter was doubtful that people could be compelled to display a motto on their license plates that they found religiously or politically objectionable. Nevertheless, his staff and a Supreme Court brief that carried his name argued that the motto facilitated identification of licenses as New Hampshire plates, while also promoting appreciation of the state's history, individualism, and pride. Terming the Maynards' action "symbolic speech" and rejecting the state's arguments as inadequate to justify the compulsory display of mottoes people found offensive, Judge Bownes and others on a three-judge federal district court granted the relief sought. The argument that display of the motto was required for vehicle identification, the panel observed, was "belied by the fact that only passenger cars are required to have license plates that contain the motto." Besides, the state's name on license plates clearly identified them as New Hampshire licenses. By a 6–3 vote, the U.S. Supreme Court concurred.[118]

Souter's stance in the license motto case attracted criticism. A Massachusetts woman wrote him to attack his defense of the challenged requirement. Noting that she was a New Hampshire native, she called for "a grassroots revolt against the tyranny of such officious, arrogant officials as those among us who would cram down our throats any philosophy contrary to individual thinking in the name of promoting state pride or history or tradition or tourism. This could be easily accomplished if more of us would stop behaving like sheep and show the intestinal fortitude and willingness to personally sacrifice at any cost in the manner of George and Maxine Maynard."[119]

In his reply, Souter expressed regret that "the action of the New Hampshire Legislature in placing the state motto on automobile registration plates leaves you embarrassed and ashamed." But the issue litigated, he asserted, involved the validity of the state's action under the U.S. Constitution. "The desirability of taking this sort of action raises, of course, a separate question. If you believe that the motto should not be placed on registration plates, I can only suggest that you communicate with the members of the Legislature to suggest that the law be amended." As noted previously, Souter doubted the constitutionality of the motto display requirement but considered it his legal responsibility as attorney general to defend the law in court.[120]

The attorney general's defense of another Thomson initiative would be a particular source of concern during Souter's confirmation proceedings. At the slightest provocation, the governor regularly ordered the lowering of flags on state property to half-mast. When President Carter signed the Panama Canal treaty and granted amnesty to Vietnam draft dodgers, for example, the flags came down. In 1976, Thomson began ordering that New Hampshire and U.S. flags fly at half-mast on Good Friday to, as his proclamation put it, "memorialize the death of Christ on the Cross." The New Hampshire Civil Liberties Union complained in 1976 that Thomson's conduct was "an utterly inappropriate usurpation of power" and announced that its members were "deeply distressed" when the governor repeated the action in 1977. Several local clergy had also complained that such exercises violated the establishment clause; in 1978, five clerics, represented by a Civil Liberties Union lawyer, filed a federal court suit seeking to prevent a repeat of the previous years' directives.[121]

The governor was hardly dissuaded. The next day, he told reporters he had dusted off the 1977 proclamation and changed its date, once again directing that the flags be lowered "to memorialize the death of Christ on the first Good Friday." Three Unitarians, an Episcopal priest, and a Jewish rabbi were plaintiffs in the suit. Calling their court complaint a "nuisance action," the governor asserted that most of the plaintiffs "apparently do not believe in recognizing Christianity as symbolized by Good Friday, by Easter and by all other Christian holidays."[122]

Judge Hugh Bownes had recently been elevated to a seat on the Court of Appeals for the First Circuit in Boston, and the Concord district court bench had not yet been filled. Thus, Walter Skinner, a Boston federal district judge, heard the flag case. Souter assigned Bill Glahn and Steven McAuliffe to defend the governor. But Glahn, as he later recalled, "was consulting with David all the way." The case went through the federal judicial system with remarkable speed—at that point, Glahn believes, probably "the fastest case ever to go from a complaint to the U.S. Supreme Court."[123]

Judge Skinner ruled for the plaintiffs, holding that the governor must have a secular rather than a religious purpose for any flag-lowering venture. The court of appeals quickly reversed, concluding that the plaintiffs had failed to file their case in a sufficiently timely fashion; the governor, after all, had first begun to issue his Good Friday proclamations two years earlier. "David was ecstatic," Glahn remembers, "the governor was happy, and I went home that night and had a couple of good, stiff drinks." But almost immediately word came down that the plaintiffs had filed an appeal in the Supreme Court, and a 5–4 majority there granted a stay of the First Circuit's ruling pending further review of the case.[124]

In a brief for the case that Glahn wrote but Souter signed and, Glahn later said, "would have approved of," the state contended that Thomson's proclamation neither advanced nor inhibited religion and thus did not violate the three-pronged religious establishment test announced by the Supreme Court in *Lemon v. Kurtzman* (1971), which required that policies affecting religion have a secular purpose and a primary effect that neither advanced nor harmed religion, while also avoiding excessive church-state entanglement. "The lowering of the flag to commemorate the death of Christ no more establishes a religious position on the part of the State or promotes a religion than the lowering of a flag for the death of Hubert Humphrey promotes the cause of the Democratic Party in New Hampshire."[125]

The day after the Supreme Court ruling, however, Governor Thomson, following discussion with Souter, issued a new proclamation giving Good Friday flag-lowering a more secular cast. Now, the exercise was to honor "the historical impact on Western civilization of the life and teachings of Jesus Christ." But Judge Skinner never issued a ruling on that declaration, and the case, as Souter remarked during his Senate confirmation hearing, "just petered out at that point."[126]

During the flag controversy, a Massachusetts lawyer wrote Tom Rath, asking if Souter would "use some discretion in deciding whether or not to defend the Supreme Executive Magistrate [the New Hampshire constitution's quaint description of gubernatorial authority] on matters concerning his personal preferences regarding the height of the United States flag?" In two days, Souter replied. "My standard, in flag cases and any others, has been simply this: this office will represent any governor in a proceeding brought against him in his official capacity whenever his action cannot reasonably be judged patently illegal or unconstitutional." As attorney general, he added, he would "act as a lawyer guided by generally applicable principles. I don't believe any other standard is possible." The only alternatives: "an attorney general who is a political rubber stamp or one who is a political spokesman for political opposition to the governor." Souter found neither option acceptable. "Although I don't want to sound testy," he concluded, "I don't believe your political objection to the governor's action can reasonably be translated into legal or political objections to the principles adopted by this office in providing representation to the governor in his capacity as an official of the state." Particularly in view of the strong commitment to church-state separation he would later embrace as a justice, a commitment based largely on Supreme Court precedents that predated Meldrim Thomson's administration, Souter probably had little sympathy for the governor's religious agenda. Again, however, he considered himself bound by his legal duty as attorney general, whatever his personal views.[127]

Souter, as Bill Glahn phrased it, caught "a lot of flack" about the flag case during his confirmation proceedings. But the dispute did provide its lighter moments. One day, Steven McAuliffe later recalled, he, Glahn, and Souter were standing in the attorney general's office discussing how to proceed with the case. "Bill was doing the talking; David was listening. At one point, Bill said, 'You know, since it's Good Friday and the claim is that church-state separation is being violated by lowering the flag in honor of Christ's death on Good Friday, why don't we just go the whole way and raise it again [Easter] Sunday morning.' [David Souter] never cracked a smile. He just stared with his black eyes and said, 'I trust you'll not breathe a word of that outside this office—particularly not mention that suggestion to the governor.' We all broke out laughing."[128]

2

New Hampshire Judge

IN 1977, THE YEAR after David Souter became New Hampshire's attorney general, a vacancy arose on the state supreme court. Warren Rudman and Tom Rath, among others, urged Governor Meldrim Thomson to choose their friend. Eventually, Rudman later wrote, Souter and Rath went to see Thomson. "While they were talking, Thomson left the room to take a phone call, and when he returned he told David—seemingly in some distress—that he couldn't put him on the supreme court, but that he'd gladly appoint him to the superior court. David declined the offer and continued as attorney general. Tom Rath [was] convinced that the call came from [*Union Leader* publisher] William Loeb, vetoing David's appointment to the supreme court."[1]

Early the next year another seat became available on the supreme court, and the governor again offered Souter a superior court seat, although adding on this occasion that after a few years of trial court experience, promotion to the supreme court would be an easier proposition. Souter initially declined but then accepted, urged on by Rudman, who "assumed that [his friend] would be so outstanding on the superior court that some future governor would promote him to the supreme court."[2]

On February 24, Meldrim Thomson submitted Souter's superior court nomination to the executive council, along with his choice of Tom Rath to become attorney general. The governor's action prompted the usually reserved Souter to exclaim, "Of course, I'm honored in the extreme and at the same time, I'm very happy that apparently Tom Rath will succeed me." By that point, the council had not yet confirmed the governor's supreme court nominee, Louis Wyman, a controversial lawyer who had served several terms in the U.S. House of Representatives before losing a wild 1974 U.S. Senate race that ended with such a close vote and so many hotly disputed returns that the Senate had ordered a second election. A *Union Leader* reporter speculated that the governor had picked Souter for a superior court judgeship in an effort to appease the council, which was said to prefer Souter over Wyman for the high court. If that was Thomson's ploy, however, it did not work. Wyman had to accept a superior court seat, too.[3]

During its March 10 session, the executive council unanimously confirmed Souter's appointment to be a justice, as superior court judges are designated in New Hampshire. Tom Rath won unanimous approval as attorney general as well. On April 6, Thomson administered the oath to the two at a testimonial dinner for Souter at the Concord Country Club. The new judge's father had died in 1976, but Helen Souter attended the ceremony, and the next day's *Concord Monitor* carried a photograph of Souter pinning a corsage on his delighted mother. Thomson presented Souter a gift of a small desk flag flying at half-staff in honor of the Good Friday flag case. Rath, who had become principally responsible for dealing with the Clamshell Alliance's protest against the Seabrook nuclear facility, received a white T-shirt with the words "Eat Clams" inscribed on the front.[4]

Riding Circuit

With Souter's appointment, the state superior court, first created in 1901, consisted of thirteen associate justices and Chief Justice William H. Keller. Judges, like those on the New Hampshire Supreme Court, receive lifetime appointments. Superior court judges sit individually, hearing felony and major civil cases, divorce and other domestic relations suits, and appeals from state district court judges' rulings in misdemeanor cases. Superior court judges ride circuit, but Souter would try cases mainly in Merrimack (Concord) and Hillsborough (Manchester) County.

A stickler for propriety, Souter invoked a demanding recusal policy on the trial bench. He refused, for example, to preside over cases in which counsel included attorneys from his old law firm or lawyers with whom he had worked in the attorney general's office. When asked about his friend's tenure on the superior court bench, Orr and Reno's Ronald Snow had "one vivid memory." On one occasion, Snow was asked to represent a woman in a divorce action who would later become a major Boston television personality. "At the time she was living in New Hampshire and getting an absolutely uncontested divorce. She was not asking for any alimony. It was all sort of friendly. And the plan was to get [it] done in Hillsborough County, Manchester, in about a thirty-minute proceeding." The court clerk agreed, asking that Snow and his client arrive at court at noon on the appointed day.[5]

When they appeared at the courthouse, the clerk told them to wait in a conference room while he got one of the sitting judges to preside. "In a few minutes, the clerk returned with a pretty exasperated look on his face and said, 'Justice Souter is [the only judge] sitting here today, and he won't hear you.' And I said, '. . . Did you explain to Justice Souter that this is uncontested; there's no challenge, there's absolutely nothing that's disputed? The other side isn't even going to appear; it's just pro forma.' And the clerk replied, 'Yes, I did, in spades, and he's not going to hear you.'"[6]

Snow sent the clerk back to Souter, hoping that some way could be devised to resolve the matter and send his client, spouseless, on her way. The clerk soon returned, explaining that the justice had made the clerk a special magistrate for the day, so that he could handle the divorce. "About five minutes later, the girl turned to me and said, 'Is that all there is?' And I said, 'That's it; it's over.'" But Snow had hardly been surprised at Souter's stance. "That's my friend Souter, whose ethics are so uppermost in his mind that even a hint of doing a favor for a friend, in a matter that no one could have ever heard about, predominated over friendship. And for that I admire him."[7]

Not unexpectedly for those familiar with Souter's reputation in the attorney general's office, he was, as Tom Rath put it, "a demanding trial judge. He liked to begin and end on time. He wanted you to be prepared, not knock off at two o'clock in the afternoon." Lawyers seemingly oblivious to their responsibilities were a particular source of concern and irritation to the justice. Jack Middleton, a veteran Manchester attorney, was once scheduled for a motion hearing before another judge; opposing counsel failed to appear. "Just plain wasn't there. And that judge, kindly I thought from the point of view of the other counsel, just continued the hearing to another date."[8]

Justice Souter was assigned the case for that second court appearance. And again, the other lawyer was not present. But Souter granted no further continuance, nor did he merely rule in Middleton's favor. Instead, "Justice Souter came into the courtroom, and we had a full-scale hearing on the motion. I had no opposition. But I was invited to argue to him until he satisfied himself that there was some merit to the motion rather than simply rubber-stamp it. And I was impressed, because even in those days, judges were pressed for time and judicial resources were scarce. Yet he took the time to look into the matter. And frankly, at the end of the hearing, when he granted my motion, I was fairly sure that nothing on earth was going to change the result. . . . He was obviously distressed, as I was, that this matter had been scheduled a second time; and the second time around the lawyer again had not shown up in court. And there was no explanation for it that any of us were aware of."[9]

Souter also quickly gained a reputation as a jurist who treated everyone in the courtroom with respect. "One of the things I heard a lot about from folks at the time," Tom Rath remembers, "was that he was extraordinarily considerate of jurors and followed the practice of meeting privately with the jury [in each case] and thanking them for their service." On at least one occasion, his courtroom habits drew comment from a juror as well. Souter liked to paint and had even tried his hand at sketches. His friends Bill and Hansi Glahn found one effort that he showed them "actually very good." During superior court proceedings, the justice often sketched on the bench. He thought it particularly important during a long trial, Bill Glahn has said, "to remember what the witnesses looked like. And a little sketch helped him [remember]." One day, though, a juror asked, "Were you drawing those witnesses?" And Souter had to admit he had been caught in the act.[10]

Souter treated those in court, including defendants, with dignity. Mark L. Sisti is one of New Hampshire's premier criminal defense lawyers. As Manchester attorney Bruce Felmly put it, "If somebody chops up more than one person, Sisti probably [represents that] defendant." As a public defender, Sisti appeared before Souter in superior court "in just about every type of criminal matter you could possibly appear before him on." Both as a public defender and later in private practice, he also argued cases before Souter on the New Hampshire Supreme Court. On the trial bench, Sisti recalls, Souter "treated a lot of our clients that most folks wouldn't even take a second look at with the utmost respect." Sisti's law partner Paul Twomey agrees. "Even when he was sentencing someone to prison for years, he always treated the defendant with dignity."[11]

Souter's treatment of defendants was the same, Sisti has said, "even when they didn't respect him." One of Sisti's clients was a young man who was part of a ring stealing gold from "small 'Mom and Pop' coin shops" throughout New Hampshire and Massachusetts. Most of the gang got away, but Sisti's client was arrested for illegal hitchhiking after his car broke down on an interstate highway, then quickly connected with the coin-shop thefts. Convicted in Justice Souter's court, he could have received the maximum sentence as he had a prior record and had served time in San Quentin, among other prisons. Souter, moreover, typically imposed stiff sentences. Paul Twomey remarked, "When sentencing [time] came, he was not the guy you wanted to be before." Perhaps out of consideration for the defendant's youth,

Souter set a somewhat lighter sentence than the statutes authorized. But the defendant was hardly grateful. "He was a California-based kid, and he was a tough kid. . . . He stood up," Sisti remembers, "and spat toward the bench. Justice Souter, instead of reacting angrily, just looked at him, waved to a bailiff, and said, 'Just take him away.' He didn't hold him in contempt; he didn't up the sentence; he just blew him off, which I thought was an interesting reaction and one that showed the utmost restraint." It was also, Sisti added, hardly the usual reaction of judges to such courtroom behavior.[12]

Although a tough sentencer, Sisti and Twomey also found Souter to be a compassionate jurist. In one case, Twomey represented a man charged with stealing a dollar from his employer. "They had it on videotape. . . . He had previously been convicted of a number of things [under] an old version of a three-strike law that made [the client's offenses] a felony if he had prior convictions. The state told him that if he went to trial, he was going to get a four- or five-year sentence. They offered him a two-year sentence, which he accepted over my advice." When the plea was being formalized in court, Twomey told Souter he had advised his client against the plea bargain. "Judge Souter refused to take the plea because it was cruel and inhumane to put someone in prison for two years for stealing a dollar. I don't remember any other judge ever doing that."[13]

Despite Souter's background as a prosecutor, Sisti and Twomey also quickly decided that the justice was not "pro-state," but instead was "pro–fair trial," willing to suppress illegally seized evidence and confessions "even when it pained him. . . . [He] would follow the right path." One of Sisti's clients was Al Jaroma, a Hookset, New Hampshire, man with "a record that had to be a mile long. He was an habitual burglar and thief, receiving stolen property. . . . He was a con artist. . . . He literally had an entire home furnished and stockpiled with stolen material. What made it more aggravating was that his next-door neighbor was the police chief. In fact, part of the allegation was that he stole items from the chief of police. . . . We are talking literally of tons of materials stolen throughout [the area]. . . . I think, in fact, there may have even been stolen evergreens and azaleas he literally dug up from people's [yards] and replanted."[14]

On May 12, 1982, Manchester police, acting on a search warrant, entered Jeroma's house and found several items taken in a recent burglary. A Hookset police officer along on the search spotted other items he thought were stolen and obtained a second search warrant. The second search produced an inventory of stolen goods sixty-seven pages long![15]

Sisti raised a number of evidentiary claims in a motion to suppress the evidence before trial in Justice Souter's court. After a lengthy hearing, Souter declared much of the seized evidence inadmissible. In a sixteen-page order, he held that the warrant on which the second, much more productive, search was based was invalid. Agreeing with Sisti, he concluded that the second warrant was unduly broad and that the police lacked probable cause to justify such a sweeping search. Souter acknowledged that the defendant's home amounted to "a virtual warehouse of stolen goods" but determined that most of it could not be used as evidence against him. Based on Souter's ruling, the prosecutor dismissed seventeen counts for possession of stolen goods and one count making it illegal for a convicted felon to possess a firearm. "What outraged him more than anything [else] in the case," Sisti later said, recalling Souter's stern reaction to the searches in court, "was that the police department searched [Jeroma's] home and then opened his home up to the local television station and allowed them to walk through the house with TV cameras, and run for the nightly news the search itself. . . . He found that to be just absolutely outrageous and unreasonable, that the police department was going beyond the search itself for their own self-aggrandizement."[16]

Sisti and Twomey also represented Susan Beardsley, a woman charged with arson and second-degree murder in a fire at a large Manchester tenement building in which a child died. Before the jury was selected, Beardsley's counsel brought to Souter's attention possible tampering with the evidence. "Early on in the case," Sisti has observed, "we were able to get an investigator into the complex and shoot film inside the complex. When the fire took place, obviously the electricity was cut off and the clocks were frozen at the time. [The time on clocks in the tenement] didn't fit . . . with the state's case very well. We moved to preserve the building intact and to have it secured, which [Justice Souter] granted. . . . When we went back into the building prior to the trial starting and the jury taking a view [of the fire site], we noticed that the clocks had been changed." To extract a confession, police had also told Beardsley they would take her child from her unless she cooperated with their investigation, after which she signed a statement indicating that she must have set the fire even though she had no memory of it. When the defense brought the police practices to Souter's attention in a written motion to suppress, Sisti recalls, "This was not a happy judge." The attorney general's office moved for dismissal of the case, ending the prosecution.[17]

According to Paul Twomey, the Manchester police chief "blasted" Souter's suppression of evidence in the Beardsley case. Souter's ruling in another arson case was also controversial. During a bicycle race in Concord, the local Ramada Inn was set on fire. "Every room was occupied," Sisti remembers. "Everybody got out alive, thank God, but [the fire] may have taken out a floor or two of the hotel." Sisti represented the defendant, a young man named Larry Cooper, who was charged with arson in the case. "[Cooper] was mentally challenged, to say the least. . . . There was just an unbelievable amount of publicity about the case, and people were screaming for [Cooper's conviction]." But Souter was hardly one to yield to public pressure. After holding a two-day competency hearing, he declared the defendant incompetent to stand trial. "He was the kind of guy who could take it," Sisti remembers; "he thought that the law trumped" public outcry.[18]

The Barney Siel Case

Souter's controversial trial rulings did not always favor defendants, however. In 1980, a Strafford County grand jury indicted Barney Siel, whose mother was an assistant to the Merrimack County clerk in Concord, for first-degree murder and attempted robbery of one Joseph Woodside. In a jury trial before another judge, the defendant was found guilty on both counts and sentenced to life imprisonment without possibility of parole. On the motion of Siel's counsel, however, the trial judge set aside the verdicts and ordered a new trial on the basis of flaws in his instructions to trial jurors prior to their deliberations.[19]

In preparation for further proceedings and as part of a defense strategy to shift suspicion to others, Siel's counsel subpoenaed Laura Meade and Joel Brown, two student newspaper reporters at the University of New Hampshire in Durham. Defense lawyers wanted the reporters to appear at a discovery proceeding and give evidence relating to articles they had written about Joseph Woodside's involvement in drug dealings and presence in Durham the week before his death. The defense believed that the articles showed that other people in Durham would have known that Woodside was a drug dealer and might have had a motive to rob or kill him. Moving to quash the subpoenas, Meade and Brown contended that they had no personal knowledge of Woodside's involvement in drug dealing or his whereabouts the week before his murder. They further claimed that, as reporters, they were privileged under the First Amendment and the New Hampshire constitution from being required to disclose information about the case.[20]

After a hearing, Justice Souter upheld the reporters' privilege claims and also rebuffed Siel's efforts to avoid a second trial. In *Branzburg v. Hayes* (1972), the U.S. Supreme Court had rejected a reporter's challenge to a subpoena requiring him to testify before a grand jury and his argument that compliance with the subpoena would inhibit confidential news sources, thus restricting the free flow of information vital to a free society. In his opinion for the 5-4 *Branzburg* majority, Justice Byron White emphasized that it was more important to do something about crime than write about it. White also dismissed as highly speculative press claims that compliance with subpoenas would impose a meaningful chilling effect on confidential sources, especially given the fact that most journalists had long enjoyed close relationships with confidential informants even without recognition of a First Amendment testimonial privilege.[21]

Justice White appeared to reject any such privilege absent a showing of government bad faith. In a concurring opinion, however, Justice Lewis Powell, the critical fifth member of the *Branzburg* majority, construed the Court's opinion to require a judicial balancing of competing interests in any case in which journalists resisted testifying before grand juries.

In upholding the reporters' claims in the *Siel* case, Justice Souter, like most other judges, embraced Powell's interpretation of the *Branzburg* ruling. A unanimous state supreme court affirmed, adopting what the justices characterized as "the well-reasoned position that the trial judge developed at length in his rulings and holding that defendants could overcome a press privilege to withhold confidential news sources only when they could establish that they had unsuccessfully exhausted reasonable alternatives for acquiring the information sought, that the information was relevant to [the] defense, and that there was a reasonable possibility that the information sought would affect the verdict in the case."[22]

In his ruling, Souter made the following observations:

Defendant seeks the identity of the reporters' informants in this case to strengthen his claim that others in Durham would have had an opportunity to learn that Woodside carried drugs or money, or dealt in drugs. On the basis of such evidence, he would argue that other persons had an opportunity and motive to rob for the money or drugs, whether simply to obtain them or in revenge for unsatisfactory dealings. I should note that defendant seeks the identity of the sources solely as a means of leading him to such evidence. There is no basis on the record that would suggest that the sources, or any of their sources, could provide more definite evidence that any other person did in fact have such motives or did in fact kill Woodside.

The high court concurred with Souter's assessment, agreeing that there was only a suspicion that the reporters' sources might have information that would assist Siel but not "the level of certainty needed to overcome the reporters' privilege."[23]

Following Siel's second trial and conviction, Souter released the defendant pending appeal on a bond his parents had posted. When Siel went scuba diving at Rye Beach, then disappeared, people initially speculated that he had faked his drowning to escape punishment for his crime. Siel's body was recovered several months later, but not before Justice Souter had required his grieving parents to forfeit the bond. After the body was discovered, the bond was returned to the parents. But Paul Twomey thought Souter's initial action unduly "harsh," a sentiment many other Concord citizens apparently shared.[24]

At the time of his U.S. Supreme Court nomination, leaders of press groups praised Souter's ruling and rationale in the *Siel* case as something of a landmark in media law. In ruling on testimonial press privilege claims, they noted, other courts had considered the relevance of the evidence sought from journalists and whether alternative sources of the information were available. But Souter had also asked whether requiring a reporter's testimony would create a "reasonable possibility" of affecting the verdict in a case. Souter's decision had been the first in a New Hampshire case involving press privilege claims in a criminal case. Jane Kirtley, the executive director of the Reporters Committee for Freedom of the Press, found the decision "quite extraordinary, especially for a trial judge. When I came across this decision, I said this guy is very good for us."[25]

Justice Souter's reputation as a tough trial judge, albeit one willing to honor precedents expanding the rights of criminal defendants, was also enhanced in a 1981 case. There, he rejected two attempts by defense counsel to plea-bargain down the sentence of a woman who had pleaded guilty to stealing a .357 Magnum handgun during a burglary. The justice sentenced her to serve nine months of a one-and-a-half to three-year term and placed her on four years' probation, conditional on drug rehabilitation and completion of a high school equivalency program. To the prosecutor who had agreed to more lenient plea arrangements, he caustically observed: "This is a Class A felony, and when somebody breaks into a house and steals one of the most powerful handguns that one can steal, one is intentionally raising the risk of injury, serious harm or death to other people."[26]

Abortion and Parental Consent

As attorney general, it will be recalled, Souter had expressed opposition to "unlimited abortions" and his concern that New Hampshire could become the nation's "abortion mill" were all the state's abortion regulations repealed in the wake of the *Roe* decision. On the superior court bench he went further, registering his opposition to parental consent legislation that permitted minors to seek a judge's approval if they were unable to secure the permission of parents.

By that point, the Supreme Court had approved such judicial bypass measures. In 1981, however, Souter wrote a letter on behalf of his colleagues to the chair of a New Hampshire legislative committee. In the letter, he urged legislators to defeat a bill that would have authorized judges to approve abortions for minors unable to obtain their parents' permission. Because the Supreme Court had been willing to approve parental consent abortion laws only if they included a judicial bypass provision, abortion opponents were vigorous supporters of such legislation. While the New Hampshire bill was pending, Elizabeth Hager of Concord, a state legislator and board member of the National Abortion Rights Action League (NARAL), telephoned Justice Souter, the only judge she knew well enough socially, she later said, to feel "comfortable picking up the phone and having this conversation." Hager told Souter about the judicial bypass proposal and expressed hope "he would read it and talk to his fellow judges, because I didn't think they would want to be dealing with minors obtaining abortions. He agreed and he talked to his fellow judges, and he drafted the letter, and they approved it, and he sent it to the committee." The bill failed to pass. When the bill was revived four years later, Hager again called Souter. He was then on the state supreme court but referred her to Richard Dunfrey, who had become superior court chief justice. "I sent [Dunfrey] a copy of the [Souter] letter and he made a couple of minor changes and sent it to the Legislature over his signature."[27]

In 1990, when Souter was nominated to the U.S. Supreme Court, Hager told a reporter that the letter had "been a critical part of preventing passage of parental consent legislation" in New Hampshire for the past nine years. She insisted, however, that "the tone of the letter clearly indicates his purpose was to defend the judicial system against the bypass, and not take a stand against the legislation"—a favorite of abortion opponents. National pro-choice interests were concerned, moreover, that the conception of the judicial function embraced in the letter was more in line with that favored by the first Bush administration than the more flexible approach to constitutional interpretation on which *Roe v. Wade* and related decisions had been based. In language reflecting the concerns of conservatives, Souter complained in the letter that the proposed legislation would "leave it to individual justices of this court to make fundamental moral decisions about the interests of other people without any standards to guide the individual judge" and based on "only the individual judge's principles and predilections." Critics of the judiciary, he asserted, had contended that their interpretations of constitutional provisions are "no more than the imposition of individual judges' views in the guise of applying constitutional terms of great generality." The proposed bill "would force the superior court to engage in such acts of unfettered personal choices." Urging the legislature to reject any parental consent bill that involved "the exercise of judicial choice," he warned that since only "some judges" could not in good conscience issue an abortion order, enactment of the bill would lead to "shopping for judges" willing to allow abortions.[28]

Souter's opposition to the judicial bypass proposal seems clearly to have been based, as he asserted, on his aversion to giving judges authority to substitute their judgments for those of parents, or minors, in abortion cases, rather than on opposition to a parental consent restriction on a minor's choice. In the U.S. Supreme Court, as noted earlier, Souter's high regard for precedent has obliged him to reaffirm the essence of *Roe* and also to uphold parental consent regulations with a judicial bypass option. As a jurist, he also has consistently embraced substantive due process, the constitutional doctrine protecting individual liberties, including abortion and other rights not mentioned specifically in the Constitution's text, from unreasonable government interference. Writing on a clean slate under that doctrine, without *Roe* and its progeny on the books, Souter would probably have accepted some degree of constitutional protection for abortion rights yet also have recognized considerably broader governmental authority over abortions than *Roe* and later cases have embraced. On a purely personal moral level, moreover, the one-time candidate for the Episcopal priesthood probably viewed abortion with considerable distaste. Against that backdrop, the tone of his comments about the judicial bypass measure, and earlier abortion statements as New Hampshire attorney general, hardly seem surprising.

By all accounts, Souter enjoyed his tenure on the superior court. "He actually liked to travel around," Bill Glahn has said, "because he got to see different lawyers, and cases that you hear in [more rural sections of a superior court's jurisdiction] are much different than cases you're going to hear [in Concord or Manchester]. You're going to get small cases, and you're going to have farmers and loggers. . . . There's only one judge [on the bench], and you get everything. You get the domestic violence cases; you get the commercial cases; everything that's on the docket. David loves New Hampshire; he loves everything about it. And he deals equally well with the governors and senators and the people who run the general store." Sitting on the superior court bench gave him the opportunity to interact with people from all walks of life.[29]

State Supreme Court Justice

In 1983, however, a combination of factors led to Souter's elevation to the New Hampshire Supreme Court. In 1980, Warren Rudman won a U.S. Senate seat, and Democrat Hugh Gallen brought an end to Meldrim Thomson's reign in the governor's office. John Sununu, a state legislator, had lost to Rudman in the Republican primary but agreed to serve as Rudman's campaign manager in the general election where, Rudman believed, the anti-abortion, Catholic Sununu could help his candidacy among Catholics troubled by Rudman's pro-choice abortion stance. Two years later, when Sununu ran for governor, Rudman became honorary chairman of his friend's campaign. On election night, when Sununu came from behind to win, New Hampshire's next governor threw his arms around Rudman, telling the senator he would never forget his support in the campaign. "Warren," Rudman later quoted Sununu as saying, "anything you want in this state, you've got." Rudman immediately took Sununu up on his offer, asking that David Souter be appointed to the next vacancy on the state supreme court. Sununu did not know Souter then, but promptly replied, "Warren, it's done."[30]

In the fall of 1983, Sununu kept his promise, nominating Souter to replace Justice Bois, who was retiring from the high bench. On September 7, the executive council unanimously confirmed the lifetime appointment. In an article by Associated Press reporter Norma Love that appeared in the *Concord Monitor*, Tom Rath described the new justice as "one of the most analytical people that I know." When the U.S. Coast Guard attempted to exert control over Lakes Winnipesaukee and Winnisquam and the Merrimack River, Rath reported, he and then Attorney General Souter had spent weeks preparing for the confrontation, even reading ancient maps of the lakes. U.S. Transportation Department secretary William Coleman arrived at a Washington meeting on the issue flanked by staff, lawyers, and a huge collection of pertinent documents. "Souter walked into the office where the legal pads and the files were voluminous and he just walked in and sat in a chair without a piece of paper in his hand and argued his case." The Coast Guard, Rath added, abandoned its plans.[31]

The profile included what, by that point, were familiar references to Souter's attire, work ethic, demeanor, and lifestyle. When he dressed casually, a friend jokingly remarked, "he unbuttons one more button on the vest of his three-piece suit." People were amazed, Rath said, that such a staid personality and conservative dresser had "a wicked sense of humor that can skewer the most stuffed shirt." Following up on a Rath reference to Souter's weekend stints in the attorney general's office, reading "every single piece of incoming or outgoing correspondence," the writer cited the new justice's "voracious appetite for literature," as evidenced by "his farmhouse, where stacks of books can make navigating the living room perilous." Souter had remarked, she added, "It looks as though someone is moving a bookstore and stopped"— perhaps the first of many uses of that line in Souter profiles. Rath acknowledged that Souter might be unduly reserved in public: "At times I wish he would let people see more of his human side." But Souter himself indicated that he was just as content hiking in the White Mountains; if companions were not available for such a trek, he went anyway. "I'm very happy to go off alone."[32]

The article was not entirely flattering. One unidentified lawyer said that Souter had often sided with the government as a superior court judge. "If I had a progressive case (challenging the power of government) I would want a more progressive judge. But those are few and far between in New Hampshire." The writer also referred to the "sting" a recent Souter ruling had given members of New Hampshire's state employees association. The association's board of directors had authorized an employee "sick-out" for June 17. At midnight, Governor Sununu called Souter to hold a hearing. At 3:45 A.M., the justice ordered the employees to return to their work or face possible fines. He also threatened to impose fines of $5,000 a day against the union and $500 daily against its leaders. The board soon met and voted to comply with Souter's ruling. But the union's executive director termed it a "unique order," adding, "We don't recall any other organization, public or private, faced with such severe penalties in the state."[33]

Ronald Snow was no doubt correct, however, when he observed years later that Souter's elevation to the state's highest tribunal "was not controversial at all. Everybody said, 'Yeah, that makes a lot of sense. This guy has been a great trial judge. And instead of a political guy who's getting a payoff, . . . which is one of the things that happens occasionally, this is a guy that really had been in the trenches as a trial judge and gained the respect of the trial bar.'"[34]

Beginning in 1895, the chambers of the New Hampshire Supreme Court were located next to the state house in Concord. In 1970, however, the court moved to new quarters on Concord Heights, across the Merrimack River from the city's main business district and most other government buildings.[35]

Then, as now, the court was composed of five justices: four associates and a chief justice. John W. King had been chief justice since 1981. Each justice had two law clerks. Two secretaries did the typing and related clerical work for the associate justices, and the chief justice had a separate secretary.

Karen Brickner worked as a secretary at the court from 1983 to 1996. She recalls that she and one other secretary during Souter's tenure there were the only ones who could decipher his tiny, elegant, but almost illegible handwriting. She also remembers Souter as an exceptionally considerate justice. "He was very kind and gentle with you. If he wanted something done, his manner was 'please' and 'thank you.' He was a 'please' and 'thank you' person. The manner was always there. Some people, when they get under pressure, . . . just throw things at you—'I need this done; I need this done!' He was not that way. . . . You could tell sometimes from the look on his face that he needed [something done] promptly; there was a little bit of a rush . . . there. But he never forgot to say 'please' and 'thank you.' I'll always remember that." Sometimes, Brickner saw Souter at Shaw's supermarket doing his grocery shopping after court. The justice was invariably friendly to her there as well. On one occasion, she joined Souter and his law clerks on a hike into the White Mountains. After a grueling trek, she informed the justice, "Thank you very much; this will be my last hike."[36]

Souter's routine of working on weekends did not end with his elevation to the state's high court. "He was a workaholic," Ronald Snow remembers. "I had a habit of jogging about every day. And my Sunday loop from east Concord . . . would take me by the supreme court over there on the Heights. And his car would be parked there every damned Sunday afternoon. I would tease him about it occasionally, and he would say, 'Oh, I'm so far behind; I have so many cases. We don't have enough staff, and I'm working.' But he really cared about the law. That was the bottom line."[37]

During oral argument before the court, each side was normally allotted twenty minutes. Souter typically took the lead in raising questions from the bench. James Duggan, a 1969 Georgetown law graduate, opened a public defender office in Manchester in 1972. He then became a visiting professor at the Franklin Pierce Law Center in Concord. In 1980, while teaching at Franklin Pierce, he started an appellate defender office, representing indigent defendants appealing their convictions to the New Hampshire Supreme Court. In that capacity, he regularly argued cases before the high court until his own appointment to the court by Democratic governor Jeanne Shaheen in 2001.

Duggan had appeared before Justice Souter in superior court on only a few matters but estimated that he argued around a hundred cases before the state supreme court during Souter's tenure there. During oral argument, Duggan recalls, Souter

> was a very attentive judge, . . . very persistent in his questioning. He was extremely well-prepared. When we prepared for arguments in our office, we always knew that he would pick out the toughest part of the case and question us about it. He would get right to the nub of the case and ask us really hard questions, and we would prepare for those kinds of questions. Sometimes they would come from other judges as well. But we could always count on him to get right to the heart of the case and to ask us not just one or two questions, but a series of questions about the toughest part of the case. . . . He was demanding, and if he disagreed with you, he would let you know that he disagreed with you. And if I disagreed with him, I would let him know. . . . It was an argument after all. He was courteous. There were times when he and I had very quick exchanges where it was obvious that we disagreed about something. But there was never anything personal about it. . . . From my point of view as a litigant, . . . I enjoyed the challenge, and I enjoyed the fact that he forced the case out of the shadows into the light at the argument. . . . Some of our cases were not very good, since they were all court-appointed cases, and we didn't have any choice about who we represented. But if we had a reasonably good argument and a reasonably good case, it came out that way [with Souter].[38]

Asked to compare Souter to the justice's state supreme court contemporaries, Duggan hesitated ("You're getting me into trouble here"), then responded, "He was certainly the one who in almost every case you expected would be asking questions, and almost always very good questions. . . . During the time he was there, he was always [among the few] justices who were asking most of the questions, obviously prepared for the argument, and on top of the issues. He rarely asked an informational question. . . . He asked questions that were more probing than that. It was a sign that he had prepared the case so that he had gotten to the point where he pretty much had digested the relevant law and facts and was ready to proceed to the next level of analyzing the case."[39]

Court Leader

Veteran defense attorneys Mark Sisti and Paul Twomey had similar memories of oral argument before Justice Souter. "He was leading the supreme court," Sisti has remarked. "When you argued at the supreme court before Justice Souter, you better know it all. And you better be prepared to be questioned by him, because basically he was doing it all. When you walked in there, there were five people sitting there, but there was one person asking questions. He had read all the briefs; he was absolutely prepared. There was nothing he didn't lead." Oral argument before Souter, Twomey adds, "was the kind of thing that wouldn't be pleasant if you went in unprepared. . . . I remember one case where he did a withering examination of me. . . . I remember at one point being very uncomfortable."[40]

Others agreed. At the time of Souter's nomination to the U.S. Supreme Court, John Broderick, who was then president of New Hampshire's bar association and in 1995 would also be appointed to the state high court, told a reporter that Souter "would ask you in one question the issue that got to the bottom line and you would spend 36 pages [in your brief] trying to get there." In a 1990 case, a majority struck down a workers' compensation law that had created a presumption that firefighters diagnosed with cancer incurred the disease while employed as firefighters, thereby imposing additional financial burdens on local governments. The court based its decision on a state constitutional provision prohibiting the state from imposing new programs or financial obligations on local governments unless they were fully funded by the state. During oral argument, Souter asked Richard Galway, the lawyer challenging the law, whether he was arguing that a law that costs a town more money was, for that reason, unconstitutional. When Galway acknowledged that he was, the justice asked whether, pursued to its logical conclusion, the lawyer's stance meant that the state was obliged to pay for any changes in the law that cost communities money. For example, asked Souter, what if the state got rid of laws immunizing towns from lawsuits? That would certainly cost them money, but hardly amounted to a program. Did a law, the justice asked, have to require towns to *do* something as well as spend something before state funding was required? Souter, joined by Justice Stephen

Thayer, dissented, recommending a remand for further review of certain (in their judgment, unresolved) issues raised in the case. When, in a brief filed in another case, counsel for one party thoroughly researched the history of the relevant law, Souter probed opposing counsel about the soundness of his opponent's position. After several fumbling attempts to respond, the lawyer finally confessed that he knew nothing about the history of the law in question. (The lawyer lost the case.)[41]

In another case, a couple replaced their one-car garage with a two-car structure after securing the required variance from the local zoning board. Neighbors opposing the variance appealed to the supreme court after losing their case in superior court. In defending the variance during oral argument, a lawyer argued that the smaller, one-car garage had posed the "unique" hardships necessary for granting a zoning variance. Souter repeatedly pressed counsel to explain what had created the unique hardship. At one point, the lawyer argued that the lot on which his clients lived could support the larger garage and the new structure created no housing density problem. "There's nothing unique about that," Souter rejoined. The attorney then turned to the findings of the master who had heard the case in superior court. "The master indicated," said counsel, "that a garage is a necessary appurtenance to a single-family residence, and finally with regard to . . ." Souter lost his patience. "What's that got to do with it? What we're arguing about here is the difference between a one-car garage which doesn't require a variance and a two-car garage that does. What possible use is it to know that garages are normal appurtenances?" Reversing the zoning board and superior court, Souter later observed for the court, "It is difficult to imagine a set of facts less apt to satisfy the condition that hardship be unique to the applicant's parcel, distinguishing it from others in the area."[42]

Once the justices had heard oral argument and taken a vote in a case, a member of the majority was designated to write an opinion of the court. Since the days of Chief Justice John Marshall, custom in the U.S. Supreme Court gave the prerogative to the chief justice, if in the majority, to write the Court's opinion announcing its decision and rationale or assign that task to another majority justice. If the chief justice dissented, however, that role fell to the senior associate justice in the majority.

In the New Hampshire Supreme Court, by contrast, opinions were randomly assigned to a justice in the majority. John King, the court's chief justice from 1983 to 1986, explained that "there was an old silver bowl somebody had left. We'd put the case numbers in the bowl. I would take the bowl around and we'd each pick out case numbers." Souter wrote 217 opinions of the court and separate opinions during his years on the high bench. During his Senate confirmation testimony, he summarized his approach to opinion writing:

> The way I happen to work on opinions was to ask a law clerk whom I would assign to that particular case to draft an opinion which followed a rough outline that I would give the clerk of the points that I wanted to cover and the basic reasoning that I wanted to go through. What I wanted the clerk to do was not to write me an opinion which I was necessarily going to use—because, in fact, on the New Hampshire Supreme Court I never did use a clerk's draft ultimately. What I wanted the clerk to do was, in effect, to make the run-through, help me with the research, reduce down the amount of reading that I personally had to do of the most important authorities, and to give a further preliminary look at whether there was some flaw in our reasoning that I was not catching or that the other judges in the majority with me were not catching.
>
>   . . . After the clerk's draft came back, I would then work my way through the [lawyers'] briefs again . . . read the portions of the record sent up to us that were germane to the decision . . . [and] go through my own research process of rereading cases . . . that the parties had relied on.
>
>   At that point, I would make a final assessment myself as to whether there was any reason to change my view from what it had been when the court voted. If there was, I would either go back to the court or I would draft an opinion indicating the change and circulate that [to other justices] and explain why I was doing it. If there was no change I would then write my own opinion. I would revise it an unfortunate number of times. And then I would let the clerk have a go at it again, and the clerk would try to tear it to pieces. Usually, another clerk would review it then, and ultimately it would circulate to the rest of the court, at which point I might or might not be in trouble.[43]

Court secretary Karen Brickner well remembers the justice's major role in the process. "I definitely would see his [distinctive and extensive] handwriting on draft opinions. He would 'cut and paste' his clerks' drafts," as well as make substantive revisions.[44]

Much of the court's caseload involved applications of statutes and common law principles, with rulings often turning on narrow, technical questions. Because New Hampshire has no intermediate appeals court, the caseload was extensive and varied. Souter seemingly thrived on technical issues before the justices. In one case, a woman given the pseudonym "K" to protect her privacy sued the Mary Hitchcock Memorial Hospital at the Dartmouth-Hitchcock Medical Center. Two days after being discharged from the hospital following her baby's birth, K began to experience the symptoms of herpes. In an effort to establish that the infection was contracted at the hospital, her counsel sought a report of the hospital's nurse epidemiologist and minutes of its Infections Committee relevant to her claim. Citing a state law, the hospital contended that the documents sought were privileged. The court, speaking through Souter, agreed.[45]

K's counsel argued that the only documents privileged under state law were the records of hospital committees specifically designated "quality assurance" committees. But in an elaborate analysis of the applicable statute's use of indefinite ("a") as well as definite ("the") article adjectives and the law's legislative history, Souter concluded that any hospital committee concerned with evaluating the care and treatment of patients was entitled to the privilege, whatever its formal name. "One may reasonably ask," he wrote, "whether there is any significance in the mixture of definite and indefinite articles. Should the definite reference to 'the quality assurance committee' in [one part of the statute] be thought to imply that a given hospital is permitted to have only one such committee as a font of statutory privilege, or were the indefinite references to 'a quality assurance committee' and 'a hospital committee organized to evaluate'. . . meant to indicate that a hospital may have more than one, each identified by reference to its functional responsibility?" Souter agreed with the hospital that the second interpretation was correct.[46]

Like other state high courts, the New Hampshire Supreme Court's caseload had a largely state statutory and common law thrust considerably different from the sorts of federal constitutional issues Justice Souter would later confront on the U.S. Supreme Court. As a state justice, however, he participated in a relatively significant number of cases suggestive of the stance he might assume in higher court opinions involving the proper role of judges in construing constitutional provisions, the weight he has accorded precedent cases, and his approach to specific constitutional issues.

Constitutional Interpretivist

On the U.S. Supreme Court, it will be recalled, Souter was to embrace the sort of flexible, evolving interpretation of constitutional provisions that the second Justice John Marshall Harlan had earlier advanced. Like Harlan, however, he also rejected the notion that courts could ignore the language of constitutional provisions, evidence of their framers' intent, or long precedent merely to achieve what a majority viewed as a worthy result in a particular case. Souter assumed the same position as a New Hampshire Supreme Court justice in a dissent he registered for the 1986 case of *In Re Estate of Henry Dionne.*

The *Dionne* majority, speaking through Chief Justice King, struck down as a violation of Article 14 of the New Hampshire bill of rights a statute requiring parties to pay a special fee to probate judges for conducting special sessions. King conceded that the number of days set by statute for regular probate court sessions was insufficient to handle the probate caseload. He also recognized that probate courts must be readily available to citizens and that their judges were entitled to adequate compensation for their work. The chief justice held for the court, however, that the fee system "smack[ed] of the purchase of justice, and [was] therefore anathema" to the Article 14 requirement that "every subject of this state is entitled . . . to obtain right and justice freely, without being obliged to purchase it." In the court's judgment, the fee arrangement also violated "the spirit, though not the letter," of a constitutional provision declaring that salaries, not fees, for supreme and superior court justices were "not only the best policy, but [also best] for the security of the rights of the people." That same concern, the chief justice observed, applied equally to the state's other courts and judges, including the judges of probate. Quoting the 1980 report of a retired probate judge, King concluded, "The New Hampshire court system cannot be considered as having joined the twentieth century until the fee system has been totally abolished."[47]

In his lone dissent, Justice Souter readily conceded that, as a matter of policy, the fee system should be condemned. In fact, in his judgment, "the majority opinion [was], if anything, moderate in its condemnation." Were he evaluating the system in terms of "notions of good public policy," he declared, "I would join with the court in bringing the system to an end." Because, however, the issue before the court was the fee's constitutionality, not its wisdom, the justice was compelled to dissent. Quoting from an 1863 opinion of the justices, reaffirmed as recently as five years earlier, Souter declared that "the language of the Constitution is to be understood in the sense in which it was used at the time of its adoption." Invoking that interpretive approach to constitutional construction—an approach based on the intent of a provision's framers and other historical evidence of its meaning—the justice sought evidence of the meaning of the state constitutional guarantee that people were "entitled to obtain right and justice freely, without being obliged to purchase it," in two sources: scholarly and judicial commentary on the meaning of a clause in the English Magna Carta of 1215 and "the history of

New Hampshire statutes providing not only for probate fees, but specifically for fees in lieu of probate judges' salaries or as supplements to such salaries." New Hampshire and other courts, he contended, had interpreted the Magna Carta "to abolish, not fixed fees, prescribed for the purposes of revenue, but the fines which were anciently paid to expedite or delay law proceedings and procure favor." At the time the constitutional provision at issue was enacted as part of New Hampshire's 1784 constitution, moreover, judicial fees were in effect, including a six-shilling fee for those attending any probate dispute, payable as a cost of litigation and to be divided equally between the judge and the register of probate. Thus, observed Souter, "Many of the same legislators who proposed the adoption of article 14 understood its provision to be consistent with probate fees payable as judicial compensation." Later statutory developments, he argued, were to the same effect. "This consistency of statutory history with the accepted interpretation of the original Magna Carta provision demonstrates beyond any serious doubt that the people who framed and adopted article 14 meant principally to guard against bribery of the sort that had corrupted the early medieval judiciary. They did not mean to outlaw all statutory fees related to judicial services."48

Souter also adhered closely to prevailing precedent, even in a case overturning one of his superior court rulings. In *State v. Roger M.* (1981), the justice had been reversed when he construed a state statute to prohibit annulment of a defendant's conviction and sentence in cases in which a fine was part of the sentence, rather than probation or a conditional discharge alone. *State v. Meiser* (1984) reaffirmed and extended *Roger M.* In a separate opinion, Souter indicated that he continued to agree with his rationale and Justice Bois's dissent in *Roger M.* "Nonetheless," he added, "I accept the defendant's eligibility to [seek a record annulment] on the basis of the majority opinion in *Roger M.* The consequences of what I believe was an unsound conclusion in that case are not serious enough to outweigh the value of *stare decisis*."49

The Bosselait Brothers

Souter's at times seemingly cold-hearted stance in a number of family law, privacy, gender, and related discrimination cases also, on closer examination, proved to be more complex and precedent-based than they might at first have appeared. In one case, two elderly brothers, Albert and Edward Bosselait, seventy-six and seventy-nine years old, respectively, were denied unemployment compensation because they were not ready, willing, and able to perform full-time work. The brothers had shared a single, full-time janitor's position at a North-field youth center for twenty-two years, each working four hours a day. When the center outsourced its custodial services in 1986, they lost their jobs. Denied unemployment benefits by the state department of employment security, they filed an appeal within the agency. During a hearing, Albert Bosselait (the seventy-six-year-old brother) indicated that he had a "weak back [that] goes out of joint when least expected." His brother said he was limited by partial eyesight and angina. Insisting that he was "not gonna play with [his] health," Edward further testified, "We don't dare to work more than four hours a day at our age." When informed that under the law, applicants for unemployment compensation must be available for, and seeking, full-time work, Edward contended that the statute was "discriminatory against old fellas . . . old people."[50]

Based on their refusal (inability) to seek full-time employment, the administrative tribunal rejected the brothers' appeal. They then obtained counsel, who asked that the employment security department reopen their case based on federal and state equal protection claims as well as contentions that the department's action violated state and federal statutes forbidding discrimination against mothers, the handicapped, and people over sixty-five. In further proceedings, the department's appellate division conceded that Albert and Edward were physically able to work only four hours a day but rejected their counsel's claims that the state unemployment law violated equal protection under the New Hampshire constitution or provisions of the federal Rehabilitation Act of 1973.

A unanimous state supreme court, per Justice Souter, affirmed the appellate division's decision. Citing the failure of the brothers' counsel to raise their statutory and constitutional claims in an appropriate and timely fashion, Souter asserted "in candor . . . that if the state of the record had been adequately disclosed to us we would not have accepted this appeal." But as the appellate division had "[seen] fit to deal with an issue under the [federal] Rehabilitation Act" and to rule that there had been no state equal protection violation, the justice saw "some utility in speaking to [those] issues."[51]

The Bosselait brothers were hardly to benefit from that exercise. Souter saw no conflict between the state's restriction of benefits to those available for full-time employment and the Rehabilitation Act's prohibition against the denial of benefits "solely by reason of [a person's] handicap." To claim the Rehabilitation Act's protection, the brothers had "to prove not only that they suffered from handicaps but that the handicaps, and the handicaps alone, rendered them unable to work a full day." The brothers, Souter asserted, had failed to meet that burden. "It is neither common knowledge, nor do the plaintiffs claim, that a weak back, poor eyesight, or angina necessarily prevents an individual who can work four hours a day from working eight."[52]

Turning to the brothers' state equal protection claim, the justice rejected their argument that their denial of benefits was subject to "the so-called middle-tier test" established by the New Hampshire Supreme Court in *Carson v. Maure* (1980). The *Maure* court, drawing on U.S. Supreme Court constructions of the federal equal protection guarantee, held that legislation limiting enjoyment of an "important substantive right" was to be "reasonable, not arbitrary," and bear a "fair and substantial" relationship to a legitimate governmental objective. In holding gender classifications subject to such a standard under the federal Constitution, the U.S. Supreme Court had relied in part on the "immutability of sex" as an individual characteristic. The brothers argued that age was as immutable as gender, and because the challenged statute arguably had a disparate impact on the elderly, it should be subjected to middle-tier review. Souter was not impressed. Citing cases in which the high Court had rejected strict or heightened scrutiny for age discrimination, applying instead a lenient, rational-basis standard of review to age classifications, the justice saw "no basis to claim that State equal protection should grant the middle-tier scrutiny that federal equal protection would provide, because federal equal protection does not provide it."[53]

Under the rational-basis formula, Souter concluded, the challenged statute was reasonably related to a legitimate state interest in conserving available funds for those who needed them most, "those with no source of income except their paychecks" and thus most likely to seek full-time employment." The legislature had also been entitled to assume, he observed, that an applicant ready to take full-time work had a better chance of getting a job quickly—and thus no longer requiring unemployment benefits. Souter realized that "the scheme as so rationalized will not, admittedly, produce an exact equality of benefits and burdens among the variously identifiable segments of employable people. But the standard of equal protection makes no such demand . . . any more than it requires a court . . . to ignore the other societal benefits, such as social security, that are available to responsible and commendable job applicants like the plaintiffs, whose age prevents their acceptance of full-time work."[54]

Most people, and certainly someone as solicitous of elderly family members and friends as David Souter is reputed to be, would sympathize with the Bosselait brothers' plight. But the U.S. and New Hampshire Supreme Courts had refused to accord meaningful judicial scrutiny to regulations that had a disparate impact on the elderly. And for Souter, such precedents, like those in other fields, trumped any natural concern for the brothers' pitiful circumstances.

Rape Victims and the Constitution

Regard for precedent also overcame Souter's likely natural sympathy for rape victims in another case decided the same year. In *State v. Colbath* (1988), the justice spoke for a unanimous court in holding that the trial judge should have been allowed to consider evidence of the victim's public behavior in the hours preceding the rape as a matter bearing on the defense of consent. Richard Colbath became acquainted with the victim when he and several companions visited the Smokey Lantern tavern in Farmington. "There was evidence," wrote Souter, "that [the complainant] directed sexually provocative attention toward several men in the bar, with whom she associated during the ensuing afternoon, the defendant among them." The defendant, in fact, had "testified that he had engaged in 'feeling [the complainant's] breasts [and] bottom [and that she had been] rubbing his crotch' before the two of them eventually left the tavern and went to the defendant's trailer."[55]

Once in the trailer, they had intercourse, forcible according to the victim, consensual according to Colbath. Before they left the trailer, a young woman who lived with the defendant kicked the trailer door open, violently assaulted the complainant, and dragged her outside by the hair, an attack that ended only when Colbath and a third woman intervened. The complainant accused Colbath of rape as soon as she returned to Farmington, and he was promptly arrested.

At Colbath's trial, the prosecution sought a ruling from the bench forbidding witnesses to testify about the complainant's behavior in the tavern with the defendant and other men. After extensive argument on the motion, the trial judge excluded such testimony on the ground that it was immaterial as evidence of the complainant's character and also forbidden under New Hampshire's rape-shield law, which barred evidence of "prior consensual sexual activity between the victim and any person other than" the defendant. Despite his ruling barring the defense from presenting such evidence, the judge allowed a prosecution witness to testify that the complainant had left the tavern with various men several times during the afternoon; also admitted was that witness's statement to the police, in which she said she had seen "a girl with dark hair hanging all over everyone and making out with Richard Colbath and a few others." In his charge to the jury, however, the judge reiterated that the complainant's "conduct with other individuals is not relevant on the issue of whether or not she gave consent to sexual intercourse."[56]

Viewing the judge's instructions as tantamount to an order "striking the testimony about the complainant's openly observed behavior with other men during the course of the afternoon," Justice Souter struck it down as an improper application of the rape-shield law. Despite the statute's seemingly absolute language, Souter pointed out that state supreme court constructions of the law since its adoption in 1975 had consistently limited its reach out of regard for the right of defendants to confront their accusers. In *State v. Howard* (1981), for example, the court held that a rape defendant must have the chance to demonstrate that the "probative value [of the statutorily inadmissible evidence] in the context of [a] particular case outweigh[ed] its prejudicial effect on the prosecutrix."[57]

Weighing this prejudicial and probative force in *Colbath*, Souter reasoned, required a ruling in the defendant's favor. "On the one hand, describing a complainant's open, sexually suggestive conduct in the presence of patrons of a public bar obviously has far less potential for damaging the [victim's] sensibilities than revealing what the same person may have done in the company of another behind a closed door. On the other hand, evidence of public displays of general interest in sexual activity can be taken to indicate a contemporaneous receptiveness to sexual advances that cannot be inferred from evidence of private behavior with chosen sexual partners." The jury, for example, could have considered her conduct "toward a group of men as evidence of her probable attitude toward an individual within the group." The close proximity in time between the "publicly inviting acts" and "the alleged sexual assault by one such man," added the justice, "could have been viewed as indicating the complainant's likely attitude at the time of the sexual activity in question."[58]

Souter considered such evidence particularly significant because "visible injuries" to the complainant could have been inflicted by the defendant's "jealous living companion" rather than by Colbath himself. "The fact of intercourse," after all, "was not denied." And the jury could have regarded the companion's "attack as a reason for the complainant to regret a voluntary liaison with the defendant, and as a motive for the complainant to allege rape as a way to explain her injuries and excuse her undignified predicament.

With the sex act thus admitted, with the evidence of violence subject to exculpatory explanation, and with a motive for the complainant to make a false accusation, the outcome of the prosecution could well have turned on a very close judgment about the complainant's attitude of resistance or consent."[59]

Viewed in isolation from precedent cases, Justice Souter's opinion in *Colbath* might be considered callous, not to mention inconsistent with the prevailing general belief that the admission of trial evidence about a rape victim's prior sexual history may prejudice a jury on the critical issue of consent. For Souter, however, the earlier cases construing the New Hampshire rape-shield law had rejected an absolute application of that rule as inconsistent with the defendant's right to confront accusers. And again, his regard for precedent prevailed.

Two years earlier, precedents broadly construing the right of confrontation had also prompted the justice to require further probing at trial of a rape victim's sexual background. In that case, he spoke for the court in reversing a trial judge's refusal to admit evidence regarding a young male victim's prior sexual conduct or hold a hearing midtrial on that issue. The defendant had paid two young boys for sex with him over a two-year period. The defense had argued that evidence about the sexual past of the victim named in the indictment would help to establish that his knowledge of sexual practices that he described on the witness stand was not necessarily based purely on his experiences with the defendant. In opposing a hearing, the state had argued, among other things, that the jury had heard evidence indicating that the victim was a streetwise and experienced thirteen-year-old. Souter's response: "This is true so far as it goes, but it begs the question, which is whether he was experienced enough to have known about the sexual acts he described unless he had experienced them with the defendant. We may, indeed, have our suspicions, but on the evidence before the jury there could be nothing more than that. [Our precedents] . . . teach that the due process right of confrontation requires more." Thus, whatever his personal sympathy for child rape victims, earlier rulings embracing an expansive right of confrontation carried greater weight with the justice.[60]

The "Real World"

Souter's opinion in a 1990 divorce case later prompted questions whether he was sufficiently familiar with the "real world" to sit on the U.S. Supreme Court. In *Yergeau v. Yergeau*, the New Hampshire high court, per Souter, held that postseparation adultery could be the basis for a divorce decree. Under state law, a spouse deemed to have committed adultery was at a serious disadvantage when a judge divided a divorced couple's property, set alimony, and decided child custody issues. Elizabeth Cazden, attorney for the adulterous husband in the case, thought the ruling might have reflected Souter's high moral standards. "I'm speculating that, having never been married, he may be more exacting about other people's lives. I think he is very exacting about his own [life]. I know that he is really . . . a stickler on honesty and integrity. I have always assumed that carries over into his personal life. . . . He expects everyone to do the same, and he lets you know if he thinks you haven't." Cazden also had "a sense that [Souter] was out of step with the reality that people live with when they are separated. The reality is that people want to be able to start dating." Another lawyer told a reporter that he and other attorneys in his firm were telling clients to be "circumspect" about new relationships after filing for divorce. "The law and justice aren't the same thing," he added. "The responsibility of the higher court is to blend those two."[61]

Because the Court's decision was unanimous, Cazden may have been inferring too much from the opinion about Souter and the impact of his lifestyle on his judicial record. As the opinion's author, however, the justice arguably contributed more to the court's expansive conception of adultery than other justices.

Although he has never revealed his personal feelings with respect to *Roe v. Wade*, one of Souter's New Hampshire Supreme Court opinions at least suggested that he found some of *Roe*'s broader implications troubling. In *Smith v. Cote* (1986), Linda Smith was diagnosed with rubella during the second trimester of her pregnancy. Her daughter Heather was born a victim of congenital rubella syndrome. By age six, Heather was legally blind; suffered from multiple congenital heart defects, motor retardation, and a significant hearing impairment; and had undergone surgery for cataracts and her heart condition. On her own and Heather's behalf, Smith sued her physicians, who, she contended, failed to test for or discover her exposure to rubella in a timely manner, then neglected to advise her of the potential for birth defects in a fetus exposed to the disease, as a result depriving her of the knowledge necessary for an informed decision whether to give birth or have an abortion, as allowed under *Roe*. A superior court judge transferred to the state supreme court two questions: whether New Hampshire law recognized a cause of action on the part of the mother to sue for "wrongful birth," or a right of her daughter to sue for "wrongful life." Announcing the court's judgment, Justice William F. Batchelder recognized a right under state law to recover for wrongful birth, but not for wrongful life.[62]

In a brief concurring opinion, Justice Souter discussed an issue that, as Justice Batchelder noted in his opinion, had "not been raised, briefed, or argued in the record before us." The questions transferred from superior court had failed to raise, wrote Souter, the "significant issue . . . whether, or how, a physician with conscientious scruples against abortion, and the testing and counseling that may inform an abortion decision, can discharge his professional obligation without engaging in procedures that his religious or moral principles condemned." Declaring that "say[ing] nothing about this issue could lead to misunderstanding," the justice emphasized that the court had not held "that some or all physicians must make a choice between rendering services that they morally condemn and leaving their profession in order to escape malpractice exposure." Instead, he observed, "the defensive significance, for example, of timely disclosure of professional limits based on religious or moral scruples, combined with timely referral to other physicians who are not so constrained, [was] a question [still] open for consideration in any case in which it may be raised."[63]

Although conceding that the ultimate impact of *Roe* on the legal obligations of physicians was still open for review, Souter's willingness to go beyond the specific issues raised in *Cote*, and to emphasize that the courts had not yet decided such issues, arguably is evidence that, at least at this point in his career, he believed that doctors had no obligation to provide medical services in a constitutionally protected field. *Roe* and later U.S. Supreme Court cases have never imposed such requirements, but Souter's willingness to anticipate the issue suggests that he harbored doubts about *Roe*, its nature and scope.

A number of other family law cases raised sensitive issues as well. In one, ex-spouses each attempted to adopt a child for whom they had been foster parents when married. In the divorce decree, the wife was given custody of the child, and the husband was accorded visitation rights. When the woman later petitioned a probate court to adopt the child, her former husband asked to be treated as a copetitioner. The probate judge denied the man's request but granted his former wife's petition, declaring, in effect, that state law did not allow unmarried adults jointly to adopt a child. On appeal, the former husband cited the statutory categories of adults eligible to petition for adoption, pointing out that one category was "an unmarried adult." He conceded that "adult" was singular but argued that designation could fairly be construed to include two unmarried adults, especially given a New Hampshire abortion provision specifying that "singular . . . includes the plural . . . when consistent with the intent of the chapter." In defending his interpretation, he urged the justices to remember, quoting a 1980 case, that the adoption statute was passed "to facilitate the adoption of children by removing 'arbitrary and broad restrictions' on who could adopt and to enable the courts to respond to the varied circumstances of individual cases."[64]

The court, per Souter, declined the former husband's entreaty. Under the law, Souter wrote, most persons seeking to undertake an adoption "share a common characteristic: their domestic circumstances do not threaten to disrupt the living arrangements they will provide for the child to be adopted." Married applicants "jointly demonstrate a sense of common purpose." Applying alone, an unmarried applicant would offer a household that posed "no apparent risk of splitting up." A married applicant who was separated was comparable, practically, to a single person. From those categories of eligible applicants, Souter inferred the intent of the legislature to limit adoption to those who would "probably provide a unified and stable household for the child." Two unmarried applicants seeking joint adoption would not be likely to satisfy that objective. "[They] do not share living quarters," the justice observed; in fact, were a joint petition granted, a judge would then be obliged to decide the child's living arrangements, making custody decisions separate from the divorce decree itself. Yet New Hampshire law, he concluded, did not "appear to contemplate such a process. [Instead,] the statute evidently assumes the child will have one 'home,'" an assumption reflected in the law's failure to provide for an award of custody except in those instances where an adoption petition was dismissed. "Respect for such [legislative] intent," concluded Souter, "preclude[d]" giving the statute an arguably more literal construction. Clearly, the justice was unwilling to embrace a novel interpretation of New Hampshire adoption law—even one arguably consistent with its text—when such a construction seemed inconsistent with the broader goals of adoption policy, including a "unified and stable household for the child."[65]

Gay Rights

An unsigned, per curiam opinion that Justice Souter joined in 1987 offered little cause for optimism among homosexual groups regarding his likely response to gay rights claims on the nation's highest tribunal. The New Hampshire house of representatives asked the state supreme court for an advisory opinion on the constitutionality of a proposed bill prohibiting homosexuals from adopting, being foster parents, or running day care centers. In their response, the justices first assumed that the definition of a homosexual in the law was limited to persons who engaged "both voluntarily and knowingly" in oral and anal intercourse with persons of the same sex—thereby avoiding "the patently absurd result" of including victims of homosexual rape within the bill's scope. The justices also construed the bill to apply only to persons who engaged in homosexual acts "on a current basis reasonably close in time" to a petition for adoption or application for a day care license—thus excluding persons, for example, who had "one homosexual experience during adolescence, but now engage in exclusively heterosexual behavior."[66]

With those preliminary matters out of the way, the justices turned to the question of whether the proposal, if adopted, would violate the federal constitutional guarantee to equal protection of the law. Citing *Bowers v. Hardwick*, a 1986 U.S. Supreme Court case that Justice Souter would vote to overturn in 2003, the justices rejected claims that discrimination against homosexuals, like racial classifications, was constitutionally suspect and thus subject to the strictest judicial scrutiny. Nor, they concluded, were homosexuals even "within the ambit of the so-called 'middle tier' level of heightened scrutiny," applied to gender and certain other "quasi-suspect" classifications. "Sexual preference is not a matter necessarily tied to gender, but rather to inclination, whatever the source thereof." The U.S. Supreme Court had long held that discriminatory laws interfering with "fundamental rights" were subject to strict judicial review. But *Bowers* had rejected any fundamental constitutional right to homosexual sodomy, the New Hampshire justices observed, and there was also no fundamental right to adopt, to be a foster parent, or operate a day care center. As the bill thus involved no suspect or quasi-suspect classification, nor a discriminatory obstacle to the exercise of a fundamental right, the bill should be subjected only to the lenient, rational-basis standard of equal protection review under which laws were valid if rationally related to some legitimate governmental purpose.[67]

Applying that standard, under which laws almost invariably survived constitutional challenge, the justices found the foster parent and adoption bans rationally related to the bill's stated purpose of "provid[ing] appropriate role models for children," but not the bill's exclusion of gays from the operation of child care agencies. Opponents of the bill had cited studies finding no correlation between the homosexual orientation of parents and their children's sexual orientation. Observing, however, that the source of a person's sexual preference was "still inadequately understood and . . . thought to be a combination of genetic and environmental influences," the justices found that the reasonable possibility of an environmental impact on a child's sexual development meant that the legislature could rationally determine that a role model would influence a child's sexual identity. "Obviously, this theory most likely holds true in the parent-child or other familial context."[68]

The justices could see no rational basis, however, for excluding homosexuals as a class from operating all types of day care agencies. "To extend [the rationale] to all such facilities would, we believe, paint with too broad a brush. . . . This is especially evident in light of the bill's use of the term 'applicant' as the entity whose sexuality is at issue. It would often be the case that the applicant would not be a human being at all, but rather a corporation, for example. In addition, even if the applicant were a human being, he or she might have little or no contact with the children for whom services were to be provided, in which case the applicant's sexual preferences would be irrelevant." The noncontinuous nature of day care service, the justices added, further weakened the role model rationale that justified the ban on homosexual adoptions and foster care. Thus, it was only in "those living situations approximating a familial or parent-child arrangement that the role model theory provided a rational basis" for such restrictions. Although a blanket ban was not rational, the justices agreed that licensing authorities could make specific determinations to that effect in individual cases.[69]

The justices assumed essentially the same stance regarding legislative concerns that the bill might violate federal and state constitutional privacy and due process guarantees, particularly as *Bowers* had refused to extend the privacy right to consensual homosexual sodomy. Any freedom of association claim raised against the bill, moreover, would depend on judicial recognition of such privacy and related rights.

Justice Batchelder filed a vigorous dissent. The legislature had avowed that the bill's purpose was to protect children rather than punish homosexual conduct; homosexual conduct as defined by the resolution submitting the bill to the court was not criminal in New Hampshire, although heterosexual adultery was. Batchelder considered government never more humanitarian than when it protected the health of children, nor less so "when it denie[d] public benefits to a group of its citizens because of ancient prejudices against that group." Charging that the legislature had no rational basis for presuming "that every homosexual [was] unfit to be an adoptive parent or to provide foster or day care," the justice argued that reasonable alternative methods were available for evaluating the fitness of homosexual applicants.[70]

In its opinion, the majority had rejected the contention that the ban on homosexuals adopting or providing foster care was based on an irrebuttable presumption (i.e., that they would not be proper role models for children) lacking in universal or near-universal validity. In cases in which the U.S. Supreme Court had struck down such presumptions on due process grounds, the majority concluded, the presumptions at issue (e.g., that unwed fathers were unfit parents) were "immediately disprovable presumed" facts and also involved "a legally cognizable interest" (e.g., a parent's interest in the custody of his own children). On the other hand, the challenged classification proposed in the bill raised no such risk and implicated no fundamental legal interest. Batchelder disagreed. He conceded that parental fitness was less objective than the presumptions the U.S. Supreme Court had held to violate due process. But that, he insisted, was "no more than a matter of the weight of the evidence in individual determinations. In this vein, the presumed fact that homosexual parents are unfit is no less disprovable than the [presumed] fact . . . that unwed parents are unfit." Batchelder would have found all the bill's provisions unconstitutional. Souter's decision to join the Court's opinion, on the other hand, squared with his general reluctance to impose meaningful restrictions on legislative discretion in a field in which available precedent, such as the Supreme Court's *Bowers* ruling the previous year, arguably granted lawmakers extremely wide latitude.[71]

In a case decided the next year, however, Justice Souter made it clear that state efforts to protect minors from sexual abuse must conform to the requirements of procedural due process. Mark Richardson, a social worker, was discharged from his position based on his agency's finding that he had "French-kissed" a fourteen-year-old girl over whom he had responsibility. While an appeal of the discharge was pending before the state personnel commission, Richardson obtained a job at a residential home for boys; when a state official learned of his new employment, he had Richardson's name placed on the state's central registry of child abusers. Because any child care facility employing persons on the register faced a loss of its license, the residential home promptly fired Richardson. Speaking for a unanimous court, Justice Souter held that Richardson was entitled to notice and a hearing before having his name placed on the register. Souter obviously had no patience with government employees who abused those in their charge. But drawing on Supreme Court precedent in related cases, he held that Richardson had a liberty interest in continued employment consistent with his educational training that could not be breached absent notice and a hearing allowing him to contest the agency's decision.[72]

The First Amendment

In free expression cases, Justice Souter recognized broad but not unlimited power of government to regulate speech on public property. In February 1988, Michael Hodgkiss, a supporter of Libertarian presidential candidate Lyndon LaRouche, distributed pamphlets on a sidewalk next to the Manchester city hall and urged passersby to register to vote in the upcoming New Hampshire presidential primary. He also set up a card table several feet from the curb to hold extra literature and display signs. Trying to protect the table from rain, he covered it with a large umbrella, kept in place with a rope strung between a lamppost and a tree, both maintained by the city. Suspended from the rope as well was a six-foot cardboard campaign sign. That afternoon, a police officer told Hodgkiss he would need a permit for the table and sign suspended from the rope. When asked to remove the table, umbrella, and sign until he secured a permit, Hodgkiss declared two relevant city ordinances unconstitutional and continued his solicitation. Soon, another officer appeared and began reading the ordinances to Hodgkiss. Hodgkiss then began shouting that the police were "'commies' behaving like the K.G.B." Arrested for disorderly conduct, he was later charged with violating the two ordinances. A conviction for disorderly conduct was ultimately dismissed; the convictions for violating the ordinances went to the New Hampshire Supreme Court on appeal.[73]

Speaking for a unanimous court, Justice Souter overturned Hodgkiss's conviction for unlawfully encumbering the sidewalk. That ordinance, he concluded, was addressed to merchants, not to "the sort of political promotion in which defendant was engaged." But the court affirmed Hodgkiss's conviction under an ordinance prohibiting the posting of signs on public property. Finding that the provision's purpose was directed purely at the "unsightliness of postings as such, considered without regard to the substance of any message or depiction," the justice held that the ordinance was a "content-neutral" regulation that "entirely prohibit[ed] the attachment of notices and the like to the public structures to which it applies." Invoking the standard for such regulations going back at least to the U.S. Supreme Court's ruling in *United States v. O'Brien* (1968), the justice concluded that the regulation furthered a substantial government interest unrelated to the suppression of expression (the prevention of "visual pollution") and that adequate alternative modes of expression (handbilling, speaking to pedestrians) were available for communicating Hodgkiss's message.[74]

Souter invoked a balancing of interests approach in certain other First Amendment contexts as well. In *Lathrop v. Donahue* (1961) and later cases, the U.S. Supreme Court had upheld the "integrated bar" concept, under which lawyers could be required to be members of their state bar association; New Hampshire's high court also recognized the concept in 1972. In a 1986 case, Orr and Reno attorney William L. Chapman contended that use of his bar association dues to oppose tort reform legislation, including a $250,000 limit on monetary damages for pain and suffering, violated his free speech rights. Seeking to avoid declaring the association's action unconstitutional, the court, speaking through Justice David A. Brock, narrowly construed the association's constitution to limit its activities to matters directly related to the efficient administration of the judicial system; the membership and operations of the courts; and the education, ethics, competence, integrity, and regulation of the legal profession. Opposition to tort reform legislation, concluded Brock, was not within that mandate.[75]

In a concurring opinion, Justice Souter primarily took issue with Justice Batchelder's dissent, which argued that all the lobbying at issue was consistent with both the bar association's constitution and the First Amendment rights of dissenting lawyers. The bar association's right to override the personal First Amendment interests of members, asserted Souter, "extend[ed] only so far as the need to serve the counterbalancing public interests." Under that approach, an integrated bar did not have unlimited authority to lobby for any purpose a majority of its members thought appropriate. Instead, a bar association could use the dues of dissenting members only to lobby a legislative proposal promoting competence and integrity among lawyers and judges, expand public access to lawyers and courts, and develop effective methods for securing and enforcing legal rights. But bar associations could not conduct lobbying activities affecting the substance of legal rights and obligations. Souter agreed, therefore, that Chapman was correct in claiming First Amendment violations in the association's opposition to certain provisions of the tort reform legislation, including the cap on monetary awards.[76]

Justice Batchelder argued in dissent that the lobbying efforts at issue in the case served a significant state interest in the administration of justice and law practice. Justice Souter, however, contended that the balance had been struck in *Lathrop* and other cases approving the integrated bar and holding that the objectives it served outweighed the general First Amendment interests of members at odds with a bar association's position. Deciding whether a particular lobbying effort served the integrated bar's objectives did not call for further balancing, in Souter's judgment, but instead for a comparison of the lobbying's objectives with those justifying compulsory bar membership. The court's narrow construction of the bar association's by-laws, he added, would hardly obstruct lawyers wishing to oppose tort reform. At least one voluntary bar association, for example, "would lend itself to the purposes of such opposition."[77]

In another case involving restrictions on the bar, Souter embraced an expansive interpretation of the First Amendment rights of legal services lawyers. The New Hampshire Disabilities Rights Center (DRC) was established under state law to provide legal services for the poor. In a petition to the New Hampshire Supreme Court, the DRC asked that it be allowed to represent all disabled persons, not simply the poor, although indigent persons would have priority. Speaking for a unanimous court, Souter held that state statutory prohibitions on the DRC's representation of nonindigents violated the First Amendment. The justice pointed out that states had no legal obligation to provide legal services in civil cases. Drawing on Supreme Court precedents, however, he held that noncommercial litigation to bring about political and social change was protected by the First Amendment, subject only to "compelling" countervailing interests.[78]

Criminal Appeals

A good deal of a state high court's caseload typically involves appeals of criminal convictions, and the new Hampshire Supreme Court was no exception. In such cases, Souter could be impatient with appeals he considered frivolous. In 1986, for example, he chastised a defendant in a sexual assault case who, he was convinced, had challenged his counsel simply as a device to prolong his case and provide a ground for appeal. Upholding the trial court's refusal to dismiss the public defender appointed to represent the defendant after he dismissed his first lawyer, the justice declared that "a right to counsel is not a right to endless engagement in dilatory tactics."[79]

He also assumed stances on criminal justice issues that tracked—or anticipated—the U.S. Supreme Court's increasingly conservative resolution of such cases. In 1990, Chief Justice William H. Rehnquist spoke for a majority in upholding a sobriety checkpoint program set up by state police on Michigan's highways. Five years earlier, Souter had dissented in *State v. Koppel*, a 1985 case in which a New Hampshire Supreme Court majority struck down Concord's version of the same scheme. Observing that 1,680 vehicle stops in a six-month period had resulted in only eighteen DWI arrests at roadblocks, while the Concord police had made 175 DWI arrests using traditional techniques during the same period, the majority concluded that the roadblocks were not sufficiently effective to justify their interference with federal and state constitutional guarantees against unreasonable searches and seizures. In his dissent, Souter rejected the majority's notion that roadblocks must "significantly" advance the public interest in highway safety to satisfy constitutional requirements. But even under that standard, he thought the roadblocks were constitutional, especially given the brevity of the stops, their minimal intrusion on individual privacy, and the obvious importance of highway safety.[80]

The majority had quoted an Oklahoma Supreme Court opinion that raised the specter of a "police state" in condemning DWI roadblocks. If motorists could be stopped to detect liquor violations, the Oklahoma court reasoned, pedestrians could be stopped as part of a program to detect shoplifters. "The justices of that court," wrote Souter, "thus see roadblocks as the thin end of a constitutional wedge." But the justice was by no means convinced. "Shopping, like most other normal public pursuits, is not so fraught with risk to others as to be a regulated activity. Driving a car, conversely, is a public pursuit that raises just such a risk and is pervasively regulated in order to mitigate its potential danger. Measures that would be reasonable in policing activities of great risk would not be reasonable as intrusions into the characteristically safe and innocent pursuits of social life."[81]

Justice Souter also spoke for a majority in upholding against a state constitutional challenge police use of pen registers, a mechanical device used to detect outgoing signals produced on a telephone line when a number is dialed—decoding the signal, printing the number, recording date and time, and indicating whether the call was answered. In *Smith v. Maryland* (1979), a divided U.S. Supreme Court held that installing and using a pen register did not amount to a search within the meaning of the Fourth Amendment guarantee against unreasonable searches and seizures. Speaking for the majority, Justice Harry A. Blackmun reasoned that telephone users had no reasonable expectation of privacy from the recording of telephone numbers, information voluntarily exposed to the phone company each time a call was made. Speaking for the state supreme court in *State v. Valenzuela* (1987), Justice Souter assumed essentially the same position in rejecting the state constitutional objection. But Justice Batchelder contended in dissent that "the necessary nonvolitional disclosure of certain facts to the telephone company [in order to use the phone] does not require the assumption that the company will voluntarily share that information with others, especially the government." In his judgment, telephone users had a reasonable expectation of privacy in the number dialed. Use of a pen register thus should require a warrant.[82]

Souter's approach to judicial federalism issues growing out of criminal justice cases arguably was also suggestive of a generally conservative posture in such suits. As the U.S. Supreme Court began to assume a more conservative stance in criminal procedure cases in the 1970s and 1980s, legal scholars and a number of judges, including Justice William J. Brennan, began to urge state courts to look more closely at state constitutions as a viable basis for the recognition of rights the national high court seemed reluctant to embrace as a part of the U.S. Constitution. Because decisions grounded in state law were largely immune from Supreme Court review, state courts could expand constitutional rights without fear of Supreme Court reversal. In *Michigan v. Long* (1983), however, a Supreme Court majority, speaking through Justice Sandra Day O'Connor, held that state court opinions must contain plain statements basing their rulings on state constitutional grounds; otherwise, the justices would conclude that a decision appealed to them from a state high court rested on federal grounds and proceed to reach those issues. In *Long*, for example, a majority concluded that a Michigan Supreme Court decision striking down a police automobile search was based on the search and seizure provisions of the federal, not the Michigan, constitution, then overturned the state court ruling.[83]

Perhaps in an effort to better insulate its decisions from U.S. Supreme Court review, the New Hampshire high court, with Souter not participating, held the year after *Long* that it would first examine state constitutional claims raised in any case, moving to a consideration of federal questions only if the state claim was rejected. "Even if it appears that the Federal Constitution is more protective than the State Constitution," Justice Charles Douglas, citing *Long*, observed for the court, "the right of our citizens to the full protection of the New Hampshire Constitution requires that we consider State constitutional guarantees. This is because any decision we reach based upon *federal* law is subject to review by the United States Supreme Court, whereas we have unreviewable authority to reach a decision based on articulated adequate and independent State grounds."[84]

The next year, the court invoked the New Hampshire constitution in striking down a search warrant and subsequent search, thereby avoiding any need to decide whether federal law would have provided greater protection for the defendant. Justice Souter joined the court's decision. But in a brief concurrence, he "express[ed] this one time my reservation about the approach to State constitutional adjudication adopted in *State v. Ball* . . . and followed here. When a federal constitutional standard is binding upon us and we do not question [its] soundness . . . I would rest the decision of the case on the federal standard. I would concentrate on the development of State constitutional law in those cases when a State rule would be different from its federal counterpart and would affect the outcome. I believe that over the long term, the adjudicatory process is likely to lead to sounder results when a practical difference is at stake."[85]

Nor was Souter inclined to find a *Miranda* or related violation in police interrogation cases. In *State v. Denney* (1987), he dissented when a majority held that the due process guarantee in the New Hampshire constitution forbade use by the prosecution of a defendant's refusal to submit to a blood alcohol test, where he had not been warned that his refusal could be used against him at trial. In dissent, Souter argued that due process required no such warning and that, even if it did, the police had provided Denney with adequate warning. The arresting officer had given the *Miranda* warnings, including the advice that anything said could be used as evidence, before asking the defendant to take the blood test. The police thus provided Denney, Souter argued, "with the very advice that the majority require as a condition for admitting evidence of [his] refusal" to take the test. But Souter would have gone further. The majority had attached significance to a provision of a state statute requiring police to inform a suspect "of the consequences of his refusal to permit a test." However, that language, Souter countered, was enacted at the same time as the statute's original version, which expressly described two consequences of a refusal to take the test: no administering of the test and revocation of the suspect's driver's license. In Souter's judgment, those were the "consequences" referred to in the statute, and no warning was required by law that the refusal to take the test could later be used as evidence at trial.[86]

Souter prevailed in an earlier DWI case in which a defendant invoked her state constitutional privilege against compulsory self-incrimination in objecting to the introduction at trial of her refusal to submit to a blood test. Speaking for the majority and citing state court precedents, the justice held that the state constitutional privilege, like its Fifth Amendment counterpart, applied only to the compulsion of testimonial evidence, not physical evidence, and that the defendant's refusal to submit to a blood test constituted her choice to suppress physical evidence—a choice given her under state law, but one not without its adverse consequences. Souter further concluded, however, that the accused's refusal to submit to a blood test, whether testimonial or physical evidence, was not compelled. In declining the test, Souter reasoned, the defendant was simply exercising a legal right created by the legislature, not a constitutional right, as there was no constitutional right to refuse a blood test. The legislature could have granted the prerogative to refuse a blood test with no strings attached. Instead, it had imposed two conditions: loss of the driver's license for up to a year and use of the refusal to take the test as evidence in any civil action or criminal prosecution of committed DWI. Exercising the option to refuse the test, Souter added, simply excluded from court more probative evidence (the test results) for less probative evidence (use of the refusal in court), a trade-off advantageous to the defendant. In his judgment, therefore, her refusal was in no way analogous to the sort of compulsion of testimonial evidence forbidden by the federal and state constitutions.[87]

Chief Justice King, joined by Charles Douglas, dissented. Although conceding that the U.S. Supreme Court had long drawn a distinction between the compulsion of physical and testimonial evidence, holding that only the latter was covered by the Fifth Amendment, King argued that the New Hampshire constitutional safeguard against self-incrimination provided the accused with broader protection than its federal counterpart. In contrast to the Fifth Amendment, which guaranteed only that no person "be compelled in any criminal case to be a witness against himself," the state constitutional guarantee protected the individual from being "compelled to accuse or furnish evidence against himself." That prohibition against the compelled furnishing of evidence, King suggested, might go further, covering "evidence otherwise considered to have been real, not testimonial, in nature." But King saw no need to reach that issue in the case before the court because the defendant's refusal to submit to the blood test was "clearly testimonial." Although not clear in the record, the defendant's refusal had to have been "manifested in the form of some communication, either verbally or by assertive conduct, which expressed the defendant's state of mind at the time to refuse to submit to a test."[88]

King also rejected Souter's assertion that the evidence had not been compelled. The defendant's refusal to submit to a blood test was not the product of a free choice, asserted the chief justice. After all, those who refused lost their driver's license. More important, admitting into evidence the defendant's refusal to take the test was comparable to a confession "and, for practical purposes, inevitably [led] to a conviction." Any attempt to rebut evidence of a refusal, moreover, would usually require the defendant's testimony; the "choice of whether to testify [was] really no choice at all, for it goes to the heart of the testimonial privilege itself, that is, protecting the defendant from the 'cruel trilemma of self-accusation, perjury or contempt.'"[89]

Souter would appear to have had the better of the argument. The dissenters' suggestion that the self-incrimination provision of the New Hampshire constitution might reach compulsion of physical evidence, such as blood or breath samples, arguably conflicted with state precedents limiting its reach, like the Fifth Amendment's, to testimonial evidence alone—precedents Souter cited in his opinion. Moreover, equating the defendant's exercise of her purely statutory option to refuse to provide a blood sample with unconstitutional coercion of testimonial evidence seems a stretch at best. By refusing to provide a blood sample, the defendant, as Souter contended, was simply choosing to have the best evidence (the test results) excluded from court while less probative evidence (her refusal to provide a sample) would be admitted.

Vincent Coppola and the Law

At least one Souter interrogation opinion would perplex those criminal defense attorneys who admired what they considered his genuine commitment even to those constitutional precedents with which he disagreed. In that case, a jury convicted Vincent Coppola for the vicious rape of a seventy-eight-year-old woman. One issue James Duggan, as appellate defender, raised on appeal of the case to the New Hampshire Supreme Court was the admission at trial of a statement Coppola made to police during their investigation of the crime. When officers made a second visit to the defendant's house, asking to talk with him again, he offered this response: "Let me tell you something; I'm not one of your country bumpkins. I grew up on the streets of Providence, Rhode Island. And if you think I'm going to confess to you, you're crazy."[90]

Although Coppola did not testify at his trial, what Justice Souter termed his "defiant remark" to police was admitted into evidence. On appeal, the defendant's counsel contended, in Souter's words, "that his boast to be Rhode Island street-wise was tantamount to" invoking his privilege against compulsory self-incrimination. Duggan also cited, among other cases, *Doyle v. Ohio*

(1976), in which the U.S. Supreme Court held that the demands of fundamental fairness inherent in due process forbade the state from impeaching a defendant with evidence that he remained silent after being arrested and given the *Miranda* warnings. Speaking for a unanimous court, however, Souter emphasized the "factual unreality of equating [Coppola's] taunt to the police with an invocation of his constitutional right to remain silent. . . . His statement cannot be read as a mere assertion that he, unlike a bumpkin, would not talk; he claimed, rather, that the police were crazy to think that someone of his sophistication would confess. By describing his choice as a refusal to confess, he implied that he had done something to confess about. It was this implication that took the defendant's retort outside the realm of allusions to the fifth amendment and affirmatively indicated his consciousness of guilt."91

The justice would not have the last word in *Coppola*. After losing in the New Hampshire Supreme Court, Duggan filed a petition for a writ of habeas corpus in the federal district court in Concord, challenging his clients' conviction and imprisonment based on the sorts of constitutional claims the state high court had rejected. The district court dismissed the petition. But a three-judge First Circuit panel, speaking through Judge Hugh Bownes, reversed the district judge, holding that the admission at trial of Coppola's statement to police had indeed placed an unconstitutional burden on his Fifth Amendment privilege.92

Emphasizing that the privilege was to be given a liberal interpretation, that its invocation did not turn on a particular choice of words, and that it was not limited to persons in custody or charged with a crime, Judge Bownes "respectfully" rejected much of his friend's rationale for affirming Coppola's conviction. In his opinion, Souter had accorded considerable weight to *Jenkins v. Anderson* (1980), a case in which the U.S. Supreme Court had held that prearrest silence could be used to impeach a defendant's credibility at trial. Bownes countered, however, that in *Jenkins* the defendant had waited until the trial to claim that he had stabbed the victim in self-defense, neither saying anything to anyone about the stabbing nor reporting the victim's death for two weeks after the incident. Coppola's statement to police, by contrast, had been used in the prosecution's case in chief. Bownes also took issue with Souter's assertion that Coppola's constitutional claim might have carried weight had he couched his refusal to talk with police "in terms of speech versus silence." The Fifth Amendment depended, Bownes reiterated, on no "special combination of words," no "semantic formula." But the First Circuit judge reserved his "most emphatic" rebuke for Souter's contention that "by describing his choice as a refusal to confess, [the defendant] implied that he had done something to confess about." Declared Bownes, "Any refusal to speak, no matter how couched, in the face of interrogation, raises an inference that the person being questioned probably has something to hide. . . . Such logic ignores the teaching that the protection of the fifth amendment is not limited to those in custody or charged with a crime." Finally, Bownes was obviously troubled by Souter's reference to Coppola's statement "as a 'taunt to the police,' a 'defiant remark' betraying petitioner's 'sophistication.'" Though having no "quarrel" with such a characterization, Bownes "wonder[ed] what bearing it has on the question whether petitioner effectively invoked his privilege against self-incrimination."[93]

Mark Sisti had represented Coppola at trial. Justice Souter, Sisti later said, "misstepped on that one, there's no question. And I think, if he'd had the chance he would have taken it back." By one count, Souter voted for positions asserted in behalf of a defendant only nine times out of eighty-two state high court opinions in criminal cases. He was most likely to favor the accused in cases involving the right of jury trial and procedures necessary to a fair trial. In a 1984 case, for example, he wrote for a unanimous court in reversing a conviction based on the trial judge's response to a question from the jury in a way that intruded on the jury's fact-finding prerogatives. In *Richard v. MacAskill* (1987), he overturned the sentence of a defendant who had entered a plea of nolo contendere, declining to contest the charge, on a finding that the accused actually had not knowingly and intelligently waived his right to a jury trial. When a judge obtained only a lawyer's consent, not the defendant's, before excusing a member of a jury during its deliberations, he also spoke for the court in reversing the accused's conviction. In other criminal procedure areas, just as in constitutional cases generally, he pursued a decidedly more conservative course on the New Hampshire Supreme Court.[94]

Even so, Sisti and other members of the state's criminal defense bar typically considered Souter a judge willing to apply the law and precedent, whatever his personal preferences. "I really, really believe that there are people who take oaths, and there are people who take oaths. And he was absolutely dedicated to filtering the facts through the prism of the Constitution." When Souter was nominated to the U.S. Supreme Court, Sisti was asked to serve on a committee set up by the National Association of Criminal Defense Lawyers to evaluate the nominee's credentials from that organization's perspective. "My sense was," Sisti later said, "that they were trying to shoot him down.

. . . We had a couple of telephone conference calls. And they said, 'He's a conservative; he's gotta be a conservative. He's from New Hampshire; Bush is putting him out there.' And I said, 'You guys are reading this thing all wrong. You've never practiced in front of this man. If you were a criminal defendant, this is the [man] you would choose to be in front of. He's not going to be a light sentencer if you get convicted. But you're going to have a fair trial on the way there. And that's really all you can ask for.' Jim Duggan and I were the contact people in New Hampshire. And . . . when I got that first phone call from them, it was like, 'How are we going to get rid of this guy?' And I thought, 'Are you kidding me? I mean, who's Bush's second choice?'"95

3

"Stealth Candidate"

WITHIN A SHORT TIME of his appointment to the New Hampshire Supreme Court, David Souter had acquired a reputation as the court's intellectual leader. When John King retired as chief justice in 1986, Souter's friends assumed Governor John Sununu would elevate him to the court's center seat. But Sununu followed tradition, choosing David Brock, who had been appointed an associate justice on the court in 1978, five years before Souter joined him there. According to Souter's friend and mentor Warren Rudman, whose high regard for the future justice accounted for his rapid rise in the New Hampshire attorney general's office, "David was disappointed. The challenge of being an associate justice was wearing thin. Once again he was uncertain about his future. He even considered leaving the court."[1]

The possibility of a federal judgeship, combined with Souter's distaste for private practice, persuaded the justice to stay on the New Hampshire bench. In 1987, a rumor circulated that his friend Hugh Bownes was considering taking senior (or semiretired) status on the Court of Appeals for the First Circuit, which would have permitted President Ronald Reagan to appoint a new judge to that circuit. But Bownes, a Lyndon Johnson appointee to the federal bench, was hesitating, reportedly because he feared that Reagan might appoint an extreme conservative as his replacement. Warren Rudman, who had been elected to the Senate in 1980, went to former Tennessee GOP senator Howard Baker, the president's chief of staff, on Souter's behalf. Baker agreed that Justice Souter would be appointed to the First Circuit if Bownes stepped down. Rudman then visited Bownes in his Concord chambers, assuring the jurist, albeit delicately, that Bownes would have a worthy replacement should he retire. "I assume you mean David Souter," Bownes replied with a laugh. Knowing Bownes's high regard for Souter, Rudman promised the jurist their friend would indeed be appointed. With Reagan in the White House, however, Bownes decided to stay put for the time being.[2]

In the October 29, 1987, issue of the *New York Times*, legal correspondent Linda Greenhouse informed her readers that "a potential nominee to the Supreme Court who has received virtually no public attention has apparently emerged as one of the leading contenders as President Reagan prepares to announce the Administration's selection" later that day. Citing an anonymous Senate source, Greenhouse reported that Souter's name had been on a list of thirteen potential nominees Howard Baker had presented to the Senate earlier and that the justice and three other candidates were now at the top of the list. The vacancy was the one to which Judge Robert Bork had originally been nominated; the other top prospects were Anthony M. Kennedy of the Court of Appeals for the Ninth Circuit in California, Douglas H. Ginsburg of the District of Columbia circuit court, and Clarence Thomas, another D.C. circuit judge. President Reagan first chose Ginsburg, but the former Harvard law professor's nomination was quickly aborted in the face of conflict of interest charges and news of his penchant for marijuana, the latter an automatic disqualifier, at least for Republican nominees. Anthony Kennedy, the White House's next choice, won easy confirmation in the Senate.[3]

Speculating about the White House's interest in Souter, Greenhouse not only quoted Warren Rudman's hardly surprising assessment of his friend as "the most brilliant legal mind" he had ever encountered; she also noted that Souter was a conservative Republican yet enjoyed high regard among New Hampshire Democrats. "On that basis," Greenhouse reasoned, "he would be an appealing choice for those in the White House eager to find a nominee who can be approved in the Senate without a bitter confirmation fight" of the sort the Bork nomination had provoked. As a Reagan nominee, she added, conservative Republican senators would also be unlikely to oppose him, "and in any case Senator Gordon J. Humphrey, a New Hampshire Republican who was a leader in the last-ditch battle to keep . . . Bork's doomed nomination alive on the Senate floor, would have political trouble opposing a nominee from his own state."[4]

In his memoir, Warren Rudman gave this explanation for the Reagan White House's passing over Souter in 1987: after the Bork debacle, Rudman telephoned Howard Baker that he had "the man you need, sitting on the New Hampshire Supreme Court." White House representatives talked with Souter and were impressed. But Attorney General Edwin Meese, according to Rudman, "held out for his fellow Californian Anthony Kennedy."[5]

Federal Circuit Judge

In 1988, Reagan's vice president George H. W. Bush won election to the White House. Seeking to obscure his (by Republican standards) moderately liberal political image, Bush had run a Reaganesque campaign, complete with thinly veiled racial appeals (most prominently, the "Willie Horton" strategy), disavowal of his opponent as a "card-carrying" member of the American Civil Liberties Union (ACLU), even a visit to an American flag factory, where he reportedly wrapped himself in one of the facility's products to underscore his patriotism. But Judge Bownes apparently had more confidence in the kind of nominee Bush might select to replace him than he had in the Reagan White House. In any event, the jurist stepped down in early 1990, and President Bush chose Souter for the vacancy on the First Circuit Court of Appeals.

Like Supreme Court nominees, candidates for seats on the lower federal bench must be approved by a simple majority of the U.S. Senate. Hearings before the Senate Judiciary Committee on lower federal court nominees, however, are typically brief and perfunctory; Souter's was no exception. He appeared on April 5 before the committee with nine other judgeship nominees. Of committee members, only Edward M. Kennedy (D-MA) and Arlen Specter (R-PA) were present for any portion of Souter's testimony, and only Kennedy questioned the nominee. Souter gave no prepared statement. But before Kennedy began his questions, New Hampshire senators Gordon Humphrey and Rudman made brief statements praising the nominee and summarizing his credentials. Senator Rudman also placed in the record a resolution of the New Hampshire Bar Association "unanimously and enthusiastically" endorsing the nomination on behalf of its 3,400 members.[6]

Senator Kennedy's interrogation of Souter was brief but pointed, focusing on two of the nominee's New Hampshire Supreme Court opinions in criminal cases. The first was *State v. Coppola*, in which Souter spoke for the court in upholding the trial judge's refusal to exclude from evidence the defendant's bold assertion to police seeking to question him at home: "I am not one of your country bumpkins. I grew up on the streets of Providence, Rhode Island. If you think I am going to confess to you, you are crazy." Souter, it will be recalled, had refused to construe Coppola's statement as an invocation of his right against compulsory self-incrimination, but instead as evidence of his guilt. In a habeas corpus proceeding, Judge Bownes had spoken for a First Circuit panel in rejecting Souter's rationale. At one point in his opinion, Bownes construed the Souter opinion in the case thus: "Any refusal to speak, no matter how couched, in the face of police interrogation, raises an inference that the person being questioned probably has something to hide. Under the reasoning of the New Hampshire court, any pre-arrest invocation of the privilege, no matter how worded, could be used by the prosecutor in his case in chief because it raises an inference of guilt. Such logic ignores the teaching that the protection of the Fifth Amendment is not limited to those in custody or charged with a crime."[7]

When Kennedy asked Souter to respond to the First Circuit's criticism of his *Coppola* opinion, the nominee recalled a portion of Senator Rudman's statement to the committee crediting the "clarity" of his judicial opinions, then added, "Apparently I was not clear enough for the first circuit." He had not intended to state, Souter testified, that in any precustodial statement by a defendant containing both inculpatory language and an "arguable invocation of fifth amendment rights," the inculpatory element of the statement should always prevail in court. Instead, he and his colleagues had simply concluded that Coppola's statement, in that case, was inculpatory rather than an assertion of the Fifth Amendment privilege. Souter readily agreed with the principle that particular "technical language usage" was unnecessary to an assertion of the privilege and that "any such invocation should be read in a fashion liberal to the defendant." He and Judge Bownes had merely disagreed over the principle's application in *Coppola*.[8]

Senator Kennedy was not satisfied. Asserting that the self-incrimination guarantee was "one of the hallmarks of our constitutional scheme of ordered liberties" and that, if "meaningful, juries must be forbidden to infer guilt from a defendant's refusal to talk to police," the senator asked the nominee what assurance he could give that "you will not take a crabbed view of the scope of that fundamental constitutional protection?" The nominee replied, "The principle that you have just enunciated goes without saying, or should go without saying, in the mind of any judge, including mine. . . . The difficulty that comes, and I think that this case illustrates, is at what point [does] a statement which is, in the first instance, or at least in its first aspect, inculpatory devolve into a fifth amendment invocation. And we saw that point [in *Coppola*] as coming later" than the First Circuit had held.[9]

Kennedy also asked Souter about *State v. Colbath*, the case in which the nominee had concluded for a unanimous New Hampshire high court that a rape victim's public sexual conduct with a group of men shortly before the rape allegedly occurred could be admitted as evidence of consent. "That ruling drew some criticism," the senator observed, "because it appeared to contradict the clear language of [New Hampshire's] rape shield law. Those laws are very important in assuring that victims of rape are not victimized a second time by the ordeal of the trial." Given Souter's position in *Colbath*, Kennedy wondered whether the nominee would "be sensitive to the privacy interests of rape victims."[10]

Assuring the committee that he would indeed be sensitive to such interests, Souter noted the "obvious tension between, on the one hand, the laudable policy of barring a rape prosecution from turning into, in effect, a prosecution of the complaining witness through embarrassing cross-examination, and on the other hand the undoubted right of" defendants to confront their accusers and present evidence favorable to their defense. He also cited *Davis v. Alaska*, a 1974 decision in which the U.S. Supreme Court had overturned a trial judge's order preventing an accused's counsel from referring in cross-examination to a prosecution witness's juvenile record, despite a state provision protecting the anonymity of juvenile offenders and the obvious interests that regulation served. "There comes a point," said Souter, "at which the testimony which, on the face, is excludable under the rape shield law becomes so relevant and so important to the issue of guilt and innocence that the statute has to yield to the constitutional interests." Given the fact that Colbath's defense was consent, he added, "the complaining witness's behavior immediately prior to their departure from the public bar [to the residence where the crime allegedly occurred] had a very high degree of significance." "Well, it is obvious," Kennedy rather lamely replied, "that it does, as you stated very clearly, present some sensitive, important privacy and constitutional kinds of issues. . . . So we welcome hearing your explanation, and also your concern."[11]

Souter won confirmation by a unanimous Senate vote, and on May 25, the First Circuit's chief judge Stephen Breyer, who would himself be appointed to the Supreme Court in 1994, administered the oath of office. During his brief First Circuit tenure, Souter took part in the decision of at least one case—the appeal of a criminal conviction on five counts of income tax evasion—joining an opinion for a unanimous three-judge panel written, ironically enough, by Judge Bownes sitting as a senior circuit judge. He also heard oral argument and otherwise participated in several other cases. But he did not take part in the opinions of those cases, because by that point his career had taken yet another turn.[12]

The Brennan Seat

As the Supreme Court's 1989–90 term ended, Justice William J. Brennan's standing as the most influential justice of his era had long been firmly established. A New Jersey Democrat and social progressive with strong labor union ties, Brennan had been appointed by a Republican governor first to a superior court trial seat, then to its appellate division, and, in 1952, with the strong endorsement of the state's distinguished chief justice Arthur T. Vanderbilt, to a seat on the New Jersey Supreme Court. There, Brennan compiled a generally liberal record—too liberal, perhaps, for the tastes of President Dwight D. Eisenhower and many in the president's inner circle. But the strong backing of Vanderbilt, as well as Eisenhower's appointments secretary, a Brennan boyhood friend, made Brennan a likely prospect for promotion to the nation's highest bench. For a president eager to bolster his bipartisan image with a largely Democratic national electorate, the appointment of the first Roman Catholic to the Court since 1949 would also do no harm, especially in 1956, a presidential election year. In October of that year, the president named Brennan, then age fifty, to a recess appointment; in early 1957, when the Senate reconvened, Brennan's selection was made permanent. On the high bench, the new justice, for whom "five"—the number needed for a majority vote—was the most significant word in the Court's lexicon, became a master of negotiation and compromise, resolutely liberal in his instincts, yet sufficiently flexible to forge winning alliances in a variety of issue areas.[13]

With Ronald Reagan's appointees making the Court an increasingly conservative institution, Justice Thurgood Marshall assured supporters, "Don't worry, I'm going to outlive those bastards." Justice Brennan, on occasion, had voiced similar sentiments. But in July 1990, Brennan was eighty-four; on more than one occasion during the preceding Court term, he and Marshall had dozed during oral arguments. He had endured a variety of medical challenges, including cancer. He had fainted during a recent trip. The time had come, Brennan decided, for him to leave the bench. On July 20, he sent President George H. W. Bush a retirement letter, citing advancing age and health. (The next year, Justice Marshall would follow his colleague's lead.)[14]

Souter's friend Tom Rath heard the news of Brennan's retirement on his car radio that Friday evening after picking up his daughter Erin from a summer camp in Massachusetts. "And I looked at my wife and said, 'Gee, if David hadn't just been put on the circuit, we might be talking about something.'"

The next morning, the telephone rang at Rath's summer condominium on Newfound Lake. It was Warren Rudman. Souter was on a very short list for the Brennan seat.[15]

After Rudman's press secretary telephoned him in New Hampshire about Brennan's announcement, Rudman had called former New Hampshire governor John Sununu, Bush's chief of staff, telling him they "had a chance to do something important for America." The next day, Rudman spoke directly with the president, telling Bush, "You've just appointed this man to the First Circuit Court of Appeals and he can easily be confirmed for the Supreme Court. I can guarantee that he has no skeletons in his closet, and he's one of the most extraordinary human beings I've ever known."[16]

Thanking Rudman for his interest, Bush was noncommittal. Robert Bork, after all, had won easy confirmation for a circuit court seat before going down to defeat in the Supreme Court proceedings. But Rudman was confident, telephoning Souter to tell him of his efforts with Sununu and Bush. Souter, on the other hand, was skeptical at best. "They aren't going to appoint me to the Supreme Court," he chided his friend. "I don't know the president or anybody important." "I take that personally," Rudman laughingly shot back; "you know me."[17]

When he graduated from Harvard College in 1961, several classmates had presented Souter with a scrapbook filled with imaginary news stories about the impressive career they were certain lay before him. One headline pasted in the book read, "David Souter Nominated to the Supreme Court." At Oxford, his Rhodes classmate Melvin Levine has recalled, Souter "told me . . . on numerous occasions that he was going to be a justice of the Supreme Court. . . . We used to tease him; we always called him Mr. Justice Souter." But Levine, whose pediatric specialty is child development, thought "there was never a doubt in [Souter's] mind that he was going to be on the Supreme Court."[18]

However seriously Souter may have entertained such a notion in his youth, his wariness at Warren Rudman's enthusiasm was probably genuine rather than a display of false modesty. A few weeks earlier, when his friend John McCausland had telephoned to congratulate him on his First Circuit appointment, McCausland had jokingly asked whether the appeals court would merely be a stepping stone to the nation's highest tribunal. "No," Souter responded, "there's no chance I'll be nominated, because I come from a politically insignificant state." Indeed, of Supreme Court justices to date, only Levi Woodbury (1845–51) and Harlan F. Stone (1925–46) had been Granite State residents.[19]

A "Judicious Choice"

Even so, the Bush White House's interest in Souter should hardly have been surprising, considering the penchant in the post-Bork era for what one writer termed "judicious choices" for the high bench. Although generally conservative, Souter's record in the New Hampshire attorney general's office and on the state supreme court was unlikely to provoke intense debate. The party division in the Senate was close (fifty-five Democrats to forty-five Republicans), but the Democrat-controlled body was unlikely to confirm a doctrinaire conservative, at least a white conservative, along the lines of Chief Justice William Rehnquist or Justice Antonin Scalia. Souter's sponsor, Senator Rudman, was a political moderate respected and liked on both sides of the Senate aisle. Finally, Souter, unlike Robert Bork, had no lengthy paper trail of controversial off-the-bench writings. In fact, his only publication, other than several newspaper columns, was a tribute to Justice Laurence Ilsley Duncan, who served on New Hampshire's high court from 1946 to 1976.[20]

Justice Duncan, like Souter, had served on the New Hampshire Superior Court before being elevated to the state supreme court. Seeking total mastery of the facts of a case, Duncan was admired as "the outstanding technician of his court." He also possessed, Souter wrote, the great virtue the legal positivist H. L. A. Hart once accorded Justice Oliver Wendell Holmes: "that if he was wrong, he was wrong clearly." But Duncan possessed more than mere technical skill; he was also bent on doing "right by litigants, whatever the right might be." His opinions tended to be the court's most detailed and far longer than those of his colleagues. They also were the "hardest hitting," yet never reflecting annoyance. "Often there was some fun. But in the main they were weapons of debate, and in reaching judgment within the Court he lived by the sword." In dealing with his law clerks, on the other hand, "[Duncan's] directness gave way, and he would try to coax the best out of them. He was a kind man, and he had a gentleman's sense of the appropriate." Concerned about the form and tone of the court's opinions, as well as their substance, he became the "de facto editor of headnotes and opinions," pressing his colleagues to eliminate needless words. His widow told Souter, moreover, that "he worked just about all the time," his briefcases stuffed even when she packed him off to Kennebunkport, Maine, for a much-needed vacation. Most interesting, perhaps, Souter wrote that Duncan "the boy would become the most private of men, though he would spend a lifetime quietly serving cultural and philanthropic organizations and the collegiate interests of the courts," including a lengthy tenure, like Souter, on the board of the Concord Hospital. The justice particularly guarded the privacy of his personal life. "He did not say why, and probably would have thought his privacy was beside the point of any interest the world would have in him." Duncan "was my kind of judge," Souter concluded. "He was an intellectual hero of mine, and he always will be."[21]

In his tribute to Justice Duncan, Souter appeared to be describing himself. But nothing in the piece could be considered controversial. Moreover, while, as we have seen, Souter had signed many advisory opinions, memoranda, and letters during his years in the attorney general's office, issued a number of important superior court orders, and had already authored 217 opinions as a state supreme court justice, that work product placed him along neither extreme of the contemporary political spectrum.

Whatever Souter's own misgivings about the likelihood of his imminent elevation in judicial rank, the Bush White House clearly found him an appealing prospect for a contention-free confirmation. Soon after talking with Rudman, Souter called back. C. Boyden Gray, the White House counsel, had tracked him down in his Concord chambers where, characteristically, he was working that Saturday afternoon. (Earlier, Gray had telephoned Souter's mother in an effort to locate her son. Thinking the president's lawyer might be a prank caller, Helen Souter had initially hesitated to provide Gray her son's private number at his chambers, but finally relented.) Souter had been asked, he told Rudman, to fly to Washington the next day for a Monday meeting with President Bush. "We had a pretty intense discussion," Rudman later wrote. "His attitude, at least at first, was 'What have you done to me now?' He said, in effect, that he didn't want to go through [the] exercise, that there were other candidates who were better known and more politically connected, and it just wasn't going to happen." But Rudman was confident his friend was the "perfect candidate": superb professional credentials, no skeletons in his closet, and no Bork-type paper trail of provocative writings the opposition could exploit.[22]

Later that day, Souter called Rudman again. Was it possible to fly directly to Washington from Manchester? Rudman assured him a direct flight was available and even insisted on driving him to the airport, "lest he miss the plane." That night, Souter telephoned yet again. He would not go to Washington, he vowed, if anyone was going to ask him his stance on *Roe v. Wade*. "I won't take a litmus test. I'll discuss judicial philosophy with them, but I won't go down there and be compromised. I won't discuss how I might rule in future cases. They ought to know that beforehand. It might save us all a lot of time."[23]

After Rudman made a call to John Sununu, obtaining assurances that absolutely no questions would be raised about the abortion issue, or indeed Souter's likely response to any specific issues that might come before the Court, Souter agreed to go to Washington, albeit still certain that he would not be the president's choice. When Rudman dropped the future U.S. Supreme Court justice off at the Manchester airport on Sunday, Souter got out of the car, his "ancient, battered suitcase" in tow, but then turned to Rudman, a pained expression on his face. Pulling out his wallet, Souter revealed that he had only three dollars with him. Rudman gave him a hundred dollars. "I ought to pin a tag on you," he remarked, only half-jokingly. "You know, one that says, 'Please take this boy off the plane in Washington.'"[24]

President Bush had been on Air Force One, preparing to return to Washington after several days of fishing and politics in the West, when he learned of Justice Brennan's retirement. After calling the justice to accept his resignation, Bush called John Sununu, scheduling a White House meeting with senior advisers for 8:00 the next morning. During that session, Bush, Sununu, Boyden Gray, and Attorney General Richard Thornburgh went through a dozen or so dossiers of Supreme Court possibilities compiled since the president's election. In that session, Sununu apparently held back, permitting Gray and Thornburgh to make the case for Souter. By the end of the meeting, the list had been reduced to around eight. Bush asked for more specifics about each, then retired for the weekend to the presidential retreat at Camp David. According to press reports, Sununu then began working behind the scenes on Souter's behalf, asking Warren Rudman, for example, to fax a supporting letter to be included in a packet delivered to the president at Camp David. On Sunday, Bush narrowed the field to five candidates: Souter, Fifth Circuit Court of Appeals judge Edith Jones of Houston, Solicitor General Kenneth Starr, and D.C. federal appeals judges Lawrence Silberman and Clarence Thomas, the former chairman of the Equal Employment Opportunity Commission, who would take Justice Marshall's seat in 1991 after rancorous confirmation proceedings focusing on Thomas's alleged sexual harassment of former colleague Anita Hill. As Bush had met neither Souter nor Jones, they were invited to Washington for the Monday morning meeting with the president.[25]

After spending Sunday night at the home of Michael Luttig, an assistant attorney general later appointed to a seat on the Court of Appeals for the Fourth Circuit, Souter was taken to the Treasury Department, then, to avoid media, through a tunnel leading from Treasury to the west wing of the White House. Following a meeting with Boyden Gray and other White House staff members, he entered the Oval Office for an interview with President Bush. Later, Mrs. Bush joined them. As Sununu had promised, Bush discussed Souter's general conception of the judiciary without broaching any specifics. "As I had expected," Warren Rudman later wrote, "David and the president hit it off extremely well. They came from similar backgrounds: Yankee, white Anglo-Saxon Protestant families that believed in the old values of hard work, integrity and public service. The president was impressed by David's intelligence, modesty and sense of duty, and he was shrewd enough to anticipate that the Senate and the nation would be impressed by those qualities too."[26]

Judge Jones, with whom Bush also met that morning, was clearly a more familiar figure nationally than Souter. But she was also more likely to provoke the confirmation battle the White House wanted to avoid. Until her appointment to the Fifth Circuit by President Reagan in 1985, Jones had been a member of the Houston law firm in which Bush secretary of state James A. Baker was a partner for many years. Unlike Souter, she had been active in partisan politics, serving, for example, as general counsel to the Texas Republican Party in 1983–85. Jones was a frequent speaker at meetings of the Federalist Society, the organization of conservative lawyers and judges Antonin Scalia had helped to found. In 1988, she had rebuked a lawyer in a death penalty case for what she considered his filing of a spurious, last-minute appeal for a stay of execution. In another death penalty case, she complained that a lawyer's last-minute appeal had forced her to miss the birthday party of one of her sons.[27]

The other reported finalists for the Brennan seat seemed equally problematic, given the White House's interest in avoiding a serious confirmation debate. Judge Silberman was closely identified with the Rehnquist-Scalia wing of the federal judiciary. Only two weeks earlier, he had joined a ruling overturning one of Oliver North's convictions in the Reagan administration's Iran-Contra scandal. The White House probably considered an African American such as Clarence Thomas unlikely to draw much opposition from Senate Democrats, considering the demographics of the American electorate, but Bush was probably holding him for Justice Marshall's anticipated retirement, or death. Even in those pre-Clinton years, moreover, Solicitor General Kenneth Starr was closely connected with the GOP's most conservative wing.[28]

After his interview with the president, Souter telephoned Tom Rath in New Hampshire. "I've had this discussion," he told his friend. "I don't know what's going to happen. Call my mother and tell her I'm okay." Later, he called back. "I'm in the anteroom of the Oval Office, and the President of the United States has just told me he's going to appoint me. We're about to walk down the hallway to the press room."[29]

At 5:00 P.M., President Bush announced his choice to reporters, praising Souter as "a remarkable judge of keen intellect and the highest ability, one whose scholarly commitment to the law and whose wealth of experience mark him of the first rank." His selection, the president assured the nation, "was not geared simply to any legal issue"; he had applied no "litmus test." At the same time, Bush insisted, he had selected a jurist "committed to interpreting, not making the law," one who recognized "the proper role of judges in upholding the democratic choices of the people through their elected representatives within constitutional constraints."[30]

When the president called for questions, Helen Thomas of United Press International promptly asked whether Bush had asked his nominee's views on abortion. "Do you know what his views are? And affirmative action—all of these things that have become so controversial, the major issues of the day."

Bush replied that "it would have been inappropriate to ask [Souter] his views on specific issues. . . . I am familiar with him, with his general views; but I did not and would not, as I think I've said before when I talked about . . . the litmus test approach—I wouldn't go into that with him." But reporters pressed on. "Sir, does that mean you do not care what he thinks on these issues?" "It means," Bush shot back, "that I have selected a person who will interpret the Constitution and, in my view, not legislate from the Federal bench." Asked if he were uncertain how the nominee would vote on abortion questions, the president reiterated his preference for a justice who would "interpret" the Constitution, not legislate. "I've pledged to seek out excellence," he added, "and I've pledged to look for somebody who would interpret the Constitution, and I am satisfied that I have found the best in that regard."

Leslie Stahl of CBS News inquired whether Souter had written anything on the abortion issue. Bush rejoined that he thought it would be inappropriate for the nominee to comment on any specific issue, but added, drawing laughter from his audience, "I'll let him make up his own mind" on the matter. Asked whether the Senate could properly raise such questions of the nominee, the president answered, "I would let the Senate do whatever they want."

At the suggestion of press secretary Marlin Fitzwater, Bush then turned the podium over to Justice Souter. But the nominee was no more cooperative than the president. Decidedly less poised than he was to be before the Senate judiciary committee, Souter made the following statement: "Thank you, Mr. President. . . . If it were possible for me to express to you the realization that I have of the honor which the President has just done me, I would try, and I would keep you here as long tonight as I had to do to get it out. But I could not express that realization, and I'm not going to try to do the impossible. Beyond that, I hope you will understand that I think I must defer any further comments of mine until I am before the Senate in the confirmation."

Justice Souter said no more, but the press were not about to let President Bush off the hook. Citing the nominee's connection to John Sununu, "recognized as the champion of the conservatives in the White House," one reporter wanted to know if the nomination was designed to appease the "conservative right," disgruntled with Bush over his recent "flip-flop" on his "no-new-taxes" 1988 campaign pledge. Claiming that "there was almost a certain recusal on the part of Governor Sununu" in the nomination process, Bush assured journalists that "excellence came to the top" with Souter's selection, that "there [was] no politics of this nature in this kind of appointment."

Reporters were hardly convinced. After getting the president reluctantly to concede that Souter's background had been subjected to considerable investigation, one member of the press corps noted that Souter owed his New Hampshire Supreme Court appointment to Sununu, and that the opposition of both the president and his chief of staff to *Roe v. Wade* was well-known, then asked, "Why should we not believe that [abortion was] a factor in your selection—even in making a list?" "Because I've told you it's not," Bush testily responded.

Like Souter's other friends, Malcolm McLane watched the announcement on television. "David gets a terrible five o'clock shadow," he later said; "he's a dark-looking fellow. He looked a little nervous." McLane's assessment was perhaps unduly generous. White House staff members, not to mention the nominee himself, described him as "dazed" and in a "state of shock" during and after the news conference, and he did indeed look haggard and drawn. Afterward, he was taken immediately to Sununu's office to begin planning the confirmation process. About an hour later, he has recalled, "the Governor came in, and he said that the President believed I could probably stand some refurbishing. And I thought, well, the President finally got it right this afternoon." The nominee was taken up to the family quarters, where the president and Mrs. Bush were watching the news. "The President gave me a drink to compose myself. And after a couple of minutes of conversation, Mrs. Bush said to me, 'How is your mother taking this?'"[31]

Helen Souter was then living at Havenwood, an assisted living facility in Concord. Souter told Barbara Bush he had called his mother and could "report that the mother was taking things a lot better than the son was." "What's her phone number?" the president asked. Souter gave Bush the number, and he called her. "Now, look, Mrs. Souter," the nominee would remember the president telling his astonished mother, "I want you to know he's okay. We've got him up here, and we're watching the news, and he's having a drink. And we'll look after him, and he's going to be all right."

Following a New York meeting that morning, Warren Rudman had flown to Washington's National Airport. There, he received a message asking that he rush to his office, that Souter's nomination was about to be announced. Following the news conference and the nominee's visit with President and Mrs. Bush, Souter was taken to Rudman's office. "It was bedlam there," the senator later recorded. "We went into my office and embraced and we both wept. I was so proud and happy for him, truly overwhelmed."[32]

Souter had planned to be in Washington only one night, but learned at the White House that he would be expected to remain in the capital until the weekend, meeting members of Congress and planning confirmation strategy. When Rudman invited him to stay at his apartment, the frugal Souter readily agreed. As the week progressed, his attire grew increasingly familiar to reporters trailing him around Capitol Hill. Finally, one reporter could no longer resist: "If I could ask you a personal question. Someone pointed out that you seem to be wearing the same [pin-striped] suit." To that point, the nominee had been reluctant to respond to media questions. On that occasion, he made an exception. "I came down on very short notice. . . . Frankly I had no expectation of staying for very long, so they're right, somebody's got good eyes. It's the same suit." He promised to have a different suit soon.[33]

As the nominee made the rounds of capital offices that week, he increasingly displayed the composure and wit so familiar to his New Hampshire friends. Asked about his feelings when nominated, he replied, "The best news I have is that the blood is circulating to the brain well enough now so that I'm beginning to have some feelings." When news photographers crowded into the office of Arlen Specter, the only Republican on the judiciary committee who voted against Robert Bork's confirmation, the Pennsylvanian remarked, "I haven't had this many photographers since Judge Bork was here." "Can't you find another precedent?" asked Souter, in a stage whisper. Specter quickly obliged: "Since Sandra Day O'Connor was here." When Senator Strom Thurmond, ranking Republican on the judiciary committee, gave the nominee a copy of the Constitution, Souter responded, "This will not be my first reading, but I am grateful." Vermont Democrat Patrick Leahy, another judiciary committee member, told the nominee he planned to spend the Senate's August recess reading his New Hampshire Supreme Court opinions. "You'll have no trouble sleeping," said Souter. But Souter perhaps found his match in Senate Republican leader Robert Dole of Kansas. As the nominee's meeting with Dole was about to begin, someone asked Souter if he was "going to be sorry to leave New Hampshire." "I don't know that anyone wants to leave New Hampshire," Souter replied. "I did," quipped Dole, whose 1988 bid for the Republican presidential nomination had run aground in the New Hampshire primary.[34]

These initial courtesy calls went well for Souter. Senator Leahy, for example, found the nominee "not at all like Bork" in temperament. Leahy termed Souter "quiet, pleasant and obviously intelligent." From the moment the nomination was announced, however, politicians and the national press had begun dubbing Souter the "stealth candidate" and "Justice Who," expressing frustration at his refusal to respond to questions and the paucity of information about his views on contemporary legal issues, especially the all-consuming abortion question. When George Bush told the nation he had not asked Souter's thoughts on *Roe v. Wade*, conservative columnist George Will, who had attended the same Oxford college as Souter, caustically charged that the president "either [was] not telling the truth or . . . telling a terrible truth about himself—that he is willing to buy, and asking the Senate to buy, a pig in a poke." In a recent book, Robert Bork had opined that presidents wishing to avoid future confirmation battles were "likely to nominate men and women who have not written much, and certainly nothing that could be regarded as controversial by left-leaning Senators and groups." Writing for the *Wall Street Journal*, Paul Gigot contended, in a column entitled "Don't Say Robert Bork Didn't Warn Us," that President Bush, "the artful dodger himself," had done just that. As information about Souter's background began to surface, interest groups found mixed signals in his background disturbing. On learning of the nominee's 1981 opposition to including a judicial bypass provision in a state parental consent abortion law, the legal director of the National Abortion Rights Action League (NARAL) expressed concern that Souter might uphold a consent law that did not include a judicial bypass option, as well as other abortion restrictions. But Bush's insistence that he had not probed the nominee's views on abortion or other hot-button issues also alarmed the president of the American Life Lobby, an anti-abortion organization. "As soon as he said, there is no litmus test," she told a reporter, "I thought, 'Uh-oh, that's it for pro-lifers.'"[35]

Liberals found troubling reports that John Sununu, the most conservative member of the White House staff, had engineered his fellow Granite Stater's selection. "At the press conference announcing Souter's nomination yesterday," wrote columnist Jimmy Breslin, "it was stressed that John Sununu . . . had virtually nothing to do with naming Souter. Sununu, as governor of New Hampshire, named Souter to the State Supreme Court. Sununu now is in the White House. He is said to have knocked down everybody else in the White House so he could have room to wave his hands in making a point while speaking alone to the president. Therefore, it makes sense that Sununu had absolutely nothing to do with the appointment."[36]

Perhaps in an effort to head off having his friend tainted among Democrats by his ties to Sununu, as well as being reluctant to share credit for securing Souter's nomination, Senator Rudman emphasized shortly after Bush announced his choice that "it would be a mistake to associate this nomination in any way with John Sununu. John Sununu did not know David Souter at the time that he appointed him to the New Hampshire Supreme Court, other than casually." Later, Rudman reacted testily to reports that Souter was Sununu's "protégé or an ideological twin." Declaring that the Bush chief of staff hardly knew Souter when he appointed him to the state high court, Rudman insisted that he "pushed him for that, I told Ronald Reagan about him, I pushed him for the Circuit Court job and I urged Bush to choose him this time. He's not Sununu's man." But Rudman's assurances hardly quieted speculation or fears that Souter might be another Bork. Speaking on the floor of the House of Representatives, Ohio congressman James Traficant assured colleagues, "You could bet your booty that David Souter's personal legal philosophy is right out of Robert Bork's personal writings. . . . Tricky, tricky, tricky."[37]

The Marshall Outburst

One may assume that the suspicions of Representative Traficant, who would later be expelled from the House following bribery, racketeering, and tax evasion convictions, carried little weight on Capitol Hill. But the repudiation of Souter and President Bush by one of the giants of the modern civil rights movement—however inconsistent with the standards of judicial propriety—was potentially a different matter. Never known for his reticence, Justice

Thurgood Marshall had become increasingly outspoken in recent years, condemning what he considered to be the Reagan administration's assaults on civil rights, rejecting the notion that African Americans had any reason to celebrate the bicentennial of the Constitution (in contrast to adoption of the Civil War amendments), and otherwise delivering himself of pronouncements sitting judges typically avoid. In an interview with television reporter Sam Donaldson, broadcast on the ABC News program *Prime Time Live* on Thursday after the Monday announcement of Souter's nomination, the justice shared with the nation his low opinion of President Bush. "It's said," Marshall remarked, "that if you can't say something good about a dead person, don't say it. Well, I consider him dead." It was obvious to Marshall that John Sununu was "calling the shots" in the selection of a successor for his longtime friend and Court ally, William Brennan. "If [Sununu] came up for election," he added, "I'd vote against him. No question about it." Of the president's choice, the exasperated justice observed, "I just don't understand what he's doing. I don't understand it." Did Marshall know Justice Souter? Donaldson asked. "No," the justice replied, "never heard of him." When Donaldson noted the obvious, that the New Hampshire jurist might replace Brennan, Marshall shot back, "I still never heard of him. When his name came down I listened on television. And the first thing, I called my wife. 'Have I ever heard of this man?' She said, 'No, I haven't either.' So I promptly called Brennan, because it's his Circuit," said Marshall in a reference to Brennan's supervisory responsibilities over the First Circuit. "And his wife answered the phone, and I told her. She said: 'He's never heard of him either.'"[38]

Administration spokespersons and Souter's friends rushed to the nominee's defense. President Bush declined any comment on Marshall's statements, saying simply that he had "a very high regard for the separation of powers and for the Supreme Court and [that] the people can get along without a comment from me." Attorney General Thornburgh said that Marshall's remarks "saddened" him and were, he believed, "the first time any Supreme Court justice has ever criticized in our history an appointment and indeed the president who made the appointment." Characteristically, Senator Dole was less restrained, scorning what he termed the justice's "cheap shots" and "partisan and demeaning political statements," and Senator Rudman called it "absurd" for Marshall and other critics to charge that the nominee had no record to examine. Citing Souter's more than two hundred state supreme court opinions, Rudman contended that his friend had "a paper trail that is a mile long and a mile deep." It was not Souter's fault, he added, that he had not dealt extensively with issues "on people's minds." Not surprisingly, Justice Souter declined comment on his future colleague's remarks. Asked by a reporter if he had ever heard of Justice Marshall, Souter replied, "I trust there is no one in the United States who has not heard of Justice Marshall."[39]

As Linda Greenhouse of the *New York Times*, among others, suggested, Justice Marshall's comments may have raised more questions "about the 82-year-old Justice's own mental competence and about the impact his remarks might have on a Court that Judge Souter would [probably] soon join," than about the nominee's fitness for the position. The massive volume of early news stories and commentary on the nomination included, moreover, two thoughtful and prophetic analyses of the sort of justice Souter might prove to be. Columnist Anthony Lewis took his lead from a remark Warren Rudman made the day Souter's nomination was announced. Asked whether the nominee especially admired any past members of the Supreme Court, Rudman had speculated that Oliver W. Holmes, subject of Souter's Harvard senior thesis, and the second Justice John Marshall Harlan were the nominee's favorites. During the late nineteenth and early twentieth centuries, a shifting majority on the Supreme Court had embraced laissez-faire, regularly declaring unconstitutional federal and state regulations of business and industry. Justice Holmes dissented in many such cases, urging judicial deference to the policy choices of the voters' elected representatives. At the same time, Holmes generally endorsed broad interpretations of freedom of speech and related civil liberties guarantees against majority tyranny. The second Justice Harlan, wrote Lewis, took cases as they came. "He had no agenda. He did not go into a case with certainty about how it should come out. He struggled to be disinterested. That did not mean unconcerned; he cared deeply. It meant that he tried genuinely to understand both sides of the argument." Harlan was also respectful of the past, even joining the application of precedent cases in which he had originally dissented. "But his mind," added Lewis, "was open to fresh applications of the Constitution to meet new threats." He had declared the Connecticut law forbidding the use of contraceptives unconstitutional four years before a Warren Court majority followed his lead. Although a Wall Street lawyer and "thorough gentleman," Harlan "had the rare empathetic ability to see issues from the viewpoints of others with different backgrounds and different premises," speaking for the Court during his last term, for example, in rejecting state authority to punish people for the mere public display of offensive epithets. Souter had been described as a conservative. But

Lewis suspected he had come "to this great appointment with no ideological agenda: no list of legal wrongs he is determined to right." Conservatives and liberals seemed "discontented with that. They want to make him register his votes in advance. . . . I think that is a terrible idea. Requiring a nominee to fill out a score card on particular issues would be contemptuous of the Court and of the judicial process. . . . It would reduce the Supreme Court to sheer politics and wound an institution on which all of us ultimately depend for our freedom."[40]

Interviewed for an article in a legal newspaper, University of Virginia law professor A. E. Dick Howard cautioned that the nominee should not necessarily be judged by John Sununu's support. Noting that Souter had described himself as an "interpretationist," Howard termed the justice's choice of words "meticulous," adding, "He is clearly too bright to use that word unwittingly." An interpretationist, Howard explained, embraces a strict construction of the Constitution's language but reads its words "in light of contemporary conditions, and is not bound by [the framers'] original meaning." Souter, Howard suspected, would reject the contentions of Reagan attorney general Edwin Meese and others that the Constitution's provisions should be construed according to the "original intent" of their framers at the time of their adoption.[41]

On Friday, July 27, Souter and Rudman returned to New Hampshire aboard Air Force One with the Bushes, who were en route to their Kennebunkport, Maine, summer home for a cousin's wedding that weekend. Again avoiding reporters' questions, Souter told them he did not wish to "ruin" his reputation for reticence, adding that he had only two words for them, "hello and goodbye." On landing at Pease Air Force Base in Portsmouth, New Hampshire, he announced that it felt "damn good" to be home. Asked by reporters if he was "excited" and "having fun," he replied, "I'm trending in the right direction." After a visit with his mother in Concord, he returned to his house in Weare. That evening, a photographer caught a picture of an incredibly exhausted-looking Souter, in shirt sleeves and tieless, standing in the doorway of his home.[42]

Media Frenzy

The media, of course, had not waited until Souter's return to descend on New Hampshire. Shortly after he telephoned Tom Rath from the White House the previous Monday, telling him President Bush would soon announce his nomination, the telephone at Rath's home rang again. It was David Broder.

When Rath's daughter Erin told the columnist her father would call him back, Broder responded, "I think his phone is going to be real busy for the rest of the day. I'll just hold." Reporters bombarded Souter's other friends as well. CBS anchorman Dan Rather put Ronald Snow on live from Manchester one evening. While waiting to go on the air, Snow received a telephone call from CBS reporter Leslie Stahl, a former Boston television reporter and friend of long standing. "And she said, 'I'm going to follow you tonight. I just need to know from you straight out, is David Souter for real? Are there skeletons there? . . . Is this guy gay?'" Snow laughed and offered to provide Stahl with the names of Souter's former girlfriends. "Leslie," Snow later recalled telling the reporter, "the guy is absolutely straight; he's smart as hell. He's a little introverted, but he's the funniest guy in the world if you get to know him." But Snow and other friends found journalists very suspicious. "They'd been out to the house [and thought,] 'Oh, my God! This guy must be a recluse!'"[43]

Soon, magazines and newspapers were filled with stories and photographs covering the nominee's life and career. High school classmates shared their memories. Extensive play was given a yearbook photograph depicting Souter—the "most sophisticated" senior boy—dressed in caveman attire, dragging his female counterpart Marjorie MacLeod along by the hair of her head. So, too, were his initial plans to enter the Episcopal priesthood, continued devotion to his church, and preference for the 1928 Book of Common Prayer over the 1970 modernized version. At Hopkinton's St. Andrews Episcopal Church, more than one journalist reported, he served on the vestry and wheeled an elderly amputee woman into church each Sunday.[44]

Few details of Souter's personality, habits, and lifestyle were ignored. His love of mountain climbing, his standard lunch of an apple and cottage cheese (or yogurt—there were even articles devoted to which). His voracious appetite for rare prints and books, which he purchased at Goodspeed's in Boston or at the Sykes & Flanders bookshop near his home, where he had recently purchased a first edition of the letters of Charles Francis Adams, son of John Quincy Adams. His very frugal nature, especially his penchant for ancient cars (including the 1987 Volkswagen Golf he was then driving) that, as the New York Times put it, "he drives (and drives and drives)," and chronic complaints about electric bills—which invariably prompted friends to feign amazement that he even had electricity in his house. The affection of his law clerks, among them Boston attorney Jane Cetlin, who had asked Souter to be her daughter's godfather and who once received a bar of soap from the justice after using "colorful" language in his presence. His net worth ($621,252.41, including his house, valued at $150,000, $46,000 in cash, $160,000 in bank stock, and $191,000 in personal property). His freedom from debt. Indeed, in a profile entitled "Thoroughly Unmodern Souter," the *Legal Times* speculated that Souter "seem[ed] to be a man uncomfortable with the modern world, and therefore not a candidate for creating new and expansive ways of addressing a justice's role." Most telling, according to the paper, was "the simple fact that at age 50, he has apparently accumulated zero debt: no mortgage, no credit cards, no unpaid bills."[45]

Armed with names provided them by Souter's friends, anxious to dispel suspicions the nominee was gay, journalists also contacted former girlfriends. Anne Cagwin, now married to Concord native Gunnar Hagstrom and living in Maine, compared Souter to "someone from another century." Ellanor Fink, the Wheaton College student the nominee had dated in law school, characterized him as "tremendously fair-minded." Responding to concerns that Souter had little conception of the "real world" and its problems, Fink expressed confidence that he would "have the empathy" to understand women's issues. "It's not as though he's lived in a cave for the last 25 years. He has many friends and I'm sure many women friends and I'm sure he's very aware of the impact of abortion on women's lives and men's lives as well." Calling Souter "Hackett," the middle name he apparently preferred at Oxford and in law school, Fink thought that Souter's New Hampshire roots were an excellent clue to the sort of justice he would prove to be. "It's a very special kind of place," she said. "It respects individuals and it's very tolerant of others." Souter's Oxford classmate Melvin Levine was equally certain his friend was well-suited to resolve constitutional issues. Around Souter, he told a *Time* reporter, "you really feel as if you are with one of the Founding Fathers."[46]

Nor were Souter's Weare house and neighbors spared. Soon after the nomination, Warren Rudman later wrote, "reporters and television crews arrived at his isolated farmhouse and began peering in windows and climbing on the roof, trying to see inside. Some used floodlights to film the books in the library. They went to local video stores to see what videotapes he was renting. Presumably they were hoping he watched porn, but the exercise was pointless since David didn't own a VCR—he only reluctantly owned a [black and white] TV. Reporters even invaded the nursing home where David's mother lived and represented themselves as doctors to try to gain access to Mrs. Souter. Eventually, the state police had to protect David's home from intruders."[47]

Two *Los Angeles Times* reporters provided this description of Souter's Weare house:

At the foot of a dirt dead-end road sits the Souter family farmhouse, an unkempt old pile under a siege of waist-high weeds. The brown paint is peeling and . . . the bare wood windows sag under years of dirt, cobwebs cling to the door and an ancient bird's nest perches above the porch light. There are five lightning rods along the roof, no television antenna.

Inside, no piece of furniture is less than half a century old. The ancient refrigerator is powered by an electric motor on the top and the antique stove has white cast-iron handles. Boxes are piled to the ceiling, and the study is a warren of magazines, phonograph albums and books—reference books, novels, oversized art books, books on foreign lands and long-ago battles, books of laws, books about laws and books about the men who make laws.

It is hard to believe anyone lives in this creaking museum, except perhaps an aged hermit, counting out his days rummaging through faded numbers of *Collier's* and the *Saturday Evening Post*. Yet this wreck of a house raised and still shelters U.S. Appeals Court Judge David Hackett Souter, President Bush's 50-year-old nominee for the Supreme Court.

"Only the dining room—with its antique chairs and lace table cloths," other reporters discovered, was "free of clutter."[48]

Souter's Weare neighbors were supportive and protective. But like his other friends, at times their remarks to reporters helped to reinforce the media image of a reclusive eccentric. Sylvia Peterson said she had played "kick the can" with the nominee as a child, but also volunteered that his room "was always cluttered with books, a small chemistry lab, and toys that he never played with." "His light stays on 'til midnight up there," an elderly neighbor added. "You know he's reading his books. . . . He's a loner."[49]

According to his friends, Souter found press intrusion on his neighbors' privacy deeply distressing. The feeling was mutual. Weare's citizens were perhaps understandably suspicious of outsiders. When the flood control dam constructed decades earlier inundated the village's center, residents commemorated the act with a historical marker pointing out that "their beautiful community was sacrificed by the Everett Flood Control Project." Now, Susan Gilman "watched with mounting anger," the *Concord Monitor* reported, "as some media walked on Souter's grass, peered through his windows or sat on his porch." She was pleased her three children were not present to witness the spectacle. "We've taught our kids to respect his property. It really bothers me to see people all over his house. One thing we do is respect each other's property." Like others, Gilman had quickly tired of reporters' questions. "The biggest question is," she said, "do we go out and socialize together. And we don't. He's friendly when we see him."[50]

Television and print media were not the first outsiders to come to Weare with inquiries about the village's most prominent citizen. When Souter was being considered earlier that year for appointment to the First Circuit, FBI agents interviewed Weare residents as part of the agency's investigation into his background. Nellie and Lyhl Perrigo had a "friendly conversation" with an agent one afternoon at their dining table. According to a reporter, "[The agent] asked how long they had known the judge (since he was a boy), what was he like (like a son to them), and how he was in school (wonderful)." "I think he was wanting to know all the good things we knew," Nellie Perrigo remembered. " 'Course, there was nothing else we could tell him."[51]

If friends and neighbors were determined to do nothing intentionally to jeopardize Souter's appointment, journalists investigating the nominee's New Hampshire roots obviously wanted whatever information and opinion they might uncover about the elusive nominee, positive or negative. They were largely disappointed in their quest. Speaking with a Concord reporter, Nina Totenberg, the legal affairs correspondent for National Public Radio who had first broken the story of Justice Brennan's retirement as well as Reagan nominee Douglas Ginsburg's proclivity for marijuana, expressed the frustration many reporters had begun to feel shortly after arriving in New Hampshire: "I have no confidence that I will have more than the most generic sense of this person by the time I leave. I mean, he's a very private person and by most modern standards, a peculiar person. He's so solitary. . . . This is one man I don't think we're going to very successfully intrude on, unless there is some horrible skeleton in his closet, which I frankly doubt." Vexed at her "inability to get beyond the one-dimensional element of a man from another century, who wrote mainly about the most arcane and uninteresting state issues," she wanted to know much more about the nominee and assumed the Senate Judiciary Committee would also. In her twenty-two years covering the Supreme Court, she said, she had never known so little about a nominee. "I can't think of a nominee . . . that when he was named and walked out with the president, I didn't know who he or she was."[52]

Totenberg and two assistants had spent the previous day interviewing Souter's acquaintances, examining records in the attorney general's office and the nominee's judicial opinions, even tracking down his favorite area bookstore. She confessed that she had gone "fishing," but insisted that she was not looking for damning information, just something that would give her a "sense of [a] nominee" about whom very little was known. But she was skeptical about the "hymn of praise" his friends and legal associates were singing.

"I think his friends, of whom there are many, view him through their own prejudices," seeing themselves in him. "I think they all think he shares their view of life, if not of particular questions, and of the law, if not a particular case. But it can't be true; it can't possibly be true." What she had found in the records of the attorney general's office was "boring," the nominee's judicial opinions not very illuminating. "I'm not denigrating his credentials, but the lack of a paper trail was obviously one of the reasons he was picked." Virtually nothing was known of his views on abortion and other major issues. About all she could conclude, in fact, was that he was "conservative," looking for "black-and-white" answers in the law. Totenberg also intimated that she shared the concerns of those worried that Souter possessed a keen intellect but lacked the life experiences necessary to make "wise" Supreme Court decisions. At the same time, she predicted he would weather the confirmation process with little difficulty: "For this nomination to get really lively, something dramatic has to happen. There has to be some new revelation; he has to screw up in the hearings; something has to happen." Considering such possibilities unlikely, the real test for Souter, she concluded, lay on the Supreme Court: "I don't know of any justice who [has] gone to the Supreme Court and not been overwhelmed for years."[53]

"Dog in a . . . Meat Wagon"

Whatever the difficulties Totenberg and other journalists encountered, a complicated media portrait of Souter's style, record, and reputation on the New Hampshire bench began to emerge. One prominent Manchester lawyer compared Souter, in his relentless pursuit of attorneys during oral argument on the state high court, to "a dog in a goddamned meat wagon." For illustration, an article in a legal newspaper quoted extensively from the oral argument transcript for *Kiluk v. Potter*, a 1990 case in which a state district judge had exceeded his sentencing authority under the New Hampshire constitution in a case involving a defendant convicted on two misdemeanor assault charges.[54]

During oral argument, Mark Howard, an assistant attorney general, cited a state statute purportedly authorizing the sentence the district court had imposed. Justice Souter wanted to know the constitutional source of the legislature's power. When Howard instead noted the absence of any constitutional provision prohibiting such laws, Souter was incredulous: "Are you taking the position that the legislature as one branch, or the government in general, can do anything under the sun that the constitution does not prohibit?" "Well," Howard replied, "that's an obviously broad, sweeping term." "Right," Souter shot back. "And your answer is no." Howard: "That's right. It is no." Souter: "Because the basic scheme of the constitution is a limitation of powers. And one of the things that [this court's precedents] indicated was that there was no power to impose such . . . penalties, and there was no power in the legislature to authorize them to do it. . . . What you are asking us to do is to recognize a power in the district courts that [this court] specifically held they didn't have."[55]

Eventually, Howard, recognizing "the ice getting thinner and thinner under my feet," sought to move to another phase of the case. "You will always have to be careful when Justice Souter tries to be helpful," Justice Stephen Thayer interjected at that point. "I thought," said Souter, that "you were going to tell me that consistency is the hobgoblin of little minds and go to something else." Howard lost the case. A unanimous court, citing the state constitution, held that district courts could impose sentences of up to a year in county correctional facilities, but not the heavier state prison sentence state law authorized for defendants with two prior convictions.[56]

Lawyers appearing before Souter made it clear, though, that he was, as one put it, "not argumentative in a ranting way, but intellectually insistent." Ever the gentleman, he sent a note of apology to an attorney he had subjected to a particularly probing round of interrogation.[57]

Souter's reputation on the New Hampshire trial bench as a harsh sentencer tough on criminal defendants also received ample coverage. Particular attention was devoted to his remarks during the 1981 sentencing of one Daniel Berry, a chronic alcoholic convicted in superior court of negligent homicide in the deaths of three teenagers a drunken Berry struck with his car. Applying the criminal justice principles that sentences should be proportionate to the gravity of the offense, have a reformative effect on the accused, serve a deterrent function, and promote protection of public safety, Souter first declared that "flagrant cases should not be dealt with leniently" and that, "short of murder," Berry's offense was "as flagrant . . . as it could be." Given the defendant's prior record of DWI convictions, Souter doubted that any sentence would have a rehabilitative influence on the accused. But he was reasonably certain that anything less than a "heavy" sentence would have no reformative effect. He was equally skeptical that anything but a severe sentence would have any deterrent effect "on the next drunk who decides to risk as many deaths as there are people in the motor vehicles that he is reasonably likely to meet in the road." Finally, citing the defendant's three previous DWIs, repeated arrests for public drunkenness, and the three deaths Berry had caused, the justice characterized the defendant as "in the most dispassionate sense of the term a menace to the people who drive on the highways of this state. He is a dangerous man. He is dangerous in the same sense that he would be dangerous if he stood out on the highways shooting loaded guns. So that, I think, public protection has something to demand."[58]

Terming Berry's offense the most flagrant case of negligent vehicular homicide he had ever seen, Souter sentenced the defendant to consecutive maximum terms of three and a half to seven years for each of the three deaths—ten and a half to twenty-one years—but also conceded, "One of the things which I personally think is wrong with the sentencing scheme in this state is that we are forced to use inflated rhetoric." With time off for good behavior, Berry would be eligible for parole in about six years. Even so, eligibility for parole did not mean automatic release, and Souter had a proposition for Berry. If his conduct in prison was exemplary and he also continuously participated in a program of counseling and therapy for his alcoholism while incarcerated, the defendant would be allowed to petition for a reduction in sentence six months before becoming eligible for parole.[59]

At the same time, Souter refused to release Berry on bail pending any appeal of his conviction.

> I believe it is about as close to certain as tomorrow morning's sunrise that if this defendant is released pending appeal, he will be drunk and he will be behind the wheel of a car. . . . He knows what is hanging over him. He knows the severity of the sentence. And I don't think it takes a great deal of imagination to figure the way he is going to react to it. He's going to react to it by getting drunk. And when he gets drunk, he commits offenses again and again and again. . . . If he does not have a period of time of enforced drying out, . . . he's going to do it again. I don't have to shut my eyes, and I don't have to turn off my mind. I know what he's going to do. . . . And I'm going to deny bail on the alternative grounds that in my judgment it is a reasonable measure for the protection of public safety because, otherwise, I think it is highly probable that he will repeat his offenses . . . and he will again run the risk which has brought us here today.[60]

Souter's proclivity for long sentences did not mean, of course, that he had invariably favored the prosecution. One of the state's witnesses in Daniel Berry's case, for example, was a "cadologist," an expert witness who reconstructs accidents. Upon questioning the man's credentials, Souter discovered

that his "doctorate" was actually an honorary degree from a college of op-
tometry. The justice threw the charlatan out of court and later delighted in
mimicking the man's sputtering replies to his grilling. "It shocked the hell
out of me—I'd never had it happen before," the former prosecutor who tried
the case told a reporter. "This guy had testified before, was well-known. Some
judges would have let it go by, but not Souter."[61]

Not all members of the local bar, of course, thought that Souter had a pro-
prosecution bias. Mark Sisti, who had served as a public defender when the
nominee was on the superior court bench, conceded the nominee's reputation for harsh sentences, but insisted that Souter favored neither side in his
interpretation of constitutional guarantees to fundamentally fair criminal
proceedings. Bjorn Lange, a Concord public defender, agreed, emphasizing
that Souter held police and prosecutors to high standards, throwing out evidence when police exceeded their authority. As an example, both cited the Al
Jaroma case, in which the justice, it will be recalled, ruled inadmissible a "virtual warehouse" of stolen goods unlawfully seized by police from the defendant's residence. Gregory Swope, a state prosecutor when Souter was on the
trial bench, remembered his asking "a lot of probing questions about [police
and prosecutorial] conduct." Jim Duggan, the appellate defender and law professor, told a reporter that Souter was given to a "narrow reading of constitutional rights" but had also demonstrated an eagerness to protect the accused's
rights. "There are a lot of judges around," observed Duggan, "who never reverse criminal convictions. Souter is not closed to that. He's a true intellectual
who understands the system and knows you have to apply the rules."[62]

The New Hampshire legal community was also divided with respect to
Souter's broader constitutional philosophy and likely approach to specific issues on the nation's highest tribunal. While respectful of his intellectual credentials, a female Manchester lawyer expressed concern about how he might
deal with abortion. In a play on one of George Bush's campaign slogans,
Bruce Friedman, a professor at Concord's Franklin Pierce Law Center, conceded, "He's smart and diligent," but doubted Souter would "be a general in
the war for a kinder, gentler America." Friedman's colleague Jim Duggan cautioned, however, that the nominee's "streak of Yankee independence . . .
makes him somewhat unpredictable." Although Duggan would later acknowledge that he had never discussed the abortion issue with the nominee,
he speculated to a reporter that Souter was "against abortion, and I'm sure he
thinks Roe v. Wade was wrongly decided." But he perceptively added, "What
is impossible to measure is whether he's prepared to overturn a Supreme

Court precedent. I think his thinking would be that he would not, unless he felt it was egregiously wrong." Others also emphasized Souter's high regard for precedent, even those he opposed. The comments of some of Souter's associates, of course, raised more questions than they answered. John McCausland, Souter's friend who had become an Episcopal priest in Weare after years of law practice, predicted that the nominee would be "very conservative as a Justice, but . . . the kind of conservative who can fool the people who appointed him." He would be, McCausland added, "technically conservative, but not ideologically conservative, not like a Scalia. He might well . . . be a swing vote. He is not a crusader for any cause."[63]

Souter spent the weekend after his nomination in seclusion, not even attending Sunday services at Hopkinton, lest he and other parishioners be accosted by the press. On Monday, he made another visit to his mother's residence. As a beaming Helen Souter stood in the doorway, watching her son depart, a wire service photographer captured the moment. ("THAT'S MY BOY," at least one newspaper captioned the photograph.) The next day, the nominee was back in Washington for further meetings with senators and administration officials. As before, Senator Rudman took the lead, escorting his friend around Capitol Hill for visits with eight or ten senators a day.[64]

At the end of that second week in Washington, Congress began its August recess, and Souter and Rudman returned to New Hampshire to begin preparing for the confirmation hearings. During an intense two days at Tom Rath's Newfound Lake condominium, the trio, joined by Bush White House counsel Fred McClure and A. B. Culvahouse, former counsel to President Reagan, held brainstorming sessions and watched videotapes of four confirmation proceedings, especially the Bork and Anthony Kennedy hearings. For the balance of the summer, Souter continued to prepare, carefully studying several large notebooks the administration had compiled.[65]

The Souter Record

By that point, of course, news reports about Souter's decisions as a state's attorney and judge were providing grist for questions members of the Senate Judiciary Committee were certain to ask—and for which the nominee would be expected to provide satisfactory responses. The press and congressional staffers explored every element of his background that might provoke controversy: his intervention in the Clamshell Alliance's protests against the Seabrook nuclear facility, his opposition to New Hampshire's becoming, in his words, the nation's "abortion mill," his defense of voter literacy tests and reluctance to furnish federal officials data regarding the race, national origin, and sex of state and local employees, his defense of Governor Meldrim Thomson's Good Friday flag-lowering exercises, his concern for physicians with moral scruples against performing abortions, his notion that spouses in the process of securing a divorce were guilty of adultery if they started dating before the divorce decree became final, his flexible interpretation of New Hampshire's rape shield law and defense of highway sobriety checkpoints, his condemnation of "affirmative discrimination." Political liberals were particularly concerned about such elements in the nominee's record. Trying to be helpful, Governor Thomson told reporters that Souter had disapproved of his Good Friday order to fly the flag at half-mast on state office buildings to commemorate the death of Christ. Various colleagues claimed responsibility for certain of the controversial briefs with which he was associated in the state attorney general's office. The nominee's supporters contended, moreover, that Souter was hardly the sort of doctrinaire conservative President Bush might have chosen.[66]

But liberals were not the only ones troubled about Souter's positions—and the ambiguities in his record. Illustrative of the misgivings of conservative ideologues was an op-ed piece judicial scholar Gary McDowell wrote for the *Wall Street Journal*. As a Reagan administration official, McDowell had ghost-written Attorney General Edwin Meese's speeches attacking liberal Supreme Court records on a variety of fronts. He had been one of Robert Bork's most vigorous advocates. Now, he compared Souter to the main character in *Being There*, a book, later turned into a Peter Sellers movie, about, wrote McDowell, "a strange little man who, through no fault of his own, was suddenly thrust into the whirl of American politics. A simple fellow who had grown to maturity tending to his business was an instant hit in official Washington; it had not seen his like before. His every utterance was taken with the utmost seriousness; he was acclaimed profound. All the world hung on his every word." The problem was, McDowell continued, that he was truly "a simple man, with simple thoughts. . . . His depth was added by his audience; the little man had no depth at all. The joke was that his audience did not know that; indeed, they did not care. He spoke to their fears and their hopes and in so doing gave them what they both wanted and needed. Enter Judge David H. Souter."[67]

McDowell readily conceded that the nominee was "a very nice man: kind to friends and family; a quietly pious fellow; a hard worker; an old-fashioned frugal Yankee." But those virtues had not gotten him the nomination. "What got him to the courthouse door is the notion that he is brilliant; he is, we are assured, 'a scholar.'" Yet, "in a legal career that has spanned nearly three decades, Judge Souter has published nary a word [off the bench] on the law; delivered no memorable speeches; and . . . has not so much as engaged in spirited discussions with his closest friends and associates about the most intellectually interesting ideas of our time. By all accounts, the great public issues of our day do not interest Judge Souter very much. This should be troubling to conservatives and liberals alike."[68]

To be entitled to Senate confirmation, McDowell argued, Souter should be required to prove that "he is a scholar worthy of the Supreme Court. . . . The Constitution and the country deserve at least that much." That would not happen, he was certain, if the judiciary committee "allow[ed] the process to slide into the abortion mire, there to sink beneath the surface of reason." Instead, the committee should not ask a single question about abortion, but focus on "more permanent concerns": "How does Judge Souter understand the idea of separated powers; of federalism; of the role of the founders' intention[s] in constitutional construction? What is his view of *stare decisis*, the binding power of precedent? Does he believe precedents are sacrosanct or does he, with Thomas Hobbes, believe that precedent merely shows what was done, not what was done well?" The Senate should also probe the nominee's views regarding "the relationship of higher law to the Constitution." It should "ask the judge, for example, to share his views of Justice James Iredell's rejection of natural law in constitutional construction and Justice Samuel Chase's defense of it in the 1798 case *Calder v. Bull*. . . . The acrimony of the Bork debacle can be avoided if the Senate chooses to examine this man's scholarly credentials in a scholarly way. That, after all, is what advice and consent should be about."[69]

One suspects McDowell thought such a review would reveal a nominee more devoted to precedent, less concerned about modern precedents expanding the scope of judicial review, civil liberties, and national political authority over the states, and more flexible in his approach to constitutional construction than McDowell would prefer. Other conservatives had similar concerns as well as misgivings about Souter's lifestyle. One conservative leader warned John Sununu that a fifty-year-old bachelor might be a closet homosexual. Pat McGuigan of the Coalition for America, a lobbying group headed by Paul Weyrich, met with Sununu to express such misgivings. Afterward, McGuigan distributed a confidential memorandum, later leaked to the press. According to that document, McGuigan had told Sununu, "You guys could have hit a home run if you had picked Edith Jones, [the] Texas judge [also on Bush's short list]. Instead, you hit a blooper single which has barely cleared the mitt of the first baseman who is backpedaling furiously and almost caught the ball." "Pat, you are wrong," Bush's chief of staff reportedly responded. "This is a home run and the ball is just about to leave Earth orbit." Although "there were no words exchanged that would constitute any specific assurances on any specific issue," McGuigan assured his followers in the memorandum, "The general thrust of the discussion definitely made me feel better." Sununu and other White House staff members also assured McGuigan and other conservative leaders that there was absolutely no truth to gossip that the nominee was gay. Shortly after circulation of the memorandum, the Coalition announced its full support for the nomination. But conservatives remained nervous about Bush's choice.[70]

The Gay "Issue"

Judiciary committee chairman Joseph R. Biden, a Delaware Democrat, had scheduled the confirmation hearings to begin September 13. On August 2, Iraq's Saddam Hussein ordered his troops to invade neighboring Kuwait; on August 7, Operation Desert Shield forces left for Saudi Arabia to protect U.S. interests in the Persian Gulf. For a time, national interest in Iraq diverted media attention from Souter's nomination, but not enough to suit the very private nominee. He could tolerate press comparisons of his appearance to that of comedian Pat Paulsen, known mainly for his satirical presidential campaigns, and the media image of a recluse out of touch with the realities of modern life. But he resented press intrusions on his privacy, that of his friends and neighbors, and especially his mother, and he was especially irritated at continuing speculation about his sexual preferences.

Not long before the confirmation hearings were to begin, according to Warren Rudman, media friends informed them that a gay newspaper in New York was planning to expose the nominee as a homosexual. "In fact," Rudman later wrote, "the story never appeared, and if it had, it would have been either someone's fantasy or a deliberate lie." But the senator had been sufficiently concerned to alert Joe Biden and offer to produce the names of several women to rebut any article that might appear.[71]

Senator Biden laughingly declined the offer, but the incident further confirmed Souter's misgivings about the entire affair. Over supper at Rudman's apartment the night they first learned of the possible "outing," a distressed Souter declared, "Warren, if I had known how vicious this process is, I wouldn't have let you propose my nomination." The senator entirely understood Souter's feelings. "Clearly the attacks had pained him personally, but I think he was even more disturbed by their impact on his mother and close friends." The threat was simply the "last straw." Nevertheless, Rudman was determined that Souter would realize what he considered his friend's "destiny" to sit on the Supreme Court. Souter, he confidently—and prophetically—predicted, "was going to blow the Judiciary Committee away." They talked most of the night. Gradually, Souter's "inner strength took over—for David, for all his mildness, is one of the toughest people I know." By 3:00 A.M., he had agreed not to withdraw. "After that he never looked back."[72]

As the hearing date approached, Souter returned to Washington, studying Supreme Court cases and participating in mock hearings at the Executive Office Building next to the White House. Bush's counsel Boyden Gray, William Kristol of Vice President Dan Quayle's staff, and various Justice Department attorneys took turns questioning the nominee. Kenneth Duberstein, a Washington public relations specialist who had served as White House congressional liaison in the Reagan administration, had also worked with Souter since the beginning. Indeed, as Souter walked away from the podium after President Bush announced his nomination, he had been introduced to Duberstein.[73]

In early September, Souter's prospects for confirmation received a further boost when the American Bar Association's Committee on Federal Judiciary endorsed the nomination. Formed in 1946, the fifteen-member committee investigated the professional credentials of nominees to federal judgeships, assigning each a rating. As the ABA's image had grown more liberal over the years, Republican administrations had become increasingly critical of its place in the federal judicial selection process. Four ABA Judiciary Committee members had assigned Robert Bork an "unqualified" rating, and another voted "not opposed." Neither the Reagan nor the Bush White House had completely forgiven the committee for its role in Bork's defeat. The Bush administration had reinstated the practice of seeking the ABA's evaluation—an arrangement dropped during the Reagan years (and at the beginning of the second Bush's tenure)—only after the association agreed to delete any reference to ideology from its criteria for evaluating nominees.

As part of the ABA committee's review of Souter, two teams of law professors examined the nominee's judicial opinions, and another group of lawyers, headed by Reagan administration solicitor general Rex Lee, conducted a similar study. Based on such evidence, a unanimous committee, whose members included William J. Brennan III, son of the justice, gave the nominee its highest rating of "well-qualified," reserved for those who met "the highest standards of integrity, professional competence, and judicial temperament." Forgetting momentarily the administration's differences with the ABA, Attorney General Thornburgh cited its vote as proof that President Bush had "selected a man of superb intellect and qualifications." "This just about means," an ecstatic Justice Department official told reporters, "it's all over."[74]

The Association of the Bar of the City of New York, which had also split over Judge Bork, was more reserved in its assessment of Souter. Although confident that he possessed the requisite professional qualifications, the group was concerned that little was known of his position on constitutional issues. A resolution adopted by the association indicated that, after Souter's Senate testimony, it might "wish to revisit" certain areas of concern. Spokespersons for various liberal interest groups voiced similar concerns. Arthur Kropp, president of the action fund of People for the American Way, declared that Souter's "technical qualifications"—the basis for the ABA rating—"were never in question"; the outcome of the confirmation hearings would turn instead on his judicial philosophy. Nan Aron, director of the Alliance for Justice, an association of liberal public interest legal groups, expressed hope that the Senate judiciary committee would probe Souter closely on abortion, women's rights, and other issues.[75]

The "Justice from Nowhere"

Members of the press continued to express frustration about the nominee's lack of a paper trail revealing his positions, as well as their suspicions that the Bush White House actually knew Souter's stance on abortion and related questions he would confront as a justice. In August, Michael Kinsley of *The New Republic* declared that the president was "either a liar or a fool when he says he has no idea where David Souter stands on abortion, affirmative action, and the other hot constitutional issues." In an editorial published three days before the hearings were to begin, the *New York Times* was equally scornful: "Having pandered to right-wing calls for a less liberal-minded Court, Mr. Bush now professes to know little about the legal views of his own nominee. This may avoid some political problems, but it's a stance of deniability better suited to covert action than lifetime appointments to the highest court." Emphasizing the Senate's "equivalent authority" in the appointment process, the *Times* urged the judiciary committee "to draw the fullest possible picture of Mr. Souter's character, credentials and qualifications with instructive and deliberate confirmation hearings." Souter might prove to be a suitable replacement for Justice Brennan, "but the proof is in the hearings."[76]

As the White House had hoped, however, Souter's status as the "Justice from Nowhere" had made it difficult to mount an organized campaign of opposition to his confirmation. Kate Michelman, director of NARAL, argued that the burden should be on the nominee to establish that he deserved a seat on the Court, not that there was simply inadequate evidence to defeat him. But of groups in the anti-Bork coalition, only the National Organization for Women (NOW) declared its outright opposition before the hearings and scheduled a rally against the nomination. The ACLU had revised a fifty-year-old bylaw to oppose the Bork nomination; it decided to remain silent on Judge Souter.[77]

In a C-SPAN interview taped for broadcast on the eve of the hearings, four of Souter's close friends—Ronald Snow, Steve McAuliffe, Bill and Hansi Glahn—got an opportunity to praise the nominee, discuss his background, and answer what they considered media distortions of his personality and record. The session got off to a shaky start when the moderator asked the group about Souter's reputation as a "very witty and funny" person, then added, "But nobody can point to any particular or good description of that." Ronald Snow launched into an account of a mildly amusing practical joke the nominee had once pulled on an Orr and Reno secretary "who has since gone to her reward." Bill Glahn cited his friend's gift for mimicry, particularly his imitation of New Hampshire's eccentric former governor Meldrim Thomson. But Souter's wit is largely contextual and difficult to capture in a few words, and the moderator was skeptical. "Remember, he's got a national reputation now for being witty and humorous. I know it's difficult to recreate humor."[78]

Souter's friends were more engaging when they described the nominee's frugal side and "creaking museum" of a house, particularly Souter's suggestion, according to Glahn, "that after this is all over, one way or the other, . . . it might be appropriate to turn his home into a theme park." So, too, were their stories about the nominee's love of mountain climbing, affection for their children (and theirs for him), personal charm, and genuine empathy for others, as well as their obvious respect for his professional talents. McAuliffe related a story a clerk at a small market in Concord had recently shared with him. Souter was in the store when a man whose car had run out of gas came in seeking help. "[David] immediately turned to the man and [asked,] 'Do you have a gas can?' And the man said no. And he said, 'Well, I have one. Get in my car, and we'll go get it.' . . . He drove him three miles off to get a can of gas, drove him back. Didn't think anything of it. That's the kind of man he is."

Bill Glahn even managed to turn one media example of Souter's extremely private nature to advantage. Glahn had teased his friend about a legal newspaper's recent survey of more than five hundred members of Souter's Harvard law class. "The overwhelming sentiment was that nobody could remember him." Souter's response: "He tried to spend as little time at the law school as possible."

The interview was broad-ranging, covering various names ("Soutie," "Hackett," "David") the nominee and his acquaintances had favored at various stages of his life; his elegant but calligraphic handwriting; a law school photograph that had appeared in the press, picturing Souter smoking a cigar ("a *Lampoon* picture," Ronald Snow explained. "That was a joke. . . . I'm sure he doesn't smoke"); the nominee's girlfriends; and a host of other matters. But mainly his friends sought to answer questions the press and segments of the public found troubling about the nominee. When the moderator cited articles describing him as an eighteenth-century mind in the twentieth century, Bill Glahn conceded that they often teased Souter for embracing the assertion of the Duke of Cambridge "that any change of any thing for any reason is to be deplored." But Glahn also agreed that his friend could indeed be called an eighteenth-century man if by that one "meant a man who has the kind of intellectual breadth I think the true intellectuals in prior centuries had—or probably do in the twentieth century." Steve McAuliffe pointed out, moreover, that the nominee had been the first to hire female assistant attorneys general in New Hampshire, adding, "That's not 18th century thinking; that's 21st century thinking."

When asked about media reports that, despite his lengthy career, Souter had left no paper trail of off-the-bench writings, McAuliffe minced no words: "You know, that's one of the things that really has . . . irked me in this whole process. . . . The man has written 200 supreme court opinions. He's written countless letters and correspondence as attorney general. He's tried cases. . . . If you mean [by paper trail] some record of a scholarly intellect, some record of his capabilities, some record of his thought processes, there is more than enough. Most of the people looking at it probably wouldn't be able to comprehend what he's written."

McAuliffe also had some advice for members of the Senate Judiciary Committee. He had worked for committee chairman Joe Biden in the senator's unsuccessful 1988 bid for the Democratic presidential nomination. "I got to know him reasonably well," he told the C-SPAN audience. "And . . . one of the things I told him [recently], I said, 'You know, seriously, you should tell the senators that they should have their brightest aides sitting at their elbows, because this man is so smart and so charming that you're going to hear a lot of senators say, 'You know, I never thought of it quite that way, judge.'"

The Senate Hearings

On Wednesday, September 12, the day before the hearings were to begin, Warren Rudman gave Souter a look at Room 215 of the Hart Senate Office Building, the huge room in which the proceedings were to take place. The next day, the senator escorted the nominee back to the now crowded hearing room. At 10:05, Senator Biden began the session with opening remarks; each of the thirteen other committee members gave ten-minute presentations as well. New Hampshire's senators Rudman and Gordon Humphrey then introduced the nominee, applauding his record and, in Humphrey's case, even comparing Souter to another "scholarly" bachelor, "one of the Nation's most eminent and humane Justices, the great Benjamin Cardozo."[79]

A few days earlier, after a letter to the *New York Times* had also compared Souter favorably to Cardozo, a Baltimore lawyer wrote a caustic rejoinder: "When Cardozo . . . was appointed, . . . he was viewed by Democrat and Republican to have the finest legal mind in America. Cardozo had as a judge in New York written four brilliant books on legal and judicial philosophy and scores of opinions that were models for all America. Judge Souter's supporters should eschew hyperbole."[80]

Souter's performance before the judiciary committee, however, would quickly resolve the doubts of most skeptics. In an opening statement Souter had decided to prepare, he did an adroit job of humanizing the remote, impersonal figure, out of touch with the problems of modern life, that media coverage had typically portrayed. "Whatever court we are in, whatever we are doing, whether we are on a trial court or an appellate court," he assured committee members, "at the end of our task some human being is going to be affected. Some human life is going to be changed in some way by what we do."[81]

From the outset, the nominee also quickly displayed the sense of humor his friends had sought to demonstrate in the C-SPAN interview. Senator Biden began his interrogation of the nominee with the inevitable question whether Souter believed the Constitution included protection for unenumerated rights. "My colleague Warren Rudman," noted Biden, "has said—he has said many things." "You should have been staying with him for the last 10 days," Souter shot back.[82]

When the laughter subsided, Biden continued. The second Justice John Marshall Harlan, Rudman had said, was one of the Supreme Court justices Souter most admired. The committee chairman wanted to know if Souter agreed with Harlan's separate opinion in *Griswold v. Connecticut*, the landmark 1965 case in which Harlan, although widely regarded as a conservative jurist, asserted that the word "liberty" in the Fourteenth Amendment's due process clause included a privacy right of married couples to use birth control. Avoiding the trap that helped to doom Robert Bork's confirmation, Souter readily acknowledged that he did indeed "believe that the due process clause . . . does recognize and does protect an unenumerated right of privacy." At the same time, he refused to say whether he would adopt "every word" in Harlan's opinion. Nor, he said, did he think it "appropriate" to express a specific opinion on the exact result in *Griswold*, particularly as the reasoning of the justices there was "a predicate toward the one case which has been on everyone's mind and on everyone's lips since the moment of my nomination—*Roe v. Wade*, upon which the wisdom or the appropriate future of which it would be inappropriate for me to comment." Moreover, although conceding that marital privacy was among unenumerated constitutional guarantees, he refused to go further in cataloguing the scope of such rights.[83]

Even with those conditions, though, Souter made it clear that he, unlike Judge Bork, would not limit the Constitution's meaning to guarantees stated in its text. The Constitution's "concept of limited government," he asserted, was "not simply to be identified with the enumeration of those specific rights or specifically defined rights that were later embodied in the" Bill of Rights. "If there were any further evidence needed for this," he added, "we can start with the ninth amendment." The meaning of the Ninth Amendment—providing that "the enumeration in the Constitution, of certain rights, shall not be construed to deny or disparage others retained by the people"—had long "bedeviled scholars," he said, and he conceded that he had nothing new to add to current scholarship with respect to the amendment's meaning. But he thought the amendment was "an acknowledgment" that the enumeration of certain rights in the Constitution "was not intended to be in some sense exhaustive and in derogation of other rights retained." Indeed, observed Souter, one argument that he had with the "incorporation doctrine"—the thesis that the Fourteenth Amendment was intended to embody the specific guarantees of the Bill of Rights, a notion the second Justice Harlan consistently rejected—was the proposition that those explicit rights were "meant to exhaust the meaning of enforceable liberty" protected by the amendment's due process clause.[84]

Strom Thurmond, ranking minority member of the committee, was the first Republican to question the nominee. As he had with other Supreme Court nominees during his lengthy career, the 1948 Dixiecrat presidential candidate turned Republican senator hoped to elicit verification from Souter that the national government and its judiciary had usurped state authority. He was to be disappointed. The nominee conceded that he had once complained about "an erosion of power all in the direction of the National Government from the States." But that erosion, he now explained, "began with the fact that there were problems to be solved which the States simply would not address and the people wanted them addressed and therefore the people looked to Washington." The Tenth Amendment reserved to the states powers the Constitution did not delegate to the national government nor deny to the states. Souter insisted, however, "that any approach to the 10th amendment today is an approach which has got to take into consideration constitutional developments outside of the 10th amendment which we cannot ignore, and . . . would have astonished the Framers"—especially Congress's ever-expanding use of its enumerated authority over interstate commerce since the Depression of the 1930s and its power under the Fourteenth Amendment to enforce civil rights. From time to time throughout the hearings, Souter returned to the theme that the modern national government had merely reacted to the "vacuum" created by state inaction in areas of pressing public need.[85]

Thurmond was no more successful when he turned to the Supreme Court's criminal procedure rulings, particularly the senator's major Warren Court bugaboo, *Miranda v. Arizona*. Since 1971, the high Court had gradually restricted *Miranda*'s application. Thurmond wondered what Souter thought of such rulings. It would be a mistake, the nominee replied, for any court "to be unwilling ever to reexamine the wisdom of" its decisions. But he also insisted that the Court should never be swayed "by the politics of the moment," that it should remain "above the momentary furor." *Miranda* had been a "prag-matic" attempt to assure the voluntariness—and thus the admissibility at trial—of confessions; it had been "on the books" a long time. "We are [thus] faced with a practical obligation, if one wants it modified or expanded or contracted," Souter observed, "to ask very practical questions about how it actually works." Later, in response to a question from Iowa Republican Charles Grassley, Souter characterized *Miranda* as "a very pragmatic procedure that would cut down on the . . . degree of possibility that confessions would turn out to be involuntary" and excluded from court. In his judgment, the burden lay on *Miranda*'s opponents to demonstrate that it had not served that pragmatic objective.[86]

Throughout the hearings, Massachusetts Democrat Edward Kennedy would be Souter's most skeptical interrogator. Citing Souter's defense of New Hampshire's refusal in the 1970s to supply federal officials with the racial composition of its state and local government workforce, Kennedy claimed that no other public or private employer had taken a position "so hostile to civil rights." In response, Souter noted that he had been acting at that time as a lawyer with the state as his client and that New Hampshire had no history of employment discrimination that would have warranted federal acquisition of the data sought. The nominee assumed the same stance in defending New Hampshire's opposition to a national congressional ban on voter literacy tests, tests the Supreme Court had previously upheld as constitutional. Kennedy also scored statements attributed to Souter that granting illiterates access to the ballot would "dilute" the votes of literate citizens and that illit-erates would cast their votes "at random, utterly without comprehension." The nominee, said Kennedy, appeared "to interpret the [civil rights] powers of Congress so narrowly that we cannot achieve our purpose—even [in] fun-damental areas such as race discrimination and the right to vote."[87]

But Souter had an effective rejoinder:

> With respect, Senator, let me address a couple of points that you raise. Maybe the best place to start is with the fundamental one. That is about me today, as opposed to me as an advocate in a voting rights case 20 years ago.
>
> I hope one thing will be clear and this is maybe the time to make it clear, and that is that with respect to the societal problems of the United States today there is none which, in my judgment, is more tragic or more demand-ing of the efforts of every American in the Congress and out of the Congress than the removal of societal discrimination in matters of invidious discrimi-nation which we are unfortunately too familiar with. . . .

The second thing that I think must be said . . . is that I was not giving [a judicial] interpretation 20 years ago. I was acting as an advocate, as a lawyer, in asserting a position on behalf of a client.[88]

Senator Kennedy also inserted into the record the 1978 petition for certiorari to the Supreme Court that Souter, as New Hampshire attorney general, had signed in the *Meloon* gender discrimination case. In the petition, it will be recalled, Souter had criticized the middle-tier or heightened scrutiny the Supreme Court had recently begun applying in gender discrimination cases. That standard was intended to provide women and men greater protection against such discrimination, the senator observed, yet the nominee "urged the Court to reexamine and perhaps eliminate the new standard." "So," asked Kennedy, "do you think the Court should go back to uphold statutes that discriminate by sex if there is any plausible reason for the distinction?"[89]

Again emphasizing that he was acting as the state's advocate in his certiorari petition, Souter responded that his concern was with the "looseness of the [middle-tier] equal protection test." The "rational basis" formula applied to economic and most other types of discrimination could be rather easily applied; government need cite only some rational relationship between the discrimination in question and a legitimate government objective to withstand judicial scrutiny. The "strict scrutiny" standard invoked against racial and related forms of discrimination was also relatively easy to apply; virtually any regulation subjected to that test was doomed. Under the middle-tier formula, however, gender discrimination had to bear a "substantial relationship to an important governmental objective." Souter considered that standard of review "unfortunate" in that "it leaves an enormous amount of leeway to the discretion of the court that is doing the reviewing." Its vagueness made it possible for "a court, as a practical matter, to read it back down to the lenient [rational-basis] level of scrutiny, if it is inclined to do so." But his position, Souter emphasized, should in no way be construed to suggest that he opposed heightened scrutiny for gender classifications. "To compare sex discrimination with common economic determinations seems to me totally inappropriate. The question is, what is a workable and dependable middle-tier standard for scrutiny." In his brief, Kennedy responded, Souter had "talk[ed] about even eliminating that test." "I also talked," the nominee shot back, about "making the test more clear and eliminating this kind of protean quantity."[90]

During his initial questioning of Souter, Utah Republican Orrin Hatch sought to minimize any damage Senator Kennedy's questions might have done—questioning the extent of the nominee's actual involvement with the civil rights briefs with which he had been associated, stressing Souter's role as an advocate with a duty to defend any plausible legal position of state officials, and pointing out that New Hampshire had always obeyed federal law and court rulings when its officials lost such battles. But even without Hatch's help, Souter's friends and congressional supporters thought he had done an excellent job deflecting what Warren Rudman later described as Kennedy's "bumbling attempt to cross-examine the nominee." During a morning break in the proceedings, Souter and Tom Rath had retreated to the nearby office of Republican Alan Simpson, Wyoming's folksy, acerbic, and at times obnoxious junior senator, who was also a member of the judiciary committee. A boyhood fan of Saturday matinee westerns, Simpson compared Souter's encounter with Kennedy to celluloid hero Roy Rogers's final shootouts with the outlaws. "It always ended up," said Simpson, "with the bad guy biting the dust. And some old codger would say, 'You don't mess with Roy Rogers.' Judge, that's what I thought when you finished with Ted Kennedy: 'You don't mess with old Roy.'"[91]

That day, Souter continued to avoid responding to specific questions about *Roe v. Wade* yet also attempted to demonstrate his empathy for women facing an unanticipated and unwanted pregnancy. Asked by Senator Howard Metzenbaum (D-OH) to discuss his personal feelings about women in such situations, the nominee replied, "Senator, your question comes as a surprise to me. I was not expecting that kind of question, and you have made me think of something I have not thought of for 24 years." He went on to say that a freshman student "in pretty rough emotional shape" had come to him while he was a dormitory proctor at Harvard. The student's girlfriend was pregnant and "about to try to have a self-abortion." She was afraid to tell her parents or the student health service. Souter had spent two hours "listening to her and trying to counsel her to approach her problem in a way different from what she was doing."[92]

Metzenbaum said he "appreciate[d]" Souter's response but questioned where the nominee's sympathies actually lay, given his expression of concern in *Smith v. Cote* (1986) for the moral scruples of doctors opposed to performing abortions, his equating (as New Hampshire's attorney general) of abortion with "the killing of unborn children," and his opposition to repeal of the state's criminal abortion statutes even after *Roe*. Again declining to state a position on *Roe*, Souter cited his counseling session (although never indicating the advice he had given), as well as his service on the Concord Hospital board at the time it decided to permit abortions there, in assuring the committee of his open mind on the issue. "What you want to avoid," he added, "is a judge who will not listen, and I will ask you when these hearings are over to make a judgment on me as to whether I will listen or not. I think I have a record as a judge which indicates that I will [listen]."[93]

Metzenbaum was also interested in Coalition for America director Pat McGuigan's memorandum regarding his meeting with John Sununu. The senator wanted to know what this "advocate for the right" had found so reassuring about that session. "Judge Souter," asked Metzenbaum, "what does John Sununu know about you that we do not know?" Had Souter had conversations with Sununu "or others at the White House either before the nomination or since the nomination concerning any matter of issues, points of view," that would console the national conservative movement, or individual conservatives, such as the president's chief of staff? The nominee emphatically denied any such discussion with the president or any other official.[94]

Not surprisingly, other Democrats on the judiciary committee raised sensitive questions as well. On the second day of Souter's three days of testimony, Senator Paul Simon of Illinois asked about the commencement address years earlier when the nominee had referred to affirmative action programs as "affirmative discrimination." In his reply, Souter expressed the "hope that was not the exact quote because I don't believe it." Whatever his language, he was referring, he said, only to "discrimination in the sense that benefits were to be distributed according to some formula of racial distribution, having nothing to do with any remedial purpose but simply for the sake of reflecting a racial distribution." Because any affirmative action program would by definition have some sort of remedial objective, Souter's testimony hardly clarified his choice of words in his commencement speech. He did assert, however, that judicial power to remedy proven discrimination was not limited to stopping it. "The appropriate response, wherever possible, is to say undo it. That is a judicial obligation to make good on the 14th amendment." The extent of congressional power "to address a general societal discrimination as opposed to a specific remedy," he added, was still being developed, but he endorsed recent Supreme Court decisions giving Congress greater flexibility than state and local governments in remedying the effects of past discrimination through affirmative action programs.[95]

In his second round of questions, Senator Kennedy probed Souter's ultimate defense of Meldrim Thomson's Good Friday flag lowering as a ceremony honoring Jesus as a "historical" rather than religious figure, terming Souter's rationale "kind of demeaning [to] religion, Christianity." Kennedy also characterized as "hostile and really . . . heartless" Souter's justification for the denial of unemployment compensation to the Bosselaits, the elderly brothers unable to work full time and thus ineligible for benefits. "It seems to me to be remarkable," observed Kennedy, drawing laughter from the audience, "that these two brothers were working at all, quite frankly." Souter sought to defend what, to Kennedy, was "a technical and excessively legalistic ruling" in that state supreme court case largely by reference to applicable law. He also insisted that his opinion for a unanimous court reflected, "in fact, how admirable we believed these men to be." Had the Good Friday proclamation been his rather than the governor's, he asserted with reference to that suit, Kennedy's observation "would be a very fair objection to it. My own religion is a religion which I wish to exercise in private and with as . . . little expression in the political arena as is possible. . . . Whether or not my client, at the time, believed it was demeaning, I do not know. I am sure he did not intend it in a demeaning way."[96]

Committee liberals may well have found the nominee's responses to queries about affirmative action, the Good Friday dispute, and the fate of the Bosselait brothers at least mildly troubling, but they were no doubt heartened by his reply when Herbert Kohl of Wisconsin asked the witness how he thought Justice Brennan would be remembered. "Justice Brennan is going to be remembered," Souter unhesitatingly answered, "as one of the most fearlessly principled guardians of the American Constitution that it has ever had and ever will have." Under questioning from Senator Leahy, moreover, he refused to attack *Lemon v. Kurtzman* (1971) and other Supreme Court precedents demanding strict separation of church and state. Reminded of his willingness to defend school prayer as New Hampshire's attorney general, the nominee first clarified what he had actually said in that situation: "that if the law were called into question, in a lawsuit, that I would defend the law." But he then observed, "Quite frankly, I think if we had reached [that] point, which we never did, I think probably I would have had to state to the court, that following *Lemon*, that the law couldn't be enforced." Pressed by Leahy on the issue whether he might join Supreme Court justices who favored overruling *Lemon* and embracing a narrow construction of the religious establishment clause, he responded, "I do not have the view, if I were to go on the Court, that that doctrine should be changed. I am not approaching it with an inclination to upset the law in that respect." *Lemon's* long status as precedent, he meaningfully added, must also be taken into account. "Let's assume that we found that the establishment clause had a very narrow [originally] intended meaning, do we ignore, essentially, the development of the law for the last 40, or 200 years? The answer is, no; we don't deal with constitutional problems that way."[97]

At various points in his testimony, the nominee also helped to reassure liberals—while alarming conservatives—about his approach to constitutional construction. In *Estate of Dionne* (1986), it will be remembered, Souter had drawn on the intent of the framers in dissenting from a majority holding that a state constitutional provision forbade probate judges to assess special fees in addition to their salaries. Critics were concerned that Souter's approach to constitutional meaning would align him with opponents of *Roe* and other decisions considered to be at odds with the original intent of the Constitution's framers. Souter made clear, however, that the state provision at issue in *Dionne* was much more "specific" than such guarantees as equal protection and due process, about which debates over constitutional interpretation most often arose. Responding to a question from New Hampshire's Gordon Humphrey, moreover, Souter placed his philosophy under "the broad umbrella of interpretivism," yet emphasized "that the search that I am engaged [in] is a search for principle as opposed to specific intent. . . . What I am searching for is the meaning, which in most cases is a principle, intended to be established [by a constitutional provision] as opposed simply to the specific application that the particular provision was meant to have and that was in the minds of those who proposed and framed and adopted it in the first place." In short, Souter embraced the position that the meaning to be assigned a constitutional provision must be determined in its contemporary context. In defining, for example, the "liberty" protected from undue government interference by the due process clause, he "preferred the approach of the late Mr. Justice Harlan above all others, and . . . we are making a search on his approach into the principles that may be elucidated by the history and tradition of the United States, and ultimately . . . a search for the limits of governmental power, because it seems to me if there is one point that is clearly established by both State and National constitutional history, it is that the powers of the Government were not intended to be unlimited, that the grant of legislative power was intended to have limits, and those limits are reflected in the liberty concept."[98]

Referring to the *Griswold* case, in which the Supreme Court had recognized an unenumerated constitutional right of marital privacy, the conservative Senator Humphrey seemed relieved that Souter preferred Justice Harlan's use of due process as a basis for the privacy right recognized there rather than Justice William O. Douglas's majority opinion declaring the right to be within the penumbra of, or implied by, various specific Bill of Rights guarantees: "If you cannot ever find a better explanation than penumbras formed by emanations [from explicit rights], maybe you ought to conclude that you ought to leave it to the legislative body to deal with it. I mean that is real rot gut." The senator did not appear to realize that Justice Harlan's approach, and thus Souter's, to defining the scope of constitutional liberties was potentially more open-ended than the *Griswold* majority's rationale, which at least required unenumerated rights to be tied in some way to explicit constitutional guarantees. But others no doubt found the nominee's approach to interpretivism reassuring.[99]

Some of Souter's testimony, especially his description of his counseling session with the pregnant Harvard undergraduate, sounded scripted. In the main, however, the nominee was an extraordinarily well-prepared, articulate, and persuasive witness. The only major gaffe in his testimony, in fact, occurred when he was being questioned by Senator Simpson. Trying to be helpful to the nominee in the aftermath of Senator Kennedy's questions regarding his stance on literacy tests and other racial issues, Simpson asked, "David Souter, are you a racist?," adding, "A crazy question to ask, is it not?" "Well, far be it for me to say that a question from you, Senator, is crazy," Souter replied, to laughter from the committee and audience. But he also emphasized, of course, that he indeed was not a racist, that "never once, ever in my house," when he was growing up, had he ever heard his parents "refer to any human being in terms of racial or ethnic identity. . . . And if there is a kind of homely vision for America, in my mind, it is simply the vision of my home." Sitting in the row behind him, he added, were "two of my closest friends in this world"—Warren Rudman, who had talked to him "about what it was like to be discriminated against when he was a kid because he was Jewish," and Tom Rath, whose grandparents remembered when signs around Boston read, "No Irish need apply."[100]

But Souter went further. Denying that he was a racist, he said, "might have been impressive to some people if I had grown up in a place with racial problems. . . . The State of New Hampshire does not have racial problems." When Joseph L. Rauh Jr., general counsel to the Leadership Conference on Civil Rights, appeared before the judiciary committee on September 18, the day after Souter's testimony ended, Rauh brought with him for insertion into the record a huge collection of newspaper clippings and other materials detailing New Hampshire's racial difficulties and related matters: the 1979 harassment of black students at Daniel Webster College in Nashua, site of Souter's 1976 attack on "affirmative discrimination"; a 1987 state legislative proposal to make English the nation's official language; a state senator's racist joke about civil rights leader Jesse Jackson; the 1989 spray-painting of a swastika on a Jewish temple in Concord; a Manchester social club's discriminatory practices; a town's employment of a Ku Klux Klan member as a part-time police officer; Governor Thomson's 1986 praise for the white government of South Africa; and Governor Sununu's appointment, later withdrawn, to the state human rights commission of a man whose construction firm the commission had found guilty of discriminating against a black worker. Only New Hampshire and Montana, Rauh further noted, had yet to endorse a state holiday honoring Dr. Martin Luther King, the slain civil rights leader. "It is a fact," he exclaimed, "that [a] judge of the Supreme Court ought not be one who cannot see what is right under his nose: the terrible racial problems in New Hampshire."[101]

According to Rauh, the Leadership Conference's membership ranged from organizations "formally" opposing to those "deeply troubled" by Souter's nomination. But they were unanimous in urging that the nominee be called back before the committee for further inquiry. In their testimony and documents filed with the judiciary committee, leaders of other groups, as well as individuals, both liberal and conservative, also voiced their misgivings. Kate Michelman of NARAL urged the committee to withhold consent unless "absolutely certain" Souter would "respect and protect our fundamental right to privacy, including the right to choose." The president and general counsel of the Mexican-American Legal Defense Fund decried the nominee's "extreme and cold" positions on discrimination issues while in the New Hampshire attorney general's office. Condemning the "abortion holocaust" *Roe v. Wade* had created, Conservative Caucus chairman Howard Phillips contended that he was "absolutely certain" Souter had a "permissible view toward abortion" and declared that "it would be no more convincing for an Adolph Eichmann to say that his personal views on gas chambers had no bearing on legal decisions he might make as a member of a Nazi high court than it is now plausible for a David Souter to argue that his role as an accomplice to abortion [presumably on the Concord Hospital board] has no bearing on his suitability to be a Justice of the U.S. Supreme Court." Based largely on the assurances of Mark Sisti, members of the National Association of Criminal Defense Lawyers (NACDL) were "reasonably confident that [Souter] is capable of becoming sensitized to the critical role that constitutional rights play in everyday life in America" and chose not to oppose his confirmation. In its prepared statement, however, NACDL detailed his "crabbed" approach to criminal procedure rights, particularly in pretrial stages of a prosecution.[102]

Two witnesses disagreed over the degree to which the nominee had demonstrated sensitivity to racial issues during his years at Harvard, a period of growing civil rights fervor in the nation. Wesley S. Williams, an African American Washington attorney who attended law school with Souter, thought his classmate, "while not disposed to be in the fray," was moved by the civil rights struggle, "awakening to it . . . like most Americans at that time." After hearing Williams's testimony, however, Haywood Burns, a past president of the National Lawyers Guild who had spent two years with the nominee at Harvard College, testified, "I did not find him mean-spirited. I did not find him biased. But certainly I did not find that he had any understanding of human rights or any concerns expressed in this very turbulent time when we were in college together, living in the same dorm, sleeping under the same roof, eating in the same dining hall."[103]

But the committee chose not to call Souter back for further questioning regarding the complaints of critics, and the testimony of a lengthy list of supporters tended to neutralize opponents of confirmation. John Broderick of the New Hampshire Bar Association introduced that organization's unanimous endorsement of his appointment. Deborah Cooper, one of the first two women Souter had named assistant state attorneys general, attested to his support for genuine gender equality. Steve McAuliffe, widower of *Challenger* astronaut Christa McAuliffe, was perhaps most eloquent:

> Let me tell you what I think David Souter is not. He is not isolated. His friends are many and diverse. . . . He is not sanctimonious. . . . He is not pretentious. He is easily teased and teases easily.
>
> He is not an elitist, either intellectually or socially. David Souter, as you have seen, is a humble and insatiable student of life, learning from and curious about everyone. He is not humorless. He laughs easily and easiest at himself. Neither is David Souter perfect, except in recognizing the imperfections that we all share.[104]

McAuliffe had been present during portions of the hearing when questions were raised about Souter's "capacity for understanding and human feeling." Noting that he had "some experience with personal pain," he assured the committee "that David Souter feels and shares and understands the pain of others with great compassion and great dignity." The witness also took a shot at those "on opposing sides [who] seem to predict with ease, yet contrarily, this nominee's unknown and unknowable future vote on current social-legal issues. No one knows how David Souter will vote—no one. David Souter does not know. . . . David Souter, the judge, simply does not prejudge cases. . . . Those who believe that David Souter is somehow committed or is an ideologue or is known by the White House better than by the Senate, are mistaken."[105]

The hearings had been largely free of rancor or disruption. At one point, a dozen members of Act-Up, a homosexual rights group, were arrested by Capitol police when they interrupted the proceedings with shouts that a gay or lesbian should be appointed to the Supreme Court. When Molly Yard and other leaders of women's rights groups appeared as witnesses, they grimaced at Senator Thurmond's reference to them as "a lovely group of ladies." Senator Simpson rushed to his colleague's defense, characterizing their glances as "tiresome arrogance." "You don't say to men, gentlemen, you all look lovely," Yard responded. "Well," snorted Simpson, "we don't have to quack around in that stuff." Later, Yard complained to the press that the Wyoming senator had "lectured us like schoolchildren."[106]

Pro-choice leaders were also distressed that Susan McLane, Souter's New Hampshire friend but a staunch *Roe* supporter, sat in the front row of spectators during the nominee's testimony. McLane had visited the hearings en route to London. Some abortion rights leaders, she told a reporter, did not want her there, fearing she might send a false message that Souter was sympathetic to the abortion cause. But McLane declined their entreaties. "I'm a close friend of David's," she said, "and I'm also a strong abortion rights advocate. I greatly admire David and I hope I'm right that he's pro-choice, but I don't know that."[107]

The hearings ended on September 19. Some liberals suspected a "confirmation conversion" on Souter's part, questioning the sincerity of the relatively broad and flexible conception of civil liberties and the role of the Supreme Court he had embraced before the judiciary committee. Benjamin Hooks, the executive director of the NAACP, announced that his organization would urge the Senate to reject the nomination. Several women's rights and pro-choice groups joined NOW in opposing confirmation. Editorially, the *New York Times* complained that the judiciary "committee can't do its job properly without calling back the nominee for some better answers. For example, how does he justify his willingness to uphold certain rights like free speech [in his testimony], yet insist on saying virtually nothing about women's rights?" But conservatives seemed most distressed. "Everyone on the conservative side is very alarmed," Gary McDowell told one reporter. Souter's testimony, Terry Eastland, another Reagan administration Justice Department official, said, "confirm[ed] my worst fears." Judiciary committee member Arlen Specter's reaction to the nominee's judicial philosophy, willingness to give unenumerated rights constitutional recognition, and assumption that the courts had a duty to fill in "vacuums" left by political inaction, was probably no comfort to conservatives either. "I don't think you'll find a more liberal statement anywhere. It was out of [Justice] Brennan's left pocket."[108]

But whatever the public and press reaction to the quality, consistency, and implications for the future of Souter's testimony, the clear consensus was that the nominee, as his friends had predicted, "blew the judiciary committee away." Despite her paper's concerns, Linda Greenhouse of the *Times* pronounced his performance a "masterly exercise in self-definition from a nominee who began the process as a virtual unknown." Duke law professor Walter Dellinger, who had clerked for Justice Hugo Black and would serve as acting solicitor general in the Clinton administration, called Souter "the most intellectually impressive nominee I've ever seen," adding, "It shows you don't have to be an ideologue in order to have a brain." Judiciary committee chairman Joe Biden had come to that realization early in the proceedings, referring to Souter on the second day of his testimony as the "soon-to-be Supreme Court Justice." Symbolically, Souter's celebration during his testimony of his fifty-first birthday on September 17—the 203rd anniversary of the adjournment of the 1787 Constitutional Convention in Philadelphia—could have done no harm either. Nor did the nominee's willingness to permit the senators to do much of the talking. After Senator Simpson, as one television critic put it, "warbled on for most of his [allotted time] without asking a question," the senator applauded the nominee for being "a listener." Several of Simpson's verbose colleagues did also. "The judge listened," the reporter recorded, "and did not crack a smile."[109]

Not surprisingly, when the judiciary committee voted on September 27, only Senator Kennedy opposed confirmation. Senator Biden conceded that Souter was "not the sort of judge I would nominate if I were President," but thought he was "about the best we can expect in the divided Government situation we now face." On the abortion issue, added Biden, the nominee was "about the best we are going to do on this score from the Administration."[110]

Souter listened to the vote on a radio in Tom Rath's Concord law office.

"He called me within a minute of the time the committee voted," Warren Rudman told a reporter. "We just kind of rejoiced together. He felt very good about it." For his part, Souter thanked committee members for their "courtesy and consideration." He was, he said, "gratified by their action." He then left the state with his mother for a visit with relatives.[111]

By that point, six senators, all Democrats, had announced they would oppose confirmation. Alan Cranston of California, the Senate Democratic whip, was the first to announce his plans to vote against Souter on the chamber floor. As his reason, Cranston cited the nominee's selective refusal to discuss constitutional issues on the ground they might come before the Court, as well as his reluctance to extend the right of privacy beyond marital relations to unmarried persons. New Jersey Democrats Bill Bradley and Frank Lautenberg soon joined Cranston, as did Barbara Mikulski (D-MD).

But confirmation was never in doubt. Despite its continuing concerns, the *New York Times* declared the paper "For David Souter, With Hope," on the day the judiciary committee voted. Terming the nominee "his own best witness," the *Times* praised "his sharp, analytical testimony and his grace in enduring sloppy, often aimless questions" from judiciary committee members. For the paper, Souter's "refusal to appease conservative senators by bashing the Supreme Court was one of the strongest features of his testimony." The *Times* remained skeptical about his stance on abortion. Souter's "abrupt burst of spontaneity" in recalling his counseling, more than two decades earlier, of a pregnant student contemplating self-abortion had "arrived with a false ring." But the nominee had given "decent grounds for hope," according to the paper, "that he can be fair-minded on this explosive question." Beyond the abortion issue, his "record, for all its gaps, portrays a pragmatic moderate. He is so moderate as to disturb the Republican right wing. It's reassuring that his judicial hero is the enlightened conservative John Marshall Harlan and that he ungrudgingly salutes the greatness of Justice William Brennan." The *Times* would have preferred a fuller portrait. "But enough is now known about his character and intellectual capacity to permit supporting his nomination with hope."[112]

Senate liberals no doubt agreed with Joe Biden that Souter was the best they could expect from George Bush, and conservatives in both parties, whatever their doubts, really had no choice but to support the confirmation, although several, including even Gordon Humphrey of the nominee's own state, suggested that they were undecided at one point or another in the process. After a perfunctory four-hour debate on October 2, the Senate confirmed Souter by a vote of 90–9. (Not voting was California Republican Pete Wilson, home campaigning for governor.) The nominee spent much of that day doing chores at his Weare farmhouse, then went to Tom Rath's office to watch the conclusion of the Senate floor debate and vote on television. Still cautious about the outcome, he refused to allow friends to uncork a bottle of champagne until the final vote was cast. Later, in New Hampshire's executive council chamber, he said that he had "read in more than one place remarks by members of the Supreme Court that nothing prepares you to assume the responsibility of that office. I believe very strongly that I am going to feel that same way, because nothing has prepared me to stand here right now." Stephen Merrill, one of Souter's successors as New Hampshire attorney general, told other well-wishers that "David Souter is living proof that your mother was right. If you live a good life, study hard and keep your nose clean, you can truly get ahead." Steve McAuliffe predicted that, twenty years from now, his friend would be "credited for being the major source on the U.S. Supreme Court for continuity. He will be the man who ties the history of the Court and its traditions together."[113]

Two days after the Senate vote, Souter—looking comfortable in a mustard-green tweed jacket with elbow patches, brown trousers, and muted houndstooth tie—sat with Tom Rath in Rath's office, talking with two *Boston Globe* reporters. Asked where he placed himself on the "judicial spectrum," Souter declined to say "smack in the middle," preferring instead to consider himself "closer to the center than some but still on the right side." He and Rath also discussed the confirmation process. Souter conceded that Rath and Rudman had finally conditioned the reluctant nominee to agree "that you have to be willing to talk about yourself." Among judiciary committee members, Rath said, they had been especially concerned about Senator Kennedy, who had led the coalition that defeated Robert Bork. At a minimum, they feared the Massachusetts senator would delay the proceedings and organize interest group opposition to the nomination. That fear proved unfounded. "Kennedy told Rudman," according to Rath, "I'm going to do what I have to do but I'm not going to have [actor] Gregory Peck do commercials," as he had in the anti-Bork campaign. "That sent us a message," Rath said, "and Kennedy also did not speak about his opposition until the committee vote." Rath had also been concerned about irritating "the right," since Souter, in his judgment, was "far more moderate than they wanted" and deeply admired Justice Brennan. The nominee's praise of Brennan had angered conservatives. But Rath had been equally fearful that Souter might be asked whom he most admired on the current Court. His answer, said Rath, would have been Thurgood Marshall, the Court's most liberal justice, even though Marshall had ridiculed Souter's nomination. "David calls Marshall one of the giants of the century."[114]

The Supreme Court had started its 1990 term on Monday, October 1, with the Brennan seat vacant. The justices had contacted their future colleague to offer their congratulations but also to share with him their eagerness that he join them soon in order that tie votes on controversial cases could be avoided. The wait was not long. On October 8, Chief Justice Rehnquist administered the constitutional oath of office to Souter in a brief White House ceremony, the new justice's hand resting on a Bible held by Tom Rath's daughter Erin. Standing before an audience that included the justice he was succeeding, Souter promised to use his authority "as best I can, according to the light that God gives me and, in due course, I will try to pass it to another in as vigorous condition as I have received it this afternoon from Justice Brennan." In a development that probably pleased the frugal and private Souter, if no one else, a temporary government shutdown—part of a Capitol Hill budget impasse—meant that "Mr. Bush's first appointment to the High Court," as the press reported, "was not even given a reception." The next day, the chief justice, in a ceremony lasting barely five minutes, administered the judicial oath at the Court, and the new justice took his seat on the bench. Beginning at 10:15 A.M., the justices heard oral argument in four cases, issued orders in more than a hundred, and accepted six new appeals for argument. "I got to work on time this morning," Souter had told reporters earlier. "I'm starting off on the right foot."

Two days before, columnist James Jackson Kilpatrick had gleefully predicted that Souter's appointment would return conservative domination to the Court. The nominee "went out of his way during his confirmation hearings to lavish praise upon the departed Brennan," the journalist conceded. But Kirkpatrick assured his readers that "Brennan and Souter look at the Constitution from opposite poles," adding, "Tides ebb and tides flow. Over a period of 35 years, extending roughly from 1935 through 1970, liberals could look forward to a term of court in a sense of pleasant anticipation. Their justices set the agenda. Earl Warren and Bill Brennan wrote the key opinions. They effectively changed the Constitution. With Souter aboard, it's the conservatives' turn."[115]

Concluding his speech during Senate floor debate on the new justice's confirmation, however, Wisconsin Democrat Herbert Kohl voiced the sentiments of those who ultimately had taken the nominee at his word. "If Justice Souter turns out to be a rigid ideologue, and not the moderate that he appeared to be," Kohl declared, "then both the Senate and the American people will have been deceived."[116]

When David Souter was eleven, his family moved from Melrose, Massachusetts, where he was born in 1939, to this farmhouse on Cilley Hill Road in the village of East Weare, New Hampshire. On first seeing Weare and the ramshackle house, in which the justice still lives, some reporters concluded that the Supreme Court nominee was a recluse out of touch with modern national problems. During the Court's summer recesses, the justice, unlike most of his colleagues, returns home to the solitude of Weare and the New Hampshire mountains. (Author's 2002 photograph)

When the family left Massachusetts, Joseph Alexander Souter, the justice's father, became an officer with the New Hampshire Savings Bank in Concord. (Promotional photograph, New Hampshire Savings Bank)

At a 1978 Concord country club dinner in his honor, Souter pins a corsage on his mother, Helen Hackett Souter, before taking the oath of office as a New Hampshire superior court justice. (*Concord Monitor*)

David Hackett Souter
"Soutie"

Nicknamed "Soutie" at Concord High School, when Souter brought a genuine leather briefcase to school, classmates immediately dubbed him "Suitcase Soutie." (1957 Concord High School yearbook)

Considered something of a "bookworm" and hardly a social lion, the senior class salutatorian was nonetheless popular with classmates and included in the yearbook superlatives section as "Most Likely to Succeed," "Most Sophisticated," and "Most Literary." (1957 Concord High School yearbook)

MOST SOPHISTICATED

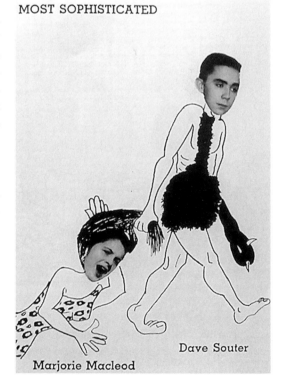

Dave Souter

Marjorie Macleod

Harriett Moulton Bartlett, a prominent medical social worker, was the daughter of an official with the Boston and Maine Railroad, for whom the justice's grandfather, Joseph M. Souter, worked for many years as a blacksmith and foreman. A distant relation whom David Souter affectionately called "Aunt Harriett," Bartlett was an important mentor and role model for the future justice. (Harriett Moulton Bartlett Papers, Simmons College)

As New Hampshire's attorney general (1976–78), Souter was obliged to defend the actions of New Hampshire's colorful, reactionary, and at times outrageous governor Meldrim Thomson, including the governor's decision to have flags at state buildings lowered to half-mast on Good Friday. (New Hampshire Historical Society)

In 1977, Souter joined a successful campaign against efforts by Governor Thomson and conservative newspaper publisher William Loeb to bring government-run casino gambling to New Hampshire. Pictured here with a stern-faced Souter during that legislative battle are the future justice's close friends Tom Rath (left), who would succeed Souter as state attorney general, and Warren Rudman, who preceded Souter as attorney general and, as a U.S. senator from New Hampshire, would become his friend's chief sponsor for a seat on the U.S. Supreme Court. (*Concord Monitor*)

At Warren Rudman's urging, Governor Thomson appointed Souter to a seat on the New Hampshire Supreme Court (which he held from 1983 to 1990). Here, the justice is pictured on the bench with colleague David Brock, who in 2000 would be acquitted in impeachment proceedings tried in the state senate. (AP-Wide World Photos)

Governor Thomson (right) shakes hands with John Sununu, a New Hampshire governor who became chief of staff to President George H. W. Bush. Pressed by Warren Rudman and others, Sununu brought Souter to President Bush's attention but later expressed disappointment at the justice's relatively liberal Supreme Court record. (New Hampshire Historical Society)

President Bush announces Souter's Supreme Court nomination to the press while the nominee, appearing hardly enthusiastic about the honor, looks on. (George Bush Presidential Library)

Senator Rudman and Souter walk to the hearing room for the first day of his confirmation hearing. The nominee's national obscurity and vigorous efforts to guard his personal privacy had led pundits, politicians, and at least one Supreme Court justice to question whether this "stealth candidate" was qualified for a seat on the nation's highest tribunal. But Souter's masterful performance before the Senate judiciary committee quickly dispelled most such doubts. (AP-Wide World Photos)

With Tom Rath's daughter, Erin, holding the Bible, Rath, Senator Rudman, and President Bush watch as Chief Justice Rehnquist administers the oath of office to the new justice in a White House ceremony. (George Bush Presidential Library)

A 1990 portrait of the Supreme Court taken shortly after Justice Souter took his seat. Seated, front row: Associate Justices Harry A. Blackmun and Byron White, Chief Justice William H. Rehnquist, Associate Justices Thurgood Marshall and John Paul Stevens. Standing, back row: Associate Justices Anthony Kennedy, Sandra Day O'Connor, Antonin Scalia, and David Souter. (Photographed by Joseph H. Bailey, Courtesy of the Supreme Court of the United States)

A portrait of the Supreme Court, taken in 1994, after Justices Ruth Bader Ginsburg and Stephen Breyer had replaced Justices Byron White and Harry A. Blackmun. Seated, front row: Associate Justices Antonin Scalia and John Paul Stevens, Chief Justice William H. Rehnquist, and Associate Justices Sandra Day O'Connor and Anthony Kennedy. Standing, back row: Associate Justices Ruth Bader Ginsburg, David Souter, Clarence Thomas, and Stephen Breyer. (Photograph by Richard Strauss, Smithsonian Institution, Courtesy of the Supreme Court of the United States)

4

Common Law Justice

THE SUPREME COURT David Souter joined in October 1990 had long been the target of a battle for its jurisprudential soul—a struggle waged, with varying degrees of intensity on and off the Court, since Chief Justice Earl Warren's 1969 retirement. In his 1968 presidential campaign, Richard Nixon had vowed to place "strict constructionists" on the Court—justices who would overturn or substantially restrict the expansive civil liberties precedents of the Warren era. Before the Watergate scandal forced him from office, Nixon appointed Minnesota native and conservative federal appeals court judge Warren Burger, a vigorous critic of Warren Court decisions expanding the rights of criminal defendants, to replace Warren and named as associate justices Burger's boyhood friend Harry Blackmun, distinguished Richmond lawyer and former president of the American Bar Association Lewis Powell, and William H. Rehnquist, head of the Nixon Justice Department's Office of Legal Counsel. During his brief tenure as Nixon's successor, Gerald Ford chose federal court of appeals judge John Paul Stevens to replace William O. Douglas in 1975, and in 1981, Ronald Reagan nominated Sandra Day O'Connor to join the Nixon-Ford appointees and Warren Court holdovers William Brennan, Byron White, and Thurgood Marshall on the high bench.

Thus, by 1981, six of the nine justices on the Burger Court were appointees of Republican presidents. Even so, the constitutional counterrevolution Warren Court critics and supporters had hoped for and feared never really materialized. In dissents, Justice Rehnquist registered objections to the incorporation doctrine under which the Court had applied First Amendment freedoms, the right to counsel, and most other Bill of Rights safeguards to the states via its interpretation of the Fourteenth Amendment's due process clause. Rehnquist also contended that the First Amendment establishment clause was intended to ban only government preference for particular religious groups, rather than all government accommodation of religion in public life. A Burger Court majority did curb the Fourth Amendment exclusionary rule and the *Miranda* doctrine, and in *National League of Cities v. Usery* (1976), a 5–4 Court, speaking through Justice Rehnquist, struck down a congressional exercise of the commerce power on federalism and state sovereignty grounds for the first time since 1936. But another 5–4 majority overturned *Usery* in 1985, declaring once again that the political process, not judicial review, was an adequate safeguard against alleged abuses of congressional regulatory authority, absent encroachment on a specific civil liberties guarantee. Warren Court civil liberties precedents remained largely undisturbed and in certain instances were even expanded. It was the Burger Court, after all, that produced *Roe v. Wade*, substantially expanding the privacy concept by including within its scope a broad abortion right. And while Chief Justice Burger preferred a narrow ruling with little value as precedent, Justice Blackmun, under pressure from most of their colleagues, ultimately drafted an extraordinarily expansive opinion for the *Roe* Court, with only Justice White, a 1962 Kennedy appointee, and Justice Rehnquist in dissent. Justice Powell, another Nixon appointee, cast the decisive vote in the 1978 *Bakke* case, permitting race-conscious affirmative action admission programs, though not racial quotas, in state universities. And Justice Stevens was to become the most liberal justice on the Rehnquist Court following the retirements of Justices Brennan and Marshall.

President Ronald Reagan not only appointed Justice O'Connor, but on Chief Justice Burger's retirement in 1986 had the opportunity to move William Rehnquist to the Court's center seat and replace Rehnquist as associate justice with conservative law professor and federal appeals judge Antonin Scalia. In 1987, Reagan selected Anthony Kennedy to replace Justice Powell after false starts with Robert Bork and Douglas Ginsburg. Following the appointment of Justice Souter to replace William Brennan in 1990, the first President Bush chose Clarence Thomas to fill the seat vacated by Thurgood Marshall's 1991 retirement. In 1993 and 1994, President Bill Clinton nominated Ruth Bader Ginsburg and Stephen Breyer to replace Justices White and Blackmun, respectively. Those would be Clinton's only appointments and the only justices chosen by a Democratic president on the Court at the beginning of the new century. Even so, at this writing, the Rehnquist Court, like the Burger Court, has hardly developed the consistently conservative record President Reagan and the elder Bush had anticipated. Only the chief justice and Justices Scalia and Thomas, of the Reagan-Bush I appointees, have favored a complete dismantling of *Roe v. Wade* and other controversial Warren- and Burger-era expansions of civil liberties, while Justices O'Connor and Kennedy have pursued a more moderately conservative course. David Souter would figure prominently in the partial failure of the Reagan-Bush Supreme Court agenda.

Adjusting to Washington

On December 27, 1990, the New Hampshire Bar Association and Governor Judd Gregg hosted a reception for the new justice at the executive council chamber in Concord. For more than two hours, an estimated fifteen hundred people, from government secretaries to partners in major firms, filed past, at one point making a line that stretched from the council's second-floor capitol chamber down the stairs and out into the state house plaza. Souter, who had breakfast earlier that day with Warren Rudman and former governor Thomson, seemed genuinely touched by the outpouring of affection. When John and Peggy Dellea approached, the grin on Souter's face widened. "I married these two," he told Rudman, adding that John Dellea had clerked for him on the New Hampshire Supreme Court. The usually reserved Souter even honored a state legislator's request for a photograph, smiling as Representative Kenneth W. Malcolm put his arm around the justice while a governor's aide snapped a picture. "Most of these people didn't have much contact with him, since he was a judge and all," Malcolm said. "But it shows how much they liked him. And he's talked to them for two hours. He's a regular Joe."[1]

For Souter, the Concord affair was no doubt a welcomed respite from what, by all accounts, had been the justice's rather difficult adjustment to life in Washington and work on the Court. Not surprisingly, given his frugal nature and Spartan Weare lifestyle, he decided to lease a small apartment in southwest Washington rather than purchase a home. When filling out the lease application, the question about salary ($118,690) stumped him; he had never bothered to ask how much Supreme Court justices make. The lodging he chose was apparently satisfactory. "He rents the very same apartment that he moved into the first day he was there, with basically the same furniture and the same configuration," Tom Rath reported years later. At one point, the wife of Souter's Oxford classmate Melvin Levine "offered to go to his apartment and clean it up and hang pictures." The justice declined her kind offer.[2]

His penchant for aged cars would also persist after his move to Washington. Once, as he drove into the Court's underground parking garage, someone noticed that the justice was leaning back in the driver's seat at an unusual angle. Later, it was learned that the seat was simply broken and Souter had neglected to have it repaired.

Named by the *Washington Post* soon after his arrival as one of the capital's ten most eligible bachelors, the justice quickly became the reluctant target of vigorous matchmaking efforts and a host of social invitations. Single friends eager to meet him contacted the wives of male colleagues. Unknown women telephoned the Court asking to speak with him. One insisted that the telephone operator pass on to the justice her recipe for meatloaf, a dish, she explained, that someone living alone could easily prepare. At a White House dinner for the Hungarian prime minister, Barbara Bush seated the dateless justice next to an unmarried Bush cousin. On Souter's other side at the table was the wife of Hungary's minister of international economic relations. Unable to find a common living language, they ultimately conversed in Latin.[3]

A future filled with such social engagements was obviously not an appealing prospect for David Souter, who much preferred, at most, small gatherings with close friends. Nor was it compatible with the grueling schedule he had set for himself on the New Hampshire Supreme Court and continued to observe in Washington: seven-day work weeks, twelve-hour days, an apple and cottage cheese in his chambers for lunch, supper at home most evenings. "He works all the time," Tom Rath would say in 2002. "He gets to work by nine or before, and he works almost twelve hours. And when he gets home, he will jog [near Ft. McNair] and work out for an hour, have a late dinner, and start all over the next day. He works literally seven days a week. And if he's going to take a break for dinner with me [or someone else], he goes back to the Court [afterward]."[4]

Relatively soon after his appointment, the justice began to curtail his social calendar dramatically. "He's not much for functions," Rath has reported. "He'll do the ones he thinks he needs to do, but he will not seek them out. He will turn down things like the Gridiron [Club dinners] or [similar] sorts of Washington events. Even things like the State of the Union. If he doesn't have to do it, he won't." From the beginning, he gave few interviews, then stopped granting them almost entirely. With rare exceptions, he turned down lecture invitations. Asked after more than a decade on the Court to participate in a lecture series honoring a distinguished constitutional scholar, he declined, explaining in a brief note that he enjoyed neither attending nor giving lectures and saw little value in them. Given his reserved lifestyle and personality, *Washingtonian* magazine quickly compared him in dress and manner to Gordon Gekko, the evil investment banker essayed in the motion picture *Wall Street*, while a snide article in *Spy* magazine concluded that Souter "brings out the schoolyard bully in us," adding, "[He] is said to be impossibly erudite, but his anodyne dweebishness is alarming, a type we haven't seen close up since we quit going to MENSA meetings."[5]

According to most reports, however, Souter's wit and manner quickly charmed Court staff and his new colleagues. He also took in stride his status and duties as the Court's newest member. Traditionally, the junior justice acts as doorkeeper during the Court's closed conferences, relaying messages to and from the justices and their clerks. Justice Kennedy gladly turned that chore over to his new colleague. "It's really true. That's my job," Souter told a reporter. "I opened the door just this morning." He lost no time, however, continuing another tradition of new justices: the opportunity to borrow five works of art from the National Gallery, to be hung in his chambers.[6]

Souter's wit extended to his occasional appearance before congressional committees in the Court's behalf. When questioning before a House subcommittee in 1999 turned, for example, to the Court's request for data-processing and related technological support, the justice promptly confessed that, "to the extent you want to get into technological detail, you are, unfortunately, addressing an ignoramus." Justice Thomas, who was testifying with Souter that day, confessed that his law clerks had eventually "shamed" him into using word processors. "I'm shameless," Souter promptly added.[7]

Not surprisingly, the justice's tenure has avoided any hint of scandal. At times, however, he has become caught up in disputes involving the New Hampshire courts, with the press and critics attempting to display him in an unflattering light. When a former Souter clerk on the state supreme court represented a client of the justice's friend Bill Glahn in a dispute over attorney fees, the *Concord Monitor* reported that Souter had declined his clerk's luncheon invitation, citing his close association with Glahn. But friends insisted that the justice simply wanted to stay out of local cases.[8]

In 2000, Souter would also figure in a highly publicized scandal on the New Hampshire Supreme Court that led to the resignation of Justice Stephen Thayer and impeachment proceedings against Chief Justice David Brock. Brock was ultimately acquitted in the state senate. But one article of impeachment alleged that, in the 1980s, the chief justice had attempted to pressure a trial judge to issue a decision favorable to Edward C. Dupont Jr., a prominent businessman and majority leader of the senate. When Justice Souter and other members of New Hampshire's high court overturned that judge's ruling against Dupont, he complained that the decision was politically motivated. The impeachment process against Brock also questioned the chief justice's practice of permitting Souter and other justices to review drafts of opinions and participate in conferences of the justices regarding cases from which they had recused themselves because of a possible conflict of interest.[9]

Two weeks before Brock's acquittal by the senate, the conservative Manchester *Union Leader* took an editorial potshot at Justice Souter. During Brock's impeachment trial, a specialist in judicial ethics testified that the chief justice violated the judicial code of conduct when he permitted colleagues to participate in cases from which they were recused, but was reluctant to speculate about whether Souter and other associate justices were also guilty of ethics violations. To Jack Kenney, author of the *Union Leader* editorial, the reason for the witness's reticence was obvious. "[He] would be on dangerous ground if he accused [the associate justices] of ethical violations. For they include . . . David Souter. . . . And it would be unwise to even suggest that David Souter, sanctified, beatified and all but canonized by the New Hampshire legal establishment, might have engaged repeatedly in an unethical judicial practice." The previous summer, Kenney noted, the state house judiciary committee considered a motion to subpoena Souter as a witness. "It was voted down overwhelmingly. Removing David Brock remains a possibility, albeit an unlikely one. But bring David Souter down from his pedestal? Never!"[10]

Souter's clerks would hardly share the *Union Leader*'s skepticism. Justices usually form close and enduring ties with their law clerks, the recent top graduates from mostly prestigious schools who assist the justices they serve with research, opinion drafting, and a host of other tasks. Justice Souter was no exception. For years, Supreme Court clerks were recruited directly from law school for the enormous responsibilities they assumed. By the time of Souter's appointment, however, they had typically held a clerkship on a lower federal court before taking a position in a justice's chambers. Each associate justice was entitled to hire four clerks each term, and clerks usually served a single term. As of the end of the 2001–2002 term of the Court, Souter had recruited forty-seven clerks, only one of whom (Peter Rubin, a Harvard law graduate) served two terms. Most came from Harvard (seventeen) and Yale (fifteen), but there were also recruits from Columbia (four), Chicago (four), Stanford (three), Michigan (three), New York University (one), and Boston College (one). Within a few years of his appointment, one and sometimes two of the clerks Souter hired each term were women. With two first-term exceptions, all had clerked on a lower court before clerking for Souter, although that number included Paul Salamanca, a Boston College law graduate whom Souter initially recruited to clerk for him on the Court of Appeals for the First Circuit. Michael Barr, who clerked for Souter during the 1993–94 term, had previously clerked for a federal district judge; the rest, through the 2001–2002 term, first clerked on a federal court of appeals.[11]

On occasion, Souter hired clerks based on the recommendations of personal associates. Harris Berman, one of Souter's friends in high school, wrote the justice a letter on behalf of his son's best friend, a Yale law graduate who, like Souter, had attended Harvard as an undergraduate and Oxford on a Rhodes scholarship. "I wrote David a letter saying that I had never met a young man who was as much like you were as this fellow. And he became his law clerk. . . . This kid was first in his class at Harvard, just a brilliant kid. He was in the same trajectory that David was. And when they met each other, I think David thought so, too."[12]

Typical of Supreme Court clerks, Souter's clerks left his service to become law professors at Harvard, Michigan, Georgetown, George Washington, Boston University, Boston College, New York University, and other schools, or associates with major law firms, including Covington and Burling and Wilmer, Cutler, and Pickering in Washington. They also left the Court with feelings of affection and respect bordering on adoration for their justice. Although declining, under the terms of their confidentiality agreement as clerks, to be interviewed for this study, more than a few of Souter's clerks expressed their high regard for what one called "the great man." When Souter's New Hampshire friend Bill Glahn encountered one of the justice's former clerks while working on a case, he was hardly surprised that she thought Souter "walked on water. . . . David inspires unbelievable loyalty in the people who work for him or around him. And part of it is the way he approaches things. You never feel like David Souter feels he's intellectually superior to you." Glahn also suspected that the justice's rapport with his clerks came from his tendency to pick staff on the basis of their personality as well as intellectual capacity. "I know that his relationship with his clerks is always a very informal one. And my guess is . . . that the people he picks are also the people that he tends to be able to get along with. He has to have four good people in his chambers. And he's going to pick the people he thinks are the brightest and most capable. But he's also going to pick people on the basis of who he thinks he's likely to enjoy working with. That's certainly what he wanted to do in the [New Hampshire] attorney general's office."[13]

Law and bar groups would also find Souter an affable, witty, and charming addition to the high bench. At the reunion of his law class shortly after his nomination, it will be recalled, few of his classmates remembered him. But he was a star at the first reunion after going on the Court. "He was delightful," classmate Robert Brinton has said. "All of a sudden, he went from being the person that nobody knew about to being someone who was very much being engaged by everybody and was very responsive." Jack Middleton, who tried cases before Souter in the New Hampshire courts, remembers the justice's attending a meeting of the American Bar Association after being named an honorary fellow of the American Bar Foundation. "They had a receiving line for the fellows. This is a formal dinner, and they had a receiving line. And Justice Souter arrived early for the event and dropped into the line to greet the guests as they arrived. And someone said, 'You know, Mr. Justice, you don't need to do that.' But he was very gracious and said, 'No, no, that's fine; I'd be glad to.'"[14]

Souter's reputation as a justice, of course, would ultimately depend on his work at the Court. On October 9, 1990, the day Chief Justice Rehnquist administered the judicial oath to his new colleague, Souter and the other justices heard oral argument in four cases, accepted six more for later argument, and issued orders (typically denying review) in a hundred cases. From that day to the end of the year, the Court heard oral argument in thirty-eight cases. Souter asked no questions during his first week on the bench. During argument of *McNary v. Haitian Refugee Center* in his second week as a justice, he asked his first questions, but they were essentially technical, offering little clue to his likely approach to constitutional issues.[15]

Most of the other questions Souter raised in oral argument during his first autumn on the bench were equally unrevealing. As a Supreme Court fellow for the National Association of Attorneys General, Laurie Loveland, North Dakota's solicitor general, had an opportunity to observe the new justice in all the arguments in which he participated through the end of 1990. In many ways, her observations mirrored those of lawyers who had appeared before Souter in the New Hampshire Supreme Court. Drawing on another researcher, she characterized Souter as a "fundamentalist," that is, a justice whose questions during oral argument focus largely on the "legal and factual nuts and bolts of the case," "often . . . hard questions, reaching to weak points of the argument, but . . . generally foreseeable." Loveland found, for example, that Souter did "not hesitate to challenge what he [saw] as weak points or inconsistent arguments." He also "like[d] an orderly progression in the argument and answers to his questions," even prompting attorneys to repeat parts of their argument in pursuing a systematic progression in his questions. Not surprisingly, she found his manner "polite and professional," while further noting his "sense of humor" and "relaxed" demeanor on the bench. "Since his first day on the bench," she added, the justice's questions had "not appeared to be premeditated or written out. . . . Souter seems a jurist comfortable with the rhythm of his domain."[16]

Questions the justice raised during oral argument of one case early in his tenure prompted much media and interest group speculation regarding his likely stance in abortion cases. At issue in *Rust v. Sullivan*, argued during his second week on the bench, were administrative regulations promulgated under Title X of the federal Public Health Service Act. The regulations, issued by the Reagan administration in 1988, forbade doctors at federally funded family planning clinics to provide abortion counseling or referral services to patients. About fifteen minutes into Bush administration solicitor general Kenneth Starr's defense of the regulations, Justice Souter asked what option a Title X physician had when a patient's pregnancy created an "imminent danger to [her] health." Under those circumstances, Souter asked, could the doctor tell the patient that an abortion was advised? To tell the patient that "your health is in danger is absolutely fine," Starr answered, but "to actually go forward, as I understand the hypothetical, and to counsel 'you need an abortion' is beyond the mandate." Seemingly incredulous, Souter emphasized that the doctor in his hypothetical was not advising an abortion for purposes of "family planning," but solely to protect the patient's health. Although describing the hypothetical as "extreme," Starr held his ground, even when Souter brought up a patient with high blood pressure that could lead to a stroke within an hour. "You are telling us the physician cannot perform his normal professional responsibility," the justice declared. "I think you are telling us that in some circumstances the secretary, in effect, may preclude professional speech."[17]

Ultimately, Souter would join a majority to uphold the regulations at issue in *Rust*. But abortion rights activists were elated by the tone of the questions the justice raised during oral argument. Judith Lichtman, president of the Women's Legal Defense and Education Fund, told a reporter she was "definitely more optimistic" about Souter's appointment. Duke law professor Walter Dellinger flatly stated that the justice would vote to strike down the restrictions at issue in *Rust*. Laurence Tribe, who had argued the case for those challenging the regulations, was more cautious, but saw the justice's questions as a "source of encouragement." Although obviously discouraged by

Souter's questions, anti-abortion leaders attempted to put them in perspective. James Bopp, counsel to the National Right to Life Committee, termed the questions an "appropriate line of inquiry," and Edward Grant, vice president of Americans United for Life, predicted that exceptions in the regulations for "emergencies" would satisfy the justice and that he would "rule in our favor." Some abortion rights advocates, on the other hand, were predicting as much as a 7–2 majority to invalidate the regulations. Legal journalist Tony Mauro underscored the uncertainties Souter's questions actually created: the justice might "turn out to be a closet moderate." But arguments in earlier cases, Mauro reminded his readers, had "brought forth liberal-sounding noises" from Justices O'Connor and Kennedy, who then had voted to restrict *Roe*'s reach.[18]

In his first opinion for the Court, handed down February 19, Justice Souter rejected Georgia's efforts to bar the Court's review of a federal constitutional jury claim. Interestingly, *Ford v. Georgia* bore some resemblance to another Georgia case that had attracted the interest of Souter's jurisprudential mentor, the second Justice Harlan, early in Harlan's tenure on the high bench. In March 1953, Aubrey Williams, an African American, was convicted of murder by a Georgia jury and sentenced to death in the state's electric chair. Two months later, the Supreme Court, in *Avery v. Georgia*, reversed the conviction of another black man tried in the same county where Williams was convicted, holding that the method of jury selection used there violated equal protection. The scheme—a tidy arrangement in which the names of white prospective jurors were placed on white cards and black jurors' names on yellow cards—was obviously discriminatory. But the Georgia Supreme Court had dismissed Williams's appeal, citing a state procedure requiring defendants to challenge juries at the time they were impaneled. Bowing to the doctrine of abstention, under which the Supreme Court typically refuses to decided federal constitutional issues in cases in which state defendants failed to follow state procedural rules in raising their claims, the Supreme Court declined to rule on Williams's jury challenge. Based on research conducted at Justice Harlan's request by one of his clerks, the Court also emphasized that the Georgia high court had discretion in deciding whether to apply the jury challenge rule in particular cases, expressing hope that the *Avery* ruling would be honored in Williams's case. Unmoved, the Georgia Supreme Court reaffirmed Williams's conviction and death sentence. The U.S. Supreme Court denied further review, and the defendant was executed.[19]

James Ford would fare better with Justice Souter and the Court. Charged with the kidnapping, rape, and murder of a white woman, Ford, an African American, filed a pretrial motion to restrict the Coweta County prosecutor's racial use of peremptory challenges during the jury selection process. In support of the motion, Ford's lawyer claimed that the prosecutor, "over a long period of time," had excluded blacks from juries in cases in which the defendant was black and the victim white. Opposing the motion, the prosecution cited *Swain v. Alabama* (1965). In *Swain*, the Supreme Court had recognized that the purposeful exclusion of members of a defendant's race from a trial jury would violate equal protection but required defendants to prove a pattern of such discrimination in prior cases as well as their own to mount a successful challenge to the jury system. The trial judge denied Ford's motion; in "numerous or several" cases, he declared, he had seen the prosecutor strike prospective white jurors while leaving black jurors in the jury box for trials of black defendants.

During jury selection, the prosecutor exercised nine of his ten peremptory challenges to strike black jurors, leaving one black on the jury. Following his conviction and death sentence, Ford moved for a new trial, claiming that the prosecutor's racially based use of peremptory challenges had denied him an impartial jury. The defendant's motion was denied, and the Georgia Supreme Court affirmed the conviction. While Ford's petition for a writ of certiorari was pending before the U.S. Supreme Court, however, the Court decided *Batson v. Kentucky* (1986), which dropped the *Swain* rule requiring proof of prior discrimination and held that prosecutors must provide racially neutral explanations for peremptory challenges to prospective jurors of a defendant's race. Based on *Batson*, which the Court later applied retroactively to all cases pending on direct appeal or not yet final when *Batson* was decided, the Court vacated Ford's conviction and remanded his case for further proceedings in the state courts.[20]

On remand, the Georgia Supreme Court, without briefs or arguments from the parties, held that Ford's equal protection challenge to his jury was procedurally barred. The defendant, the court reasoned, had raised a *Swain* claim before his trial; that claim was decided adversely to him on appeal and could not be further reviewed. The Georgia high court then suggested that Ford had not raised a *Batson* claim at trial; but if he did, he had not raised it in a timely manner. Under a state procedural rule announced in *State v. Sparks* (1987), the court asserted, a *Batson* claim must have been raised after the jury was selected and before the trial started; Ford, the court concluded, had not met that requirement. Thus, review of his claim was barred under *Sparks*.[21]

Following the Georgia court's ruling, the Supreme Court again granted certiorari to review the issue whether *Sparks* constituted an adequate and independent state procedural bar to review of Ford's *Batson* claim. Speaking for a
unanimous Court, Justice Souter rejected the contention of the state's counsel
and the holding of its high court. In conceding that Ford had properly raised
a *Swain* claim in his pretrial motion challenging racial use of peremptory
challenges, yet arguing that motion was insufficient to raise a *Batson* claim,
the state, Souter declared, "assumes a distinction between the holdings in
those two cases that does not exist." Both *Swain* and *Batson*, after all, had
"recognized that a purposeful exclusion of members of the defendant's race
from the jury selected to try him would work a denial of equal protection."
Swain had merely required proof of prior discrimination for a defendant to
prevail with such a claim, while *Batson* did not. "Because *Batson* did not
change the nature of the violation recognized in *Swain*, but merely the quan-
tum of proof necessary to substantiate a particular claim," observed the justice, "it follows that a defendant alleging a violation of equal protection of
the law under *Swain* necessarily states an equal protection violation subject to
proof under the *Batson* standard of circumstantial evidence as well."[22]

Nor would Souter accept the state supreme court's conclusion that any
Batson claim Ford had raised was untimely and thus barred from state court
appellate review under the *Sparks* decision. Georgia had conceded that Ford's
Swain claim was timely, and the Court had already held that an equal protection violation asserted under *Swain* in effect encompassed a *Batson* claim as
well. "It would [thus] be reasonable to conclude," Souter observed, "that the
state court's concession of timeliness under *Swain* must [also] govern its treatment of the *Batson* claim." Souter agreed that *Sparks*, as construed by the
Georgia Supreme Court, required a jury objection to be raised after jurors
were chosen. Citing earlier Supreme Court precedent, however, he emphasized that only a "firmly established and regularly followed state practice"
could be used by a state to prevent review of a federal constitutional claim,
such as that Ford had raised. The Georgia court's application of *Sparks* in
Ford's case, declared Souter, did "not even remotely satisfy [that] requirement." *Sparks* was decided more than two years after Ford had filed his jury
challenge and long after his trial. "To apply *Sparks* retroactively to bar consideration of a claim not raised between the jurors' selection and oath," wrote
the justice, "would . . . apply a rule unannounced at the time of petitioner's
trial and consequently inadequate to serve as an independent state ground
within the meaning of" the Court's requirement that state procedural bars to

review of federal constitutional claims be based only on "a firmly established practice." Contrary to Supreme Court precedent, he added, the Georgia court had also not consistently followed the *Sparks* ruling.[23]

For their baptism into the role of Court spokesman, freshman justices are typically assigned unanimous cases dealing with relatively settled issues. *Ford v. Georgia* was no exception. But Souter's maiden effort was entirely satisfactory and may have helped to soothe those concerned that the new justice might be unduly deferential to state courts in criminal procedure cases. At the time of Souter's appointment, Mark Sisti and other members of the New Hampshire criminal defense bar had sought to assure skeptics that the justice would vigorously enforce precedents expanding the rights of suspects and defendants. Souter's stance in *Ford* lent further credence to their confidence in the new justice.

"Walking through a Tidal Wave"

Less than three weeks before the decision in *Ford* was announced, the justice had again returned to his native state for a nostalgic, sentimental speech to the New Hampshire Bar Association. Addressing the question "Why me?" Souter was appropriately—and no doubt sincerely—humble, crediting luck, the friendship of many Granite State lawyers, and the conjunction of tradition and history. Nearly three decades earlier, Justice Potter Stewart had appeared before the association, noting that the New England seat on the Supreme Court had vanished but predicting that the tradition would be reinstated once John Kennedy, the incumbent president, remembered where he won his first presidential primary victory. "Justice Stewart," Souter observed, "was just a few years off." The justice recalled for his audience signing the first Justice Harlan's Bible, a tradition for every new justice since the turn of the century. "I got to the end of the long list [of justices' names]. I looked at it for a long time. Late at night, in the quietness of that great building, I signed my name." That experience, he said, "was the most humbling thing I have ever done in my life." Souter had been assigned chambers Justice William O. Douglas had once occupied. Recently, he said, he had read a *National Geographic* article Douglas had written about hiking in New Hampshire's White Mountains, a favorite Souter pastime. "I realized, as I was leaning against the desk, that I was reading the old article in the room where he had written it. . . . It was eerie and it is eerie still."[24]

The New Hampshire affair was obviously a touching event for the Supreme

Court's newest member. Long before that point, though, Souter had conceded the greater than usual difficulty he was experiencing adjusting to the Court. In an interview for *The Docket Sheet*, the Court's in-house publication, he acknowledged becoming overwhelmed soon after taking his seat on the bench. "I really see myself less as working than as trying to keep from being inundated by the flow of things to be done. . . . Somebody used the phrase that coming here is like walking through a tidal wave, and it is."[25]

Souter's approach to opinion writing was clearly part of the problem. Increasingly, Supreme Court justices have become editors rather than authors, reviewing and modifying their clerks' opinion drafts rather than composing their own initial efforts. On New Hampshire's high court, however, Justice Souter had largely written his own opinions, using clerks primarily for research. Press reports indicated that he was attempting to continue that pattern in his new position. Never a modernist in any respect, he also refused to use labor-saving word-processing equipment.[26]

The result was that by late May, as the hectic final weeks of the term approached, most Court watchers, as the *Boston Globe* put it, were "struck less by what Souter had done than by what he has not done—write." Apart from his *Ford* opinion in February, he had not produced a single majority, concurring, or dissenting opinion. By the same period in her first term, on the other hand, Justice O'Connor, who had also come to Washington from a state supreme court, had already written seven majority opinions, three dissents, and five concurrences. Observers were again referring to Souter as the "stealth justice" and now dubbed his chambers a "black hole." In an article blaming Souter's "anemic" opinion output for the Court's end-of-term gridlock, *Newsweek* quoted a former clerk: "There's just one reason and that's the total breakdown in one chamber." Although unable to confirm his assertion, ABC legal correspondent Tim O'Brien even reported that, earlier in the term, Chief Justice Rehnquist had stopped assigning opinions to Souter in an effort to relieve the Court's backlog.[27]

Souter's first dissenting opinion—challenging the Court's holding that a federal trial judge must give prior notice to the parties before increasing a defendant's sentence beyond that recommended in a guilty plea agreement— did not appear until June 13, near the end of the term. Souter finished his first term with the lowest opinion-writing rate of all the justices: eight opinions for the Court, two concurring opinions, and two dissents, compared with a Court average of 12.55 majority opinions, 4.88 concurrences, and 11.22 dissents. At the same time, he had the highest rate of agreement with the majority in all cases (91 percent), as well as nonunanimous decisions (84 percent). Overall, he was more likely to join conservative or pro-government majorities, especially in criminal cases. In *Schad v. Arizona* (1991), for example, a plurality, per Souter, held that juries need not unanimously agree on alternative theories of premeditated or felony murder in order to convict a defendant in a capital case. Not surprisingly, his lowest rates of voting agreement were with the Court's liberals: Justices Blackmun (61 percent), Marshall (55 percent), and Stevens (52 percent). But his highest rate of agreement was with the moderate conservatives, Justices O'Connor (91 percent) and Kennedy (85 percent), rather than the Court's most conservative justices, Rehnquist (81 percent) and Scalia (72 percent). For the first term, then, Souter appeared to be positioned roughly in the Court's center, more moderate than might have been expected on certain issues and a swing voter, along with O'Connor, White, and Kennedy, between Rehnquist and Scalia at one end of the Court and Marshall, Blackmun, and Stevens on the other end. By the same token, Souter, at least in his first term, was clearly no Justice Brennan. In a survey of the justice's record for the 1990–91 term, for example, Professor Robert Smith found fifty-three issues of disagreement between Souter's vote and the likely position of the justice he replaced.[28]

Brennan would no doubt have been pleased, though, with his successor's first opinion in a free press case. In *Cohen v. Cowles Media Company* (1991), Dan Cohen, a political party campaign worker, gave newspapers court records about another party's candidate after receiving a promise of confidentiality from reporters for the St. Paul *Pioneer Press* and the Minneapolis *Star Tribune*. When Cohen lost his job after the newspapers revealed his identity in their stories, he sued the publishers for breach of contract and misrepresentation. After a 5–4 Supreme Court majority, speaking through Justice White, held that judicial enforcement of the confidentiality agreement did not violate the First Amendment and that Cohen's identity should have been held confidential by the newspapers, the Minnesota Supreme Court ordered the publishers to pay Cohen $200,000 in damages. Originally, Souter voted with the majority. Ultimately, however, he filed a dissent. Applying the sort of balancing approach his jurisprudential mentor Justice Harlan embraced in First Amendment cases, Souter, joined by Marshall, Blackmun, and O'Connor, concluded that the public interest in the publication of Cohen's name outweighed the interest in penalizing the newspapers' violation of the agreement. "The propriety of his leak to respondents," reasoned the justice, "could be taken to reflect on his character, which in turn could be taken to reflect on the character of the candidate who had retained him as an adviser. An election could turn on just such a factor; if it should, I am ready to assume that it would be to the greater public good at least over the long run."[29]

During his first term, however, a liberal Souter vote was most likely in discrimination and civil rights cases, with the justice helping to form a majority to uphold the rights at issue. Two cases extended the *Batson* ban on race-based peremptory challenges. *Powers v. Ohio* permitted the accused to raise a *Batson* claim even if of a different race than the excluded jurors, and another case applied *Batson* to the selection of jurors in private civil cases as well as criminal prosecutions. He also joined expansive interpretations of the federal Voting Rights Act, upholding its application to statewide elections of state supreme court judges, as well as the election of trial judges in single-member districts. And in *UAW v. Johnson Controls*, he joined Justice Blackmun's opinion for a 5–4 majority that affirmed a challenge under Title VII of the 1964 Civil Rights Act to a company's fetal protection policy excluding women capable of childbearing from certain jobs against the contention that the employer's rule constituted a bona fide occupational qualification.[30]

An Independent Streak

On two occasions in which Souter helped to form a conservative majority, moreover, he filed a concurrence suggesting the independent streak that was to characterize his later tenure on the Court. In *Payne v. Tennessee* (1991), he joined a 6–3 majority in holding that victim impact statements could be admitted in evidence as part of the penalty phase of a capital case. *Payne* reversed two recent precedents, *Booth v. Maryland* (1987) and *South Carolina v. Gathers* (1989). Speaking for a 5–4 majority in *Booth*, Justice Powell had concluded that the presentation of victim impact evidence shifted the focus of sentencing hearings away from the accused's blameworthiness and toward such irrelevant factors as the relative worth of the victim's character and the impact of the crime on the victim's family, factors about which the defendant may have had no prior knowledge or capacity to anticipate. Chief Justice Rehnquist declared for the *Payne* majority, however, that a jury or judge could properly consider the harm a defendant's crime had caused in deciding whether to impose the death sentence and victim impact statements were an appropriate source of such evidence.[31]

In a concurrence that Justice Kennedy joined, Souter disputed the premise of *Booth* and *Gathers* that only a "defendant's anticipation of specific consequences to the victims of his intended act [was] relevant to sentencing." That sort of "detailed foreknowledge," declared the justice, did "not exhaust the category of morally relevant fact" that could legitimately be brought to bear on the sentencing decision.

> Every defendant knows, if endowed with the mental competence for criminal responsibility, that the life he will take by his homicidal behavior is that of a unique person, like himself, and that the person to be killed probably has close associates, "survivors," who will suffer harms and deprivations from the victim's death. Just as defendants know that they are not faceless human ciphers, they know that their victims are not valueless fungibles; and just as defendants appreciate the web of relationships and dependencies in which they live, they know that their victims are not human islands, but individuals with parents or children, spouses or friends or dependents. Thus, when a defendant chooses to kill, or to raise the risk of a victim's death, this choice necessarily relates to the whole human being and threatens an association of others, who may be distinctly hurt. The fact that the defendant may not know the details of a victim's life and characteristics, or the exact identities and needs of those who may survive, should not in any way obscure the further facts that death is always to a "unique" individual, and harm to some group of survivors is a consequence of a successful homicidal act so foreseeable as to be virtually inevitable. . . . It is morally both defensible and appropriate to consider such evidence when penalizing a murderer, like other criminals, in light of common knowledge and the moral responsibility such knowledge entails.[32]

In Souter's judgment, failure to take such factors into account would smack more of an undue "act of lenity" toward the defendant than their consideration would invite arbitrary sentencing. "Indeed, given a defendant's option to introduce relevant evidence in mitigation, . . . sentencing without such evidence of victim impact [seemed to Souter to be] . . . a significantly imbalanced process."[33]

Souter had also decided that *Booth* created such an "unworkable" and "arbitrary" standard of factors constitutionally relevant to the sentencing process "as virtually to guarantee a result far diminished from [*Booth's*] promise of appropriately individualized sentencing for capital defendants." The justice based that conclusion on the interaction of three facts: that *Booth's* restriction of relevant sentencing facts to what the defendant knew and considered in deciding to kill applied to any evidence, "however derived or presented"; that details about a victim and survivors of which the accused was unaware would usually be disclosed during the guilt phase of the trial anyway; and that the jury that determined guilt usually would also determine, or make recommendations about, imposition of the death sentence. *"Booth* thus raise[d] a dilemma with very practical consequences." Were specific facts unknown to an accused excluded from the guilt phase of a trial, jurors would be deprived "of those details of context that allow them to understand what is being described." Were the rules of evidence left in place, on the other hand, a separate sentencing jury, unexposed to facts regarding victims and survivors about which defendants were unaware, would be necessary. That would be a "major imposition on the States" that the justice assumed no one would "seriously consider." Even if *Booth* were extended to "exclude completely" all facts about victims and survivors unknown to the accused, however, arbitrary sentencing could still result. Drawing on a hypothetical of a minister robbed and killed in the presence of his wife and daughter, the justice noted, for example, that the child could have screamed, "Daddy, look out," immediately before the murder. The defendant would thus have been aware of the daughter's existence, and that fact would have been relevant to the sentencing process. "Resting a decision about the admission of impact evidence on such a fortuity," declared Souter, "is arbitrary."[34]

Given Souter's apparently strong commitment to the principle of stare decisis, one might think it surprising that he would join the *Payne* majority in overturning two precedents, especially rulings of such recent vintage. In his concurrence, however, Souter clearly attached greater weight to precedent than Rehnquist embraced in the Court's opinion; Justice Scalia, in another concurrence, even appeared scornful of the doctrine, dismissing it as resting on little "more than administrative convenience." Souter emphasized the "fundamental importance" of stare decisis to the rule of law, declaring that even in constitutional cases, in which precedent had traditionally been applied less rigidly than in nonconstitutional contexts, "the doctrine carries such persuasive force that we have always required a departure from precedent to be supported by some 'special justification.'" The arbitrary sentencing results *Booth* arguably invited, as well as the Court's own stare decisis precedents, provided such justification, in Souter's judgment. "In prior cases, when this Court has confronted a wrongly decided, unworkable precedent calling for further action by the Court, we have chosen not to compound the original error, but to overrule the precedent. . . . Following this course here has itself the support not only of precedent but of practical sense as well."[35]

The justice assumed a stance even more distinctive from the majority's in the concurring opinion he filed for *Barnes v. Glen Theatre* (1991), which upheld a state ban on nude dancing. Speaking for a plurality, Chief Justice Rehnquist concluded that the public decency law at issue in the case had only an incidental impact on any expressive message nude dancers conveyed and that it also furthered important governmental interests unrelated to the expression of ideas—specifically, the state's interest in promoting public morality. The law thus satisfied the requirements of *United States v. O'Brien* (1968), a Warren Court decision regarding government regulations of symbolic speech unrelated to the suppression of expression. Justice Souter concurred in the judgment but declined to rest his vote "on the possible sufficiency of society's moral views to justify" the nude dancing ban. Instead, he preferred to rely on what he considered the state's "substantial interest" in preventing secondary crimes encouraged by nude dancing establishments, including increased prostitution and sexual assault.[36]

The four dissenters, per Justice White, argued that a ban on nude dancing based on fears that it might provoke sex crimes was inherently related to the suppression of expression. Souter disagreed: "To say that pernicious secondary effects are associated with nude dancing establishments is not necessarily to say that such effects result from the persuasive effect of the expression inherent in nude dancing. It is to say, rather, only that the effects are correlated with the existence of establishments offering such dancing, without deciding what the precise causes of the correlation actually are. It is possible, for example, that the higher incidence of prostitution and sexual assault in the vicinity of adult entertainment locations results from the concentration of crowds of men predisposed to such activities, or from the simple viewing of nude bodies regardless of whether those bodies are engaged in expression or not." In a note to Justice White, Justice Stevens, another dissenter, took a swipe at Souter's reasoning: "If I understand him correctly, he seems to be saying that with respect to speech of this kind the Government can directly regulate its content in order to make it less persuasive, and thus reduce its secondary effects. Under his reasoning, I suppose the State could regulate the kinds of gyrations that the dancers can employ and, perhaps, even require them to appear fully clothed." Souter's emphasis on the secondary effects of nude dancing establishments, however, probably simply reflected his uncertainty at that point about what position such expression should occupy in First Amendment law. In a 2000 case, discussed in a later chapter, he required evidence of such effects and declined any longer merely to assume that nude dancing establishments inevitably fostered crime.[37]

Justice Souter's first-term record clearly separated him from the Court's most conservative members. In *Barnes*, for example, he was unwilling to embrace the Rehnquist plurality's narrow conception of constitutionally protected expression. His stance in *Payne*, moreover, appeared to reflect less a reluctance to interfere with state death penalty policies than a desire to assure that judges and juries take into account all aggravating and mitigating factors in their death penalty decisions.

Nor was he as anxious as some of his more conservative counterparts to embrace the "harmless error" doctrine. Under that rule, developed most extensively in *Chapman v. California* (1967), the Supreme Court had long held that a constitutional error in a criminal prosecution could be held harmless— and thus the conviction affirmed—if it appeared "beyond a reasonable doubt that the error complained of did not contribute to the verdict" in the case. The *Chapman* Court also indicated, however, "that there are some constitutional rights so basic to a fair trial that their infraction can never be treated as harmless error," including in a footnote the use of coerced confessions among the latter constitutional violations. In *Arizona v. Fulminante* (1991), Souter joined a 5–4 opinion of the chief justice partially overruling *Chapman* and extending the harmless error doctrine to the admission of involuntary confessions. Even so, there were limits to his willingness to embrace such claims. In *Yates v. Evatt* (1991), another first-term case, he spoke for the Court in reversing a state supreme court's unduly expansive construction of the doctrine.[38]

Confirmation Conversion?

Among liberals, the justice's first-term performance aroused concerns that the moderately liberal philosophy Souter purportedly embraced during his testimony before the Senate judiciary committee might simply have been a pose, a "confirmation conversion." Souter's vote to uphold the abortion counseling ban at issue in *Rust v. Sullivan* was particularly frustrating, especially given his strong intimation during oral argument that the regulation unduly interfered with the professional speech of physicians in federally funded facilities. Speaking for the 5–4 *Rust* majority, Chief Justice Rehnquist based the Court's conclusion that the ban on abortion counseling violated neither First Amendment freedoms nor the abortion right largely on decisions holding that those guarantees did not include a right to government funding of their exercise. The chief justice emphasized, moreover, that physicians affected by the regulation were in no way forced to give up abortion-related speech entirely; they were merely required to keep such activities separate and distinct from federally funded projects.[39]

During the Court's deliberations in *Rust*, Souter had shared with Rehnquist his concern that the majority make clear that voluntary acceptance of government funds was "not an answer to every First Amendment objection" raised in such cases. He had also suggested language for Rehnquist's opinion indicating that, under certain circumstances, the doctor-patient relationship would include free speech safeguards, "even when subsidized by the Government." To secure Souter's concurrence, the chief justice, as noted earlier, incorporated some of his colleague's suggestions into the Court's opinion, albeit in considerably diluted form.[40]

Given, again, Souter's high regard for precedent, the justice's ultimate decision to join the *Rust* majority was not unexpected. But his vote obviously disappointed those concerned about the future of abortion rights. When he drove into the Supreme Court's parking garage the morning after the decision was announced, he was booed by a group of abortion rights advocates. Judith Lichtman of the Women's Defense Fund proclaimed that the justice had now shown "his true colors," and Souter's law school classmate Laurence Tribe, who had argued the case for family planning clinics, found "far less basis now than there was at the time of his confirmation hearings to think that he is likely to play an important centrist role" on the high bench. Suspicions that Souter's background and lifestyle gave him little acquaintance with, or empathy for, the "realities" of life emerged again as well. While praising the justice's "extraordinarily impressive . . . command of legal doctrine and his fairminded analysis" of issues during the confirmation proceedings, Yale law professor Paul Gerwitz questioned, for example, whether Souter "was someone who distinctively knew life and distinctively molded his views around a hardheaded feel for the way the world really operates."[41]

Nor did critics focus only on the justice's vote in *Rust*. When Justice Marshall's retirement—and the opportunity for President Bush to make another appointment—was announced on the last day of the term, California Democrat Alan Cranston, one of the few senators to vote against Souter's confirmation, predicted a tough confirmation battle over Marshall's replacement if the president "picks another 'stealth' candidate like David Souter, whose views remained a mystery throughout his hearing." Added Cranston, "Given the votes that David Souter has cast in his first term, we now ought to know better."[42]

Shifting to the Left

But a single term does not a Supreme Court record make. Souter's votes and opinions in the 1991–92 term would begin the trend in which he was to become, in most issue areas, one of the most liberal justices of the Rehnquist Court. The justice continued to assume a generally conservative stance in criminal procedure cases. In fact, when the Court, in early May 1992, handed down its decision in *Keeney v. Tamayo-Reyes*, further restricting inmate access to federal habeas corpus proceedings, the *New York Times* editorialized that the votes of Souter and Clarence Thomas, the latest Bush appointee, with the *Tamayo-Reyes* majority had made "moderates" of dissenting justices O'Connor and Kennedy, two Reagan appointees. Souter also went along when the Court, over the dissents of Justices Stevens, Blackmun, and O'Connor, upheld federal district court jurisdiction over a Mexican national kidnapped and forcibly returned to the United States for trial in connection with the kidnap-murder of a federal Drug Enforcement Administration agent and his pilot, reversing lower court holdings that the abduction violated the U.S. extradition treaty with Mexico. When the Court lifted the latest in a series of stays of execution granted a convicted murderer and demanded that federal courts permit no further delays "except upon order of this Court," Souter also joined that majority over the opposition of Blackmun and Stevens. Joined by Justices Scalia and Thomas, moreover, Souter dissented in a 1992 case when the Court, in his judgment, gave an unduly narrow interpretation to *Teague v. Lane*, the 1989 decision restricting the retroactive application of "new" procedural rights to cases in which defendants had exhausted their direct appeals before the new rule was announced.[43]

Souter's vote in criminal cases, however, was not entirely predictable. In *Doggett v. United States* (1992), he spoke for a 5–4 majority in a rare decision overturning a conviction on speedy trial grounds. Doggett was indicted on federal drug charges in 1980, but left the country before DEA agents could arrest him. The government knew Doggett was later jailed in Panama but failed to follow up on its request that he be expelled to the United States. On learning that Doggett had left Panama for Colombia, moreover, the DEA made no further attempt to locate him and thus was unaware when he reentered the country in 1982, married, earned a college degree, found steady employment, lived under his own name, and apparently broke no laws. When eventually located during a routine credit check of fugitives, Doggett was arrested in September 1988, eight and a half years after his indictment.[44]

In holding that Doggett's trial at that late date would be unconstitutional, Justice Souter drew on the criteria for evaluating speedy trial claims announced in *Barker v. Wingo* (1972): whether the delay before trial was uncommonly long, whether the prosecution or the accused was more responsible for the delay, whether the defendant duly asserted his or her speedy trial right, and whether the accused suffered prejudice as a result of the delay. In a dissent, Justice O'Connor noted that "the only harm to petitioner from the lapse of time was potential prejudice to his ability to defend his case," adding that, under *Barker*, "we have not allowed such speculative harm to tip the scales." In a separate dissent joined by Rehnquist and Scalia, Justice Thomas contended that Doggett had not suffered the "major evils" against which the speedy trial guarantee was directed—"undue and oppressive incarceration" and the "anxiety and concern accompanying public accusation"—particularly as the Court was obliged to "assume that [the accused] was blissfully unaware of his indictment all the while." Speaking for the majority, however, Justice Souter rejected the government's claims that Doggett had known of his indictment before his arrest and that it had pursued his prosecution with due diligence. The justice conceded that the government had not intentionally delayed the prosecution in an effort "to gain some impermissible advantage at trial." But in the face of its "persistent neglect" in bringing the accused to trial, Souter did not consider a showing of "specific prejudice to [Doggett's] defense" necessary to his speedy trial claim. But for the government's "inexcusable oversights," the defendant would have faced trial six years earlier, even though lower courts had generally found postindictment delays "presumptively prejudicial" if they approached even one year. "When the government's negligence thus causes delay six times as long as that generally sufficient to trigger judicial review [of speedy trial claims] . . . , and when the presumption of prejudice, albeit unspecified, is neither extenuated, as by the defendant's acquiescence [in the delay] . . . , nor persuasively rebutted, the defendant," declared Souter, "is entitled to relief."[45]

Souter was also in the majority when the Court, during its 1991–92 term, overturned a defendant's conviction in a federal child pornography case. An entrapment defense is difficult to establish; an accused must show not merely that the government encouraged and assisted in the commission of a crime, but also that the defendant had no predisposition to commit the offense charged. The defendant in *Jacobson v. United States* (1992), however, was targeted in a federal "sting" operation based on a single order of two magazines featuring photographs of nude boys, publications that were legal under state and federal law. He was induced into purchasing child pornography only after twenty-six months of repeated government mailings and communications as a target of the sting. In conference, according to Justice Blackmun's notes, Souter had cast a "weak" vote to affirm Jacobson's conviction or to dismiss the writ of certiorari in which the Court had granted review of the case. But following negotiation with Justice White regarding his colleague's opinion, Souter joined a 5–4 holding that the government's conduct constituted entrapment in violation of Jacobson's right to due process.[46]

During the 1991–92 term, Souter assumed a moderately liberal stance in other civil liberties issue areas as well. In a case brought by the International Society for Krishna Consciousness, Chief Justice Rehnquist concluded for the Court that an airport terminal did not constitute a public forum with First Amendment obligations in upholding a New York Port Authority ban on the repetitive solicitation of money within the terminals of the New York City area. In a companion case, however, a majority, over a Rehnquist dissent joined by White, Scalia, and Thomas, summarily struck down a Port Authority ban on the distribution of literature in the terminals.[47]

Justice Souter concurred in the Court's rejection of the prohibition on distribution of literature, but dissented in the solicitation case. Refusing to limit the public forum concept to a "static category" of "archetypes" traditionally included in that classification—"streets, parks, sidewalks, and perhaps not much more"—the justice contended that such a narrow definition of public forums with First Amendment obligations had "no warrant in a Constitution whose values are not to be left behind in the city streets that are no longer the focus of our community life. If that were the line of our direction, we might as well abandon the public forum doctrine altogether." Drawing on a more elaborate separate opinion Justice Kennedy had filed in the case, Souter thought any public property could be classified as a public forum if expressive activity was compatible with its physical characteristics and the use to which it was normally put. "One can imagine a public airport of a size or design or need for extraordinary security that would render expressive activity incompatible with its normal use," he declared. "But that would be no reason to conclude that one of the more usual variety of metropolitan airports is not a public forum," he added, and he had "no difficulty concluding that the unleased public areas at airports like the metropolitan New York airports at issue in these cases [were] public forums."[48]

Nor could Souter agree with the Port Authority's justifications for a total ban on the solicitation of money in the public areas of the terminals. Such

regulations were constitutional only if narrowly tailored to further a significant state interest and if ample alternative channels of communication were
provided solicitors. In the justice's view, the regulations at issue served no
such interest. The claim that the solicitation ban furthered the government's
interest in preventing fraud and coercion struck Souter as "weak." Pedestrians
could simply walk by or away from solicitors, and the evidence of fraudulent
solicitations in the past was "virtually nonexistent": only eight complaints,
none of them substantial, over an eleven-year period when the ban was not
enforced. "This," asserted Souter, "is precisely the type of vague and unsub-
stantial allegation that could never support a restriction on speech." Even if
the government had an interest adequate to justify some degree of regulation, moreover, a flat ban had an unduly broad sweep. The port authority
could simply prohibit and punish fraudulent misrepresentations. Because the
ban forbade only solicitations for immediate payment, Justice Kennedy, in
voting to uphold the ban, had suggested that solicitors could distribute
preaddressed envelopes in which potential contributors could mail their donations. For Souter, however, that was hardly the ample alternative means of
communication required when government regulated the time, place, and
manner of expression. "The practical reality of the regulation," he declared,
"is that it shuts off a uniquely powerful avenue of communication and may,
in effect, completely prohibit unpopular and poorly funded groups from receiving funds in response to protected solicitation."[49]

Commencement Prayers

The justice's stance in two second-term cases would prove most heartening to
liberals, while confirming conservative doubts about John Sununu's claim that
the Bush White House had hit a "home run" with the Souter appointment. The
first was *Lee v. Weisman* (1992), in which the justice not only joined Justice
Kennedy's opinion for the Court striking down a public school commencement prayer but also filed a concurrence embracing a broad interpretation of
the First Amendment religious establishment clause. In conference, Souter had
voted to strike the prayer down, contending, among other things, that student
attendance at graduation ceremonies was not "fully voluntary"; Justice
Kennedy had voted to uphold the school and initially circulated a majority
opinion embracing that position. When Kennedy decided that his original
vote and draft were "quite wrong," Souter joined the new majority that
Kennedy's defection created, as well as his colleague's opinion of the Court.

While among the dissenters, Souter had informed Justice Blackmun that "because [*Lee*] is the first one on the Establishment Clause since my arrival, I will write something to stake out my ground." When the vote changed, he converted his dissenting opinion—somewhat unkindly dubbed his "grand essay on the Establishment Clause" by a Blackmun clerk—into a concurrence. In his separate opinion, Souter "fully agree[d]" with Kennedy's conclusion that "public school graduation ceremonies indirectly coerce[d] religious observance," even if student attendance at commencement exercises was ostensibly optional. Joined by Justices Stevens and O'Connor, however, Souter also wrote separately to underscore his belief that the establishment guarantee extended to governmental practices that did "not favor one religion or denomination over others" and to reject the notion that "state coercion of religious conformity, over and above state endorsement of religious exercise or belief, is a necessary element of an Establishment Clause violation."[50]

Going back to Justice Hugo Black's assertion for the Court in *Everson v. Board of Education* (1947) that the establishment clause forbade not only state practices that "aid one religion . . . or prefer one religion over another," but also those that "aid all religions," the justice first summarized the Court's many precedents invalidating practices that in no way discriminated among religious sects, preferring one or some over others. "Such is the settled law," he observed, his devotion to precedent (even that with which he might not personally agree) clearly in view. "Here, as elsewhere, we should stick to it absent some compelling reason to discard it."[51]

William Rehnquist had long embraced a nonpreferentialist construction of the establishment clause, most notably in a dissent registered for *Wallace v. Jaffree*, the 1985 case in which a Burger Court majority struck down an Alabama law setting aside moments of silence for prayer and meditation in that state's public schools. Rehnquist, among others, argued that the First Amendment's framers had not intended that it "require government neutrality between religion and irreligion [or] prohibit the Federal Government from providing nondiscriminatory aid to religion." While conceding in his *Lee* concurrence that "a case [had] been made" for the nonpreferentialist position, Souter did not consider such arguments "so convincing as to warrant reconsideration of our settled law." Instead, he found "in the history of the Clause's textual development a more powerful argument supporting the Court's jurisprudence following *Everson*." The Congress that drafted the establishment clause, Souter observed, had indeed considered, but rejected, drafts that would have permitted nonpreferential government aid to religion. The phrasing ultimately adopted provided that "Congress shall make no law respecting an establishment of religion." "What is remarkable," declared the justice, "is that, unlike the [earlier versions], the prevailing language is not limited to laws respecting an establishment of 'a religion,' 'a national religion,' 'one religious sect,' or specific 'articles of faith.' The Framers repeatedly considered and deliberately rejected such narrow language and instead extended their prohibition to state support for 'religion' in general." Given the clause's final language, acceptance of the nonpreferentialist interpretation, asserted Souter, quoting Douglas Laycock, a prominent scholarly student of the clause, "require[d] a premise that the Framers were extraordinarily bad drafters—that they believed one thing but adopted language that said something substantially different, and that they did so after repeatedly attending to the choice of language."[52]

In defending nonpreferentialism, Rehnquist had cited early government actions supporting religion, including presidential proclamations of days of prayer and thanksgiving and President Thomas Jefferson's signing of a treaty provision authorizing funding of a Roman Catholic priest and church for Indians. Souter dismissed the ceremonial proclamations as "at worst trivial breaches of the Establishment Clause" and warned, with respect to the grant Jefferson had approved, that if the guarantee permitted special funding for a particular sect, "it forbids virtually nothing." Perhaps recalling the Good Friday flag suit and other experiences from his days in the New Hampshire attorney general's office, the justice further noted that the willingness of government officials to accommodate religion "prove[d] only that public officials, no matter when they serve, can turn a blind eye to constitutional principle." Because even nonpreferentialism prohibited government favoring of particular religions over others, the obligation of nonpreferentialists to distinguish between "ecumenical" religious practices that government could assist and "sectarian" practices it could not aid also drew Souter's attention. Such inquiries "invite[d] courts to engage in comparative theology," and the justice could "hardly imagine a subject less amenable to the competence of the federal judiciary, or more deliberately to be avoided where possible." He was equally dubious about the nonpreferentialists' notion that government "should promote a 'diversity' of religious views." After all, there would have to be some limit to the number of religions to be sponsored and the time devoted to each. "The judiciary," he cautioned, "should not willingly enter the political arena to battle the centripetal force leading from religious pluralism to official preference for the faith with the most votes."[53]

Souter next turned to the view of Justice Kennedy, among others, that state-sponsored affirmations of religious belief were unconstitutional only if they coerced support for religion or participation in religious observances. The "coercion" interpretation of the establishment clause could be embraced, Souter argued, only by the Court's abandonment of "settled law, a course that, in [his] view, the text of the Clause would not readily permit." In many earlier cases, the Court had struck down government practices endorsing religion without any showing of coercion: the display of a nativity scene on public property, Alabama's moment of silence scheme, a state ban on the teaching of evolution in public schools, and state "creation science" policies, for example. "Our precedents may not always have drawn perfectly straight lines," he observed. "They simply cannot, however, support the position that a showing of coercion is necessary to a successful Establishment Clause claim."[54]

Because the First Amendment included a prohibition on interferences with the free exercise of religion as well as the establishment clause, the justice also found it difficult to square the coercion argument with constitutional text. Coercive laws "would virtually by definition violate [the] right to religious free exercise," Souter reasoned. "Thus, a literal application of the coercion test would render the Establishment Clause a virtual nullity." Nor did he find adequate support for the coercion doctrine in early, noncoercive government endorsements of religion, such as presidential prayer proclamations. They "prove, at best," he asserted, "that the Framers simply did not share a common understanding of the Establishment Clause, and, at worst, that they, like other politicians, could raise constitutional ideals one day and turn their backs on them the next." Despite his strong belief in church-state separation, for example, James Madison had called for days of thanksgiving and prayer on four separate occasions during the War of 1812, after having refused to do so during the first three years of his presidency and condemning them, as well as government-funded legislative and military chaplains, once out of office. Within a decade of proposing the First Amendment, moreover, Congress had adopted the Alien and Sedition Acts; yet those "measures [were] patently unconstitutional by modern standards." Early political actions, declared Souter, were thus merely "relevant," not "determinative," evidence of constitutional meaning.[55]

Souter readily accepted some degree of government accommodation with religion short of official endorsement. He even appeared sympathetic to Madison's realization "that his contemporaries were unlikely to take the Establishment Clause seriously enough to forgo a legislative chaplainship," as well as the founders' suggestion that the practice be accepted as a "trifling" interference with the establishment guarantee. Government officials invoking "spiritual inspiration entirely for their own benefit," after all, were not "directing any religious message at the citizens they lead." In Souter's judgment, however, such logic permitted no "winking" at the commencement prayer at issue in *Lee*. "When public school officials, armed with the State's authority, convey an endorsement of religion to their students, they strike near the core of the Establishment Clause. However 'ceremonial' their messages may be, they are flatly unconstitutional." Given Souter's regard for precedent and a long line of Warren- and Burger-era rulings forbidding even voluntary state-directed religious exercises in the public schools, his stance in *Lee* was also hardly surprising.[56]

The *Casey* "Troika"

It was Souter's vote and opinion writing in the major abortion case of the 1991–92 term, though, that was most troubling to conservatives. In *Webster v. Reproductive Services* (1989), a badly fragmented Court had passed on an opportunity to overturn *Roe v. Wade*. Chief Justice Rehnquist, joined by Justice White, another *Roe* dissenter, and by Justice Kennedy, favored discarding *Roe*'s "rigid" trimester approach to abortion regulations; Justice Scalia argued for *Roe*'s outright rejection. But Justice O'Connor cast the decisive fifth vote in *Webster*. In earlier cases, O'Connor had been critical of the trimester framework, urging instead a more flexible formula forbidding government to impose any "undue burden" on a woman's decision to abort a pregnancy. But she thought that the abortion controls at issue in *Webster* were constitutional even under *Roe* and the Court's other abortion precedents. "Where there is no need to decide a constitutional question," she concluded, "it is a venerable principle of this Court's adjudicatory processes not to do so. . . . When the constitutional validity of a state's abortion statute actually turns on the constitutional validity of *Roe v. Wade*, there will be time enough to reexamine *Roe*. And to do so carefully."[57]

When the Court agreed to decide *Planned Parenthood v. Casey* in the 1991–92 term, conservatives hoped that *Casey* would be the vehicle for that reexamination—and reversal—of *Roe*. *Roe* dissenters Rehnquist and White were already on record as opponents of any meaningful abortion right, as was Justice Scalia. Given her previous opinions, Justice O'Connor would support only *Roe's* dilution, not its rejection. But Kennedy, Souter, and Thomas might well provide the decisive votes for reversal.[58]

Justice Thomas would indeed join other *Roe* opponents on the Court, even though during his Senate confirmation proceedings he had denied ever having discussed the case, much less formed an opinion on its validity. But Souter and Kennedy were not prepared to go that far. Justice Blackmun's notes for the Court's April 24, 1992, conference discussion of *Casey* suggest that Kennedy was prepared at that point to overrule parts of *City of Akron v. Akron Center for Reproductive Health* (1983), which had reaffirmed *Roe*, based on stare decisis. Souter, on the other hand, indicated support at the conference for Justice O'Connor's undue burden approach to abortion issues. The previous January, moreover, when the justices were drafting questions to be reviewed in *Casey*, Souter's clerk Peter Rubin had informed a Blackmun clerk that Souter was trying to have the questions written "in such a way as to *avoid* overruling *Roe*." Apparently, Souter was ultimately able to persuade Kennedy that *Roe* should not be rejected. On May 29, Kennedy sent Justice Blackmun, *Roe's* author, a brief note. "I need to see you as soon as you have a few minutes," Kennedy wrote. "I want to tell you about some developments in *Planned Parenthood v. Casey*, and at least part of what I say should come as welcome news." Kennedy's "news," of course, was that he, O'Connor, and Souter had decided to prepare a rare joint opinion in which they refused to overrule *Roe*.[59]

In their opinion, the "troika," as one of Blackmun's clerks quickly labeled them, rejected *Roe's* trimester framework. Instead, they concluded, as O'Connor had earlier proposed, that government merely could impose no "undue burden" on a woman's decision to obtain an abortion prior to the point at which a fetus becomes viable. They thus preserved what they termed the "essence" of the abortion right *Roe* had established, as well as *Roe's* acceptance of state authority to forbid nontherapeutic abortions after viability. But they also recognized legitimate interests in protecting the woman's health and fetal life throughout a pregnancy, so long as such regulations did not unduly interfere with the woman's choice.

Joined by *Roe* opponents, the trio formed a majority upholding most of the regulations at issue in *Casey*: a requirement that a woman give her informed consent to an abortion and be provided information on which to base her decision at least twenty-four hours before the procedure was performed; a provision, with a judicial bypass option, mandating at least one parent's consent for minors seeking abortions; an exemption of medical emergencies from the consent and waiting period regulations; and reporting and record-keeping requirements for abortion clinics. However, a different majority, consisting of the trio, *Roe*'s author, Justice Blackmun, and Justice Stevens, who substantially embraced *Roe*, struck down as an undue burden on the abortion right a spousal notification provision.

In an important portion of the joint opinion, primarily drafted by Justice Souter, the trio concluded that principles of stare decisis counseled against *Roe*'s reversal. Souter readily conceded the controversy *Roe* had provoked. But he insisted that the *Roe* precedent had proved workable, that millions of women had come to rely on it, that it was by no means a doctrinal anachronism discounted by current society, and that the basic factual premises underlying *Roe* remained substantially unchanged. The justice and his colleagues seemed particularly determined, however, that the Court avoid any appearance of caving in to the intense political debate that continued to swirl around *Roe*. "A decision to overrule *Roe*'s essential holding under the existing circumstances," he declared, "would address error, if error there was, at the cost of both profound and unnecessary damage to the Court's legitimacy, and to the Nation's commitment to the rule of law. It is therefore imperative to adhere to the essence of *Roe*'s original decision, and we do so today."[60]

In biting separate opinions, Chief Justice Rehnquist and Justice Scalia scorned the notion that *Roe* should be even partially reaffirmed as a symbol of judicial solidarity against opposition to the Court's decisions. Scalia characterized such thinking as "frightening":

> It is a bad enough idea, even in the head of someone like me, who believes that the text of the Constitution, and our traditions, say what they say and there is no fiddling with them. But when it is in the mind of a Court that believes the Constitution has an evolving meaning . . . unrestrained by meaningful text or tradition—then the notion that the Court must adhere to a decision for as long as the decision faces "great opposition" and the Court is "under fire" acquires a character of almost cynical arrogance. We are offended by these marchers who descend upon us, every year on the anniversary of *Roe*, to protest our saying the Constitution requires what our society has never thought the Constitution requires. These people who refuse to be "tested by following" must be taught a lesson. We have no Cossacks, but at least we can stubbornly refuse to abandon an erroneous opinion that we might otherwise change—to show how little they intimidate us.[61]

For his part, *Roe*'s author praised the joint opinion as "an act of personal courage and constitutional principle," attempting to cast it in a light most favorable to preservation of abortion rights. Although Blackmun clearly would have preferred a full reaffirmation of *Roe*, he and his clerks realized that the troika's approach was the best they could expect and that the trio would pay a price for their decision. "Once this opinion comes out," one Blackmun clerk wrote the justice, "there will be no more speculation about a Vice President O'Connor or a Chief Justice Kennedy—and, as DHS himself recognized, I suspect Barbara Bush will find herself another most-eligible-bachelor to include on the White House invite list." (The reclusive Souter, she might have added, doubtless would have been entirely happy to pay that price for his role in the joint opinion.) Even so, Justice Blackmun also realized the fragile foundation on which even *Roe*'s "essence" rested. "I am 83 years old. I cannot remain on this Court forever, and when I do step down, the confirmation process for my successor well may focus on the issue before us today. That, I regret, may be exactly where the choice between the two worlds will be made." Fortunately for proponents of choice, those fears would not prove prophetic when the justice retired from the high bench in 1994.[62]

Editorially, the *New York Times* also appeared both frustrated and relieved by the decision. The paper doubted that the undue burden standard could be applied with "uniform humaneness" and expressed regret that *Casey* would "allow states to impose new burdens on, especially, poor women." But the *Times* also proclaimed that the Court had "preserved liberty for American women and, because of three moderates, honor for itself." Though hardly fans of *Roe*, the paper asserted, Justices O'Connor, Kennedy, and Souter had decided that "overturning it for no more reason than a change in membership would damage the Court's reputation." They had thus bolstered their own reputation as "a core of judicious moderation on a rightward moving Court."[63]

In an article written in the wake of the commencement prayer decision the previous week, *Times* reporter Linda Greenhouse concluded that "effective control of the Court" had passed to the "moderately conservative" trio, adding, "The group's hallmarks appear to be a generally cautious approach to deciding cases, a hesitancy to overturn precedents and a distaste for aggressive arguments, whether those presented to the Court or those made by the Justices themselves in written opinions." Solicitor General Kenneth Starr offered support for Greenhouse's theme. "There's a Kennedy-Souter center to the Court now, and that's a very cautious center," he told her. "As Kennedy and Souter go, so goes the Court, and I see in them the spirit of Lewis Powell," who had often been the classic swing justice during his years on the bench.[64]

As an example of the trio's distaste for aggressive advocacy, Greenhouse cited the oral argument for *Lee v. Weisman*, in which former Reagan assistant attorney general Charles J. Cooper argued for the school board that the commencement prayer at issue had no coercive effect on students, who could skip the ceremony if they wished and still receive their diploma. "In our culture," Kennedy shot back, "graduation is a key event in a young person's life." Greenhouse conceded that it would be impossible to know whether Cooper lost Kennedy's vote at that time. But she noted that "almost the exact words" the justice used that day appeared in his *Lee* opinion.[65]

Speculating that the centrist trio might also be "responding almost viscerally to the swashbuckling reach of opinions" by the Court's conservatives, particularly Scalia and Thomas, Greenhouse cited an "unusually sharp" separate opinion Justice O'Connor had filed in *Wright v. West* (1992), a recent federal habeas corpus case. Previously, O'Connor and Kennedy had appeared eager to limit the scope of federal habeas review of state convictions and sentences. But when Thomas, joined by the chief justice and Scalia, embraced an extremely narrow view of federal jurisdiction in a *Wright* plurality opinion, O'Connor invoked such words as "misdescribes" and "mischaracterizes" in her point-by-point rebuttal of Thomas, while also pointing out that Congress had refused on thirteen occasions to require greater federal court deference to the decisions of state judges in habeas cases.[66]

Because Souter based his *Wright* vote on narrow grounds, he did not, as he put it in a concurrence, "take a position in the disagreement between Justice Thomas and Justice O'Connor." But during a sailing trip with his Harvard classmate and friend John McCausland, the rector of Souter's Weare congregation, Souter expressed concern that the Court needed a center. McCausland recalled the justice saying that "there was too much individual judicial posturing" among his colleagues. "He has a great concern for stability," the cleric told a reporter, "and that things won't be overturned by a single vote or by demonstration outside the Court."[67]

Souter dissented from only eight of the Court's decisions for the 1991–92 term, tying with Justice Kennedy for the fewest dissents. By contrast, Rehnquist and Thomas, on the Court's right, dissented nineteen and twenty-three times, respectively, and Blackmun and Stevens, the Court's most liberal members, each dissented twenty-one times. For the balance of the first five terms, Souter became increasingly liberal in his voting patterns; in fact, during the 1994–95 term, the first after Justice Blackmun's retirement, only Justice Stevens had a more liberal voting record in civil rights and civil liberties cases: a 65 percent liberal voting record for Souter compared with Stevens's 86 percent. In the previous terms, moreover, Blackmun, Stevens, and Souter had liberal voting records of 71, 64, and 58 percent, respectively. During his first term, by contrast, Souter had only a 35 percent liberal record in civil liberties cases. His most conservative voting for the five-term period was in criminal procedure cases, in which he supported rights claims only 44 percent of the time. In First Amendment and civil rights cases, on the other hand, he had a support rate of 74 and 58 percent.[68]

Wall of Separation

The justice's liberal positions in a number of civil liberties cases during the remainder of his first five terms were particularly notable. As in *Lee v. Weisman*, he continued to advance the broad construction of the religious establishment clause the Court had embraced during much of its modern history. In the *Kiryas Joel* school district case, for example, he spoke for a 6–3 majority in striking down a New York law that had created a village school district consisting entirely of members of the Satmar Hasidic sect, followers of a strict form of Judaism. The village school board ran a special education program that only handicapped Hasidic children attended, while other village children attended private religious schools. It thus appeared obvious that the special public school district had been created purely because the Hasidic adherents could not afford to provide the special educational services for their children and opposed their education in religiously and culturally mixed public schools. Souter found the arrangement an impermissible aid to religion, especially as alternative methods were available to fill the students' needs. Given growing criticism on the Court of the *Lemon* establishment test, the justice made little reference to *Lemon* in his opinion—much to the glee of Justice Scalia, *Lemon*'s harshest critic and a *Kiryas Joel* dissenter. But Souter made numerous approving references to precedents based on *Lemon* and to its progenitors, including *Abington v. Schempp*, the 1963 ruling invalidating state-directed Bible reading and prayer in public schools. Thus, even when speaking for the Court, the justice's devotion to precedents obliged him to attempt to preserve as much of their substance, if not their rhetoric, as he possibly could.[69]

Along similar lines, Souter urged caution when a majority invoked free speech doctrine to blur the lines between church and state, allowing government funding of religion. In *Rosenberger v. Rector and Visitors of the University of Virginia* (1995), the justice dissented when the Court overturned the university's denial of funding to a student organization for publication of *Wide Awake*, a newspaper with a Christian editorial viewpoint. The money would have come from a university fund created to make payments to outside contractors for printing costs connected with student publications, and the majority held that the university could not discriminate on the basis of viewpoint when it subsidized private speech. Justice Kennedy rested the decision largely on *Widmar v. Vincent* (1981) and other cases in which the Court had forbidden public universities and schools to set aside space and facilities for secular student groups while denying religious organizations equal access. Because Justice O'Connor saw no government endorsement in evenhanded university funding of secular and religious student organizations, she concurred in the ruling. Joined by Stevens, Ginsburg, and Breyer, however, Justice Souter registered a forceful dissent. In cases of the *Widmar* variety, he asserted, government had simply created a limited public forum, then denied access to religious groups; the only government support for religion there was the "incidental state spending" required to maintain the facilities in which religious as well as secular speech, among other activities, took place. University funding of student publications advocating religious viewpoints was hardly analogous. Instead, it amounted to "direct funding of core religious activities by an arm of the State," a type of government support for religion the Court had never before condoned.[70]

Justice Souter also called for a reexamination of a controversial 1990 precedent diluting the scope of the First Amendment free exercise guarantee. The modern Supreme Court had long held that laws and other government action interfering with religious practices were subject to strict judicial scrutiny, struck down unless found to be the least restrictive means available to promote a compelling governmental interest. But in *Employment Division v. Smith* (1990), decided the term before Souter's appointment, a majority, speaking through Justice Scalia, held that religious practices must conform to generally applicable, religiously neutral laws, whether or not such enforcement served a compelling interest. In *Smith*, two drug counselors were fired from their jobs based on their ritual use of peyote as members of the Native American Church, then denied unemployment compensation because they had no "good cause" for loss of employment. In the future, Justice Scalia declared, only laws directed at particular religious practices were to be subjected to strict judicial review.[71]

Responding to concerns among religious liberals and conservatives about *Smith*'s impact on free exercise rights, Congress enacted legislation to overturn, in effect, *Smith* and require strict judicial review of all governmental interferences with religious practices. As discussed in a later chapter, the Court soon reaffirmed *Smith* and struck down the law, emphasizing the final power of the courts—and ultimately the Supreme Court—to construe the Constitution's meaning. But Justice Souter, who had not been on the Court when *Smith* was decided, had already used a 1993 case to reveal his misgivings about that decision.

In *Church of Lukumi v. Hialeah* (1993), the Court struck down an ordinance that prohibited the ritual sacrifice of animals, holding *Smith* inapplicable since most other forms of animal slaughter remained legal. Souter concurred in the judgment but questioned "whether the *Smith* rule merits adherence" and recommended that it be reexamined in some future case involving its application. Earlier cases, the justice contended, citing numerous illustrations, had "applied the same rigorous scrutiny to burdens on religious exercise resulting from the enforcement of formally neutral, generally applicable laws as we have applied to burdens caused by laws that single out religious exercise." Nor did he believe revisiting *Smith* would conflict with the principle of stare decisis to which the justice was so firmly committed. For one thing, neither party in *Smith* had squarely addressed the claim that the free exercise guarantee was irrelevant in such cases—the core of the *Smith* majority's rationale. For another, Justice O'Connor had demonstrated in a *Smith* concurrence that the Court, given the state's important interest in enforcing its drug laws, could have reached the same result in *Smith* under established free exercise jurisprudence. "The [*Smith*] majority," asserted Souter, "never determined that the case could not be resolved on the narrower ground, going instead to the broader constitutional rule. But the Court's better practice, one supported by the same principles of restraint that underlie the rule of *stare decisis*, is not to 'formulate a rule of constitutional law broader than is required by the precise facts to which it is to be applied.'" In Souter's judgment, a thorough review of the free exercise clause's history and judicial construction would provide a "powerful reason to interpret the Clause to accord with its natural reading, as applying to all laws prohibiting religious exercise in fact, not just those aimed at its prohibition."[72]

Free Expression

In free expression cases during the remainder of his first five terms, the justice also continued to assume a moderately liberal stance. In suits involving protests at abortion clinics, Souter joined the majority not only in upholding limited restrictions on such demonstrations to protect patients and staff from undue interference, but also in refusing to equate anti-abortion protests with conspiracies to obstruct interstate travel forbidden by a Reconstruction-era civil rights statute. He filed a partial dissent in one case, however, reasoning that private persons who prevent state officers from giving normal police protection to women seeking abortions were subject to federal legislation prohibiting conspiracies to prevent state officials from securing all persons equal protection of the laws under the Fourteenth Amendment.[73]

Although abortion rights and congressional power partially trumped free speech claims for Souter in abortion protest cases, he spoke for the Court in a 1995 decision overturning application of a state's public accommodations law to the decision of a private group organizing the traditional St. Patrick's Day parade in Boston to exclude a gay rights organization from the event. A state clearly had the authority to forbid discrimination in public accommodations. At the same time, it could not declare the speech of parade sponsors to itself be a public accommodation. In the past, the justice conceded, the parade organizers had been lenient in admitting participants. But that in no way meant that they had thereby forfeited their First Amendment right to exclude messages and messengers they did not like.[74]

One can be reasonably confident that David Souter is no fan of rap music. Nevertheless, when Acuff-Rose Music, Inc., accused the rap group 2 Live Crew of copyright infringement for its "Pretty Woman" parody of a country-western song, the justice spoke for the Court in holding that the commercial nature of a satire did not create a presumption against fair use of the original composition and that 2 Live Crew had not drawn excessively on the earlier work in its parody. In another case, he concluded in a partial dissent that the First Amendment forbade the forfeiture of an obscenity defendant's "expressive material in the absence of an adjudication that it is obscene or otherwise of unprotected character."[75]

Discrimination

Souter's position in discrimination cases followed a similar pattern. When the Court extended its growing distaste for race-conscious policies to majority-minority congressional redistricting, Souter joined the majority in conference but later filed a dissent. Emphasizing the bizarre configuration of North Carolina's twelfth congressional district, Justice O'Connor concluded for the

Court in *Shaw v. Reno* (1993) that redistricting plans so extremely irregular that they rationally could be understood only as an effort at racial segregation must be subjected to strict judicial scrutiny by trial courts. In his dissenting opinion, on the other hand, Souter cited several reasons why the Court traditionally had subjected redistricting issues involving race to more deferential judicial scrutiny than equal protection challenges to other forms of racial classification. He also lamented the *Shaw* majority's break with past precedent. As long as members of different races shared common interests and racial bloc voting persisted, Souter viewed some consideration of race as necessary to ensure that districts that state legislatures created would not dilute minority voting strength—dilution forbidden by federal voting rights law. Unlike the use of racial criteria in affirmative action programs and other areas, he added, race-conscious redistricting did not work to the advantage of one race at the "obvious expense" of those in a different racial group. Being placed in one congressional district rather than another denied no one a right or benefit extended to others. "All citizens may register, vote, and be represented. . . . One's constitutional rights are not violated merely because the candidate one supports loses the election or because a group (including a racial group) to which one belongs winds up with a representative from outside that group."[76]

Joined by Stevens, Ginsburg, and Breyer, Souter also dissented when the Court revisited *Missouri v. Jenkins* (1995), Kansas City's protracted school desegregation battle, and rejected, among other things, provisions of a district court's order designed to attract nonminority students from outside the school district and requiring across-the-board salary increases for teachers and staff to promote desegregation in the city's school district. The majority considered such provisions interdistrict remedies forbidden by the Court's holding in *Milliken v. Bradley* (1974) that school desegregation decrees must generally be confined to school districts with a history of de jure segregation, or otherwise beyond the remedial authority of district courts. But Souter contended that the majority had reached out to decide an issue that the Court had not accepted for review in the case, that need not be reached to answer the questions actually raised, and that the Court had specifically refused to answer in a previous certiorari petition in the case. He took a similar position when a majority held in *Adarand Constructors, Inc. v. Pena* (1995) that federal affirmative action programs, which the Court previously had accorded considerable deference, were to be subjected to the same degree of strict judicial scrutiny accorded state and local programs. The scheme at issue in *Adarand*,

Souter argued in a dissent joined by Ginsburg and Breyer, was constitutional under *Fullilove v. Klutznick* (1980), one of the earlier cases embracing a deferential approach to federal affirmative action programs, and Adarand Constructors had not "identif[ied] any of the factual premises on which *Fullilove* rested as having disappeared since that case was decided." Stare decisis thus compelled, he concluded, continued adherence to *Fullilove*.[77]

Criminal Procedure

Even in criminal procedure cases, in which Souter's overall civil liberties support rate was lowest, the justice was hardly the Court's most conservative member during the balance of his first five terms on the bench. In *Stone v. Powell* (1976), the Burger Court had held that state prisoners could not raise search and seizure challenges to state convictions if they had been given a full and fair opportunity to raise such claims in their trials and on direct appeal of their convictions. Based on earlier holdings that the Fourth-Fourteenth Amendment exclusionary rule was a judicially created device designed primarily to deter police misconduct, rather than a constitutional command, the *Stone* Court concluded that extension of the exclusionary rule generally to federal habeas proceedings would not appreciably enhance the rule's deterrent effect on police. In *Withrow v. Williams* (1993), however, the Court, per Souter, refused to extend *Stone* to habeas cases involving claims that state convictions rested on confessions secured in violation of the *Miranda* warnings. Unlike the Fourth Amendment exclusionary rule, the justice declared, *Miranda* safeguarded a fundamental trial right based on the Fifth Amendment guarantee against compulsory self-incrimination and served as a further barrier to the use of unreliable statements at trial. Most important, eliminating habeas review of state inmates' *Miranda* claims would hardly reduce the caseload of federal courts, given the probability that virtually every barred *Miranda* claim would simply be recast as a general due process claim that particular convictions rested on involuntary confessions. Given *Miranda's* twenty-seven-year vintage, Souter also doubted that such claims would be so frequently raised in federal habeas proceedings that they would seriously strain relations between federal and state courts.[78]

There were other cases during Souter's first five terms reflecting his concern for procedural rights. In *Arizona v. Evans* (1995), he joined the Court's extension of the "good faith" exception to the exclusionary rule to situations in which the clerical errors of court employees resulted in an illegal seizure of evidence. In a brief concurrence, however, he wondered "how far, in dealing with fruits of computerized error, our very concept of deterrence by exclusion of evidence should extend to the government as a whole, not merely the police, on the ground that there would otherwise be no reasonable expectation of keeping the number of resulting false arrests [and illegal seizures of evidence incident to arrest] within an acceptable minimum limit." Taking partial issue with the majority's treatment of a *Miranda* claim in another case, he declared, "When law enforcement officials 'reasonably do not know whether or not the suspect wants a lawyer,' . . . they should stop their interrogation and ask him to make his choice clear." In a 1995 case, the justice spoke for a 5–4 majority in reversing a defendant's murder conviction on the ground that the prosecution had suppressed evidence in violation of *Brady v. Maryland* (1963) and its progeny. The excluded evidence included statements of eyewitnesses and a police informant, as well as a computer printout of the license numbers of cars parked at the crime scene the night of the murder, a printout that did not list the number of the defendant's car. As required by *Brady*, Souter found a "reasonable probability" that disclosure of the suppressed evidence to the defense would have led to a different trial outcome. By contrast, Justice Scalia, joined by Rehnquist, Kennedy, and Thomas, declared in dissent that the "massive core of evidence" presented at trial showed that the defendant was guilty and had lied about his guilt, while any effect "that the *Brady* materials would have had in chipping away at the edges of the State's case [could] only be called immaterial."[79]

On the Court, as in his Senate confirmation testimony, Souter continued to embrace the second Justice Harlan's conception of substantive due process as a "rational continuum which . . . includes a freedom from all substantial arbitrary impositions and purposeless restraints" on individual freedom. He thus rejected, of course, any notion that constitutional rights were limited to particular guarantees mentioned in the Constitution's text. Nor did he believe, as he put it in a 1994 case, "that the Constitution's application to a general subject (like prosecution) is necessarily exhausted by protection under particular textual guarantees addressing specific events within that subject (like search and seizure), on a theory that one specific constitutional provision can preempt a broad field as against another more general one." At the same time, he thought that application of due process should be reserved "for otherwise homeless substantial claims," especially in view of the difficulties inherent in "subjecting governmental actors to two (potentially inconsistent) standards for the same conduct and needlessly imposing on trial courts the unenviable burden of reconciling well-established jurisprudence under [specific safeguards] with the ill-defined contours of some novel due process right." In *Albright v. Oliver* (1994), for example, the Court rejected the contention that arrest without probable cause violated an arrestee's claimed substantive due process rights sufficient to support a federal civil rights action, holding instead that the constitutional right violated, if any, was the Fourth Amendment freedom against unreasonable seizure. In a concurrence, Souter agreed that the case presented no substantial burden on individual liberty beyond that covered by the Fourth Amendment and rejected reliance on substantive due process merely to duplicate a right that a more specific constitutional safeguard, such as the Fourth Amendment, already protected.[80]

On March 24, 1995, as Justice Souter neared the end of his fifth term on the Court, Helen Souter died in Concord. The justice had visited his mother only a week earlier, later telling a Weare friend that she "was doing real well." Characteristically fearful that any publicity about her death would inevitably focus on her only son, Souter asked that there be no obituary and arranged for a private funeral service. But news articles in New Hampshire papers recounted her life and delight at her son's success ("I'm a very happy mother. I'm very happy that I produced a judge"). On learning of his nomination in 1990, a Manchester *Union Leader* reporter reminded readers, Mrs. Souter had said, "I think a teardrop fell."[81]

For the unmarried justice, the death of his mother must have been a particularly terrible blow, but at least Mrs. Souter had the satisfaction of knowing that her son's difficult first term on the bench was to be no measure of his ultimate reputation as a justice. By that point, Souter was no longer the "stealth justice." Early in his tenure, a woman approaching his table in a restaurant turned out to be looking for a restroom, not an autograph. But he had quickly become a celebrity in New Hampshire, besieged by autograph seekers the summer after his first term on the high bench. When a twelve-year-old girl stopped him in the supermarket one day, asking that he sign her chewing gum wrapper, he readily agreed, but asked why she wanted his autograph. "Because," she replied, "my mother says you might be famous someday."[82]

Inside the Court

Soon the justice was also drawing attention in Washington—to his extreme distress, on one occasion. As Souter told the story to his Concord friend Ronald Snow, he was walking home from the Court one night. "And this group of really tough-looking twenty-year-olds are coming right at me. And I say to myself, 'You dumb-dumb; you've done it now. You're going to end up in the hospital, if not worse.' And I thought, 'If I keep my head down and I sort of ease by, things will be okay.' And I did, and as I eased by, a guy said, 'Hey!' And I thought, 'Oh, my God.' And the hair on the back of my neck went up. I turned around and said, 'Yes?'—and they wanted my autograph!"[83]

At least by the end of his third term, Souter was also widely regarded as one of the high bench's intellectual leaders—easily the match for Antonin Scalia on the Court's right. Moreover, while Scalia's attack-dog opinion style and often scornful wit detracted from his obvious brilliance, permanently damaging his relationship and influence with several justices, Souter's quiet charm and humor had the opposite effect. Nor did he have difficulty poking fun at himself—and his at times convoluted opinion-writing style. In a skit for the annual law clerks' party in 1994, the justice read aloud a long-winded and tediously worded telegram to Ruth Bader Ginsburg, impersonating a Western Union clerk. Ginsburg listened patiently, cut out unnecessary verbiage in Souter's lengthy message, then telegraphed, "Happy Birthday, Mom." On the bench, Souter and Scalia would often be seen exchanging smiles and whispered pleasantries. But as it became clear that Souter not only was no Clarence Thomas but a decidedly more formidable jurisprudential opponent than initial doubts about his appointment suggested, Scalia appeared to grow increasingly frustrated with his colleague. Often, for example, he attacked Souter by name in his opinions—eighteen times in his *Kiryas Joel* dissent alone. Scalia also treated with apparent disdain Souter's penchant for British spellings, especially "enquire" rather than "inquire," regularly surrounding them with quotations when attacking his colleague's reasoning.

On rare occasions, Souter would respond in kind. Drawing in *Kiryas Joel* on Justice Cardozo's characterization of the dissenter as a "gladiator making a last stand against the lions," Souter agreed that Scalia's dissent was "certainly the work of a gladiator," but pointedly added that his colleague "thrusts at lions of his own imagining." The Scalia dissent embraced the nonpreferentialist construction of the establishment clause, accusing the Court of declaring the Satmar sect New York's established church. The "license" Scalia had taken in that characterization, Souter shot back, "was only one symptom of his inability to accept the fact that this Court has long held that the First Amendment reaches more than classic, 18th century establishments." Acceptance of Scalia's interpretation, Souter conceded, would make the Court's task easier. "But that," he asserted, "would be as blind to history as to precedent."[84]

Ordinarily, however, Souter good-naturedly deflected his colleague's jabs. Speaking for a plurality in a 1992 case, the justice drew on legislative history in construing a provision of the National Firearms Act. In an opinion concurring in the Court's judgment, Scalia reiterated his well-known disdain for such inquiries. Souter's response: "Justice Scalia upbraids us for reliance on legislative history, his 'St. Jude of the hagiology of statutory construction.' . . . The shrine, however, is well peopled (though it has room for one more) and its congregation has included such noted elders as Justice Frankfurter." (Souter was not alone. During Souter's first term, Justice Stevens took a more pointed, albeit private, jab at Scalia's opposition to judicial reliance on legislative history following Scalia's assertion in a dissent that 1982 amendments to the Voting Rights Act were adopted in response to the Court's decision in a case. "Sherlock Holmes, accompanied by a large, menacingly silent dog," Stevens wrote Scalia, "has just paid me a visit. He wanted me to tell him how you found out that the [amendments] were adopted in response to our decision in *City of Mobile*. Despite his inherently coercive interrogation, I refused to bark. The legislative history is still safely hidden in a locked cabinet.")[85]

Judicial scholars and the press regularly took note of Souter's growing influence on the Court, especially in the wake of the *Casey* decision reaffirming the essence of *Roe v. Wade*. In "Justice Souter Emerges," an important and perceptive 1994 profile for the *New York Times Magazine*, historian David Garrow drew on a variety of unattributed sources in concluding that the justice had been adamant from the beginning that *Roe* must not be discarded and also was the primary author of the *Casey* joint opinion.[86]

Garrow and others speculated about the possible reasons for Souter's increasingly liberal record following his first term. Off the record, some cited his close association with other justices, especially the jurist he had replaced. Journalists had frequently noted Souter's harmonious relations with his colleagues, for example, that he had spent his second Thanksgiving on the Court with Justice O'Connor and her husband. But most press attention, as well as the gossip of Court insiders, focused on Souter's growing friendship with Justice Brennan. Although retired, Brennan continued to maintain chambers at the Court. The two visited each other almost daily, and many wondered whether the elder justice, one of the most persuasive charmers ever to sit on the high bench, was subtly recreating Souter in his own image.[87]

Souter did regularly pay homage to Brennan. The two were Harvard law graduates, and in the fall of 1991, Souter gave a toast to his colleague at an event honoring Brennan sponsored by the Harvard Club of Washington. During his remarks, Souter extolled the justice's "greatness," referred to Brennan as "our great contemporary," and applauded his enduring impact on "our constitutional landscape today," adding, "The fact is that the sight and sound and thought of our contemporary world today is in great measure the reflection of Justice Brennan's constitutional perceptions."[88]

When Brennan died in 1997, Souter delivered an intensely personal eulogy at his friend's funeral mass. The justice, he said, had "made us members of a huge family by adoption, and when we were with him every one of us always felt like the favorite child." Souter was particularly poignant in describing his day-to-day relations with Brennan:

> I'd stick my head in his chamber door and he'd look up and say, "Get in here, pal," and when I was ready to go he'd call me pal again. He wouldn't just shake my hand; he'd grab it in both of his and squeeze it and look me right in the eye and repeat my name. If he thought I'd stayed away too long, he'd give me one of his bear hugs to let me know that I'd been missed. And he might tell me a few things that were patently false, which he thought I might like to hear anyway. He'd bring up some pedestrian opinion that I'd delivered, and he'd tell me it was not just a very good opinion but a truly great one, and then he'd go on and tell me it wasn't just great but a genuine classic of the judge's art. And I'd listen to him, and I'd start to think that maybe he was right. Maybe it was pretty good. And then, inevitably, I'd know it wasn't, but I'd still feel great myself. I always felt great when I'd been with Bill. I bet you did, too. . . .
>
> How do we say farewell to the man who made us out to be better than we were, and threw his arms around us in Brennan bear hugs, and who simply gave his love to us as the friends he'd chosen us to be? I can only say it the way I learned from him. When I'd been to see him in his chambers and it was time to go, I'd turn when I got to the door and look back. He'd say, "So long, pal," and I'd give him a wave and say, "So long, Bill."

Souter captured his feelings for Brennan most succinctly, however, in a PBS documentary that aired the previous year. "The Brennan mind," Souter said then, "has met its match in the Brennan heart. And in their perfect match I think lies the secret of the greatness of our friend."[89]

Justice Souter was nearly as solicitous of Harry Blackmun, the Nixon appointee who, like Souter, initially appeared to be developing the conservative record supporters of his nomination had anticipated, but beginning with his *Roe* opinion had become an increasingly liberal voice on the Court. On completing law school, Blackmun had applied unsuccessfully for a position with a prominent Boston firm for which Souter's Concord friend Bill Glahn worked at the beginning of his career. Glahn's law school roommate later clerked for Blackmun. When the justice learned of Glahn's connection with the Boston firm, he expressed disappointment at not landing a position there himself. Glahn later shared that story with Malcolm Perkins, one of the firm's senior partners. "Perkins looked up from his papers," Glahn has recalled, "and said in a very dry way, 'Tell him to reapply.'" Glahn told Souter the story; "David told Blackmun. And he got a big kick out of it. David had a great affection for Blackmun, [although] I think he was closer to Brennan."[90]

Even before the joint *Casey* opinion preserving the essence of *Roe*, Justice Blackmun had become reasonably confident that Souter would be no certain vote for the Rehnquist-Scalia-Thomas bloc on the Court. In a 1992 interview with law dean and judicial biographer James F. Simon, the justice said of Souter, "His vote is conservative, but it's not an automatic knee-jerk vote. He doesn't do what some of the others do: 'I agree with the Chief' or 'I agree with Scalia,' something like that. He may agree with them, but he has his own reasons for doing it. . . . I think this is good. And he's a very nice person."[91]

Like their colleagues, Blackmun quickly became a target of Souter's gentle wit. In the fall following *Casey*'s announcement, Souter favored the justice with a postcard depicting two men fishing, one in a boat, one wading. Its caption: "Roe v. Wade: the Great Western Fishing Controversy."[92]

In one letter to Souter, Blackmun recalled hearing as a child that a relative had been hanged years before in New Hampshire. That was all the incentive Souter required. The next day, he wrote his colleague that he was making "a direct inquiry" into the matter and furnished Blackmun with a copy of a letter he had written New Hampshire attorney general John Arnold. Soon, the justice produced a typescript of what he purported to be an 1897 article that had appeared in the *Granite Monthly*, as revised after New Hampshire's last execution in 1939. "From a purely informational standpoint," Souter reported, "the essay is an embarrassment of riches. You may not use that term in its entirety yourself, however, for the author describes the execution of not one, but six Blackmuns." The list included Esmerelda Blackmun, who poisoned her lover with a raspberry tart; Esmerelda's brother Jebediah "The Butcher" Blackmun, who decapitated several neighbors; and another relation nicknamed "The Hatchetman." Souter was "amaz[ed] . . . that none of this ever came up while your nomination to the Court was pending in 1970. The Press would have had a field day, and even if the information got generally known today, I can imagine some reporter casting a sinister light on the souvenir baseball bat that you have on display in your chambers. I guess you've just been lucky." The justice assured Blackmun, however, that neither he nor Attorney General Arnold "will do anything indiscreet to turn your luck around now."[93]

When Blackmun got to the account within the "article" of "a particularly vicious murderess" named Lydia Pinkham Blackmun, he quickly caught on to his colleague's joke, if he had not already. In the nineteenth century, Lydia Pinkham's herbal formula for "female complaints" had been a popular patent medicine. Blackmun wrote "Obviously invented" on the front page. "I am touched indeed by the fact that one of these relatives bears the name of Lydia Pinkham," he wrote Attorney General Arnold. "As a youngster, I well remember the advertisement of her Vegetable Compound which, I suppose, is still being peddled. There were jingles about her and the Compound which we used to sing in the third grade."[94]

But Souter was hardly penitent. When a New Hampshire prison inmate sent Blackmun an admiring letter, Souter speculated that the writer was probably "drawn to you by what he's heard up there at the prison about your family history." A postscript to one of Souter's summer letters to Blackmun from New Hampshire read, "The sight of the N. H. State Prison the other day reminded me of you and your family." After Blackmun's retirement, Souter noticed a certiorari petition from one Ricky Don Blackmon, petitioner in a capital case. "Another family branch accounted for," he wrote his colleague. "Your research on family dereliction proceeds apace," Blackmun promptly responded. "I am most impressed. It is well that I have taken retirement status."[95]

At a clerks' reunion dinner in May 1994, however, Souter would be the target of what he correctly suspected was "Blackmun's revenge." The clerk selected to make remarks that evening began on a serious note, observing that "the warmth and intimacy of this gathering is less a function of our relatively small numbers than of the intensity of the connection that each of us feel with Justice David Souter." Soon, however, the clerk launched into a history of the "New York branch" of the Hackett family, provided, he said, by the New-York Historical Society. "Very little of the news is good," a "researcher" had reported. "Indeed, if there is anything noteworthy about the Hacketts, it is the rather astonishing extent to which a single family could be responsible for so much mischief." "Poor Horatio Hackett" had spent most of his life in a mental institution. Initially, Horatio had showed great promise, but "was never the same after a grade-school spelling bee in which he survived to the final round only to lose by misspelling 'inquire' with an 'e.' (The winner was a young immigrant named Salvatore Scalia.)" Emmanuel Hackett "squandered his family's wealth on poorly conceived get-rich-quick schemes," including the purchase of hundreds of "brown three-piece suits" that proved impossible to sell and a yogurt factory about a century before that product's time. "Driven to ruin, Emmanuel spent the rest of his life on the street, wearing only the three-piece suits he had purchased and eating nothing but the yogurt he had been unable to sell (along with apples that passersby would toss to him, which he'd eat core and all). Emmanuel died young, long before he could have worn all his suits or eaten all his yogurt. It is not known what happened to the rest." And on it went. Souter provided Justice Blackmun a copy. "I hope," he wrote, "it will bring satisfaction to your vengeful soul."[96]

Souter and Blackmun obviously delighted in each other's company, visiting art galleries and occasionally having lunch together, with Souter usually walking to his colleague's chambers, apple and yogurt in hand. When historian David Garrow's profile of Souter appeared in the *New York Times Magazine*, Blackmun, subject of a 1983 piece in the same publication, expressed hope that his colleague was "not displeased," adding, "I learned a few things about you from this article!" "I'm sure you did learn a few things about me," Souter responded, "but possibly not as many things as you think." Souter realized that Garrow had been "very generous" to him, "to the point that one of my former clerks suggested to me that this would probably be a very good time to retire." Blackmun had recently retired from the bench. "Perhaps," suggested Souter, "we could share neighboring chambers." "You have an imaginative clerk," Blackmun rejoined. "There is an extra fine set of chambers down here, and if you take them, we would be immediate neighbors. I shall hold those chambers for you."[97]

Try as he might, however, the gregarious senior justice could not persuade his colleague to accept speaking or related engagements beyond those required to satisfy Souter's obligations as presiding justice over the First and Third appeals court circuits. Blackmun had long been active in the Aspen Institute's annual August Justice and Society Seminars in Colorado. He, Justice Brennan, and Justice Stevens had served as seminar moderators, and Blackmun hoped to persuade Souter to lead one of the sessions or at least attend the seminar. But his efforts would be in vain. Declining the Institute's initial invitation to participate, Souter wrote Aspen president David T. McLaughlin in September 1991, "I hope you will understand that for my part I would like to leave consideration of this for further on in my tenure on the Court. After one year, one has no real perspective on the right mix of court and summer work, and from what others have told me, my guess is it will take a good three years before a sense of the appropriate begins to dawn."[98]

Despite Souter's initial reaction, Justice Blackmun remained confident that his colleague "definitely is interested in something a couple of years from now. . . . He wants to have another summer by himself, but I tried to sell him on the idea that an August week in Aspen away from New Hampshire would be nice, too." Blackmun, as he himself conceded, was "unduly optimistic." In 1993, McLaughlin's successor, Alice H. Henkin, wrote Souter "what is becoming my annual letter of invitation to you to come to Aspen next summer and attend the Justice and Society Seminar" in whatever capacity Souter might prefer. In 1994, Blackmun urged his colleague to accept an invitation to participate in 1995, but again without success. On this occasion, Souter cited additional reasons "why Aspen is not for me." First, he wrote Blackmun, he needed "some period in the year when I can make a close approach to solitude. I spend July each year decompressing and seeing people throughout the month; when August comes it is time to withdraw as best I can." Second, he needed "the restorative power of New Hampshire. The restoration comes not only from the landscape and the air, though they play their significant parts, but from the people. Although I try not to see a lot of people in August, the ones I do see are by and large my neighbors, in a narrow or broad sense. I feel a strong need to be in New Hampshire for as much of the summer as I can manage it, and I would feel that I was cheating myself to head across country on what might be a regular annual basis."[99]

Nor was Souter's tenacity confined to the Aspen Institute. In 1992, he declined a Blackmun-arranged invitation to an engagement in the south of France. On several occasions, he politely but firmly refused to give the annual lecture at Manhattan's Central Synagogue honoring Jethro, Moses's father-in-law, who advised Moses to appoint judges over the people. "If I were to venture onto the lecture circuit even in a modest way," the justice wrote Blackmun, "I expect that an invitation from these people would be among the most enticing. As it is, I could go to my grave very happily without ever giving another lecture or speech between now and the point of expiration. Which means that for the time being at least, I am going to ask to be excused from even the nice lectures." That was in 1993. In 1996, after declining another invitation from the Jethro lecture committee, Souter succinctly captured the two justices' obvious personality differences in a note to Blackmun: "I know you get a kick out of these things, but you have to realize that God gave you an element of sociability, and I think he gave you the share otherwise reserved for me."[100]

On at least one occasion, though, Souter acquiesced to Blackmun's entreaties. In 1998, a class of Florida seventh-graders made a trip to Washington. One of their number was Lisa Blackmun Elsberry, daughter of Justice Blackmun's daughter Sally. Because her father was "not up to it and . . . Justice Souter is Lisa's favorite Justice," Sally Blackmun asked that Justice Souter meet with the class. Souter readily obliged, later writing his colleague that Lisa had "asked the ice-breaker question and that she and her classmates acquitted themselves very well with their interrogatories. They struck me as extremely nice and extremely smart, and I got a real kick out of them."[101]

In a law review tribute following Blackmun's 1994 retirement from the high bench, Souter spoke of the "uniquely heavy share of the Court's . . . burden" that had befallen his colleague in *Roe*'s wake. "Although the Justices divided seven-to-two [in *Roe*]," Souter observed, "the other members of the majority seem almost forgotten, and for over twenty years *Roe*'s center of gravity has been found squarely over Justice Blackmun's shoulders." But his colleague had hardly been intimidated by the experience, Souter noted. Instead, Blackmun had "read every critical letter to reach his chambers, though he could have ignored them easily" (as Souter probably would have, the justice might have added). He had also "chosen to sally out to deliver probably more speeches than any of his colleagues" and had breakfast every weekday morning with his clerks in the Court's public cafeteria, "albeit with a police officer at the next table, just in case." During Souter's difficult first term on the Court, Blackmun had walked into his new colleague's chambers to put his hand on Souter's shoulder and gently remind him "that everyone else had been through a first year, too." Souter would always remember, he concluded, "the magnanimity of Harry Blackmun's visions of the Court as it has been and as it ought to be . . . and the pat of his hand on my shoulder."[102]

Common Law Jurist

Justice Souter's affection for his elderly colleagues, and attention to their needs, was hardly unusual for a man who regularly displayed the same sort of concern for family, other friends, and parishioners at his New Hampshire congregation. A more likely key to his apparently growing liberalism on the Court after his first term was not the Svengali-like influence of a more senior

justice—even one with Justice Brennan's considerable powers of persuasion—
but instead his commitment to an essentially common law jurisprudence and
its emphasis on stare decisis. Like the second Justice Harlan, his jurisprudential mentor and another product of Oxford and its common law tradition,
Souter considers judge-made law inevitable and largely defined through a balancing of competing societal and individual interests. But the force of precedent is also a major part of the common law tradition. And whatever Souter's
personal political preferences, the civil liberties precedents he confronted on
the Supreme Court were essentially the expansive rulings of the Warren and
Burger eras. Unlike Scalia, Thomas, and, to a somewhat more attenuated degree, Rehnquist, Souter quickly proved unwilling to uproot or substantially
modify existing precedents—what he has repeatedly referred to in his opinions as "our settled law"—absent substantial justification.

To cite but a few examples over the justice's early tenure, Souter's acceptance of an expansive construction of the religious establishment clause in *Lee
v. Weisman*, the *Kiryas Joel* case, and *Rosenberger*, among other cases, rests on
precedent going back to the 1940s and *Everson v. Board of Education* (1947), as
well as the prayer and Bible-reading decisions of the 1960s. In the face of such
"settled law," a jurist of Souter's common law instincts was unlikely to—and
did not—embrace the efforts of the Court's nonpreferentialists to reject all
that past, especially when he found little in the First Amendment's final text
or history to support such a proposition or contradict long precedent. Nor
was it surprising that such a justice would question, as Souter did, Justice
Scalia's awkward attempt to dismiss the relevance of a host of religious liberty
precedents bearing on the proper constitutional standard to apply in the
Smith peyote case. Or that Souter would object, in *Casey*, to the dismantling
of *Roe v. Wade*, a precedent on which physicians, patients, and government
officials had based repeated decisions for nearly two decades. Or that he
would be reluctant to join decisions further limiting precedents excluding illegally seized confessions and evidence in habeas corpus and other proceedings. Writing with a clean slate, Souter might have assumed a conservative
stance in each of these issue areas. As all of his close Concord associates have
emphasized, however, he is a judicial conservative, not a political conservative, and thus has been unwilling to ignore "our settled law." Given the nature of that settled law, it is not surprising that he would develop a moderately liberal voting record. Or that he would continue in that pattern over the
succeeding years of his tenure.

5

Constitutional Nationalist

A S DAVID SOUTER ENTERED the second half of his first decade on
the Supreme Court, his record became part of the 1996 presidential
election campaign. Republican Senator Robert Dole, who would go
down to defeat in a challenge to President Bill Clinton that year, selected New
Hampshire governor Steven Merrill to chair his campaign. Both Dole and
Merrill were opponents of abortion rights. But in an appearance on *Meet the
Press* as the New Hampshire presidential primary approached, the governor
defended Souter's appointment to the Court by a GOP president, despite the
justice's reaffirmation of *Roe v. Wade*'s essence in the *Casey* plurality opinion.
Terming Souter the "kind of justice that I would hope President Dole would
appoint, from an intellectual point of view," Merrill professed "enormous respect" for Souter. While conceding that they disagreed on the abortion issue
"perhaps . . . more than I initially realized that we did," he also contended
that a court candidate's abortion stance should not be a "litmus test" for judicial fitness. Instead, said Merrill, "we ought to use a litmus test of quality and
integrity and intellectual substance, and certainly David Souter has those."
The governor also defended Dole's Senate votes supporting President Clinton's nomination of Ruth Bader Ginsburg and Stephen Breyer, two abortion
supporters, to the Court.[1]

Merrill's praise of the justice promptly drew the ire of Barbara Hagan,
president of New Hampshire's Right to Life organization and a supporter of
conservative commentator Pat Buchanan's presidential aspirations. Although
their organization was unable to endorse candidates and still maintain its tax-
exempt status, New Hampshire Right to Life leaders had told their members
that Senator Dole was not "baby-friendly." Scorning Merrill's comments,
Hagan argued that a "true" abortion foe would not appoint judges who did

not oppose *Roe*. "Either [Merrill] does not understand the significance of having a pro-life view when decisions come before the Court, which may affect life and death," asserted Hagan, "or he doesn't care."[2]

By that point, Justice Souter had attracted scholarly critics as well. Most pointed, perhaps, was a 1994 law review comment that derided "Justice Souter's 'Keep-What-You-Want-and-Throw-Away-the-Rest' Interpretation of Stare Decisis." Despite the justice's "almost evangelical" rhetorical commitment to precedent, author David K. Koehler's thesis ran, Souter had actually pursued a highly pragmatic approach to stare decisis. "By picking and choosing which precedent to follow and affording much heed to sociopolitical consequences, he allows and invites the 'rule of law' to be undermined and influenced by subjective decisions and value judgments." Koehler focused especially on the joint opinion in *Casey*, contending that it substantially diluted *Roe* and its progeny while at the same time professing strong allegiance to the doctrine of stare decisis.

Arguably, though, Koehler's criticism of Souter was based on an unduly wooden conception of stare decisis, a "straw man" version to which few jurists or scholars would adhere. Common law jurists such as Souter and the second Justice Harlan embrace stare decisis as necessary to the preservation of stability in the law and the legitimacy of judicial review. As noted earlier, however, they also view precedent as gradually evolving and adaptive, not inexorably fixed. As a practical matter, Koehler's emphasis on *Casey* as support for his thesis also seems particularly misplaced. Well before *Casey*, it had become clear that neither Justice O'Connor nor Justice Kennedy supported *Roe*'s strict trimester framework and that Kennedy might even join Rehnquist, Scalia, White, and Thomas in forming a majority to reject any meaningful abortion right entirely. Had Souter joined Justices Blackmun and Stevens in an opinion reaffirming *Roe*, and not merely its "essence," the three would have formed a bloc supporting a precedent at least six members of the *Casey* Court did not accept. Such an arrangement might well have pushed Kennedy into the ranks of the four justices who voted in *Casey* to reject *Roe* outright. In that context, Souter's efforts to secure a plurality opinion at least reaffirming part of *Roe*—actually a majority stance, given the willingness of Blackmun and Stevens to go further— arguably reflect a genuine commitment to preserving as much of the *Roe* precedent as possible, whatever his personal feelings regarding the constitutionality of abortion regulations, rather than the sort of pragmatic manipulation of stare decisis Koehler saw in Souter's opinions.

National Power and the States

Whatever Souter's conception of stare decisis, he has clearly kept faith with long-established precedent in a variety of cases involving conflicts between federal and state authority, related issues of governmental power, and property rights. Until the Rehnquist era, the modern Supreme Court had focused largely on personal, noneconomic rights, leaving the scope of property rights, governmental power over the economy, and the relationship between national and state regulatory authority almost entirely to the political branches of government. From 1936 to 1976, for example, the Court did not declare a single act of Congress unconstitutional on the ground that it interfered with the states' reserved powers. Federal and state laws regulating property interests were also considered largely immune from judicial review, and the few property rights in the Constitution were narrowly construed to impose few limitations on government authority.

During Chief Justice Rehnquist's tenure, however, a narrow majority has departed from this prevailing half-century tradition in a variety of ways. In a number of cases, the Court has invalidated congressional statutes on the ground that they interfere with state authority. The justices have also dramatically enlarged the scope of state sovereign immunity from private lawsuits, even preventing citizens, in all but a narrow category of cases, from suing states for damages as a way of forcing them to obey the provisions of supreme national law. But the majority has hardly been purely states' rightist in its rulings. Arguably, the justices have also attached an inordinately broad construction to the Fifth Amendment's takings clause, which forbids government to take private property without just compensation. With little precedent on which to base its approach, a majority has held that certain government controls over property amount to "regulatory takings" for which the state must provide compensation, thereby throwing into question many zoning, environmental, and related regulations enacted by elected legislators and local officials.

Justice Souter has typically dissented in such cases, assuming a nationalist position in constitutional conflicts between federal and state power, while also challenging the recent restrictions the Court has placed on state regulatory authority. Most notable have been his opinions in a number of important cases regarding the scope of congressional power over interstate commerce. In *Gibbons v. Ogden* (1824), the first Supreme Court construction of the commerce clause, Chief Justice John Marshall, the preeminent constitutional nationalist, described congressional authority over interstate commerce, as Justice Robert H. Jackson later put it, "with a breadth never yet exceeded." The power, asserted Marshall, extended to every form of commercial intercourse that "concern[ed] more states than one," was "complete in itself, [could] be exercised to its utmost extent, and acknowledge[d] no limitations, other than are prescribed in the constitution." Nor did Marshall include the Tenth Amendment's reserved state powers clause among the constitutional limitations on otherwise valid exercises of the commerce power. Instead, he declared, "If, as has always been understood, the sovereignty of Congress, though limited to specified objects, is plenary as to those objects, the power over commerce . . . among the several states, is vested in Congress as absolutely as it would be *in a single government.*" Finally, Marshall made clear that the remedy for perceived abuses of congressional authority that abridged no specific constitutional limitations on Congress's power lay with the political processes, not the courts. "The wisdom and the discretion of Congress, their identity with the people, and the influence which their constituents possess at election, are the sole restraints on which the people must often rely solely, in all representative governments."[3]

With the exception of one, now largely discredited period in the Court's history, a majority remained essentially faithful to the broad conception of congressional regulatory power outlined by Chief Justice Marshall—that is, until the Rehnquist era. The exception, of course, was the Court's so-called laissez-faire period (roughly 1888–1937), when a shifting majority of justices, generally committed to the notion that an economy free of government regulation would produce the most prosperous society, invoked expansive interpretations of state reserved powers under the Tenth Amendment and the doctrine of substantive due process, as well as narrow readings of the commerce clause and related congressional powers, in a vigorous, if uneven, campaign against government policies aimed at the excesses of the Industrial Revolution and the consequences of the Great Depression. When Congress used its regulatory powers to forbid child labor, impose minimum wage and maximum hour laws, or regulate the economy in other ways, the Court frequently declared the law at issue an unconstitutional invasion of the states' police powers. When, on the other hand, states imposed their own economic controls on business and industry, a majority typically held that they were "unreasonably" interfering with the "liberty" and "property" of employers, contrary to the Constitution's guarantee that government not take liberty or property without due process of law. State statutes, like federal laws, thus regularly ran afoul of substantive due process, repeatedly sacrificed on the altar of the Social Darwinian thought then dominating the Court.[4]

During Franklin Roosevelt's first term, a narrow majority continued its laissez-faire campaign, striking down a substantial number of New Deal statutes and state recovery measures as well. Following Roosevelt's reelection by a massive landslide in 1936, however, the president submitted to Congress his famous "Court-packing" plan. While his proposal was pending in Congress, the Court, in early 1937, underwent its remarkable "switch in time that would save nine," bringing an abrupt end to the laissez-faire era and a return of the judicial deference to congressional authority that Chief Justice Marshall had endorsed in *Gibbons*. Thereafter, economic regulations were also to be presumed constitutional and upheld against due process and equal protection challenges unless totally lacking in any "rational basis." Semantic distinctions drawn by the Old Court between "production" (subject only to state regulation) and "commerce" (subject to congressional control) were discarded, as were the dichotomies between "direct" and "indirect" effects on interstate commerce that the pre-1937 majority had put to essentially the same ends. Any activity that exerted an "actual" substantial effect on interstate commerce, whether individually or aggregated with others, was subject to federal control. The Tenth Amendment, moreover, was held to be "but a truism that all is retained which has not been surrendered, [with] nothing in the history of its adoption to suggest that it was more than declaratory of the relationship between the national and state governments as it had been established by the Constitution before the amendment or that its purpose was other than to allay fears that the new national government might seek to exercise powers not granted, and that the states might not be able to exercise fully their reserved powers." Finally, like Marshall, the post-1936 Court emphasized that effective restraints on the exercise of congressional commercial authority were to be sought in the electoral process and the political branches of government rather than through resort to the judiciary.[5]

For decades, the Court reaffirmed this extremely deferential posture toward congressional commerce power, indeed over the entire field of federal and state economic controls. The justices also made clear, in a 1946 federal Mann Act prosecution of a Mormon polygamist, that congressional control over interstate transportation was not limited to commercial contexts. A 1971 case explicitly held, moreover, that Congress need have only a rational basis for its conclusion that a particular local activity had a substantial effect on interstate commerce and thus was within the scope of congressional authority. In *National League of Cities v. Usery* (1976), a 5–4 Burger Court majority did strike down a congressional statute extending federal wage and hour controls to state and local governments and their employees. Justice Rehnquist declared for the *Usery* Court that federal interference with "traditional" or "integral" state government functions violated principles of state sovereignty, while dissenters scorned the Court's break with long precedent. When lower courts had difficulty distinguishing "traditional" state functions from others, however, Justice Blackmun defected from the *Usery* majority in *Garcia v. San Antonio* (1985), forming a new 5–4 Court to uphold federal power over state and local governments and reaffirm, yet again, Chief Justice Marshall's relegation of relief from alleged abuses of congressional power to the political process, not the courts. States, the *Garcia* majority concluded, were represented in Congress and did not require judicial intervention to protect their interests in disputes over national and state authority.[6]

Garcia, though, was hardly the Court's last word on the issue. In *United States v. Lopez* (1995), a 5–4 Rehnquist Court majority, per the chief justice, declared unconstitutional the federal Gun-Free School Zones Act, prohibiting the possession of firearms in schools. Defending the statute, government attorneys argued that possession of guns in schools may result in violent crime that in turn would affect the national economy through increased insurance costs and the reluctance of persons to travel to areas of the nation perceived as unsafe. They also cited the substantial threat that violence posed for the educational process and thus the nation's economic well-being.[7]

Such arguments seemed entirely consistent with over a half-century of commerce clause jurisprudence. But Chief Justice Rehnquist, in language strikingly similar to that of the laissez-faire justices on the pre-1937 Court, found the connection between gun possession in schools and the national economy at issue in *Lopez* entirely too remote and speculative, "indirect," he might have said. "To uphold the Government's contentions here, we would have to pile inference upon inference in a manner that would bid fair to convert congressional authority under the Commerce Clause to a general police power of the sort retained by the States." The chief justice conceded that "some of our prior cases have taken long steps down that road, giving great deference to congressional action." The "broad language" of such opinions, he added, had even "suggested the possibility of additional expansion." But the Court, declared Rehnquist, "decline[d] . . . to proceed any further."[8]

Rehnquist intimated that the statute might have withstood challenge had

Congress included a jurisdictional provision in the statute assuring that the offenses prosecuted in individual cases actually exerted a substantial effect on interstate commerce. But the law contained no such provision, nor had Congress made formal findings regarding the impact of gun possession in schools on interstate commerce. Missing entirely from the chief justice's opinion was the repeated assertion of earlier cases, including *Gibbons*, that the remedy for abuses of the commerce power was the ballot box, not lawsuits. Instead, he focused on judicial authority and the threat the challenged law posed for state sovereignty: "If we were to accept the Government's arguments, we are hard-pressed to posit any activity by an individual that Congress is without power to regulate."9

Concurring opinions varied in the degree to which their authors were willing to break with the modern Court's past, not to mention *Gibbons*. Justice Kennedy, joined by Justice O'Connor, emphasized the narrow scope of the Court's decision and the significant role states play in regulating school safety. Justice Thomas, on the other hand, appeared to embrace the thinking of the laissez-faire justices, decrying the unfortunate post-1936 drift of the case law "far from the original understanding of the Commerce Clause" and the resulting undue expansion of congressional power over essentially local matters.10

If Thomas saw in the pre-1937 laissez-faire Court's opinions a model for construction of the commerce power, Justice Souter clearly did not. One of the three *Lopez* dissenters to file an opinion in the case, Souter focused, as Justice Stevens put it in a separate dissent, on "the radical character of the Court's holding and its kinship with the discredited, pre-Depression version of substantive due process." To Souter, the laissez-faire era had been "one of the Court's most chastening experiences," and *Lopez* was a throwback to that period. The Old Court, he declared, had combined narrow, "highly formalistic notions of 'commerce'" and an "expansive conception" of substantive due process in subjecting federal and state socioeconomic legislation to exacting, typically fatal, judicial scrutiny. The folly of that era had long been established. If Congress had a rational basis for concluding that a statute regulated an activity "substantially affecting interstate commerce" and the regulatory means chosen were reasonably adapted to that end, the law at issue, according to repeated rulings of the Court, passed constitutional muster. Such deference to legislative judgment, asserted Souter, was "a paradigm of [the] judicial restraint" to which the majority so regularly professed commitment. But the *Lopez* decision and rationale "portende[d]," Souter feared, "a return to the untenable jurisprudence from which the Court extricated itself almost 60 years ago." The justice hoped that *Lopez* might be "only a misstep, its reasoning and its suggestions not quite in gear with the prevailing standard, but hardly an epochal case." He noted, however, that "not every epochal case [had] come in epochal trappings." When the New Deal Court first began dismantling the handiwork of the laissez-faire era in *NLRB v. Jones & Laughlin* (1937) and other post-1936 cases reasserting judicial deference to federal and state regulatory authority, the majority continued for a time to invoke the semantic standards of the Old Court, albeit invariably sustaining laws that earlier would have met almost certain defeat. "But we know," cautioned Souter, "what happened."[11]

Souter also filed a dissent for *Printz v. United States* and *Mack v. United States*, companion 1997 cases striking down a provision of the Brady handgun statute that required local police to conduct background checks on handgun purchasers pending completion of a national database. Two Montana sheriffs contended that the requirement imposed an unconstitutional obligation on state officials to enforce federal law; a 5–4 majority, per Justice Scalia, agreed. Finding no basis for the Court's decision in the Constitution's text, Scalia discovered adequate justification for the ruling "in historical understanding and practice, in the structure of the Constitution, and in the jurisprudence of this Court." A number of early congressional regulations, the justice conceded, had required state courts to perform certain duties, but those laws established, "at most," an original understanding that the federal government could impose obligations on state *judges*—obligations consistent with the supremacy clause mandate that state judges were "bound" to obey federal law. Those early statutes provided no support for the notion that Congress could commandeer state executive officers into enforcing federal laws. A law of the first Congress providing for the incarceration of federal prisoners in state jails merely "recommended," asserted Scalia, that states adopt enabling legislation, and passages from *The Federalist* essays that appeared to support the challenged Brady act provision only suggested that states might "consent" to assist the new national government in meeting its obligations. Scalia agreed that a number of recent federal funding measures had required state and local participation in implementing federal regulations. But such requirements, in Scalia's judgment, were more accurately described as conditions on the receipt of federal funds, which states were free to decline, than mandates to the states of the sort the Brady statute imposed.[12]

Justice Stevens argued in dissent that nothing in the Constitution's text permitted local police to ignore a command imposed by Congress pursuant to its commercial and other delegated powers. Many of the obligations the early Congress had imposed on state courts and their clerks, added Stevens, were essentially executive rather than judicial in nature. Thus, the majority's attempt to distinguish federal enlistment of state judges and other state personnel rested, in Stevens's view, "on empty formalistic reasoning of the highest order."[13]

Justices Souter, Ginsburg, and Breyer joined Stevens's dissent. But Souter found the cases "closer than [he] had anticipated" and indicated in a separate dissent that he would not have joined his colleague's opinion based merely on what he considered isolated early instances in which the federal government had employed "state officers for executive purposes." Instead, Souter based his vote primarily on Alexander Hamilton's assertion, in *The Federalist* No. 27, that under the supremacy clause and related constitutional provisions, state officials would become "auxiliaries" of the national government, obligated to assist it in the enforcement of its laws. No. 27, as well as passages in Hamilton's No. 36 and James Madison's No. 45, persuaded Souter that the national government was empowered "to require state [executive] 'auxiliaries' to take appropriate action."[14]

At the same time, Souter concluded that no similar federal authority extended to state legislatures. Five years earlier, he had joined the Court's decision and opinion in *New York v. United States* (1992). The *New York* Court struck down on state sovereignty grounds the "take-title" requirements of a 1985 congressional statute regulating the disposal of low-level radioactive waste. Under that provision, a state or regional compact that failed to provide for the disposal of all such waste generated in the state by a particular date was required, at the request of a waste generator or owner, to take title and possession of the waste and assume liability for all damages suffered by the generator/owner as a result of the state's failure to take prompt possession. The "choice" offered state legislatures to either accept ownership and liability or regulate the waste according to Congress's instructions, Justice O'Connor held for the Court, was unconstitutionally coercive and thus a violation of the Tenth Amendment.[15]

In his opinion for the *Printz* majority, Justice Scalia faulted Souter's dissent both for its reliance on *The Federalist* essays and its interpretation of *New York v. United States*. While describing state officials as "auxiliaries" in the enforcement of federal law, Souter had quoted the following passage from Hamilton's *The Federalist* No. 27: "The Legislatures, Courts, and Magistrates of the respective [states] will be incorporated into the operations of the national government, *as far as its just and constitutional authority extends*; and will be rendered auxiliary to the enforcement of its laws." If, Scalia reasoned, *The Federalist* essays were indeed evidence that the Constitution's framers intended state officials to be "auxiliaries" of the federal government, as Souter claimed, that federal power, according to No. 27's language, extended to state legislatures as well as state courts and executives. Yet the *New York* ruling, which Souter joined, had declared unconstitutional a law in which Congress had attempted to coerce state legislatures into adopting waste disposal legislation.[16]

To defend the consistency of his having joined the *New York* majority with his *Printz* dissent, Souter agreed that under the supremacy clause all state officials were auxiliary to the enforcement of federal law. He argued, however, that the supremacy clause operated on different state officers "in accordance with the quite different powers of their respective branches." The "core" power of executive officials was "to enforce a law in accordance with its terms," declared Souter; "that is why a state executive 'auxiliary' may be told what result to bring about." The "core" power of legislators, on the other hand, was "to make a discretionary decision on what the law should be; that is why a legislator [as *New York* had held] cannot be legally ordered to exercise discretion a particular way without jeopardizing the legislative power as such."[17]

Scalia scored Souter's rationale, arguing, among other things, that although legislatures were "perhaps . . . inherently uncommandable as to the outcome of their legislation," they were clearly subject to the dictates of their state constitutions, such as provisions for annual budgets and bans on laws permitting gambling. But Souter was equally skeptical of the Scalia reading of Hamilton's description, in *The Federalist* No. 27, of the role of state officers in carrying out federal law as, in Souter's words, "nothing more than a way of describing the duty of state officials 'not to obstruct the operation of federal law.'" Souter "doubt[ed] that Hamilton's English was quite as bad as all that. Someone whose virtue consists of not obstructing administration of the [federal] law is not described as 'incorporated in the operations' of a government or as an 'auxiliary' to its law enforcement. One simply cannot escape from Hamilton by reducing his prose to inapposite figures of speech."[18]

In her opinion for the *New York* Court, Justice O'Connor asserted that "the Federal Government may not compel the State to enact *or administer* a federal regulatory program." Justice Souter's efforts to distinguish *New York* from *Printz* may have been designed, therefore, to accommodate both his reluctance to break with a recent precedent, which he joined without opinion early in his tenure on the Court, and the tremendous volume of post-1936 rulings exalting national authority in the federal system. Whatever the explanation for the rather narrow nature of his *Printz* dissent, however, the justice would assume a strongly nationalist stance in later disputes over the scope of federal and state power.[19]

Invoking *Lopez* as well as Reconstruction-era cases narrowly construing congressional civil rights authority, *United States v. Morrison* (2000) struck down a provision of the federal Violence Against Women Act (VAWA). *Morrison* grew out of the complaints of Virginia Polytechnic Institute (VPI) student Christy Brzonkala that two VPI varsity football players, Antonio Morrison and James Crawford, had assaulted and repeatedly raped her within thirty minutes of meeting her. A campus committee found insufficient evidence against Crawford, and a senior administrator overturned Morrison's two-semester suspension after she concluded that his punishment was excessive in comparison with that imposed in similar cases. After learning through a newspaper that Morrison would be returning to campus the next fall, Brzonkala dropped out of the university and filed a federal district court suit against the athletes and VPI under a provision of the VAWA authorizing civil suits for the victims of gender-motivated violence. A divided panel of the Court of Appeals for the Fourth Circuit overturned the trial court's dismissal of the case, but the full Fourth Circuit reversed the panel, holding that Congress had power to authorize such suits under neither the commerce clause nor its power to enforce provisions of the Fourteenth Amendment. A 5–4 Supreme Court majority, speaking through Chief Justice Rehnquist, affirmed the Fourth Circuit.[20]

Attorneys for Christy Brzonkala and the United States argued that the VAWA was consistent with a long line of decisions upholding congressional power over local activities that substantially affected interstate commerce. In his opinion for the Court, the chief justice agreed that congressional statutes were entitled to "due respect" and should be invalidated only on a "plain showing that Congress has exceeded its constitutional bounds." Drawing on *Lopez* as "the proper framework" for analysis of the VAWA, however, Rehnquist declared that the congressional commerce power was "not without effective bounds" and that the challenged statute did not meet the standards announced in *Lopez* for determining the scope and limits to Congress's authority. First, under *Lopez*, the activity regulated must be "some sort of economic endeavor," observed Rehnquist. Second, the *Lopez* Court found it "important" that the gun control law at issue there included "no express jurisdictional element" limiting its reach to firearms possession that had an "explicit connection with or effect on interstate commerce." Finally, *Lopez* had underscored the "attenuated" connection between gun possession in schools and any substantial effect on the national economy. Like the law at issue in *Lopez*, Rehnquist concluded, the VAWA conformed to none of those criteria: gender-motivated violence was not an economic activity; the VAWA included no jurisdictional element requiring the crimes charged to be "sufficiently tied" to interstate commerce; and although the VAWA was based on numerous congressional findings regarding the serious effect of gender-motivated violence on victims and their families, the challenged law had only a tenuous connection to interstate commerce. "The Constitution," asserted the chief justice, again drawing heavily on the rhetoric of the laissez-faire era, "requires a distinction between what is truly national and what is truly local"; Rehnquist could "think of no better example of the [state] police power . . . than the suppression of violent crime and vindication of its victims."[21]

Rehnquist gave the petitioners' Fourteenth Amendment claims even shorter shrift. They had argued that pervasive gender bias in various state judicial systems—prejudice perpetuated by "an array of erroneous stereotypes and assumptions"—had resulted in insufficient state prosecution of gender-motivated crimes, an "inappropriate focus on the behavior and credibility of the victims of that crime," and "unacceptably lenient punishment" for defendants in such cases. The VAWA was thus needed "to both remedy the States' bias and deter future instances of discrimination in the state courts." In rejecting that rationale, Rehnquist cited the *Civil Rights Cases* (1883) and other decisions limiting congressional enforcement authority to state action infringing on Fourteenth Amendment rights. The VAWA, he asserted, was aimed not at state action, "but at individuals who have committed criminal acts motivated by gender bias." The chief justice also dismissed as "naked dicta" the assertions of six justices, in concurring opinions filed for *United States v. Guest* (1966), that Congress could punish private as well as state interference with Fourteenth Amendment rights.[22]

In his *Morrison* dissent, as in *Lopez*, Justice Souter, joined by Stevens, Ginsburg, and Breyer, scored the majority's rationale as inconsistent with the Court's construction of the commerce clause through most of its history and especially after 1936. Any activity that individually or in the aggregate substantially affected interstate commerce, he declared once again, was clearly subject to congressional control. "The fact of such a substantial effect," he added, "[was] not an issue for the courts in the first instance, . . . but for the Congress, whose institutional capacity for gathering evidence and taking testimony far exceeds ours." Enactment of a statute such as the VAWA indicated a congressional conclusion that the subject regulated had a substantial impact on interstate commerce; the role of the Court, asserted Souter, was not to assess the wisdom of that decision, but merely its "rationality." Unlike the gun control law at issue in *Lopez*, the VAWA was based on four years of hearings and voluminous documentation of the effect that violence against women had on interstate commerce. "The sufficiency of the evidence before Congress to provide a rational basis for [its] finding," Souter observed, "cannot be seriously questioned." Certainly, the findings on which the challenged statute was based were "far more voluminous" than the evidence found sufficient to uphold the ban on racial discrimination in places of public accommodation against commerce clause challenges to the 1964 Civil Rights Act. And in *Wickard v. Filburn* (1942), the New Deal Court had upheld federal regulation of the planting and consumption of homegrown wheat based on the "possibility" that such practices would substantially affect the interstate wheat market. "Supply and demand for goods in interstate commerce," the justice charged, drawing on congressional findings, "will also be affected by the deaths of 2,000 to 4,000 women annually at the hands of domestic abusers," as well as "by the reduction in the work force by the 100,000 or more rape victims who lose their jobs each year or are forced to quit. . . . Violence against women may be found to affect interstate commerce and affect it substantially."[23]

Souter had no doubt that the VAWA would easily have "passed muster" under the substantial effects test at any time between *Wickard* in 1942 and *Lopez* in 1995. With *Lopez*, however, the Court had begun according the deferential post-1936 version of the test only "nominal adherence," while actually supplanting its rational basis standard with a stricter formula of judicial review reminiscent of Old Court opinions. Whereas the pre-1937 Court was driven by laissez-faire zeal, the Rehnquist Court majority was motivated by "a new animating theory that makes categorical formalism [in the commercial field] seem useful again," "a conception of federalism" that attempted to draw clear-cut (and, in Souter's judgment, artificial) distinctions between commercial activities subject to congressional regulation and those within state control alone. But the *Garcia* case had repudiated the attempt to revive such a dual federalism doctrine in *Usery*, declared the justice, and the attempt of the *Lopez-Morrison* majority "to carve out inviolable state spheres within the spectrum of activities substantially affecting commerce was . . . just as irreconcilable with [Chief Justice Marshall's] explanation [in *Gibbons*] of the national commerce power as being as 'absolut[e] as it would be in a single government.'" There were limits to the congressional commercial authority, asserted Souter, but they were to be found in "politics, not judicial review."[24]

The record of the *Morrison* case made clear to Souter, moreover, the political judgment of the states regarding federal regulation of gender-related domestic violence. Thirty-six states and Puerto Rico had filed amicus curiae briefs in support of the challenged statute; only one state had joined the respondents. "It is, then, not the least irony of these cases," the justice observed, "that the States will be forced to enjoy the new federalism whether they want it or not." And that Antonio Morrison, as Justice Jackson remarked in a different context years before, had "won the states' rights plea against the states themselves."[25]

What Souter considered the relatively tentative nature of the Court's *Morrison* and *Lopez* opinions, combined with his confidence that the current "ebb of the commerce power rests on error," made the justice doubt that the majority stance would "prove to be enduring law." The Court embraced Old Court precedents "only at arm's length" and obviously had not overruled the many modern decisions broadly construing congressional power. Clarence Thomas, the Rehnquist Court's most extreme advocate of Old Court dual federalism, had even asserted that the substantial effects test—that is, the long-held principle that Congress could regulate intrastate, or local, activities that substantially affected interstate commerce—was "inconsistent with the original understanding of Congress's power and with this Court's early Commerce Clause cases"; but not even Justice Scalia joined Thomas's thesis. "The facts that cannot be ignored today," Souter concluded, "are the facts of integrated national commerce and a political relationship between States and Nation much affected by their respective treasuries and constitutional modifications adopted by the people. The federalism of some earlier time is no more adequate to account for those facts today than the theory of laissez-faire was able to govern the national economy 70 years ago."[26]

State Sovereign Immunity

Whatever the ultimate direction of the Rehnquist Court's commerce clause jurisprudence, its expansive construction of the doctrine of state sovereign immunity from lawsuit has resulted in raising a significant additional barrier to the enforcement of supreme national law. In a number of major rulings, the Court has held that individuals ordinarily are forbidden to sue a state for damages without the state's consent, even when such lawsuits are designed to secure a state's compliance with a valid congressional statute. As in *Lopez* and other commerce clause cases, Justice Souter has raised strenuous objections to such decisions.

The Court began expanding the scope of state immunity from suit in *Seminole Tribe of Florida v. Florida* (1996). Under the portion of the commerce clause covering trade with Indian tribes, Congress had enacted the Indian Gaming Regulatory Act (IGRA). Under the IGRA, tribes were allowed to conduct gambling activities, but only to the extent consistent with a valid compact between the tribe and the state in which the gaming was located. States in turn had a duty under the law to negotiate in good faith with a tribe in seeking to form a compact, and a tribe could sue a state in federal court to compel performance of the state's IGRA obligations. When Florida's Seminole tribe filed a federal court suit under the law, the state and its governor moved to dismiss the complaint on the ground that it violated Florida's immunity from suit in federal court. The district court denied the motion, but the Court of Appeals for the Eleventh Circuit reversed, holding that Congress had no power to abrogate state sovereign immunity under its commerce power. The Eleventh Circuit further concluded that *Ex Parte Young*, a 1908 ruling allowing injunction suits against officials claimed to be violating federal law, was inapplicable to the portion of the case involving Florida's governor.[27]

In the Constitution's only provision directly related to sovereign immunity, the Eleventh Amendment forbids federal courts to hear cases brought against states by citizens of other states or by citizens or subjects of foreign nations. But Supreme Court rulings have long expanded the doctrine of sovereign immunity beyond the Eleventh Amendment's language. In the controversial *Hans v. Louisiana* (1890), for example, the Court forbade federal suits brought against states by their own citizens. In a 1991 case, moreover, Justice Scalia, the Court's self-described preeminent constitutional textualist, declared the Eleventh Amendment "to stand not so much for what it says, but for the presupposition" that each state is sovereign and state immunity from suits by individuals is inherent in that sovereignty. Under that immunity, Scalia had held, Indian tribes could not sue states in federal courts.[28]

Drawing on such decisions and overturning a plurality's contrary judgment in *Pennsylvania v. Union Gas Co.* (1989), Chief Justice Rehnquist went further in his *Seminole Tribe* majority opinion: Congress lacked authority to authorize Indian tribes to sue states, even to enforce provisions of supreme national law. Such congressional abrogation of state immunity, declared Rehnquist, violated fundamental principles of federalism. Given the history surrounding adoption of the Fourteenth Amendment, the specific limitations it imposed on state power, and the express enforcement authority it conferred on Congress, the chief justice acknowledged that Congress could authorize private suits against states in Fourteenth Amendment cases. But the commerce clause, Rehnquist reasoned, did not impose explicit restrictions on the states; its language thus provided no basis for an exception to state immunity.[29]

In a sharply worded dissent, Justice Stevens dismissed the majority's decision and rationale as "profoundly misguided" and a "shocking . . . affront to a coequal branch of our Government," while scorning as "illogical" the Court's lone exception for statutes under Congress's Fourteenth Amendment enforcement powers. Stevens expressed hope, however, that "the better reasoning in Justice Souter's far wiser and far more scholarly opinion will surely be the law one day."[30]

Although characteristically more cautious than Stevens, Justice Souter, joined by Ginsburg and Breyer, filed one of the most thoroughgoing dissents of his career in *Seminole Tribe*. Reviewing in exhaustive detail the Eleventh Amendment's text, the history surrounding its adoption, and early judicial decisions construing its impact on state immunity from lawsuit, Souter contended that the amendment applied only to cases in which federal court jurisdiction rested solely on the citizen diversity clauses in Article III's grant of power to the national judiciary. The amendment had no relevance, he concluded, to cases brought against states under Article III's grant of authority to federal courts to hear suits arising under the U.S. Constitution and laws, whoever the parties. *Hans v. Louisiana* held that states were immune from suits brought by their own citizens, even in cases involving federal legal questions (such as the scope of the Constitution's contract clause, at issue in *Hans*). But the *Hans* Court had based the immunity recognized there, according to Souter, on general notions of sovereign immunity drawn from the common law rather than on the Constitution; *Hans* had not considered whether Congress could abrogate state immunity by statute. Congress, Souter argued, clearly could abrogate state immunity resting merely on common law principles. If, on the other hand, the immunity embraced in *Hans* were indeed based on the Constitution, as the chief justice claimed, Souter found it "hard to see how a State's sovereign immunity may be waived any more than it may be abrogated by Congress. . . . After all, consent of a party is in all other instances wholly insufficient to create subject-matter jurisdiction where it would not otherwise exist." Yet states regularly waived their immunity from suit.[31]

To Souter, the Court's attempt to constitutionalize common law immunity smacked of the *Lochner* era, when a majority elevated common law property and contractual rights to the level of permanent, paramount law "while regarding congressional legislation to abrogate the common law on those economic matters as constitutionally suspect." In fact, the *Seminole Tribe* majority appeared to him "to be going *Lochner* one better." At least, asserted Souter, the laissez-faire Court resorted "to some other written provision of the Constitution, like the Due Process Clause, the very object of which [was] to limit the exercise of governmental power," in restraining congressional authority. The only other time in which the Court had subordinated "the plain text of the Constitution to judicially discoverable principles untethered to any written provision" was Justice Samuel Chase's appeal to "principles of natural justice" in *Calder v. Bull* (1798). Later jurisprudence, the justice reminded readers, had "vindicated" Justice James Iredell's *Calder* dissent, "and the idea that 'first principles' or concepts of 'natural justice' might take precedence over the Constitution or other positive law 'all but disappeared in American discourse.'" The *Seminole Tribe* majority, Souter warned, should have avoided "reviv[ing] the judicial power to overcome clear text unopposed to any other provision, when that clear text is in harmony with an almost equally clear intent on the part of the Framers and the constitutionalists of their generation."[32]

Souter would have favored hearing the tribe's suit on the basis of *Ex Parte Young* alone. In his judgment, *Young* provided "a sensible way to reconcile the Court's expansive view of immunity expressed in *Hans* with the principles [of national supremacy over states] embodied in the Supremacy Clause and Article III." By permitting a *Young* suit against Florida's governor, the Court could avoid declaring a portion of the federal Indian gaming law unconstitutional; Souter found the majority's efforts to "skirt" application of *Young* in the case unconvincing. Because the majority was unwilling to take that approach, however, the justice recommended following *Union Gas* and its recognition of congressional power under the commerce clause to abrogate state immunity. At the same time, he supported *Hans* as a matter of stare decisis. Although erroneous, the *Hans* holding that states were immune from private suits raising federal legal issues had proved workable as a doctrine of federal common law subject to congressional abrogation. Through a plain statement of its intent to abrogate state immunity in a particular context, moreover, Congress could show proper respect for state authority, even though limiting the scope of state immunity from suit. Such a statement and "the political safeguards of federalism" were an adequate "check on congressional overreaching," asserted Souter, adding, "Today's abandonment of that approach is wholly unwarranted."[33]

Three years later, when another 5–4 majority extended *Seminole Tribe* to cases brought against states in their own courts, Justice Souter again dissented. In 1992, a group of Maine probation officers brought suit in federal district court, alleging state violations of the overtime provisions in the federal wage and hour law. When *Seminole Tribe* was decided, the district court dismissed the probation officers' suit. The plaintiffs then filed an action in a state court, but it dismissed the complaint, citing sovereign immunity, and Maine's highest court affirmed the trial court. The Supreme Court affirmed the state courts, holding that Congress had no power under the commerce clause to subject nonconsenting states to private damage suits in state court and that Maine had not waived its immunity.

Speaking for a 5–4 majority in *Alden v. Maine* (1999), Justice Kennedy held that state sovereign immunity was neither derived from, nor limited by, the Eleventh Amendment, but instead was a "fundamental aspect of the sovereignty which the States enjoyed before the ratification of the Constitution, and which they retain today . . . except as altered by the plan of the Convention or certain constitutional amendments." In exercising its commercial and other Article I powers, Congress could subject states to suit only on the basis of "compelling evidence" that the states were required to surrender that portion of their immunity as part of the constitutional design. Kennedy found no such justification in the framers' understanding of the Constitution, early congressional practice, early cases, or principles of federalism. The framers' silence regarding states' immunity from suit in their own courts persuaded Kennedy not that no immunity was intended, but that the doctrine was so firmly established that no one feared the new Constitution would modify it. The early Congress enacted no laws authorizing suits against nonconsenting states in state court; early Supreme Court cases offered further support for such immunity; and the respect to which states were entitled in the federal system did as well. Indeed, to Kennedy any congressional power to authorize suits against states in their courts arguably would have been even more offensive to sovereign immunity than such suits in federal court.

Thus, because *Seminole Tribe* had rejected congressional power to abrogate state immunity in federal suits, Congress clearly had no authority to abrogate such immunity in state courts. Otherwise, Kennedy concluded, Congress would exert greater power in state courts than in the federal judiciary.[34]

In his dissent, Souter, joined by Stevens, Ginsburg, and Breyer, first chided the majority for its developing immunity jurisprudence. *Seminole Tribe* had defended state immunity through a "contorted reliance on the Eleventh Amendment." But that amendment could be applied only to federal suits. Now, the *Alden* Court had "discern[ed] a simpler and more straightforward theory . . . a State's sovereignty from all individual suits [was] a 'fundamental aspect' of state sovereignty 'confirm[ed] by the Tenth Amendment.'" The early Supreme Court's holding in *Chisholm v. Georgia* (1793) that states could be sued in federal court by citizens of other states or foreign nations had provoked the Eleventh Amendment ban on such suits. Had the *Chisholm* Court, the justice wryly observed, only "understood a State's inherent, Tenth Amendment right to be free of any judicial power, whether the court be state or federal, and whether the cause of action arise under state or federal law," the Eleventh Amendment would hardly have been necessary. But Souter found no evidence supporting the majority's Tenth Amendment thesis or the version of sovereign immunity it embraced.[35]

In his *Seminole Tribe* dissent, of course, the justice had already discussed at length his position that sovereign immunity had its basis in the common law and thus could be abrogated by Congress under its lawmaking powers. But Souter could not resist responding to Justice Kennedy's contention in a portion of his majority opinion that trial by jury and the right against unreasonable searches and seizures also had common law origins yet could not be terminated by congressional statute. Those rights, declared Souter, his exasperation barely concealed, were "constitutional [and not subject to abrogation] precisely because they [were later embodied] in the Sixth and Fourth Amendments, respectively, while the general prerogative of sovereign immunity appears nowhere in the Constitution. My point is that the common law rights that were not enacted into the Constitution were universally thought defeasible by statute."[36]

The *Alden* majority's defense of an unalterable sovereign immunity as inherent in statehood was based, Souter contended, on natural law; yet he could find no "widely held" notion of that sort in the period preceding the ratification of the Constitution and adoption of the Tenth Amendment. At the time of the Constitution's framing, of course, there was "a tendency among the state constitutions to announce and declare certain inalienable and natural rights of men." But "no State declared that sovereign immunity was one of those [natural] rights. To the extent that States were thought to possess immunity, it was perceived as a prerogative of the sovereign under common law. And where sovereign immunity was recognized as barring suit, provisions for recovery from the States were in order, just as they had been at common law in England." Among leading participants in the ratification debate, Souter added, only Alexander Hamilton, in *The Federalist* No. 81, described sovereign immunity in language associated with natural law thinking.[37]

Souter was thus convinced that the majority had no historical basis for its defense of "a fundamental or inherent theory of sovereign immunity as limiting authority elsewhere conferred by the Constitution or as imported into the Constitution by the Tenth Amendment." Even were such an immunity implicit in the Constitution, however, the justice was equally certain its application was inappropriate in *Alden*. Drawing on Justice Holmes's opinion in a 1907 case, Souter reasoned that even "under the natural law theory, sovereign immunity may be invoked only by the sovereign that is the source of the right upon which suit is brought." Congress, not the state of Maine, was sovereign with respect to enforcement of the federal wage and hour law. A sovereign immunity claim thus provided no valid excuse for the Maine courts not to hear *Alden* "simply because the State is not sovereign with respect to the subject of the claim against it."[38]

Counsel for Maine had argued that the United States could bring a federal court damage suit against the state for violation of the probation officers' federal rights. But Souter considered that hardly an adequate alternative to private suit, especially given the national government's limited litigation resources. For him, there was "much irony in the Court's profession that it grounds its opinion on a deeply rooted historical tradition of sovereign immunity, when the Court abandons a principle nearly as inveterate, and much closer to the hearts of the Framers: that where there is a right, there must be a remedy."[39]

The Takings Clause

Just as Justice Souter sees in the Rehnquist Court's revival of dual federalism and expansion of state sovereign immunity similarities to the judicial creativity of the pre-1937 Court, he has been only somewhat less reluctant to embrace another decisional trend arguably reminiscent of the laissez-faire era: an expanding construction of the takings clause. The Fifth Amendment forbids the federal government from taking private property for a public purpose without just compensation, and that guarantee has long been held applicable to state and local governments through the Fourteenth Amendment. For many years, application of the takings clause was limited to situations in which government took actual title to private property or engaged in action having essentially the same effect. In *Pennsylvania Coal Co. v. Mahon* (1922), Justice Holmes concluded for a majority that government regulation of property would be "recognized as a taking" if the regulation went "too far." But even the Old Court seemed reluctant to give the notion of "regulatory takings" much of a reach, and the post-1936 Court was even more deferential to government in responding to takings claims. In 1987, a 5–4 majority even upheld a modern version of the statute struck down in the *Mahon* case.[40]

The year after Chief Justice Rehnquist moved to the Court's center seat, however, the justices began a significant expansion of the regulatory takings concept. *Lucas v. South Carolina Coastal Council* (1992), for example, upheld a challenge to that state's uncompensated refusal to allow a developer to construct beachfront housing that constituted a threat to the coastal environment or was built in an unsafe setting. Justice Scalia concluded for the *Lucas* Court that compensation was automatically required whenever government physically "invaded" private property or denied a property owner all economically beneficial or productive use of it. In *Dolan v. City of Tigard*, decided two years later, a 5–4 majority, speaking through the chief justice, struck down as an uncompensated regulatory taking a local planning commission's decision to permit a store owner to expand her building and pave the parking lot, but only if she dedicated a portion of the land for a pedestrian/bicycle path and a greenway designed to reduce flooding. Although conceding that the state clearly had legitimate interests in flood control and the reduction of traffic congestion, the majority found an insufficient connection between those interests and the contested easement. Evidence, not mere conclusion, was necessary to justify the commission's action.[41]

In *Phillips v. Washington Legal Foundation* (1998), Rehnquist again spoke for the majority in a takings case. At issue in *Phillips* was a state program under which the client funds of attorneys were put into a federally authorized pool of funds if they were unlikely to earn net interest income for individual clients after payment of service and related costs. Interest earned from the pool was then used to finance legal services for the poor. The chief justice concluded that the interest from the pool was the property of the clients, even though individually the income they would have earned would have been entirely offset by handling costs. But the majority remanded to the lower court the issue whether the program constituted a "taking" for which "just compensation" was required.[42]

In *Lucas*, Souter would have dismissed the writ of certiorari as having been improvidently granted, thus denying review, based on what he considered the trial court's "highly questionable" assumption that South Carolina had deprived Lucas of his entire interest in the beach property at issue in the case. In *Dolan*, he declined to join the broad dissent of Justice Stevens, the Court's most persistent critic of an expansive takings doctrine, who convincingly accused the *Dolan* majority of invoking the takings clause to resurrect the substantive due process analysis of the *Lochner* era. But Souter did file a brief dissent in *Dolan*, suggesting that the Court's approach seemed inconsistent with "the usual rule in cases involving the police power that the government is presumed to have acted constitutionally." And in *Phillips*, the justice, joined by Stevens, Ginsburg, and Breyer, attacked the majority's willingness to rule in the abstract only on the issue of whether the client fund pool at issue there amounted to "property." Instead, he argued, the lower court should resolve the property question "only in connection with what is a compensable taking," as the respondents would ultimately be entitled to relief only on a finding that the "property" in question had been "taken" without "just compensation." Souter thought it unlikely the respondents could prevail on those questions. Clients with funds in the pool, after all, were effectively barred from receiving any net interest on their individual funds. It might ultimately be concluded, therefore, that the program had not actually taken any respondent's property or that the "just compensation" required was "zero."[43]

Economic Due Process

Whatever Souter's doubts about the Court's expansion of the takings clause, and despite his warnings that *Lopez* and other cases subjecting congressional regulatory authority to meaningful judicial scrutiny smacked of a return to the laissez-faire era, he joined *BMW v. Gore* (1996), in which the Court arguably invoked economic due process, one of the Old Court's favorite weapons, for the first time since 1936. When Alabama physician Ira Gore learned that his "new" BMW sports sedan had been repainted prior to sale, he sued the distributor for damages. At trial, BMW acknowledged a company policy under which vehicles slightly damaged in manufacture or transportation were repaired and sold as new without notice to the buyer. A jury awarded Gore $4,000 in actual damages and $4 million in punitive damages—an appropriate figure, the plaintiff claimed, because BMW had sold a thousand repaired cars for more than they were worth. Refusing to allow punitive damages for sales in other states, the Alabama Supreme Court reduced the award by $2 million. A Supreme Court majority, speaking through Justice Stevens, found even that figure grossly excessive and thus contrary to due process.[44]

Somewhat ironically, given their participation in the recent "regulatory takings" decisions, Justice Scalia, joined by Justice Thomas, registered a vigorous dissent against any use of due process to review the substantive reasonableness of government actions. While stopping short of an outright rejection of substantive due process in the economic field, Justice Ginsburg, joined by the chief justice, also dissented, calling the majority's application of a "vague" due process concept an unnecessary and unwise intrusion "into territory traditionally within the States' domain," particularly in view of ongoing legislative efforts to impose limits on the size of punitive damage awards. But Justice Souter joined Stevens's majority opinion.[45]

Although upholding the jury awards at issue in several earlier cases, the Court had made clear in those opinions that awards of punitive damages must be reasonable. The *Gore* opinion was thus consistent with dicta in several recent cases, an important consideration for a jurist with Souter's strong commitment to stare decisis. Application of substantive due process to reverse actions in the courts themselves, moreover, arguably reflects less judicial intrusion into governmental decision making of the Old Court variety than use of the doctrine to strike down substantive legislation and executive enactments. Beyond that, Justice Souter's jurisprudence clearly includes acceptance of due process as an independent substantive as well as procedural restriction on governmental authority, rather than merely a sort of shorthand for rights stated elsewhere in the Constitution. Even so, the justice's stance in *Gore* is further evidence that he accepts meaningful judicial review of the reasonableness of government action even in the economic sphere, despite his general agreement with the thesis that the political arena, not the courts, should be the usual remedy for perceived misuses of government regulatory powers.[46]

By the end of his first decade on the high bench, Justice Souter's commitment to the economic precedents of the post-1936 Court had been firmly established. *BMW v. Gore* demonstrated his willingness to subject economic regulations to judicial standards of reasonableness, but arguably only in extreme cases; otherwise, he preferred leaving judgments about the wisdom of economic controls to the voters and their elected representatives. As we have seen, for example, he has been reluctant to join the Rehnquist Court's dramatic expansion of the takings clause as a significant limitation on government regulatory power. Most significant, he has embraced the post-1936 Court's broad construction of congressional authority, vigorously opposing the current majority's invocation of state sovereignty notions to trump national power in *Lopez* and other cases involving conflicts between federal and state power. He has been equally disdainful of the Court's recent expansions of the doctrine of state sovereign immunity, especially its use as a barrier to private lawsuits seeking state compliance with supreme national law. In short, as Justice Souter completed the first ten years of his tenure, his judicial record clearly reflected his commitment to constitutional nationalism.

6

Traditional Republican

In the fall of 2000, when David Souter began his second decade on the Court, the nation was in the final months of what was to become the closest presidential race in history. The justice's record had already become something of an election issue that year, although not as a Democratic weapon against the GOP. Instead, Souter was a target in the continuing efforts of the modern Republican Party's most conservative elements to purge the influence of the GOP's northeastern wing, with its traditional roots in the Civil War, abolition, and Reconstruction, and its moderately liberal positions on civil rights and other social issues.

With his Supreme Court record and historic roots, Justice Souter seemed to personify the traditional Republican. Thus, when Arizona senator John Mc-Cain launched his bid for the GOP presidential nomination and chose Souter's chief sponsor, Warren Rudman, as his campaign manager, fueling speculation that Rudman might become attorney general in a McCain administration, conservatives were alarmed. Fearful that Chief Justice Rehnquist, then seventy-five, might soon retire, the *Wall Street Journal* declared in a February 29 editorial on "Chief Justice Souter?" that conservatives were "alarm[ed] . . . when they hear that Mr. McCain would delegate his judge-picking to Mr. Rudman, the man who helped put liberal jurist David Souter on the high court." In his memoir, the *Journal* reminded readers, Rudman had taken "pride in recounting how he sold Mr. Souter to gullible White House chief of staff John Sununu as a confirmable conservative. Then they both sold the judge to President Bush, who wanted above all else to avoid a confirmation battle." Rudman's "Yankee Republican liberalism," in particular his outspoken disdain for the GOP's growing Christian conservative wing, "would be disastrous at Justice," the *Journal* predicted, "especially if Mr. Rudman repeated his Souter debacle." Yet Rudman had indicated in his memoir that "he suspected all along that Mr. Souter would never overturn activist liberal precedents," even recalling "a tearfully joyous embrace with Delaware Democrat Joe Biden after Mr. Souter had voted [in *Casey*] to reaffirm *Roe v. Wade*. 'You were right about him,' he quotes Sen. Biden as saying. 'Did you read that opinion? You were right!'" Senator McCain had dismissed as "hilarious" speculation that Rudman would become his attorney general; the Granite State senator, said the candidate, was not interested. And Rudman had recently told a reporter "he'd rather be ambassador to a warm climate." But, if asked, the *Journal* "doubt[ed] he'd turn it down."[1]

In a campaign speech the previous spring, Senator McCain had attacked Christian conservatives and called his opponent, George W. Bush, a "Pat Robertson Republican." But McCain, the *Journal* declared, was going to need those votes if he became the party's nominee and hoped to win in the fall election. "The earlier he starts reassuring them, the better would be his chances in November." The next president might have the opportunity to select as many as three justices, the paper noted; "Republicans can't afford any more Souters, much less three more."

In the wake of the *Journal* editorial, John Sununu, who had endorsed George W. Bush, the son of his former White House boss, for president, acknowledged "a lot of disappointment in where David Souter has ended up on the Court," adding, "I would have rather seen him as an ally of Justice Scalia." Of the *Journal*'s description of him as "gullible," Sununu, the ultimate politico, deadpanned, "I'm not sure I'd describe myself in that way." He insisted, however, that "there's no question that Sen. Rudman and Justice Souter himself tried to make the point that he was a true conservative," or that such New Hampshire conservatives as former governor Meldrim Thomson and Justice Stephen Thayer had assured him that Souter, in the words of the *Union Leader*, "would fit nicely with Bush's conservatism on abortion and other key issues." And what of Senator Rudman? "In spite of it all, he's a good friend. But I've always known that he was more liberal than he liked the world to think he was. . . . He's a good lawyer with a good legal mind, but I doubt he'll be appointed attorney general in a George W. Bush administration."[2]

Conservatives directed their criticism of Souter and his like-minded Supreme Court colleagues primarily at their positions in abortion and certain other civil liberties cases. But they also expressed alarm at the justices' expansive construction of Congress's regulatory powers under the commerce clause. Typical was an op-ed piece Harvard law professor Charles Fried wrote for the *Wall Street Journal* two weeks after the paper's editorial on the purported McCain-Rudman-Souter connection. As President Reagan's solicitor general, Fried had aggressively pursued that administration's campaign against Warren and Burger Court civil liberties precedents in the Supreme Court after Reagan's first solicitor general resigned rather than use that office—traditionally considered above politics—for what he considered unduly overt political ends. Failing to secure a Supreme Court appointment during the Reagan and first Bush presidencies, Fried took a seat on Massachusetts's highest court in 1995 but returned to Harvard in 1999.[3]

Fried had clerked for the second Justice Harlan, Souter's jurisprudential mentor. But the professor apparently did not share Harlan II's and Souter's deep respect for long-established precedent. Fried's *Journal* piece appeared the day after a 5–4 majority in *United States v. Morrison* (2000) had struck down the federal Violence Against Women Act (VAWA), holding that it exceeded congressional authority to regulate activities that substantially affected interstate commerce and ignored constitutional distinctions between national and state authority. In dissent, it will be recalled, Justice Souter, joined by Stevens, Ginsburg, and Breyer, scored Chief Justice Rehnquist's opinion as a throwback to the Court's long-discredited laissez-faire era. The political arena, not the courts, Souter argued, was the proper forum for those who believed that Congress was abusing its power and encroaching on state authority; that, at least, had been the teaching of numerous post-1936 precedents, not to mention Chief Justice John Marshall's opinion for the Court in *Gibbons v. Ogden* (1824), the first commerce clause case.[4]

Charles Fried obviously considered the political process an inadequate safeguard for state power in the federal system. Fried had been one of the lawyers for the winning side in the VAWA case. Writing in the *Journal*, he accused Souter and company of being "mired in a time warp." Had the Court upheld the law at issue, Congress would have been given "free rein" to pass any regulatory legislation it wished, whatever the traditional prerogatives of the states. "Given Congress's frequently demonstrated tendency to use the federal law as a billboard for whatever cause will attract national attention," declared Fried, "the Court's concern for the integrity of our constitutional structure is certainly warranted." Yet by their "refusal to accept the majority's attempt to breathe life into the federalism doctrine, the dissenters—who include some of the ablest minds on the court—have missed the opportunity to collaborate in fashioning a meaningful, yet practical, demarcation between the national and the local." In their "rearguard action," he asserted, "the dissenters write as if they were the students of [Harvard law professor and Supreme Court Justice] Felix Frankfurter defending the New Deal against devastation of the pre-1937 court and its 'nine old men.'" But in Fried's judgment, "There is no danger that we will return to those times when the court thought Congress lacked power to impose federal wage and hour laws or national labor laws."

Like Souter and his colleagues, the professor had no patience with the majority's recent expansion of state sovereign immunity against suits brought by private litigants seeking to secure state compliance with federal law. But he ultimately blamed Souter and company for that decisional trend. "In one [such] case [*Alden v. Maine* (1999)], state employees claimed to have been underpaid under the federal wage and hour laws." Fried thought it made no "sense" for the Court to say that Congress could impose wage and hour regulations on states, yet deny state workers the chance to sue to enforce their rights under federal law. "These nonsensical results can only have come about," he declared, "because the majority of the court lacked the confidence (or the votes) to simply say that the laws in question were an infringement of states' rights. Instead the court tried to achieve the same result through the back door, by preserving the laws but making their enforcement impossible. If the four dissenters were not mired in unyielding obstructionism, they would join with the majority to shape a more sensible federalism doctrine." For Souter, however, neither state sovereign immunity nor notions of state reserved powers largely rejected by the Court since 1936 limited otherwise valid exercises of congressional power, however "sensible" such use of federalism appeared to Professor Fried.

Bush v. Gore

When the Court became embroiled in the 2000 presidential election, Justice Souter's conservative detractors no doubt became even more convinced that his appointment to the high bench had been one of the worst miscalculations of the first Bush's presidency. That still hotly disputed contest has already been the subject of many books; my focus, therefore, is on Justice Souter's role in the lawsuit it spawned. The basic facts can be briefly summarized. Nationally, Vice President Al Gore garnered over a half-million more popular votes than his Republican opponent, George W. Bush. But the outcome of the election depended on the twenty-five electoral votes at stake in Florida. With Florida's electors, Bush would win 271 electoral votes, one more than the bare minimum necessary for victory. Without Florida, he would lose to Gore. The initial ballot count in Florida produced a margin of only 1,784 votes for Bush out of nearly 6 million cast; an automatic voting machine recount mandated for close elections reduced the Republican candidate's margin considerably. Further complicating the scenario: Bush's brother Jeb was Florida's GOP governor; the state secretary of state, the official with chief control over Florida's election returns, was also a Republican; and the punch-card balloting system used in a number of counties was fraught with difficulties, especially questions posed by "hanging" and "dimpled chads" on ballots.[5]

As allowed under Florida law, Vice President Gore asked for manual recounts in four counties. The recount began, but a state circuit court held that a seven-day statutory deadline for filing returns was mandatory and could not be extended; the secretary of state refused to include amended returns submitted after the seven-day deadline in the total vote count. After the circuit court upheld the secretary's action, Florida's supreme court, dominated by Democratic justices, reversed, extending the statutory deadline by twelve days and ordering the secretary to accept manual recounts submitted prior to the extended deadline. Professing uncertainty about the precise grounds for the Florida high court's ruling, a unanimous Supreme Court, in *Bush v. Palm Beach County Canvassing Board* (2000), vacated the lower court's judgment and remanded the case for further proceedings.[6]

While the *Palm Beach* case was pending in the Supreme Court, the Florida Election Commission certified the statewide results, declaring Bush the winner of the state's electoral votes. The next day, Al Gore filed a circuit court suit challenging the certification. Under Florida law, Gore had to allege a counting of illegal votes, or rejection of legal votes, sufficiently large to change the election outcome or place it in doubt. The circuit court concluded that Gore had failed to meet that burden, but the Florida Supreme Court partially reversed, ordering a manual ballot recount in Miami-Dade County and defining a "legal vote" as "one in which there [was] a 'clear indication of the intent of the voter.'" The Florida justices also ordered the circuit court to add a number of recounted votes in Miami-Dade and Palm Beach counties to the certified election results.

On December 9, a 5–4 U.S. Supreme Court majority granted George W. Bush's application for a stay of the Florida high court order. Treating the application as a petition for review, the majority also granted a writ of certiorari to review Bush's claims. On December 12, a 7–2 majority held, in *Bush v. Gore*, that the Florida Supreme Court's failure to establish specific standards for de-

termining voter intent violated equal protection. Under a "safe harbor" provision of federal law, the votes of a state's electors were to be considered "con-
clusive" and included in the national electoral vote totals if any dispute over
their selection had been finally resolved by the state at least six days prior to
the date established by law for the meeting and voting of electors. Because
the electors were to meet on December 18, that provision was scheduled to
expire at midnight. Citing the Florida legislature's desire to take advantage of
the safe harbor provision and the general pressure of time, a 5–4 majority refused to remand the case to Florida for adoption of appropriate recount standards and a continuation of the process. By that action, five justices gave the
election to George Bush.[7]

As Justice Souter made clear in his partial dissent for *Bush v. Gore*, he
thought the Court should not have reviewed either case or stopped the recount pending its review of *Gore*. During oral argument in the *Palm Beach*
case, Souter had suggested to Bush lawyer Theodore Olson that the proper
remedy would be to leave the dispute in Congress's hands. "Why," he asked,
"should the Court . . . be interfering in what seems to be a very carefully
thought out scheme [in federal law] for determining what happens" if Florida
sent the votes of the wrong electors to Congress? When the Court stopped
the recount while reviewing *Gore*, Souter, Ginsburg, and Breyer joined Justice
Stevens's dissent, including their colleague's assertion that "on questions of
state law, we have consistently respected the opinions of the highest courts of
the States. On questions whose resolution is committed at least in large measure to another branch of the Federal Government, we have construed our
own jurisdiction narrowly and exercised it cautiously. On federal constitutional questions that were not fairly presented to the court whose judgment
is being reviewed, we have prudently declined to express an opinion. The majority has acted unwisely." In oral argument for *Gore*, Souter and Breyer,
partly in a vain hope of securing Justice Kennedy's vote, appeared to offer an
approach to resolving the case that would provide something to both sides: a
decision that the indefinite nature of the Florida Supreme Court's mandate
violated the equal protection rights of voters, but a willingness also to allow
the recounts to resume once the state justices had established a proper
method for determining voter intent.[8]

The *Bush v. Gore per curiam* opinion overturning the Florida Supreme
Court's recount mandate addressed only the equal protection issue. But in a
concurring opinion, Chief Justice Rehnquist, joined by Scalia and Thomas,
endorsed other claims the Bush campaign had raised as well. Not surprisingly,

given the strong states' rights thrust of his judicial record to that point, the chief justice conceded that "in most cases, comity and respect for federalism compel us to defer to the decisions of state courts on issues of state law." Rehnquist hastily added, however, that the Constitution explicitly conferred on state legislatures the authority to determine the way states choose their electors and that *McPherson v. Blacker*, an 1892 case, had left the method of their appointment "exclusively" to state legislatures. Thus, any "significant departure from the legislative scheme for appointing Presidential electors present[ed] a federal constitutional question." Florida's statutory scheme reflected the state's wish to take advantage of the safe harbor provision of federal law, and the courts were obliged to ensure "that postelection state-court actions [did] not frustrate the legislative desire to attain [that] 'safe harbor.'" But by its action, the Florida Supreme Court had in effect created new law, superseding the electoral arrangement adopted by the state legislature and jeopardizing its wish to take advantage of the safe harbor provision.[9]

In separate dissents, Justices Stevens and Ginsburg rejected even the equal protection challenge to the Florida Supreme Court's ruling. But they joined all but the equal protection portion of Justice Souter's dissent; Justice Breyer joined the entire dissent, as well as filing one of his own. On the equal protection issue, Souter conceded that the Constitution did "not forbid the use of a variety of voting mechanisms within a jurisdiction, even though different mechanisms will have different levels of effectiveness in recording voters' intentions; local variety can be justified by concerns about cost, the potential value of innovation, and so on." Souter found "wholly arbitrary," however, the various rules for determining voter intent that, given the vagueness of the Florida high court's instructions to ballot counters, were being applied "to identical types of ballots used in identical brands of machines and exhibiting identical physical characteristics (such as 'hanging' or 'dimpled' chads)." At the same time, the justice saw "no warrant" for the Court's assumption that such problems could not possibly be overcome, and the recount completed, by December 18, the date set for the electors to vote. As he had intimated he might in oral argument, therefore, Souter recommended that the case be remanded to the Florida courts with instructions that they establish uniform standards "to be applied within and among counties when passing on such identical ballots in any further recounting (or successive recounting) that the courts might order." He pointedly added, "No showing has been made of legal overvotes uncounted, and counsel for Gore made an uncontradicted representation to the Court that the statewide total of undervotes is about

60,000. . . . To recount them manually would be a tall order, but before this Court stayed the effort to do that the courts of Florida were ready to do their best to get that job done. There is no justification for denying the State the opportunity to try to count all disputed ballots now."[10]

Souter gave short shrift, moreover, to other claims of the Bush campaign. Whatever the wishes of Florida's legislatures, he asserted, no state was required to conform to the safe harbor provision in order to have its electoral votes counted. Nor, in his judgment, had the state supreme court's construction of the state's election law been "so unreasonable as to transcend the accepted bounds of statutory interpretation, [thereby becoming] a nonjudicial act and producing new law untethered to the legislative Act in question." State law allowed a candidate to contest an election based on the "rejection of a number of legal votes sufficient to change or place in doubt the result of the election." But the law did not define what constituted a "legal vote," and the Florida Supreme Court had thus been obliged to look for the meaning of "legal vote" in a provision of state law dealing with damaged or defective ballots, a regulation stipulating that no vote was to be disregarded "if there [was] a clear indication of the intent of the voter as determined by [a] canvassing board." That approach and interpretation were obviously "reasonable," Souter declared. So, too, was the Florida court's conclusion that the "possibility" of a recount's changing the outcome of an election, or placing the results in doubt, rather than the "probability" the state trial court had required, was sufficient to justify the recount order. In Souter's judgment, the Florida Supreme Court had "engaged in permissible construction in determining that Gore had initiated a contest authorized by the state statute, and it proceeded to direct the trial judge to deal with that contest in the exercise of the discretionary powers generously conferred by [Florida statute on a state judge] to 'fashion such orders as he or she deems necessary to ensure that each allegation in the complaint is investigated, examined, or checked, and to provide any relief appropriate under such circumstances.' . . . Our customary respect for state interpretations of state law counsels against rejection of the Florida court's determinations in this case."[11]

In his dissent, Justice Stevens vehemently declared, "Although we may never know with complete certainty the identity of the winner of this year's Presidential election, the loser is perfectly clear. It is the Nation's confidence in the judge as an impartial guardian of the rule of law." Perhaps because of its harsh and accusatory tone, Justice Souter did not join any part of the Stevens opinion. Nor, despite their alliance on the proper approach to resolving the dispute, did Souter concur in Justice Breyer's entire dissent. Souter and Breyer were Harvard law school graduates; indeed, during a recent stroll through Harvard Square, a tourist had persuaded Souter to pose for a picture, then introduced his wife and son to "Justice Stephen Breyer"! But Breyer's *Gore* dissent, like Stevens's opinion, bristled with indignation, and the prudent Souter declined to join a section in which his colleague, drawing on Chief Justice Charles Evans Hughes's 1928 description of the infamous *Dred Scott* decision, warned that the *Gore* majority had "risk[ed] a self-inflicted wound—a wound that may harm not just the Court, but the Nation."[12]

Souter did concur, however, in a section of Justice Ginsburg's dissent in which she underscored the deference traditionally accorded state judicial constructions of state law and the rarity of instances in which the Court had "rejected [such interpretations] outright." Chief Justice Rehnquist's "casual citation" of three such cases in his opinion, Ginsburg pointedly observed, "might lead one to believe they are part of a larger collection of cases in which we said that the Constitution impelled us to train a skeptical eye on a state's portrayal of state law." Ginsburg was confident the chief justice "would be hard pressed . . . to find additional cases that fit the mold." Two of the cases Rehnquist had cited involved the "recalcitrance" of southern state high courts during the modern civil rights struggles. The Florida Supreme Court, she asserted, "surely should not be bracketed with state high courts of the Jim Crow South."[13]

Argument of the dispute in the Supreme Court had not been without its lighter moments, most notably at the expense of Joseph P. Klock Jr., attorney for Florida's secretary of state. At one point, Klock addressed John Paul Stevens as "Justice Brennan," who had died three years earlier and had not been on the high bench since 1990. Like the Harvard Square tourist, Klock next confused Justice Souter with Stephen Breyer, prompting the New Hampshire justice playfully to warn, "I'm Justice Souter—you'd better cut that out." Finally, Justice Scalia took preemptive action, explaining, "Mr. Klock—I'm Scalia," before asking the frustrated lawyer a question.[14]

Especially because seven of the nine justices had been appointed by Republican presidents, the Court's 5–4 decision in effect giving the election to George Bush provoked intense public outcry. Satirists had a field day. Editorial cartoonists depicted the five members of the majority as cheerleaders for the Bush "team." When Florida governor Jeb Bush promised to reform his state's ballot system, a late-night television host quipped, "Why fix the election system? Just fix the Supreme Court." The old saw that "the Supreme

Court follows the election returns" now read, "The election returns follow the Supreme Court." Unflattering parallels were also quickly drawn to the 1876 election, in which a party-line vote by members of a special electoral commission awarded disputed electoral votes in several states, and thus the presidency, to Republican Rutherford B. Hayes, who, like George W. Bush, had won fewer popular votes than his Democratic opponent. As a commission member, Republican Justice Joseph P. Bradley cast the deciding vote. Like other pre-Bush II presidential winners with fewer popular votes than an opponent, Hayes, quickly dubbed "His Fraudulency" by detractors, served only one term.

Participation in the case by Justices Scalia and Thomas, as well as an unfortunate election night remark by Justice O'Connor, added further fuel to the fire. Scalia's son Eugene was a partner in Gibson, Dunn & Crutcher, the Washington firm of Bush lawyer Theodore Olson, who would become solicitor general in the Bush administration; Virginia Lamp Thomas, wife of the justice, was working with the Heritage Foundation, an organization with close ties to the GOP, compiling the résumés of potential Bush administration appointees while her husband and his colleagues were deciding whether Bush would become president.[15]

Not surprisingly, given his regard for judicial decorum, Justice Souter would recuse himself from a 2001 boundary case New Hampshire brought against Maine, in which Granite State lawyers assumed a stance contrary to the position taken in a 1977 consent decree to which Souter had agreed as New Hampshire's attorney general. Later, he, Scalia, and Thomas also disqualified themselves from proceedings involving Napoleon Beazley, a young defendant sentenced to death for murdering the father of federal appeals court judge J. Michael Luttig during a car-jacking. Luttig had clerked for Justice Scalia and helped prepare Souter and Thomas for their Senate confirmation hearings. Scalia and Thomas ignored complaints, however, that they should recuse themselves in the Bush-Gore dispute.[16]

Justice O'Connor's reported election-night comment came to light only after the Supreme Court had issued its ruling in *Bush v. Gore*. During a cocktail party, she and her husband were watching election returns on television when CBS prematurely called Florida for Gore. At that point, according to *Newsweek*, the justice exclaimed, "This is terrible!" and complained to guests that the election was "over" because Gore had already carried two other swing states. "Moments later, with an air of obvious disgust," according to the magazine, "she rose to get a plate of food, leaving it to her husband to explain . . . [that] his wife was upset because they wanted to retire to Arizona, and a Gore win meant they'd have to wait another four years." Neither Justice O'Connor nor a Court spokesperson would comment on the article, but its authors claimed their story was based on information furnished by two witnesses.[17]

Coming from a Republican appointed to a seat on the high bench by the first President Bush, Souter's opposition to the *Bush v. Gore* majority decision to stop the Florida recount could hardly be claimed to carry any taint of partisanship. Nor, characteristically, was he at all inclined to carry on the debate beyond the bench. In January, seven justices played host to a conference with six Russian judges, who asked pointed questions about how a court could decide the outcome of a presidential election. Justice Breyer angrily told the visitors that the ruling was "the most outrageous, indefensible thing" in the Court's history; Justice Ginsburg asserted, "Here we're applying the Equal Protection Clause in a way that would delegitimize virtually every election in American history"; and Justice Kennedy, apparent author of the *Gore* Court's *per curiam* opinion, sought to defend the decision. Justice Souter, like Justice Thomas, declined to participate in the conference.[18]

On one occasion in the wake of the ruling, however, Souter would depart from his usual practice of confining his statements about the Court's work to the pages of his opinions. Although reputed never to grant interviews to reporters or scholars, the justice, as noted earlier, occasionally met with groups of young people. The previous November, he had participated in a discussion with high school students attending the National Youth Leadership Forum on Law in Washington. Although unable to touch on the pending Florida election dispute, he did comment on the Court's recent decision in *Santa Fe v. Doe* (2000), striking down on religious establishment grounds student-led prayer at high school athletic events. "In the Supreme Court," he said, "we have the U.S. Constitution to enforce, but the tough thing about the Constitution, and the reason cases come here, is because it doesn't use language with clear, hard edges. Although I am a religious person, I do not favor prayer at games because eliminating it doesn't prevent individuals from praying. When I was in school I never had official prayer before math class, but I can assure you, I prayed before each and every math test."[19]

Meeting with a group of students from the prep school Choate a month after *Bush v. Gore*, the justice lamented his failure to organize a majority for continuing the Florida recount. In *Planned Parenthood v. Casey*, he revealed, he had brokered a coalition with Justices O'Connor and Kennedy to preserve the essence of the *Roe* abortion decision; with "one more day—*one more day*," he told the students, he thought he could have persuaded Kennedy, though not O'Connor, to embrace his position in *Gore*. "It should be a political branch," not the courts, he said, "that issues political decisions." But he had run out of time.[20]

Souter's involvement in the election suits naturally drew comment in New Hampshire. Tom Rath and Bill Glahn had attended both rounds of oral argument. After the *Bush v. Gore* ruling was announced, Rath, a key figure in George W. Bush's New Hampshire campaign, emphasized that the justice had opposed the Court's decision to become involved in the case. "Having taken it," added Rath, "he tried to guide them through the thicket, . . . demonstrat[ing] the complexity of the issue and that it was not black and white." Souter, his friend further noted, avoided harsh rhetoric in his opinion; he realized that it "was not good to use language that was inflammatory or that deepened the division" in the nation. Martin Gross, a former Concord mayor and longtime friend of Souter's, largely echoed Rath's sentiments: "I think his opinion was the one that cut through the mess most effectively. In his usual fashion, he didn't get emotional about all this." U.S. Senator Judd Gregg, a former New Hampshire governor and another leader in the state's Bush campaign, expressed pleasure that Souter recognized the equal protection difficulties the Florida Supreme Court had posed.[21]

Even the Manchester *Union Leader's* editorial page editor Bernadette Malone Connolly, a frequent contributor to *National Review* and other conservative publications, paid Souter a backhanded compliment. "As Granite Staters," Connolly wrote, "we are relieved the unpredictable Justice David Souter of New Hampshire was one of the seven" justices who "stood tall . . . when they agreed with George W. Bush . . . [that] the Florida recounts . . . deny citizens equal protection under law." She also thought the justice "distinguished himself by being the only dissenter not to sign the unprofessional, highly partisan attack authored by Justice John Paul Stevens." But Connolly expressed regret that "Souter, unfortunately, could not bring himself to join the five-member majority opinion that effectively ended the recounting."[22]

Charles Douglas, Souter's former state supreme court colleague, was more pointed, using the occasion for a general critique of the justice's U.S. Supreme Court record. After the initial oral argument in the dispute, Douglas noted the paucity of precedent to guide the Court in reaching a decision, then suggested to the *Union Leader*, as the paper phrased it, that Souter "appear[ed] to be overly obsessed with precedent in cases that should be reexamined because they may [have been] wrongly decided." Recalling, apparently, the justice's dissents from rulings limiting the congressional commerce power and expanding state sovereign immunity from lawsuit, Douglas chastised the justice as "not a states' rights guy," adding, "He has not been with the majority in terms of giving more power to the states." Douglas was uncertain how that nationalist attitude might influence the justice's vote in *Bush v. Gore*. "David Souter may have trouble (deciding the Florida court overstepped its bounds), but he shouldn't. That is not the kind of thing he would have done himself; that would be too activist for him." Douglas also questioned the sincerity of his colleague's conservatism. "When I served with him he was being very conservative, but not in a philosophical sense. I think it was more he knew he had to be conservative to get where he wanted to get, but has been very liberal since he got there. Some of us have more of a philosophical conviction and aren't going to bend, and others bend when it's in their interest."[23]

Nationalism Revisited

Whatever Souter's ultimate motivation, he has continued in recent years to adhere largely to the constitutional approach he embraced during his first terms in Washington: a moderately liberal, strongly nationalist jurisprudence firmly grounded in a deep commitment to precedent, including those with which he apparently disagrees. In cases raising federalism issues, he has usually spoken for the Court in invoking the federal preemption doctrine to foreclose state regulations in areas of paramount national and, especially, international concern. Nor has the justice faltered in his reluctance to interfere with the exercise of state regulatory authority in ways that do not conflict with supreme national law. He joined the majority, for example, in a 2002 case refusing to extend the Rehnquist Court's expansive readings of the "regulatory takings" doctrine to "temporary" takings. He has also continued his firm opposition to the Court's expansive constructions of state sovereign immunity from private lawsuits brought against states to enforce federal law. Thus, when the Court, in a number of recent cases, upheld congressional abrogation of state immunity on the ground that the state action at issue was subject to heightened judicial review and a correspondingly broad congressional remedy, he joined the majority. When, for example, a 5–4 Court, in *Tennessee v. Lane* (2004), authorized disabled citizens to sue that state and a number of its counties for denying them convenient access to courthouses, the justice joined the Court's holding that access to courts is a fundamental right under the Fourteenth Amendment and that Congress has power to authorize such suits in a provision of the Americans with Disabilities Act (ADA) forbidding government agencies to exclude people, by reason of their disabilities, from the benefits of public services, programs, or activities. In a *Lane* concurrence, moreover, Souter not only reaffirmed his opposition to the Court's broad conception of state immunity, but also took aim at the courts' own history of "invidious discrimination" against disabled persons, declaring *Lane* "a welcome step away from the judiciary's prior enforcement of blunt instruments imposing legal handicaps."[24]

Search and Seizure

In civil liberties fields, the justice has remained somewhat more likely to side with government in criminal justice cases than in other areas, albeit less frequently so than in his early years on the Court. Most controversial, at this writing, of his more recent opinions for the Court rejecting a criminal justice claim was that filed for *Atwater v. City of Lago Vista* (2001), in which even Justice O'Connor, writing for herself and Souter's usual allies—Stevens, Ginsburg, and Breyer—registered a dissent. At issue was the authority of police to make a warrantless arrest for minor criminal offenses, such as the misdemeanor automobile seatbelt violation with which Atwater was charged. Hardly a model of professionalism, the arresting officer had verbally abused Atwater in the presence of her two young children, refused to allow her to take them to the nearby house of a friend (who fortunately soon arrived to take charge of the children), and took her to jail in handcuffs, where she was placed in a jail cell alone for an hour before being taken before a magistrate and released on bond. Charged with driving without her seatbelt fastened, failing to secure the children in seatbelts, driving without her license, and failing to provide proof of insurance, she ultimately pleaded no contest to the seatbelt offenses and paid a $50 fine, and the other charges were dismissed. When lower federal courts dismissed a federal civil rights suit she and her husband filed in the case, the Atwaters appealed to the Supreme Court.[25]

Justice Souter readily conceded that Atwater had been the victim of "gratuitous humiliations imposed by a police officer who was (at best) exercising extremely poor judgment." But he refused to conclude that Atwater's warrantless arrest violated the Fourth Amendment guarantee against unreasonable searches and seizures, as applied to the states through Supreme Court interpretation of the Fourteenth Amendment. Atwater had relied in part on the Fourth Amendment's common law roots and other historical materials to assert that the amendment was intended to permit warrantless misdemeanor arrests only in cases involving, or tending toward, violence. Based on his own succinct but copious review of such evidence, Souter rejected the petitioners' historical argument as "by no means insubstantial, [but] . . . ultimately" unpersuasive. "Small wonder, then," he added, "that today statutes in all 50 States and the District of Columbia permit warrantless misdemeanor arrests by at least some (if not all) peace officers without requiring any breach of the peace, as do a host of congressional enactments."[26]

Souter also rebuffed Atwater's fallback argument that custodial arrest should not be permitted "when conviction could not ultimately carry any jail time and when the government shows no compelling need for immediate detention." Were the Court to embrace such a balancing approach, Atwater "might well prevail," for her "claim to live free of pointless indignity and confinement," the justice observed, "clearly outweighs anything the city can raise against it specific to her case." But where police had probable cause to arrest—a matter undisputed in Atwater's case—Souter was unwilling to require "sensitive, case-by-case determinations of government need, lest every discretionary judgment in the field be converted into an occasion for constitutional review." Typically, officers were obliged to apply the Fourth Amendment "on the spur (and in the heat) of the moment." Judicial standards of reasonableness required in such settings, he reasoned, should be "sufficiently clear and simple to be applied with a fair prospect of surviving judicial second-guessing months and years after an arrest or search is made." The approach Atwater favored would frustrate that goal. Finally, the Court had no reason to suspect that the nation was faced with "anything like an epidemic of unnecessary minor-offense arrests." Asked for such evidence during oral argument, Atwater's counsel could cite only one comparable incident. "If an officer has probable cause to believe that an individual has committed even a very minor criminal offense in his presence," Souter concluded for the Court, "he may, without violating the Fourth Amendment, arrest the offender. . . . Atwater's arrest satisfied constitutional requirements."[27]

In dissent, Justice O'Connor urged adoption of a balancing approach in such cases and scorned the majority's exaltation of "administrative ease" over the Fourth Amendment's "express command" that every search and seizure be "reasonable." In the future, she feared, "a relatively minor traffic infraction may often serve as an excuse for stopping and harassing an individual." In O'Connor's judgment, the Court's *per se* rule posed "potentially serious consequences for the everyday lives of Americans" and "carrie[d] with it grave potential for abuse." Souter, however, had a ready response: "The dissent's own language (*e.g.*, 'may,' 'potentially') betrays the speculative nature of its claims. Noticeably absent from the parade of horribles is any indication that the 'potential for abuse' has ever ripened into a reality. . . . There simply is no evidence of widespread abuse of minor-offense arrest authority."[28]

Justice Souter was also the Court's spokesperson in *County of Sacramento v. Lewis* (1998), declaring the Fourth Amendment irrelevant and rejecting substantive due process claims raised in a case brought by the parents of a teenager killed when the motorcycle on which he was a passenger tipped over during a high-speed police chase and the youth was hit by the pursuing patrol car. A sheriff's deputy had given chase when the motorcycle's operator was spotted speeding and ignored the patrol car's flashing lights and the deputy's shouts. Critics have argued that the law enforcement interests that high-speed police chases serve typically are far outweighed by the fatal risks they create for public safety. But the justice found no constitutional violation: "[Deputy] Smith [and another officer were] faced with a course of lawless behavior for which the police were not to blame. They had done nothing to cause [motorcycle operator] Willard's high-speed driving in the first place, nothing to excuse his flouting of the commonly understood law enforcement authority to control traffic, and nothing (beyond a refusal to call off the chase) to encourage him to run through traffic at breakneck speed forcing other drivers out of their travel lanes. Willard's outrageous behavior was practically instantaneous, and so was Smith's instinctive response. While prudence would have repressed the reaction, the officer's instinct was to do his job as a law enforcement officer, not to induce Willard's lawlessness or to terrorize, cause harm, or kill."[29]

Early in his tenure, Souter had joined a majority in rejecting a lower court holding that police questioning of bus passengers constituted a *per se* seizure. But when the Court, in *United States v. Drayton* (2002), ruled that the pat down of two passengers by police in a drug interdiction effort was consensual, Souter, joined by Stevens and Ginsburg, dissented. The plain-clothes officers had gone through the motions of quietly and matter-of-factly asking passengers for permission to search their luggage or persons. But the bus driver had left the bus, and Souter had no doubt it had been clear to passengers that the bus trip would not resume until the police had completed their work. The language the officers had used, added the justice, invited the "reasonable inference . . . that the 'interdiction' was not a consensual exercise," that the police "would prefer 'cooperation' but would not let the lack of it stand in their way." In that setting, he declared, "no reasonable passenger" could have believed "he had any free choice to ignore the police . . . , only an uncomprehending one." Souter was unwilling to say that no search of bus passengers would be constitutional absent a warning they were "free to say no." But the circumstances in which the *Drayton* searches were conducted convinced him that more had been required of the officers "than a quiet tone of voice. A police officer who is certain to get his way has no need to shout." The justice also dissented in 2005, when a majority upheld the search of a trunk of a car stopped for speeding, based on a drug-sniffing police dog's reaction. "The infallible dog," he observed, "is a creature of legal fiction."[30]

As his New Hampshire Supreme Court record made clear, Souter had no difficulty with sobriety checkpoints designed to promote highway safety. In 2000, however, he joined the Court in striking down a drug interdiction roadblock scheme directed primarily at criminal law enforcement. When the Court, in *Illinois v. Lidster* (2004), upheld a highway checkpoint set up to obtain information from motorists about a recent hit-and-run accident at the same site, he joined a brief separate opinion in which Justice Stevens favored remanding the case for a lower court hearing on the reasonableness of the roadblock and the factual assumptions on which it was based. Moreover, when the Court has upheld suspicionless drug testing of high school students participating in athletics and other extracurricular activities, he has dissented. In short, he is willing to apply a somewhat more flexible Fourth Amendment standard when government searches serve other purposes than criminal law enforcement. But he has also favored limits on the degree of discretion allowed government in such cases.[31]

Other Rights of the Accused

The justice has also been skeptical of further restrictions on the exclusionary rule in Fourth Amendment cases. And when the Court, in *Dickerson v. United States* (2000), reaffirmed the constitutional underpinnings of the *Miranda* restrictions on police interrogation of suspects, striking down a federal law restricting *Miranda's* application, Souter joined the majority. In a 2004 case, the justice spoke for the Court in overturning a two-step interrogation scheme in which police first questioned a suspect without benefit of the *Miranda* warnings, obtaining incriminating statements, then, after a twenty-minute break, read her the warnings, secured a signed waiver, confronted her with her earlier unwarned statements, and got her to repeat her confession. "The reason that question-first is catching on" as an interrogation technique, Souter pointedly observed, "is as obvious as its manifest purpose, which is to get a confession the suspect would not make if he understood his rights at the outset." Joined by Stevens and Ginsburg, he also dissented that term when the Court upheld the trial of a convicted felon on an illegal firearms posses-sion charge, based on a pistol located as a result of statements the suspect made without benefit of the *Miranda* warnings. "In closing their eyes to the consequences of giving an evidentiary advantage to those who ignore *Miranda*," he asserted, "the majority adds an important inducement for inter-rogators to ignore the rule in that case."[32]

Early in his Supreme Court tenure, Souter had concurred in the Court's de-cision upholding the admission of victim impact statements in capital sen-tencing hearings. Even so, he has joined decisions limiting application of the death penalty and opinions favoring further restrictions on its use. He had not yet joined the Court when *Penry v. Lynaugh* (1989) upheld the execution of the mentally retarded. In *Atkins v. Virginia* (2002), however, he joined the majority when it overturned *Penry*, citing a growing national consensus against such executions. He also joined a 2005 opinion increasing the mini-mum age (at the time of an offense) at which young offenders can be sub-jected to the death penalty from sixteen to eighteen.[33]

The justice has favored close scrutiny of governmental authority in other criminal justice cases as well. In *Kansas v. Hendricks* (1997), he joined Justice Breyer's dissent when a majority rejected double jeopardy challenges to a statute that permitted the civil commitment of individuals who were likely, as a result of "mental abnormality" or "personality disorder," to engage in "predatory acts of violence," as applied to a convicted pedophile shortly be-fore he was to be released from prison. In a related area, the justice joined the Court's 2003 decisions upholding versions of "Megan's laws," statutes requir-ing the registration of sexual offenders and named for a child sexually as-saulted and murdered by a neighbor with prior sex offenses against children about which her parents had no knowledge. In one of the cases, *Smith v. Doe*, the Court held that the regulation at issue there was nonpunitive and thus its retroactive application did not violate the *ex post facto* guarantee. Souter con-curred only in the Court's judgment in that case, which he considered a close one. For him, "the fact that the Act use[d] past crime as the touchstone, prob-ably sweeping in a number of people who pose no real threat to the commu-nity, serve[d] to feed suspicion that something more than regulation of safety is going on; when a legislature uses prior convictions to impose burdens that outpace the law's civil aims, there is room for serious argument that the ulterior purpose is to revisit past crimes, not prevent future ones." In his judgment, indications of the law's punitive character were roughly equal to those related to its civil aims. Only "the presumption of constitutionality normally accorded a State's law" prompted him to give the government "the benefit of the doubt in close cases like this one."[34]

9/11 and Civil Liberties

When the Court in 2004 handed down its first decisions growing out of the tragedy of September 11, 2001, Souter also proved to be one of the justices most skeptical of Bush administration assertions of virtually unlimited presidential authority over suspected terrorists. In *Rasul v. Bush* (2004), he joined Justice Stevens's 6–3 majority opinion upholding the right of foreign nationals to raise federal habeas corpus challenges against their detention by American authorities at the U.S. Naval base in Guantánamo Bay, Cuba, an area over which the United States had acquired "exclusive jurisdiction and control" via a 1903 lease agreement with Cuba. He joined Stevens in dissent, moreover, when a 5–4 majority, per Chief Justice Rehnquist, overturned on narrow jurisdictional grounds the holding of the U.S. Court of Appeals for the Second Circuit in New York that the indefinite detention without a hearing of Jose Padilla, suspect in an al Qaeda "dirty bomb" plot, violated Padilla's due process rights. Because Padilla was being held at the Charleston, South Carolina, Naval brig, Rehnquist reasoned, the federal court in New York had no jurisdiction to review the case. Emphasizing that Padilla was in Charleston only because the U.S. military, at the direction of Secretary of Defense Donald Rumsfeld, had moved him there from his initial detention site in New York, Stevens contended that Rumsfeld was Padilla's actual custodian for habeas corpus purposes and rebuked the Court for avoiding a ruling on the merits of Padilla's claims. "Unconstrained Executive detention for the purpose of investigating and preventing subversive activity," exclaimed the justice, "is the hallmark of the Star Chamber."[35]

In the case of Yaser Esam Hamdi, another U.S. citizen detainee at Charleston, a plurality, per Justice O'Connor, agreed that Congress had authorized the detention of enemy combatants in the narrow circumstances of Hamdi's imprisonment but concluded that a citizen held in the United States as an "enemy combatant"—and thus, under a number of precedents, subject to trial by a military tribunal—had a due process right to be given notice and some sort of "fair opportunity" to contest the factual basis for that designation before a "neutral decisionmaker." Only Justice Thomas, defending an extremely deferential conception of presidential war powers, contended in dissent that Hamdi could be confined without any hearing, simply on the basis of his designation by the administration as an enemy combatant. In a somewhat surprising coalition, Justice Scalia, joined by Justice Stevens, contended in another dissent that because Congress obviously had not exercised its constitutional power temporarily to suspend the habeas corpus privilege, citizens such as Hamdi had the right to be tried for their crimes in a court—or released from custody.

In his dissent, Justice Souter, joined by Justice Ginsburg, cited legislation indicating that citizens could be detained only on the basis of clear congressional authorization. No federal statute, in his judgment, provided such authorization. The justice conceded that "in a moment of genuine emergency, when the Government must act with no time for deliberation, the Executive may be able to detain a citizen if there is reason to fear he is an imminent threat to the safety of the Nation and its people." But such an "emergency power of necessity," he added, "must at least be limited by the emergency"; Hamdi had been a detainee for over two years. As no statute authorized Hamdi's detention, no criminal charges had been brought against him, and the government had failed to show that the detention conformed to the laws of war, Souter favored remanding the case for Hamdi's release. To provide a Court majority, however, he joined the plurality in ordering a remand for the purpose of at least giving Hamdi the chance to establish that he was not an enemy combatant and thus entitled to trial in the civilian courts or release. At the same time, the justice stressed that his joining the plurality did not mean that he agreed "that the Government could claim an evidentiary presumption casting the burden of rebuttal on Hamdi [to establish that he was not an enemy combatant] . . . or that an opportunity to litigate before a military tribunal might obviate or truncate enquiry by a court on habeas."[36]

Privacy Rights

Souter has also remained committed to substantive due process, particularly the approach outlined in the second Justice Harlan's dissent in *Poe v. Ullman* (1961). In 1997, he concurred in the Court's decisions to uphold Washington and New York statutes prohibiting assisted suicide. In a separate opinion, however, he traced the history of the Court's use of due process as a basis for judicial recognition of unenumerated substantive rights and defended Harlan's *Poe* formula, which Souter characterized as a "common-law method" that "call[ed] for a court to assess the relative 'weights' or dignities of the contending [state and individual] interests." That approach, Souter, like Harlan, Frankfurter, and others before him, insisted, did not allow judges to draw on their personal predilections. Instead, the "values" to be weighed were confined "to those truly deserving constitutional stature, either to those expressed in constitutional text, or those exemplified by" the nation's traditions. Nor would a court be justified in striking down a law on substantive due process grounds merely because there was a reasonable resolution of the competing governmental and individual interests at odds with that reflected in the challenged regulation. "It is only when the legislation's justifying principle, critically valued, is so far from being commensurate with the individual interest as to be arbitrary or pointlessly applied that the statute must give way." The difficulty with the discredited pre-1937 Court's application of substantive due process in economic cases, he added, was that the *Lochner* line of cases "routinely invoked a correct [balancing] standard of constitutional arbitrariness review," yet gave it an "absolutist implementation." Applying Harlan's approach to the assisted suicide statutes, Souter concluded that the state's interests in "protecting terminally ill patients from involuntary suicide and euthanasia, both voluntary and nonvoluntary," were sufficient to bar judicial intervention, at least at that point. "While I do not decide for all time that respondents' claim [to assisted suicide] should not be recognized," he added, "I acknowledge the legislative institutional competence as the better one to deal with that claim at this time." Consistent with the joint opinion he helped write in *Casey*, however, he also joined the Court in striking down a state ban on so-called partial-birth abortions.[37]

Souter was not on the Court when a 5–4 majority in *Bowers v. Hardwick* (1986) upheld a state sodomy statute as applied to homosexuals. But he joined without opinion Justice Kennedy's opinion for the Court in *Romer v. Evans* (1996), invalidating on equal protection grounds a Colorado constitutional amendment that prohibited all legislative, executive, or judicial action designed to protect homosexuals from discrimination based on sexual orientation. He also concurred without opinion in Kennedy's 6–3 majority opinion in *Lawrence v. Texas* (2003), which drew in part on a growing state legislative consensus against sodomy laws to overrule *Bowers* and uphold a substantive due process right of consenting adults to engage in sodomy in the privacy of the home. Justice O'Connor concurred only in the Court's judgment, preferring to rest her vote on the more narrow contention that a sodomy law directed only at homosexuals—the type at issue in *Lawrence*—violated equal protection. But Souter joined Kennedy in recognizing a broad due process right, despite Justice Scalia's assertion in dissent that the ruling had daunting implications for the future of laws forbidding same-sex marriages and many other sorts of restrictions on private consensual sexual activity involving adults.[38]

In his *Poe* dissent, Justice Harlan had emphasized that the Connecticut contraceptive ban at issue there extended to married persons and thus to a legally recognized sexual relationship. But he refused to "suggest that adultery, homosexuality, fornication, and incest are immune from legal enquiry, however privately practiced," for they were "intimacies which the law has always forbidden and which can have no claim to social protection." Even so, Harlan also embraced an evolving conception of individual rights and the permissible scope of government regulatory authority. Justice Souter's willingness to join the *Lawrence* majority, therefore, may have turned largely on the growing national consensus against sodomy laws. As Justice Kennedy indicated in the Court's opinion, half the states prohibited sodomy when *Bowers* was decided. By *Lawrence*, that number had been reduced to thirteen, and only four states enforced their laws solely against homosexuals.[39]

Justice Souter is obviously aware of the dangers to judicial legitimacy an expansive conception of substantive due process poses. In *Troxel v. Granville* (2000), a majority struck down a state law permitting a court to grant visitation rights whenever such an order might serve a child's best interests, as applied to an order granting paternal grandparents, following their son's death, greater opportunity to visit his children than their mother considered appropriate. In a plurality opinion, Justice O'Connor characterized the challenged statute as "breathtakingly broad" and parents' interest "in the care, custody, and control of their children [as] perhaps the oldest of fundamental liberty interests recognized by this Court." Souter concurred only in the Court's decision to uphold a lower court finding that the law was unconstitutionally broad on its face, not the invalidation of its application to Granville, the children's mother. "I would say no more," he declared. "The issues that might well be presented by reviewing a decision addressing the specific application of the state statute by the trial court . . . are not before us and do not call for turning any fresh furrows in the 'treacherous field' of substantive due process."[40]

The Religion Clauses

In religious liberty and establishment cases, Souter has remained committed to a broad construction of the First Amendment, consistent with long precedent. Souter was part of the majority that, in 2004, dismissed on standing grounds the claim of atheist lawyer Michael A. Newdow that daily recitation of the pledge of allegiance to "one nation under God" in his daughter's public school classroom violated the Constitution. During oral argument, the justice asked Newdow, who was arguing his own case, whether the recitation had become in practice "so tepid, so diluted, so far, let's say, from a compulsory prayer that in fact it should be, in effect, beneath the constitutional radar." Had the Court reached the merits of the case, however, it is quite likely that Souter, at least in the public school setting, would have considered affirmation of a "nation under God" contrary to the establishment clause. During oral argument for *Newdow*, for example, he told Newdow at one point, "I will assume that if you read the Pledge carefully, the reference to 'under God' means something more than a mere description of how somebody else once thought. The republic is then described as being under God, and I think a fair reading of that would be: I think that's the way the republic ought to be conceived, as under God. So I think there's some affirmation there. I will grant you that."[41]

Not surprisingly, the justice did join the majority in *Santa Fe v. Doe* (2000), striking down as unduly influenced by school officials, and thus contrary to the establishment clause, student-initiated prayer at public school athletic events. The next year, the Court, speaking through Justice Thomas in *Good News Club v. Milford Central High School* (2001), struck down a public school's refusal to allow a Christian club for young children to meet on school property after hours, although secular groups were given access. Souter dissented. He had joined the Court in *Lamb's Chapel v. Center Moriches School District* (1993), rebuffing a school district policy granting after-hours access to most groups but refusing to allow a church to use school facilities for a religious-oriented film on family values and child rearing. But Souter saw constitutionally significant differences between *Lamb's Chapel* and *Good News*. Given the overwhelmingly religious nature of the Good News Club's programs, he thought it "beyond question that Good News intends to use the public school premises not for the mere discussion of a subject from a particular, Christian point of view, but for an evangelical service of worship calling children to commit themselves in an act of Christian conversion." The film series at issue in *Lamb's Chapel*, moreover, was open to the general public and directed at an adult audience, whereas the Good News program was aimed exclusively at elementary school children as young as six, an especially impressionable age group. Souter was equally concerned about the appearance of public endorsement of religion the Good News arrangement created, particularly as its meetings began immediately following the end of the official school day. "There is a good case," asserted the justice, "that Good News's exercises blur the line between public classroom instruction and private religious indoctrination, leaving a reasonable elementary school pupil unable to appreciate that the former instruction is the business of the school while the latter evangelism is not."[42]

The justice has also been a vigorous opponent of the Court's increasingly accommodationist stance in recent cases involving government aid to parochial schools. Under *Lemon v. Kurtzman* (1971), the prevailing ruling for many years, laws affecting religion were to have a secular purpose and primary effect that neither advanced nor harmed religion; nor were they to create an excessive entanglement between church and government. *Lemon* has never been formally rejected, but a Rehnquist Court majority has substantially weakened its requirements. In *Agostini v. Felton* (1997), a majority overturned two Burger-era precedents and upheld a New York scheme under which teachers paid with public funds provided remedial education to disadvantaged children in parochial schools. Speaking for the majority, Justice O'Connor concluded that the Court "no longer presume[d] that public employees will inculcate religion simply because they happen to be in a sectarian environment." Nor would the "pervasive monitoring" long held to constitute excessive church-state entanglement in violation of the *Lemon* test be required in such cases. In fact, O'Connor concluded that the excessive entanglements prong of the *Lemon* establishment test would no longer be an independent standard for determining establishment violations in parochaid cases. Instead, evidence of excessive entanglement would merely be one of three criteria used to decide if a government aid program had the primary effect of advancing religion: whether the aid at issue resulted in governmental indoctrination, whether the challenged program defined its recipients by reference to religion, and whether aid created an excessive church-state entanglement. Nothing in the record, observed O'Connor, indicated that unannounced monthly visits by government supervisors would be inadequate to assure that public employees funded under the program inculcated no religious values.[43]

In a dissent joined by Justices Stevens, Ginsburg, and Breyer, Justice Souter conceded that *Aguilar v. Felton* (1985), one of the precedents being overturned, had placed undue emphasis on the excessive church-state entanglement that state monitoring of such programs would create to avoid establishment problems. He contended, however, that the programs at issue in the 1985 cases abridged two establishment principles rooted in long precedent: "The State is forbidden to subsidize religion directly and is just as surely forbidden to act in any way that could be viewed as religious endorsement." The program at issue in *Agostini* violated both those principles, he asserted, and thus had the primary effect of unconstitutionally aiding religion. By assuming financial responsibility for a school's secular instruction, the state in effect subsidized its religious functions as well. In addition, public school teachers providing instruction in a religious institution "might inadvertently (or intentionally) manifest sympathy with the [school's] sectarian aims to the point of using public funds for religious educational purposes." Such an arrangement, he added, also created "a symbolic union of church and state that tended to convey a message to students and to the public that the State supported religion."[44]

Souter's *Agostini* dissent hardly blunted the accommodationist trend on the Court in parochial school aid cases. *Mitchell v. Helms* (2000) affirmed an arrangement in which federal funds were distributed to state and local agencies, which in turn used the funds to loan educational materials and equipment to public and private schools, including religious institutions. Over many years, the Supreme Court had required government to be neutral toward religion in the parochaid field, with governmental neutrality meaning that assistance to religious schools must have a primary effect that neither advanced nor inhibited religion. Speaking for a plurality in *Helms*, however, Justice Thomas, joined by Rehnquist, Scalia, and Kennedy, gave the neutrality concept a very different meaning: if eligibility for assistance depended on neutral, secular criteria that neither favored nor disfavored religion, and the aid provided was also secular, neutral, and nonideological, a program was neutral toward religion and did not violate the establishment clause—even if the aid at issue went directly to religious institutions and some portion of the assistance was diverted to religious uses. Thomas came close to asserting, moreover, that such neutral distribution of assistance alone immunized a program from establishment challenge.[45]

In a concurrence, Justice O'Connor, joined by Justice Breyer, scored what she termed the "unprecedented breadth" of the plurality's approach. The

Court, she insisted, had never before held that an aid program was constitutional solely because assistance was distributed on the basis of neutral, secular criteria. Nor could she accept the plurality's apparent willingness to approve some diversion of aid to religious uses. She refused to presume, however, that the religiously neutral materials at issue in *Helms* would inevitably be used to inculcate religious values, and she concluded that the evidence developed to support the contention that they actually had been utilized to promote religion was *de minimis* at best.

In his *Helms* dissent, Souter, joined by Stevens and Ginsburg, took issue with both the plurality and O'Connor, but especially with the plurality's rationale. Thomas and company, asserted the justice, assumed that the evenhanded distribution of aid to secular and religious institutions satisfied the government neutrality requirement and thus answered any establishment challenge. They also concluded that the actual diversion of aid to religious purposes, at least if relatively limited in scope, "[did] not matter." For the plurality, "there [was thus] nothing wrong with aiding a school's religious mission; the only question is whether religious teaching obtains its tax support under a formally evenhanded criterion of distribution. The principle of no aid to religious teaching [long demanded by the Court's decisions] has no independent significance." Souter would have no part of such reasoning. Nor was he impressed with the plurality's assertion that "a school's pervasively sectarian character" should have no bearing on a determination "whether aid to the school [was] likely to aid its religious mission." To Souter, that issue was "simply a matter of common sense: where religious indoctrination pervades school activities of children and adolescents, it takes great care to be able to aid the school without supporting the doctrinal effort. This is obvious." Yet the plurality had condemned such inquiries "as a remnant of anti-Catholic bigotry." The justice found the plurality's position not only illogical, but particularly ironic, as at least one of the parties and many religious groups that had filed amicus briefs in the case supported the no-aid construction of the establishment clause. "In rejecting the principle of no aid to a school's religious mission," the justice declared, "the plurality is attacking the most fundamental assumption underlying the Establishment Clause, that government can in fact operate with neutrality in its relation to religion. I believe that it can."[46]

Souter dissented again in *Zelman v. Simmons-Harris* (2002), when the Court upheld an Ohio tuition voucher plan for the Cleveland, Ohio, school district, even though 96 percent of the students participating in the program during the 1999–2000 school year attended religious schools. Speaking for the 5–4 majority, Chief Justice Rehnquist emphasized that the program distributed assistance without reference to the participants' religion and that the aid reached religious schools entirely as a result of the private choice of parents, who decided whether their children would attend religious schools, nonreligious private schools, or public schools. Any incidental advancement of a religious message, declared Rehnquist, was attributable to aid recipients, not government officials, whose role ended with the distribution of the funds.[47]

Noting that the challenged scheme was designed to provide adequate alternatives to Cleveland's failing public school system, Souter conceded that "if there were an excuse for giving short shrift to the Establishment Clause, it would probably apply here." But for him, "there [was] no excuse. Constitutional limitations are placed on government to preserve constitutional values in hard cases, like these." Quoting from his *Agostini* dissent, Souter asserted that "constitutional lines have to be drawn, and on one side of every one of them is an otherwise sympathetic case that provokes impatience with the Constitution and with the line. But constitutional lines are the price of constitutional government."[48]

Characterizing the recent Court's disregard for *Everson v. Board of Education* and its progeny as an exercise in "doctrinal bankruptcy," the justice first took issue with the majority's conclusion that the program at issue was neutral toward religion. To reach that judgment, the Court had considered not only the voucher provisions, "but . . . every provision for educational opportunity" in the district. "The illogic is patent. If regular, public schools (which can get no voucher payments) 'participate' in a voucher scheme with schools that can, and public expenditure is still predominantly on public schools, then the majority's reasoning would find neutrality in a scheme of vouchers available for private tuition in districts with no secular private schools at all. 'Neutrality' as the majority employs the term is, literally, verbal and nothing more." Only in that way, he asserted, could the Court "gloss over the very nonneutral feature of the total scheme covering 'all schools': public tutors may receive from the State no more than $324 per child to support extra tutoring (that is, the State's 90% of a total amount of $360) . . . whereas the tuition voucher schools (which turn out to be mostly religious) can receive up to $2,250." The justice also disputed the majority's notion that participants in the program had a true choice among schools. Secular private schools could accommodate few students, there was no evidence that they had many open seats, and those with higher tuitions than the maximum provided under the voucher system could afford to accommodate only a few voucher students. Thus, "the only alternative to the public schools" was religious private schools. "The criterion is one of genuinely free choice on the part of the private individuals who choose," he declared, "and a Hobson's choice is not a choice, whatever the reason for being Hobsonian."⁴⁹

Even if he had agreed with the majority's assumptions about "neutrality" and "private choice," Souter could not have joined the Court's decision. Here, he declared, the majority offered not even a "pretense that substantial amounts of tax money are not systematically underwriting religious practice and indoctrination." Yet, such a scheme violated every objective of the constitutional ban on religious establishments: respect for freedom of conscience, which James Madison thought would forbid even "three pence" of a citizen's taxes going to the support of religion; the imperative of saving the church from government corruption, such as the Cleveland program's requirement that participating schools not discriminate on the basis of religion in their policies; and protection against the political strife that government support of religion inevitably provoked. "The reality is," he sadly concluded, "that in the matter of educational aid the Establishment Clause has largely been read away. True, the majority has not approved vouchers for religious schools alone, or aid earmarked for religious instruction. But no scheme so clumsy will ever get before us, and in the cases that we may see, like these, the Establishment clause is largely silenced. I do not have the option to leave it silent, and I hope that a future Court will reconsider today's dramatic departure from basic Establishment principles."⁵⁰

The justice has also remained skeptical about the Court's dilution of the free exercise clause. In *Employment Division v. Smith* (1990), the Oregon peyote case, a majority held, it will be recalled, that all religious practices must conform to drug laws and other religiously neutral, generally applicable regulations. In the wake of *Smith*, Congress enacted the Religious Freedom Restoration Act (1993), requiring application of the compelling interest standard whenever government interfered with religion. But stressing the ultimate authority of the courts, not Congress, to construe the Constitution's meaning, a majority, per Justice Kennedy, reaffirmed *Smith* and struck down RFRA in *City of Boerne v. Flores* (1997). In a brief dissent, Justice Souter pointed out that the *Smith* doctrine had never been subjected to briefing and argument, even in *Smith*, urged such a review, and again expressed doubt about the rule's "precedential value . . . and entitlement to adherence."⁵¹

Gay Rights, the Boy Scouts, and Freedom of Association

Souter again dissented, however, when the Court, somewhat ironically given *Smith*, held that First Amendment associational rights trumped a state civil rights law. At issue in *Boy Scouts of America v. Dale* (2000) was the BSA's decision to fire an openly gay assistant scoutmaster despite a New Jersey public accommodations provision prohibiting discrimination on the basis of sexual preference. Citing, among other things, portions of the Scout Oath and Law obliging scouts to be "morally straight" and "clean," the chief justice concluded for a 5–4 majority that the BSA's philosophy included opposition to homosexuality and that requiring the Scouts to include gays in their membership would significantly impair the group's expression of that viewpoint.[52]

Justice Souter joined a scathing Stevens dissent ridiculing the evidence on which the Court based its conclusion. But in a separate dissent, Souter felt obliged to clarify one observation Stevens had made. His colleague had noted what Souter termed the "laudable decline in stereotypical thinking on homosexuality." Characteristically, Souter thought it important to point out that "the right of expressive association [did] not, of course, turn on the popularity of the views advanced by a group that claims protection. Whether the group appears to this Court to be in the vanguard or rearguard of social thinking is irrelevant to the group's rights. I conclude that BSA has not made out an expressive association claim, therefore, not because of what BSA may espouse, but because of its failure to make sexual orientation the subject of any unequivocal advocacy, using the channels it customarily employs to state its message. . . . No group can claim a right of expressive association without identifying a clear position to be advocated over time in an unequivocal way. To require less, and to allow exemption from a public accommodations statute based on any individual's difference from an alleged group ideal, however expressed and however inconsistently claimed, would convert the right of expressive association into an easy trump of any antidiscrimination law." In some future case, the justice added, a group might make an adequate contention that an individual member's presence would "so modify or muddle or frustrate the group's advocacy as to violate the expressive associational right." In such a case, a state's antidiscrimination law would be obliged to yield. Souter made it clear, however, "that our estimate of the progressive character of the group's position will be irrelevant to the First Amendment analysis if such a case comes to us for decision."[53]

In most free expression and association contexts, Justice Souter has remained committed to a broad construction of the First Amendment. In *National Endowment for the Arts v. Finley* (1998), the Court, per Justice O'Connor, upheld a federal statute requiring the NEA to take into consideration general standards of "decency and respect" for diverse American beliefs and values in reviewing grant applications. Senator Jesse Helms and other congressional conservatives had waged a successful campaign for adoption of the provision in the wake of a controversy over photographs that appeared in two NEA-funded art exhibits. But O'Connor rejected contentions that the regulation, on its face, was an overbroad interference with First Amendment freedoms or unconstitutionally vague. The provision, she observed, simply added a number of factors to be considered in the review process; it did not preclude grants for projects found to be "indecent" or "disrespectful." Moreover, when the government acted as patron rather than regulator, its officials enjoyed wide latitude in the exercise of their discretion, especially as decisions based on subjective criteria were inevitable in the arts-funding context. For the same reason, declared O'Connor, "the consequences of imprecision [in grant criteria were] not constitutionally severe. In the context of selective subsidies, it is not always feasible for Congress to legislate with clarity."[54]

Justice Souter registered a lone dissent. For him, the "decency and respect proviso" violated "the fundamental rule of the First Amendment that viewpoint discrimination in the exercise of public authority over expressive activity [was] unconstitutional." The text of the statute alone convinced the justice that it was intended to prevent the funding of art with an "offensive message." O'Connor had concluded that the challenged standards were so imprecise that they were capable of multiple interpretations and, therefore, did not constitute discrimination favoring a particular viewpoint. Souter, on the other hand, considered the provision the "very model of viewpoint discrimination, . . . penaliz[ing] any view disrespectful to any belief or value espoused by someone in the American populace. . . . The fact that the statute disfavors art insufficiently respectful of America's 'diverse' beliefs and values alters this conclusion not one whit: the First Amendment does not validate the ambition to disqualify many disrespectful viewpoints instead of merely one." Nor was he taken with the Court's assumption that a diversity requirement for members of review panels would obviate whatever First Amendment problems the challenged provision created. "That would merely mean," he asserted, "that selection for decency and respect would occur derivatively through the inclinations of the panel members, instead of directly through the intentional application of the criteria; at the end of the day, the proviso would still serve its purpose to screen out offending artistic works, and it would still be unconstitutional." The justice also challenged O'Connor's conclusion that the statute was amenable to constitutional applications (e.g., funding for art displays in schools or a children's museum, or those celebrating a particular culture), did not have a substantial chilling effect on artistic expression, and thus was not unconstitutionally overbroad in its reach. "To whatever extent NEA eligibility defines a national mainstream," he asserted, "the proviso will tend to create a timid esthetic. . . [and] 'chill the expressive activity of [persons] not before the court,'" whatever the scope of its permissible applications.[55]

The justice also dissented in 2003, when the Court upheld provisions of the Children's Internet Protection Act, requiring public libraries that receive federal funds to use Internet filters blocking obscene or pornographic images and preventing minors from accessing harmful material. Souter agreed with Justice Stevens's contention in dissent that the blocking requirements imposed an unconstitutional condition on the receipt of federal funds. But he also agreed that the rule required action that would violate free speech if taken by libraries acting alone. Souter had no doubt about governmental power to erect barriers between child library patrons and the Internet's "raw offerings." Nor would he have dissented had he agreed that, under the law, adult library patrons could obtain unblocked computer terminals "simply for the asking." But the Federal Communications Commission had declined to set a federal policy declaring when unblocking would be appropriate under the statute, and the record further indicated that unblocking could take days and might be unavailable at certain libraries. Clearly, there was no provision in the statute requiring a library to "unblock upon adult request, no conditions imposed and no questions asked." Adults would thus be "denied access to a substantial amount of nonobscene material harmful to children but lawful for adult examination, and a substantial quantity of text and pictures harmful to no one." A library, Souter asserted, could not constitutionally impose such conditions. The justice found equally unacceptable a plurality's notion that the filtering scheme was analogous to the selective process through which libraries acquired their holdings. "At every significant point . . . the Internet blocking here defies comparison to the process of acquisition. . . . The proper analogy . . . is not to passing up a book that might have been bought; it is either to buying a book and then keeping it from adults lacking an acceptable 'purpose' or to buying an encyclopedia and then cutting out pages with anything thought to be unsuitable for all adults." Souter found "no good reason . . . to treat blocking of adult enquiry as anything different from the censorship it presumptively is." He would have subjected the scheme, therefore, to strict judicial scrutiny and struck it down as an unduly broad restriction on "an adult patron's First and Fourteenth Amendment right to be free of [unjustifiable] Internet censorship."[56]

It was hardly surprising, therefore, that the justice joined the majority in 2004 when it refused to lift an injunction against enforcement of the federal Child Online Protection Act, which prohibited commercial Internet posts of erotic material "harmful to minors" but provided an affirmative defense for Web sites that restricted access by requiring use of a credit card or adopting other reasonable access controls. Although remanding the case for further proceedings to determine whether less restrictive means were available for preventing children from accessing Internet pornography, Justice Kennedy strongly intimated that filtering software currently available on the market was an adequate safeguard to prevent exposure of children to explicit sexual images—an approach that would avoid imposing a chilling effect on Web sites and unduly restricting adult access to nonobscene erotica.[57]

Early in his tenure, it will be recalled, Justice Souter had voted in the *Barnes* case to uphold a ban on public nudity, as applied to nude dancing, based on his assumptions about the secondary effects caused by such establishments, including prostitution and sexual assaults. In *City of Erie v. PAP's A.M.* (2000), however, the justice conceded a change in his approach to that issue. Rather than simply assume secondary effects associated with nude dancing, he now believed that the city had an obligation to present evidence establishing a connection between nude dancing and related crimes. "Careful readers," he acknowledged, "will of course realize that my partial dissent rests on a demand for an evidentiary basis that I failed to make when I concurred in *Barnes.* . . . I should have demanded the evidence then, too, and my mistake calls to mind Justice [Robert H.] Jackson's foolproof explanation of a lapse of his own, when he quoted Samuel Johnson, 'Ignorance, sir, ignorance.' . . . I may not be less ignorant of nude dancing than I was nine years ago, but after many subsequent occasions to think further about the needs of the First Amendment, I have come to believe that a government must toe the mark more carefully than I first insisted. I hope it is enlightenment on my part, and acceptable even if a little late."[58]

Affirmative Action

In 2003, Justice Souter also had the opportunity for the first time to reveal his position regarding affirmative action in higher education, an issue the Court had not confronted since *Regents v. Bakke* (1978). With Justice Lewis Powell casting the pivotal fifth vote on the two major issues raised there, the *Bakke* Court had declared racial admission quotas unconstitutional but also held that universities could take into consideration race and other nonacademic factors in seeking to obtain the educational benefits afforded by a diverse student body. In *Grutter v. Bollinger* and *Gratz v. Bollinger*, two University of Michigan cases, a majority reaffirmed *Bakke*, rejecting racial quotas but also concluding that universities have a compelling interest in securing diverse student bodies that justifies some consideration for race in the admissions process. Because Michigan's undergraduate admissions formula assigned bonus points to various factors, including twenty points for race, the *Gratz* majority, speaking through the chief justice, held that the point scheme smacked of a quota and struck it down as a violation of equal protection. Speaking for the *Grutter* majority, however, Justice O'Connor upheld the law school's more "holistic" use of race in the admissions process.[59]

Whatever his personal feelings about affirmative action programs, which he had once dismissed as "affirmative discrimination," Justice Souter joined the *Grutter* majority but dissented in *Gratz*. In his judgment, the undergraduate policy was "closer to what *Grutter* approves than to what *Bakke* condemns" and should have been upheld. Unlike the quota system struck down in *Bakke*, the Michigan undergraduate admissions formula did not deny any racial group the opportunity to compete for any admissions slot. "The plan here . . . lets all applicants compete for all places and values an applicant's offering for any place not only on grounds of race, but on grades, test scores, strength of high school, quality of course of study, residence, alumni relationships, leadership, personal character, socioeconomic disadvantage, athletic ability, and quality of a personal essay. . . . A nonminority applicant who scores highly in these other categories can readily garner a selection index exceeding that of a minority applicant who gets the 20-point bonus." Because universities were permitted to consider race in seeking a diverse student body, the justice found it "hard to see what is inappropriate in assigning some stated value to a relevant characteristic, whether it be reasoning ability, writing style, running speed, or minority race."[60]

Nor was Souter impressed with proposed alternative admission schemes "thrown up as preferable, because supposedly not based on race": the arrangement in some states, for example, guaranteeing admission to a fixed percentage of top students from each high school. The justice agreed there was "nothing unconstitutional about such a practice," but contended that "it . . . suffer[ed] from a serious disadvantage. It is the disadvantage of deliberate obfuscation. The 'percentage plans' are just as race conscious as the point scheme (and fairly so), but get their racially diverse results without saying directly what they are doing or why they are doing it. In contrast, Michigan states its purpose directly and, if this were a doubtful case for me, I would be tempted to give Michigan an extra point of its own for frankness. Equal protection cannot become an exercise in which the winners are the ones who hide the ball." Whatever his misgivings about affirmative action when, as a New Hampshire politician, he had termed such programs "affirmative discrimination," Souter the jurist considered himself bound by the *Bakke* precedent. Given the Court's continued acceptance of diversity as a compelling interest justifying race-conscious admissions policies, he also saw nothing unconstitutional in a state's efforts to assign some concrete weight to such diversity considerations in the admissions process.[61]

Racial Redistricting

In racial redistricting cases, the justice has remained even more deferential to race-conscious policies. In *Shaw v. Reno* (1993), a 5–4 majority held, over Souter's dissent, that North Carolina's majority-minority congressional redistricting plan raised equal protection issues, then remanded the case to the trial court for further proceedings. Souter again dissented when another 5-4 majority held in *Miller v. Johnson* (1995), a Georgia redistricting case, that race-conscious districts were subject to strict judicial scrutiny and would be struck down if found to have been based on "predominantly racial" considerations. And when a majority invoked *Miller* to invalidate North Carolina's redistricting plan on *Shaw*'s second trip to the Court, Souter registered yet another dissent for *Shaw v. Hunt* (1996) and *Bush v. Vera* (1996), a Texas case. As in the past, he questioned whether voters had standing to challenge the configuration of electoral districts and emphasized the exceptionally broad latitude state legislatures had traditionally enjoyed in that field. But Souter reserved his most pointed observations for the majority's assumption that courts could determine the "predominant" motive underlying redistricting decisions that were, by nature, highly complex, embodying a large variety of considerations and trade-offs, including the traditional political interest in protecting the reelection chances of incumbents. Only when the Court, in another lawsuit growing out of the North Carolina dispute, condemned as clearly erroneous a trial court's finding of a predominantly racial rather than political purpose in the state's latest redistricting effort, did Souter silently join the majority.[62]

The justice has taken a different position, however, with respect to gerrymandering designed to favor the candidates of one political party. In *Davis v. Bandemer* (1986), a badly fragmented Court concluded that political gerrymandering challenges raised justiciable questions, yet made them extremely difficult to prove. In *Vieth v. Jubelirer* (2004), Justice Scalia, joined by the chief justice and Justices O'Connor and Thomas, concluded for a plurality that such cases should be dismissed as raising nonjusticiable political questions. Only because Justice Kennedy retained hope that some appropriate constitutional standard might yet be devised for reviewing such claims did *Bandemer* survive at all. But in a dissenting opinion joined by Justice Ginsburg, Justice Souter rejected the plurality's "[un]sound counsel of despair." He realized that partisan considerations were invariably part of the redistricting process, but expressed confidence that the Court could "identify clues, as objective as we can make them, indicating that partisan competition [had] reached [such] an extremity of unfairness" as to be unconstitutional. Toward that end, the justice proposed use of five elements that courts could use in determining whether plaintiffs had made out a prima facie case of unconstitutional partisan gerrymandering, including a showing that a district was drawn without regard for compactness and other traditional redistricting principles.[63]

As the Court began its 2004–2005 term, then, David Souter's judicial record, if anything, would have been even more alarming to conservative Republicans than the Souter votes and opinions that had made him something of a political issue in the 2000 presidential election. In religious school establishment cases as well as suits involving devotional exercises in the public schools, he had become the Court's most vigorous and articulate defender of church-state separation—and critic of justices who saw little constitutional problem in government accommodation of religion. In cyberporn, arts funding, and related expression cases, he proved to be the justice perhaps most willing to find—and condemn—viewpoint discrimination and comparable threats to free speech. In criminal procedure cases, his commitment to precedent and long practice obliged him to uphold broad arrest powers for police, even in petty traffic cases. But he typically has opposed further restrictions on the exclusionary rule in police search and interrogation cases, as well as expansion of police authority to conduct warrantless searches. He joined the majority, moreover, in condemning execution of the mentally retarded and juveniles who were under the age of eighteen at the time of their crimes. He helped form a Court to overturn *Bowers v. Hardwick* and recognize a right of consenting adults to engage in homosexual sodomy, a position he found consistent with the Court's privacy precedents as well as his own flexible, evolving approach to defining substantive due process rights.

Consistent with the 1978 *Bakke* precedent, the justice has also been willing to support race-conscious policies in university admissions, redistricting, and other cases—one of the most contentious lines of decisions for conservative Republicans on and off the Court. Finally, of course, he has remained faithful to the constitutional nationalism that the post-1936 Court embraced until the Rehnquist era: deferring to Congress in disputes over national and state power; opposing the current majority's expansive conception of state sovereign immunity from private lawsuits, especially use of that doctrine to obstruct enforcement of supreme national law; and objecting to the Court's expansion of the takings clause as a meaningful obstacle to both national and state regulatory authority. In short, as he entered his fifteenth year on the high bench, Justice Souter had distanced himself even further from the Rehnquist-Scalia-Thomas wing of the Court and the conservative Republican judicial agenda those justices—and the presidents who appointed them, and him—embraced.

Epilogue

O NE OF JUSTICE SOUTER'S New Hampshire friends has referred to
the "Souter summer syndrome." The frugal justice has long been
one of the Court's millionaires; he could spend the summer recesses
wherever he wished. Most of his colleagues spend parts of their summers
traveling widely, collecting substantial fees for teaching and giving lectures in
various exotic parts of the world. But not Souter. In 2002, for example, he reported no teaching engagements and only one paid trip, to California for a
memorial service honoring constitutional scholar Gerald Gunther. Instead,
when the Court recesses for the summer, Souter hurries back to his beloved
New Hampshire, where his spirits seem to soar, then gradually decline as the
time for his return to Washington draws near.[1]

Orr and Reno's Ronald Snow quotes his friend as having said that "he's got
the world's best job in the world's worst city." After the September 11, 2001,
attacks, the justice expressed fear that Washington was "going to be an armed
camp." As a member of the Court's security committee, he "push[ed] for
more openness to the public, not less," Snow has recalled, but with little success. "He told me . . . about going over to the capitol for his physical
checkup. . . . He went over without a [police escort]. He didn't have the
proper papers, and they would not let him see the doctor. He said, 'I told
them I had my card, which said I was a sitting Justice of the United States
Supreme Court. And the guards made me go back.' . . . He hates the security
and the inability to just walk freely and travel to the airport by himself. He
drives home [to New Hampshire] in his little car. He doesn't fly. And you
know that the marshal service must go berserk when this guy is winding his
way up the New Jersey Turnpike in his little Volkswagen. And he has no cell
phone, so he's out of touch."[2]

An incident toward the end of the Court's 2003 term could hardly have improved the justice's impressions of the nation's capital. Early in his tenure, it may be recalled, Souter had shared with friends his immense relief that a group of youths he encountered on a late-night stroll turned out to be well-wishers. But that incident hardly made him more cautious. At night, Souter regularly jogs around the track at Fort McNair, the Army base near his southwest Washington apartment, then jogs home. When he was returning home from the track around 9:00 P.M. on Friday, April 30, 2004, two or more young men attacked him. He was not robbed, and metropolitan police seemed certain his assailants randomly chose their victim. Although Supreme Court police took the justice to the Washington Hospital Center, where he remained for several hours before returning to his apartment, a Court spokesperson reported that he had sustained only "minor injuries" and was "feeling fine." But when he returned to the bench the following Monday, his neck appeared bruised.[3]

Souter's distaste for Washington and deep affection for his native state have convinced some of his friends that he might give strong consideration to retiring once he completed fifteen years on the bench (in 2005) and was eligible for retirement at full salary. At the time this book went to press, he had given no indication that such an announcement might be forthcoming. Moreover, typically, justices leave the high Court only when their health substantially declines or they die. But as a person, if not a jurist, Souter is hardly typical; he may have little difficulty deciding to leave Washington sooner rather than later.

On the other hand, he seems clearly to enjoy his work and the association of his colleagues. Reportedly, he remains quite close to Justice O'Connor and her husband, who were very attentive to him during the somewhat difficult early days of his tenure. According to his Concord friend Bill Glahn, he also "thinks the world of Ruth Ginsburg. . . . I think Ruth is one he probably feels as much personal affection for as any of them. But I think he gets along well with [all of] them. Which is classic David. He and Scalia go at each other a lot, and undoubtedly there is a perception that Scalia has gone too far sometimes. But on a human level, he gets along great with Scalia. . . . If people have a reasoned basis for their judicial beliefs and the arguments they put forward, and he believes that they do, it wouldn't matter to him one little bit that those opinions were different from his." Not surprisingly, however, the justice considers the somewhat eccentric Justice Stevens—with whom he, Ginsburg, and Justice Breyer are most regularly allied—the Court's "smartest" justice, not Antonin Scalia.[4]

Whatever Souter's plans, it seems certain that he is not the sort of justice modern Republican presidents would be inclined to nominate as his successor on the bench. The justice's fellow New Hampshire native Harlan Fiske Stone, whose portrait hangs in Souter's chambers, became a champion of civil liberties and advocate of judicial restraint in reviewing challenges to national regulatory authority. Like Stone, Souter is deeply rooted in the traditional Republicanism of the Civil War and Reconstruction, not the new Republican Party, which depends so heavily on appeals to racially and politically conservative white southerners and religious fundamentalists for its success in presidential elections. His Great-great-grandfather Allen, after all, had played a role in securing Lincoln's presidential nomination, and other ancestors had worked in the Underground Railroad.

Most important, perhaps, Justice Souter's common law jurisprudence, with its flexible approach to constitutional interpretation and deep commitment to precedent, including expansive civil liberties rulings, makes him an unlikely model for future Republican nominees to the Court. On occasion, after Souter has rendered an opinion supporting a civil liberties claim or assertion of national regulatory power, Bill Glahn, a liberal Democrat, will telephone the justice, playfully accusing him of "turn[ing] into a damned liberal." Souter's response, Glahn reports, "is always to say, 'It's like the old New England farmer who, when asked, 'How's your wife?' said, 'Compared to what?' If I'm a liberal, it's compared to what?"[5]

As Glahn readily agrees, however, Souter's common law jurisprudence has prompted him to forge a record that is relatively liberal by any measure, and certainly by Rehnquist Court standards. It is thus a supreme irony that the first President Bush, in nominating a "stealth candidate" and thereby attempting to avoid the controversy Robert Bork's nomination had provoked, chose a justice who has proven to be the very antithesis of Bork and most of the Reagan-Bush appointees to the Court.

Bibliographic Note

A S THIS BOOK AMPLY DEMONSTRATES, Justice Souter is a very private person. He declined to be interviewed for this book, as did his law clerks. Cooperation in such a project, he told one of his friends, might offend certain of his colleagues on the Court. I naturally respect and understand that decision. At the same time, I am grateful that a considerable number of the justice's New Hampshire friends and others associated with his life and career did agree to recorded interviews. His teacher Lillian Grossman Strater provided interesting insights into his high school years, as did his classmates Ruth Houghton and Vicki McLaughlin Maiben. Dr. Harris Berman, who was a year ahead of Souter at Concord High School, furnished information about their undergraduate years at Harvard. Barbara Jackson Carpenter, who worked with Souter's mother in a Concord department store, also offered helpful insight into his youth. Malcolm McLane, who with his wife, Susan, would become Souter's close friend, served on the New Hampshire and New England selection committees for the Rhodes Scholarship. McLane discussed Souter's Rhodes selection with me. David Wilkinson and Jay W. Butler provided helpful information regarding the curriculum and routine of Oxford's Rhodes Scholars during Souter's tenure there, and the justice's longtime friend Dr. Melvin Levine provided wonderful anecdotes about their time together at Oxford and later at Harvard, where Souter was attending law school and Levine medical school. Robert L. Brinton offered recollections of Souter in law school, and a *Chicago Tribune*, September 18, 1990, profile, written by R. Eden Martin, who overlapped Souter two years at Harvard, was very enlightening. The Simmons College papers of Harriett Moulton Bartlett, whom Souter affectionately referred to as "Aunt Harriett" and who reportedly had a significant influence on his life, were also very helpful regarding the justice's college, Oxford, and law school years. Ronald Snow and Charles Leahy, partners in the Concord, New Hampshire, firm of Orr and Reno, discussed their friend's brief career in private practice, along with other aspects of his life and career, as did longtime friends and associates from his days in the New Hampshire attorney general's office, including Tom Rath and Wilbur (Bill) Glahn. Also especially helpful was the memoir of Souter's close friend and mentor Warren B. Rudman, *Combat: Twelve Years in the U.S. Senate* (New York: Random House, 1996). Jack Middleton, Mark L. Sisti, and Paul Twomey, among others, offered interesting insights as lawyers who practiced before Justice Souter in the New Hampshire Superior and Supreme Courts. So, too, did James Duggan, who started an appellate defender office in New Hampshire, representing indigent defendants before the state supreme court until his own appointment as a justice. Karen Brickner, one of the few secretaries at the New Hampshire high court who could decipher Justice Souter's handwriting, also offered helpful observations about Souter's style and routine as a state supreme court justice. Genealogical surveys conducted for me by the New England Historic Genealogical Society (NEHGS), as well as David Curtis Dearborn's "Ancestors of Supreme Court Justice David Hackett Souter," *NEXUS* 11 (1994): 31–36, an NEHGS publication, detailed the justice's family roots. The transcript of the U.S. Senate hearings on his appointment to the Supreme Court was invaluable, as was material from the George H. W. Bush presidential library. The justice's tribute to New Hampshire Supreme Court Justice Laurence Ilsley Duncan (1946–76), which appeared in the *New Hampshire Bar Journal* 24 (1983): 81, offered nearly as much insight into Souter as his subject. I also relied extensively on New Hampshire newspapers, especially the *Concord Monitor* and *Manchester Union Leader*, as well as the *Boston Globe, New York Times, Washington Post*, and various national magazines. For the four years that Justices Souter and Blackmun overlapped on the Court (1990–94), the Harry A. Blackmun Papers in the Library of Congress were an important source, as were, of course, the reported judicial opinions of the justice and his contemporaries on the U.S. and New Hampshire high courts.

Notes

Chapter 1

1. Interview with Ronald Snow, August 6, 2002, Concord, New Hampshire.

2. David Curtis Dearborn, "Ancestors of Supreme Court Justice David Hackett Souter," *NEXUS* 11 (1994): 31–36. *NEXUS* is a publication of the New England Historical Genealogical Society, which conducted several genealogical surveys for me in connection with my research on Justice Souter.

3. Brief obituaries for Joseph A. Souter are in the *Boston Globe* and *Boston Herald American*, December 10, 1976, and the *Concord [New Hampshire] Monitor*, December 9, 1976. Brief obituaries for Frank H. Hackett are in the *Boston Globe*, July 9, 1946, and *Boston Herald*, July 10, 1946. Genealogical data can also be obtained from various Internet sites.

4. Harriett Moulton Bartlett Papers, Simmons College Archives, Boston, Massachusetts.

5. Interview with Dr. Melvin Levine, November 11, 2002, Chapel Hill, North Carolina.

6. Ibid.

7. Ibid.

8. Ibid.

9. *Boston Herald*, July 10, 1946; *Concord Monitor*, September 12, 1990; interview with Malcolm McLane, January 13, 2003, Concord, New Hampshire.

10. *Concord Monitor*, July 30, September 12, 1990.

11. Ibid.

12. Interview with Lillian Grossman Strater, January 20, 2003, Cleveland, Ohio; interview with Mrs. Richard O. Blanchard, August 5, 2002, Concord, New Hampshire; interview with Ruth Houghton, January 17, 2003, Chebeaque, Maine.

13. *Concord Monitor*, September 12, 1990; *Manchester Union Leader*, August 4, 1990.

14. Houghton interview.

15. Interview with Vicki McLaughlin Maiben, January 20, 2003, Barrington, Illi-

nois; interview with Barbara Jackson Carpenter, August 6, 2002, Concord, New Hampshire.

16. Maiben interview.

17. Drawn from the 1957 Concord High School yearbook; *Concord Monitor*, September 12, 1990; and C-SPAN interview, "The Friends of Justice Souter."

18. *Concord Monitor*, September 12, 1990.

19. Concord High School yearbook; Houghton interview.

20. Concord High School yearbook.

21. Interview with Harris Berman, October 28, 2002, Waltham, Massachusetts.

22. Berman interview; interview with John L. McCausland, January 27, 2003, Weare, New Hampshire.

23. *Concord Monitor*, January 7, 1976; Learned Hand, *The Bill of Rights* (Cambridge, Mass.: Harvard University Press, 1958).

24. David Hackett Souter, "Holmes' Legal Positivism and the Criticism from a Current Position of Natural Law" (A.B. senior honors thesis, Harvard College, 1961).

25. McLane interview.

26. Interview with David Wilkinson, January 23, 2003, Hamilton, Virginia.

27. Levine interview.

28. Interview with Jay W. Butler, January 31, 2003, Bountiful, Utah.

29. Bartlett Papers.

30. Levine interview.

31. Ibid.

32. Maiben interview; Levine interview; *Concord Monitor*, September 12, 1990; *Washington Post*, September 9, 1990.

33. Levine interview.

34. Ibid.

35. Ibid.

36. Interview with Robert L. Brinton, January 23, 2003, White Plains, New York.

37. Ibid.

38. *Chicago Tribune*, September 18, 1990.

39. Ibid.

40. *Chicago Tribune*, September 18, 1990; McCausland interview.

41. *Chicago Tribune*, September 18, 1990.

42. Information drawn from the initial questionnaire Souter completed for the U.S. Senate Committee on the Judiciary as part of his confirmation proceedings. Unfortunately, the questionnaire, hereinafter cited as Senate questionnaire, is the only part of confirmation materials in the National Archives that is now available to researchers.

43. Ibid.

44. McLane interview; information about Orr and Reno drawn from a firm booklet.

45. McLane interview.

46. U.S. Congress, Senate, Committee on the Judiciary, *Hearings on the Nomination of David H. Souter to Be Associate Justice of the Supreme Court of the United States*, 101st Cong., 2d sess., 1990, p. 51 [hereinafter Senate hearings].

47. Senate questionnaire, p. 26. The unreported case was Marcou v. Jordan (1967).

48. Snow interview; Senate questionnaire, p. 26. The unreported case was Ray v. Franconia Paper Co. (1968).

49. Snow interview.

50. Leahy interview.

51. Snow interview.

52. This discussion is drawn from a retrospective account in the *Concord Monitor*, February 7, 1999.

53. Ibid.

54. Ibid.

55. Warren B. Rudman, *Combat: Twelve Years in the U.S. Senate* (New York: Random House, 1996), p. 21.

56. Ibid., p. 154.

57. Ibid.

58. Interview with Tom Rath, August 9, 2002, Concord, New Hampshire.

59. Leahy interview; Rudman, *Combat*, p. 155.

60. Interview with Wilbur Glahn, August 6, 2002, Concord, New Hampshire.

61. *Concord Monitor*, August 8, 1990.

62. C-SPAN interview, "The Friends of Justice Souter."

63. Ibid.

64. Senate hearings, pp. 553–54.

65. Ibid.

66. C-SPAN interview, "The Friends of Justice Souter."

67. Glahn interview.

68. Rath interview.

69. Glahn interview.

70. Rath interview; Rudman, *Combat*, pp. 156–57.

71. Rudman, *Combat*, p. 156.

72. *Union Leader*, November 30, 1976.

73. Ibid.

74. Reprinted in *Concord Monitor*, December 7, 1976.

75. Senate questionnaire, pp. 21–24.

76. David H. Souter to Harry M. Descotean, February 15, 1977; David H. Souter to James W. Nelson, April 16, 1976; David H. Souter to Meldrim Thomson, July 1, 1976; David H. Souter to Frank E. Whaland, January 11, 1978, Opinions of the Attorney General, State of New Hampshire, New Hampshire Supreme Court Library.

77. *Concord Monitor*, December 21, 1976.

78. *Concord Monitor*, December 28, 1976.

79. United States v. Maine, 420 U.S. 515 (1975); New Hampshire v. Maine, 426 U.S. 363 (1976).

80. United States v. New Hampshire, Memorandum in Opposition to the Motion of the United States for a Temporary Injunction, on file in the office of the Attorney General, State of New Hampshire; Lassiter v. Northampton Co. Bd. of Elections, 360 U.S. 45 (1959).

81. South Carolina v. Katzenbach, 383 U.S. 301 (1966); Katzenbach v. Morgan, 384 U.S. 641 (1966).

82. Oregon v. Mitchell, 400 U.S. 112 (1970). The three-judge court's opinion in United States v. New Hampshire is unreported.

83. Senate hearings, pp. 440–46. Judge Bownes's ruling was not reported.

84. The state's brief is no longer on file in court or state archives. But excerpts are in ibid. and the *Union Leader*, August 2, 1990.

85. United States v. New Hampshire, 539 F. 2d 277, 280, n. 4, 281, 282, n. 6 (1976).

86. Senate hearings, p. 446; New Hampshire v. United States, 429 U.S. 1023 (1976).

87. *Union Leader*, May 31, 1976; *Nashua Telegraph*, June 1, 1976.

88. Senate questionnaire, pp. 2–7.

89. Quoted in *Union Leader*, July 31, 1990; State v. Millette, 112 N. H. 458 (1972).

90. Coe v. Hooker, 406 F. Supp. 1072 (1976): Maher v. Roe, 432 U.S. 464 (1977); Harris v. McRae, 448 U.S. 297 (1980).

91. *Union Leader*, July 31, 1990; *New York Times*, July 31, 1990.

92. *Union Leader*, May 19, 1977, August 4, 1990; Planned Parenthood v. Casey, 505 U.S. 833 (1992).

93. *Union Leader*, April 14, 1977; Gregg v. Georgia, 428 U.S. 153 (1976).

94. Meloon v. Helgemoe, 436 F. Supp. 528 (1977), 564 F. 2d 602 (1977).

95. Helgemoe v. Meloon, Petition for a Writ of Certiorari, pp. 12, 17–19, reprinted in Senate hearings, pp. 77–105; Craig v. Boren, 429 U.S. at 221 (1976).

96. Michael M. v. Superior Court, 450 U.S. 464 (1981).

97. *Concord Monitor*, March 10, April 8, 1978.

98. *Concord Monitor*, July 2, 25, 1970.

99. Rudman, *Combat*, p. 25; Rath interview.

100. Leahy interview; Rath interview.

101. *Union Leader*, December 28, 1975, January 8, 1976.

102. *Concord Monitor*, January 7, 1976.

103. Leahy interview; *Concord Monitor*, January 28, April 7, 1977.

104. *Concord Monitor*, April 7, 1977.

105. *Union Leader*, April 9, 1977.

106. *Concord Monitor*, May 6, 1977.

107. Leahy interview.

108. *Union Leader*, March 6, 1976, May 28, 1977; *Concord Monitor*, May 6, 1977.

109. *Union Leader*, July 18, 20, 1976.

110. Ibid.

111. *Union Leader*, July 20, 1976.

112. Ibid.; *New Hampshire Sunday News*, July 20, 1976.

113. *Union Leader*, July 20, 1976.

114. *Concord Monitor*, April 6, 26, 29, 1978.

115. *Concord Monitor*, July 1, 1976.

116. *Concord Monitor*, July 2, 1976.

117. *Union Leader*, February 7, 1976; *Concord Monitor*, January 28, 1976.

118. Maynard v. Wooley, 406 F. Supp. 1381, 1388 (1976); Wooley v. Maynard, 430 U.S. 705 (1977).

119. Quoted in *Union Leader*, August 4, 1990.

120. Ibid.

121. *Concord Monitor*, March 20, 1978.

122. *Concord Monitor*, March 21, 1978.

123. Glahn interview.

124. Glahn interview; *Concord Monitor*, March 24, April 11, 25, 1978; Brown v. Thomson, 435 U.S. 919 (1978).

125. Glahn interview; Lemon v. Kurtzman, 403 U.S. 602 (1971). The brief is quoted in Senate hearings, p. 1059.

126. *Concord Monitor*, March 25, 1978; Senate hearings, p. 150.

127. *Union Leader*, August 4, 1990.

128. C-SPAN interview, "The Friends of Justice Souter."

Chapter 2

1. Rudman, *Combat*, p. 158.

2. Ibid., p. 159.

3. *Union Leader*, February 25, 1978. In 2000, during the administration of Democratic Governor Jeanne Shaheen, the governor established a judicial selection committee for superior court nominees, subject to confirmation by the executive committee.

4. *Concord Monitor*, March 10, April 7, 1978; *Union Leader*, March 11, 1978. Joseph A. Souter died at his Loudon Road home on December 8, 1976. A private graveside service was held in Wakefield, Massachusetts. The family suggested that contributions be made in his memory to the Weare Rescue Squad.

5. Snow interview.

6. Ibid.

7. Ibid.

8. Rath interview; interview with Jack Middleton, October 29, 2002, Manchester, New Hampshire.

9. Middleton interview.

10. Rath interview; C-SPAN interview, "The Friends of Justice Souter."

11. Interview with Bruce Felmly, January 10, 2003, Manchester, New Hampshire; interview with Mark L. Sisti, January 10, 2003, Concord, New Hampshire; interview with Paul Twomey, January 29, 2003, Concord, New Hampshire.

12. Sisti interview; Twomey interview.

13. Twomey interview.

14. Sisti interview.

15. *Concord Monitor*, July 27, 1990.

16. Ibid.; Sisti interview.

17. Sisti interview; Twomey interview.

18. Sisti interview.

19. Facts of the case are summarized in State v. Siel, 444 A. 2d 499 (1982).

20. Ibid.; *Concord Monitor*, July 30, 1990.

21. Branzburg v. Hayes, 408 U.S. 665 (1972).

22. 444 A. 2d at 503.

23. Ibid.

24. Twomey interview; Felmly interview.

25. *Concord Monitor*, July 30, 1990.

26. Quoted in *Union Leader*, August 3, 1990.

27. Bellotti v. Baird, 443 U.S. 622 (1979); *Concord Monitor*, July 26, 1990.

28. *Concord Monitor*, July 26, 1990. This article contains extensive excerpts from Souter's letter.

29. Glahn interview.

30. Rudman, *Combat*, pp. 159–60.

31. *Concord Monitor*, September 8, 1983.

32. Ibid.

33. Ibid.

34. Snow interview.

35. *Concord Monitor*, July 8, 1970.

36. Interview with Karen Brickner, August 9, 2002, Concord, New Hampshire.

37. Snow interview.

38. Interview with Justice James Duggan, August 6, 2002, Concord, New Hampshire.

39. Ibid.

40. Sisti interview; Twomey interview.

41. Workers' Compensation Fund v. Flynn, 573 A. 2d 439 (1990); *Concord Monitor*, September 11, 1990.

42. Crossley v. Town of Pelham, 578 A. 2d 319, 320 (1990); *Concord Monitor*, September 11, 1990.

43. Senate hearings, p. 113.

44. *New Hampshire Sunday News*, July 29, 1990; Brickner interview.

45. *In Re* "K," 561 A. 2d 1063 (1989).

46. Ibid., p. 1066.

47. *In Re* Estate of Henry Dionne, 518 A. 2d 178, 179, 180 (1981).

48. Ibid., pp. 181, 182, 183, 184.

49. State v. Roger M., 424 A. 2d 1139 (1981); State v. Meister, 480 A. 2d 200, 204 (1984).

50. Quoted in Appeal of Bosselait, 547 A. 2d 682, 684 (1988).

51. Ibid., p. 686.

52. Ibid., p. 687.

53. Ibid., p. 689; Carson v. Maure, 424 A. 2d 825 (1980); California v. Goldfarb, 430 U.S. 199 (1977).

54. 547 A. 2d at 690.

55. State v. Colbath, 540 A. 2d 1212 (1988).

56. Quoted in ibid., p. 1215.

57. Ibid.; State v. Howard, 426 A. 2d 457, 461 (1981).

58. 426 A. 2d at 1216, 1217.

59. Ibid., p. 1217.

60. State v. Baker, 508 A. 2d 1059, 1062 (1986).

61. Yergeau v. Yergeau, 569 A. 2d 237 (1990); *Concord Monitor,* July 26, 1990.

62. Smith v. Cote, 513 A. 2d 341 (1986).

63. Ibid., p. 355.

64. *In Re* Jason C., 533 A. 2d 32, 33 (1987); *In Re* Diana P., 424 A. 2d 178, 181 (1980).

65. 533 A. 2d at 33, 34.

66. Opinion of the Justices, 525 A. 2d 1095, 1098 (1987).

67. Ibid.; Bowers v. Hardwick, 487 U.S. 186 (1986).

68. 525 A. 2d at 1099.

69. Ibid.

70. Ibid., pp. 1101-102.

71. Ibid., pp. 1100, 1103.

72. Richardson v. Chevrefils, 552 A. 2d 89 (1988).

73. State v. Hodgkiss, 565 A. 2d 1059 (1989).

74. Ibid., pp. 1061, 1063, 1064; United States v. O'Brien, 391 U.S. 367, 377 (1968).

75. Petition of Chapman, 509 A. 2d 753 (1986).

76. Ibid., p. 761.

77. Ibid., p. 765.

78. *In Re* New Hampshire Disabilities Rights Center, 541 A. 2d 208 (1988).

79. State v. DuKette, 506 A. 2d 699, 703 (1986).

80. Michigan Dept. of State Police v. Sitz, 496 U.S. 444 (1990); State v. Koppel, 499 A. 2d 977 (1985).

81. State v. Koppel, 499 A. 2d at 985; State v. Smith, 674 P. 2d 562 (1984).

82. State v. Valenzuela, 536 A. 2d 1252, 1269–70; Smith v. Maryland, 442 U.S. 735 (1979).

83. Michigan v. Long, 463 U.S. 1032 (1983); William J. Brennan Jr., "Guardians of Our Liberties: State Courts No Less Than Federal," *The Judges' Journal* 15 (1976): 82.

84. State v. Ball, 471 A. 2d 347, 351 (1983).

85. State v. Kellenbeck, 474 A. 2d 1388, 1392 (1984).

86. State v. Denney, 536 A. 2d 1242, 1246 (1987).

87. State v. Cormier, 499 A. 2d 986 (1985).

88. Ibid., p. 993; South Dakota v. Neville, 459 U.S. 553 (1983); Schmerber v. California, 384 U.S. 757 (1966).

89. 499 A. 2d at 994.

90. Quoted in State v. Coppola, 536 A. 2d 1236, 1237 (1987).

91. Ibid., p. 1239; Doyle v. Ohio, 426 U.S. 610 (1976).

92. Coppola v. Powell, 878 F. 2d 1562 (1988).

93. 878 F. 2d at 1566, 1567; Jenkins v. Anderson, 447 U.S. 231 (1980).

94. Sisti interview; Senate hearings, p. 1103; State v. Jones, 484 A. 2d 1070 (1984); Richard v. MacAskill, 529 A. 2d 898 (1987); State v. Hewitt, 517 A. 2d 820 (1986).

95. Sisti interview.

Chapter 3

1. Rudman, *Combat*, p. 160.

2. Ibid., pp. 160–61.

3. *New York Times*, October 29, 1987.

4. Ibid.

5. Rudman, *Combat*, p. 161.

6. U.S., Congress, Senate, Committee on the Judiciary, *Confirmation Hearings on Appointments to the Federal Judiciary*, 101st Cong., 2d sess., p. 570 [hereinafter Circuit hearings].

7. State v. Coppola, 536 A. 2d 1236 (1987); Coppola v. Powell, 878 F. 2d 1562, 1567 (1988).

8. Circuit hearings, pp. 571–72.

9. Ibid., p. 572.

10. Ibid., p. 573. State v. Colbath, 540 A. 2d 1212 (1988). *Colbath* was misspelled *Kolba* in the hearing transcript.

11. Circuit hearings, pp. 573–74; Davis v. Alaska, 415 U.S. 308 (1974).

12. United States v. Waldeck, 909 F. 2d 555 (1990); Ronald M. v. Concord School Committee, 910 F. 2d 983 (1990); United States v. Gomez-Pabon, 911 F. 2d 847 (1990); Jenson v. Frank, 912 F. 2d 517 (1990); United States v. Parcel of Land and Residence,

914 F. 2d 1 (1990). He did not participate in reviewing a motion for a rehearing in *Roland M.*, 1990 U.S. App. LEXIS 23200 (1990).

13. See generally Hunter R. Clark, *Justice Brennan: The Great Conciliator* (New York: Birch Lane Press, 1995); K. I. Eisler, *A Justice for All: William J. Brennan, Jr.* (New York: Simon & Schuster, 1994).

14. Clark, *Justice Brennan*, pp. 273–74.

15. Rath interview.

16. Rudman, *Combat*, p. 162.

17. Ibid.

18. *New York Times*, July 25, 1990; Levine interview.

19. McCausland interview.

20. Mark Silverstein, *Judicious Choices: The Politics of Supreme Court Confirmations* (New York: Norton, 1991); David H. Souter, "Mr. Justice Duncan," *New Hampshire Bar Journal* 24 (1983): 81.

21. Ibid., pp. 83, 85, 86, 87; H. L. A. Hart, "Positivism and the Separation of Law and Morals," *Harvard Law Review* 71 (1958): 593.

22. "The Quiet Man," *Newsweek*, August 6, 1990, p. 14; *Union Leader*, March 25, 1995; Rudman, *Combat*, pp. 162–63.

23. Rudman, *Combat*, p. 163.

24. Ibid., pp. 163–64.

25. Richard Lacayo, "A Blank Slate," *Time*, August 6, 1990, pp. 16–17.

26. Rath interview; Rudman, *Combat*, pp. 168–69.

27. *New York Times*, July 29, 1990.

28. Lacayo, "A Blank Slate," p. 17.

29. Rath interview.

30. A transcript of the press conference is available online through the Bush presidential library.

31. This account is from the transcript of Souter's remarks at the White House ceremony, October 8, 1990, in which the president administered the constitutional oath of office to the newly confirmed justice. The transcript is available online from the Bush presidential library.

32. Rudman, *Combat*, p. 170.

33. *Concord Monitor*, July 27, 1990.

34. *New York Times*, July 26, 27, 1990.

35. *New York Times*, July 26, 27, 29, 1990; *Washington Post*, July 25, 2990; *Wall Street Journal*, July 27, 1990; Robert H. Bork, *The Tempting of America: The Political Seduction of the Law* (New York: Free Press, 1990), p. 347.

36. *Newsday*, July 24, 1990.

37. U.S. House, *Congressional Record*, July 30, 1990; *New York Times*, July 25, 1990. The transcript of Rudman's initial remarks, dated July 23, 1990, is available online through the Federal News Service.

38. *New York Times*, July 27, 1990.

39. *Concord Monitor*, July 28, 1990; *Washington Post*, July 28, 1990; *New York Times*, July 30, 1990.

40. *New York Times*, July 27, 1990. The Harlan cases to which Lewis was referring were, of course, Poe v. Ullman, 367 U.S. 497 (1961); Griswold v. Connecticut, 381 U.S. 479 (1965); and Cohen v. California, 403 U.S. 15 (1971).

41. *Los Angeles Daily Law Journal*, July 25, 1990.

42. *Washington Post*, July 28, 1990; *Concord Monitor*, July 30, 1990.

43. Rath interview; Snow interview.

44. Margaret Carlson, "An 18th Century Man," *Time*, August 6, 1990, p. 22; *USA Today*, July 25, 1990.

45. *New York Times*, July 25, 1990; *National Law Journal*, August 6, 1990; *Legal Times*, July 30, 1990.

46. Carlson, "An 18th Century Man," p. 20; *Concord Monitor*, July 28, 1990.

47. Rudman, *Combat*, p. 177.

48. *Los Angeles Times*, July 27, 1990; *Newsday*, July 25, 1990.

49. *USA Today*, July 25, 1990.

50. *Concord Monitor*, July 30, 1990; *Legal Times*, July 30, 1990.

51. *Concord Monitor*, July 27, 1990.

52. *Concord Monitor*, July 28, 1990.

53. Ibid.

54. Kiluk v. Potter, 572 A. 2d 1157 (1990).

55. *Legal Times*, July 30, 1990.

56. Ibid.; Kiluk v. Potter.

57. *New York Times*, July 25, 1990.

58. Quoted in *Legal Times*, August 6, 1990.

59. Ibid.

60. Ibid.

61. Ibid.

62. *Concord Monitor*, July 27, 1990.

63. *New York Times*, July 25, 1990; Duggan interview.

64. *Union Leader*, July 31, 1990; Rudman, *Combat*, p. 176.

65. Rudman, *Combat*, p. 176.

66. *St. Petersburg Times*, July 25, 1990.

67. Gary L. McDowell, "Senate Should Put Souter to Scholarship Test," *Wall Street Journal*, August 1, 1990, p. A14.

68. Ibid.

69. Ibid.

70. "Insider Baseball: How Sununu Sold Souter," *Harper's Magazine*, November, 1990, p. 24; Senate hearings, p. 119.

71. Rudman, *Combat*, pp. 180–81.

72. Ibid., pp. 181–83.

73. Ibid., p. 177; *New York Times*, July 26, September 12, 1990.

74. *New York Times*, September 5, 1990; *Boston Globe*, September 5, 1990.

75. *New York Times*, September 5, 7, 1990.

76. Michael Kinsley, "Here We Go Again," *The New Republic*, August 13, 1990.

77. *New York Times*, September 9, 1990.

78. C-SPAN interview, "The Friends of Justice Souter."

79. Rudman, *Combat*, p. 183; Senate hearings, p. 46.

80. *New York Times*, September 11, 1990.

81. Senate hearings, p. 52.

82. Ibid., p. 53.

83. Ibid., p. 54.

84. Ibid., pp. 55–56.

85. Ibid., p. 62.

86. Ibid., pp. 64, 244.

87. Ibid., pp. 69, 73.

88. Ibid., p. 73.

89. Ibid., p. 75.

90. Ibid., pp. 75–76.

91. Rudman, *Combat*, p. 187.

92. Senate hearings, p. 115.

93. Ibid., pp. 115, 117–18.

94. Ibid., p. 119.

95. Ibid., pp. 182–84.

96. Ibid., pp. 218–20.

97. Ibid., pp. 186, 265, 266.

98. Ibid., pp. 306, 274, 276.

99. Ibid., p. 277.

100. Ibid., pp. 122–23.

101. Ibid., pp. 466, 468–532.

102. Ibid., pp. 363, 431, 896–97, 1108, 1109–10.

103. Ibid., pp. 755, 779; *New York Times*, September 20, 1990.

104. Senate hearings, pp. 550, 553–54, 551–52.

105. Ibid., p. 552.

106. *New York Times*, September 14, 20, 1990; Senate hearings, p. 710.

107. *New York Times*, September 16, 1990; McLane interview.

108. *New York Times*, September 15, 21, 22, 1990; *Boston Globe*, September 16, 1990.

109. *New York Times*, September 15, 17, 1990; Senate hearings, p. 195.

110. *New York Times*, September 28, 1990.

111. Ibid.; *Boston Globe*, September 28, 1990.

112. *New York Times*, September 27, 1990.

113. *Boston Globe*, October 3, 1990.

114. *Boston Globe*, October 5, 1990.

115. *St. Petersburg Times*, October 6, 1990.

116. *New York Times*, October 3, 1990.

Chapter 4

1. *Boston Globe*, December 28, 1990.

2. *Boston Globe*, December 2, 1990; Rath interview; Levine interview.

3. *Boston Globe*, December 2, 1990.

4. Rath interview.

5. Ibid.; quoted in *Boston Globe*, December 2, 1990.

6. *Boston Globe*, December 2, 1990.

7. A transcript of the March 10, 1999, hearing before a subcommittee of the House Committee on Appropriations is available online from the Federal Document Clearing House, Inc.

8. *Concord Monitor*, June 3, 1999.

9. *Washington Post*, April 6, October 11, 2000; *Union Leader*, June 10, 2000; *Concord Monitor*, June 11, 2000; Home Gas Corporation v. Strafford Fuels, 534 A. 2d 390 (1987).

10. *Union Leader*, September 27, 2000.

11. This information is largely drawn from the law clerk database in the Supreme Court library.

12. Berman interview.

13. Glahn interview.

14. Brinton interview; Middleton interview.

15. McNary v. Haitian Refugee Center, 498 U.S. 479 (1991).

16. Loveland's account of her observations appeared in several legal newspapers, including *Legal Times*, January 14, 1991.

17. Ibid.; *Newsday*, October 31, 1990; *New Jersey Law Journal*, November 15, 1990.

18. *Newsday*, October 31, 1990; *New Jersey Law Journal*, November 15, 1990.

19. Ford v. Georgia, 498 U.S. 411 (1991); Avery v. Georgia, 345 U.S. 559 (1953); Williams v. Georgia, 349 U.S. 375 (1955). For an account of Justice Harlan's role in *Williams*, see Tinsley E. Yarbrough, *John Marshall Harlan: Great Dissenter of the Warren Court* (New York: Oxford University Press, 1992), pp. 153–59.

20. Batson v. Kentucky, 476 U.S. 79 (1986); Griffith v. Kentucky, 479 U.S. 314 (1987); Ford v. Georgia, 479 U.S. 1075 (1987).

21. Ford v. Georgia, 362 S.E. 2d 764 (1987); State v. Sparks, 355 S.E. 2d 658 (1987).

22. 498 U.S. at 420.

23. Ibid., pp. 421, 422; James v. Kentucky, 466 U.S. 341, 348–51 (1984).

24. *Boston Globe*, February 2, 1991.

25. *Boston Globe*, May 26, 1991.

26. Ibid.

27. Ibid.; "Souter: Slow Off the Mark," *Newsweek*, May 27, 1991, p. 4; *New Jersey Law Journal*, June 13, 1991.

28. Burns v. United States, 501 U.S. 129 (1991); Schad v. Arizona, 501 U.S. 624 (1991). For excellent surveys of Souter's first-term record, see Scott P. Johnson and Christopher E. Smith, "David Souter's First Term on the Supreme Court: The Impact of a New Justice," *Judicature* 75 (1992): 238; Robert H. Smith, "Justice Souter Joins the Rehnquist Court: An Empirical Study of Supreme Court Voting Patterns," *Kansas Law Review* 41 (1992): 11.

29. Cohen v. Cowles Media Company, 501 U.S. 663, 678 (1991); David H. Souter to Byron R. White and Harry A. Blackmun, June 17, 1991, Blackmun Papers, Library of Congress, Box 578.

30. Powers v. Ohio, 499 U.S. 400 (1991); Edmonson v. Leesville Concrete Co., 500 U.S. 614 (1991); Chisom v. Roemer, 501 U.S. 380 (1991); Houston Lawyers' Ass'n v. Attorney General of Texas, 501 U.S. 419 (1991); International Union, UAW v. Johnson Controls, 499 U.S. 189 (1991).

31. Payne v. Tennessee, 501 U.S. 808 (1991); Booth v. Maryland, 482 U.S. 496 (1987); South Carolina v. Gathers, 490 U.S. 805 (1989).

32. 501 U.S. at 838–39.

33. Ibid., p. 839.

34. Ibid., pp. 839–40, 841–42.

35. Ibid., pp. 834, 842, 843–44.

36. Barnes v. Glen Theatre, 501 U.S. 560, 582 (1991); United States v. O'Brien, 391 U.S. 367 (1968).

37. 501 U.S. at 585–86; John Paul Stevens to Byron R. White, June 19, 1991, Blackmun Papers, Box 575; City of Erie v. Pap's A.M., 529 U.S. 277, 310, 316 (2000) (Souter, J., concurring and dissenting).

38. Chapman v. California, 386 U.S. 18, 23, 24 (1967); Arizona v. Fulminante, 499 U.S. 279, 302 (1991); Yates v. Evatt, 500 U.S. 391 (1991).

39. Rust v. Sullivan, 500 U.S. 173 (1991); Maher v. Roe, 432 U.S. 464 (1977); Harris v. McRae, 448 U.S. 297 (1980).

40. David H. Souter to William H. Rehnquist, April 25, 1991; William H. Rehnquist to David H. Souter, April 29, 1991, Thurgood Marshall Papers, Library of Congress, Box 530.

41. *Boston Globe*, May 26, 1991.

42. *New York Times*, June 28, 1991.

43. Keeney v. Tamayo-Reyes, 504 U.S. 1 (1992); *New York Times*, May 7, 1992; United States v. Alvarez-Machain, 504 U.S. 655 (1992); Vasquez v. Harris, 503 U.S. 1000 (1992); Stringer v. Black, 503 U.S. 222, 238 (1992); Teague v. Lane, 489 U.S. 288 (1989).

44. Doggett v. United States, 505 U.S. 647 (1992).

45. Ibid., pp. 659, 660, 656, 657, 658; Barker v. Wingo, 407 U.S. 514 (1972).

46. Jacobson v. United States, 503 U.S. 540 (1992); David H. Souter to Byron R. White, February 13, 1991, Blackmun Papers, Box 590. The *Jacobson* conference notes are in the same file. Regarding the Court's approach to the entrapment issue, see, e.g., United States v. Russell, 411 U.S. 423 (1973); Sorrells v. United States, 287 U.S. 435 (1932).

47. International Society for Krishna Consciousness v. Lee, 505 U.S. 672 (1992); Lee v. International Society for Krishna Consciousness, 505 U.S. 830 (1992).

48. 505 U.S. at 710, 711.

49. Ibid., pp. 713–14, 715.

50. Lee v. Weisman, 505 U.S. 577, 609 (1992); Anthony M. Kennedy to Harry A. Blackmun, March 30, 1992, Blackmun Papers, Box 586; David H. Souter to Harry A. Blackmun, November 18, 1991, Blackmun Papers, Box 586; clerk memorandum to Harry A. Blackmun, December 20, 1991, Blackmun Papers, Box 586. The *Lee* conference notes are in the same file.

51. 505 U.S. at 610, 611; Everson v. Board of Education, 330 U.S. 1, 15 (1947).

52. Wallace v. Jaffree, 472 U.S. 38, 106 (1985); Lee v. Weisman, 505 U.S. at 612, 614–15 (footnote omitted), 615–16; Douglas Laycock, "'Nonpreferentialist' Aid to Religion: A False Claim about Original Intent," *William and Mary Law Review* 27 (1986): 882–83.

53. 505 U.S. at 616, n. 3, 616–17, 617–18.

54. Ibid., pp. 618, 619; County of Allegheny v. American Civil Liberties Union, 492 U.S. 573 (1989); Wallace v. Jaffree, 472 U.S. 38 (1985); Epperson v. Arkansas, 393 U.S. 97 (1968); Edwards v. Aguillard, 482 U.S. 578 (1987).

55. 505 U.S. at 621, 626.

56. Ibid., pp. 630–31.

57. Webster v. Reproductive Services, 492 U.S. 490, 525–26 (1989) .

58. Planned Parenthood v. Casey, 505 U.S. 833 (1992).

59. City of Akron v. Akron Center for Reproductive Health, 462 U.S. 416 (1983); clerk memorandum to Harry A. Blackmun, January 10, 1992, Blackmun Papers, Box 602; Anthony M. Kennedy to Harry A. Blackmun, May 29, 1992, Blackmun Papers, Box 601.

60. 505 U.S. at 869.

61. Ibid., pp. 998–99.

62. Ibid., pp. 923, 943; clerk memorandum to Harry A. Blackmun, undated, Blackmun Papers, Box 602.

63. *New York Times*, June 30, 1992.

64. *New York Times*, June 26, 1992.

65. Ibid.

66. Wright v. West, 505 U.S. 277, 303 (1992).

67. 505 U.S. at 310, n. 1; *New York Times*, July 3, 1992.

68. *New York Times*, July 3, 1992; Thomas R. Hensley et al., *The Changing Supreme Court: Constitutional Rights and Liberties* (Minneapolis: West Publishing, 1997), pp. 84–89.

69. Kiryas Joel Village School District v. Grumet, 512 U.S. 687 (1994); Abington v. Schempp, 374 U.S. 203 (1963).

70. Rosenberger v. Rector and Visitors of the University of Virginia, 515 U.S. 819, 863 (1995); Widmar v. Vincent, 454 U.S. 263 (1981); Westside Community Schools v. Mergens, 496 U.S. 226 (1990); Lamb's Chapel v. Center Moriches Union Free School Dist., 508 U.S. 384 (1993).

71. Employment Division v. Smith, 494 U.S. 872 (1990); Sherbert v. Verner, 374 U.S. 398 (1963); Wisconsin v. Yoder, 406 U.S. 205 (1972); Thomas v. Review Board, 450 U.S. 707 (1981); Hobbie v. Unemployment Appeals Commission, 480 U.S. 136 (1987); Frazee v. Illinois Department of Employment Security, 489 U.S. 829 (1989).

72. 494 U.S. at 289, 303–304, 293–94.

73. Madsen v. Women's Health Center, 512 U.S. 735 (1994); Bray v. Alexandria Women's Health Clinic, 506 U.S. 263 (1993).

74. Hurley v. Irish-American Gay Group of Boston, 515 U.S. 557 (1995).

75. Campbell v. Acuff-Rose Music, Inc., 510 U.S. 569 (1994); Alexander v. United States, 509 U.S. 544 (1993).

76. Shaw v. Reno, 509 U.S. 630, 682 (1993); clerk memorandum to Harry A. Blackmun, Blackmun Papers, Box 624.

77. Missouri v. Jenkins, 515 U.S. 70 (1995) (*Jenkins* III); Missouri v. Jenkins, 491 U.S. 274 (1989) (*Jenkins* I); Missouri v. Jenkins, 495 U.S. 33 (1990) (*Jenkins* II); Milliken v. Bradley, 418 U.S. 717 (1974); Adarand Constructors, Inc. v. Pena, 515 U.S. 200, 165 (1995); Fullilove v. Klutznick, 448 U.S. 448 (1980).

78. Stone v. Powell, 428 U.S. 465 (1976); Withrow v. Williams, 507 U.S. 680 (1993).

79. Arizona v. Evans, 514 U.S. 1, 18 (1995); Davis v. United States, 512 U.S. 452, 467 (1994); Brady v. Maryland, 373 U.S. 83 (1963); Kyles v. Whitley, 514 U.S. 419, 475 (1995).

80. Albright v. Oliver, 510 U.S. 266, 287 (quoting Poe v. Ullman, 367 U.S. 497, 543 [1961] [Harlan, J., dissenting]), 286, 287–88 (1994).

81. *Union Leader*, March 25, 1995.

82. *New York Times*, July 3, 1992; Glahn interview.

83. Snow interview.

84. *Connecticut Law Tribune*, July 11, 1994; Kiryas Joel Village School District v. Grumet, 512 U.S. at 708, 709.

85. United States v. Thompson/Center Arms Company, 504 U.S. 505, 517, n. 8 (1992); Mobile v. Bolden, 446 U.S. 55 (1980); Chisholm v. Roemer, 501 U.S. 380, 405

(1991); John Paul Stevens to Antonin Scalia, June 18, 1991, Blackmun Papers, Box 578.

86. David Garrow, "Justice Souter Emerges," *New York Times Magazine*, September 25, 1994, pp. 36–43, 52–55, 64, 67.

87. *New York Times*, July 3, 1992.

88. *New York Times*, October 25, 1992.

89. *St. Louis Post-Dispatch*, August 1, 1997. Souter's eulogy is available on the Web site of the Brennan Center for Justice, School of Law, New York University.

90. Glahn interview.

91. Harry A. Blackmun interview with James F. Simon, March 27, 1992, Blackmun Papers, Box 108.

92. David H. Souter to Harry A. Blackmun, October 15, 1992; a copy of the postcard is also in the Blackmun Papers, Box 1408.

93. Harry A. Blackmun to David H. Souter, March 26, 1992; David H. Souter to Harry A. Blackmun, March 27, 1992; David H. Souter to John Arnold, March 27, 1992; David Souter to Harry A. Blackmun, May 8, 1992. The letters and *Granite Monthly* "article" are in the Blackmun Papers, Box 1408.

94. Harry A. Blackmun to John Arnold, May 19, 1992, Blackmun Papers, Box 1408.

95. Mark Alan Waters to Harry A. Blackmun, March 3, 1993; David H. Souter to Harry A. Blackmun, March 19, 1993; David H. Souter to Harry A. Blackmun, July 12, 1993; Harry A. Blackmun to David H. Souter, December 13, 1994. The letters and cover page to the certiorari petition, on which Souter penned his note, are in the Blackmun Papers, Box 1408.

96. David H. Souter to Harry A. Blackmun, July 21, 1994. The letter and copy of the clerk's remarks are in the Blackmun Papers, Box 1408.

97. Harry A. Blackmun to David H. Souter, October 17, 1994; David H. Souter to Harry A. Blackmun, October 26, 1994, Blackmun Papers, Box 1408.

98. David H. Souter to David T. McLaughlin, September 30, 1991, Blackmun Papers, Box 1408.

99. Harry A. Blackmun to Alice H. Henkin, October 29, 1992; Alice H. Henkin to David H. Souter, September 8, 1993; Harry A. Blackmun to David H. Souter, October 17, 1994; David H. Souter to Harry A. Blackmun, October 25, 1994, Blackmun Papers, Box 1408.

100. David H. Souter to Harry A. Blackmun, December 4, 1992; David H. Souter to Harry A. Blackmun, May 17, 1993; David H. Souter to Harry A. Blackmun, July 22, 1996, Blackmun Papers, Box 1408.

101. E-mail, Wanda Martinson to Shelly Blincoe, December 1, 1997; David H. Souter to Harry A. Blackmun, April 8, 1998, Blackmun Papers, Box 1408.

102. David H. Souter, "A Tribute to Justice Harry A. Blackmun," *Yale Law Journal* 104 (1994): 5–6.

Chapter 5

1. *Concord Monitor*, February 12, 1996.

2. Ibid.

3. Gibbons v. Ogden, 9 Wheat. 1, 194–95, 197 (1824) (emphasis added); Wickard v. Filburn, 317 U.S. 111, 120 (1942) (Jackson, J.).

4. United States v. E. C. Knight Co., 156 U.S. 1 (1895); Lochner v. New York, 198 U.S. 45 (1905); Schechter Poultry Co. v. United States, 295 U.S. 495 (1935); Carter v. Carter Coal Co., 298 U.S. 238 (1936).

5. West Coast Hotel v. Parrish, 300 U.S. 379 (1937); National Labor Relations Board v. Jones & Laughlin Corp., 301 U.S. 1 (1937); United States v. Carolene Products Co., 304 U.S. 144 (1938); United States v. Darby Lumber Co., 312 U.S. 100, 124 (1941); Wickard v. Filburn, 317 U.S. 111 (1942).

6. Cleveland v. United States, 329 U.S. 14 (1946); Perez v. United States, 401 U.S. 146 (1971); National League of Cities v. Usery, 426 U.S. 833 (1976); Garcia v. San Antonio Metropolitan Transit Authority, 469 U.S. 528 (1985).

7. United States v. Lopez, 514 U.S. 549 (1995).

8. Ibid., p. 567.

9. Ibid., p. 564.

10. Ibid., p. 584.

11. Ibid., pp. 602, 603, 604, 605, 608, 614–15; National Labor Relations Board v. Jones & Laughlin Corp., 301 U.S. 1 (1937).

12. Printz v. United States, Mack v. United States, 521 U.S. 898, 905 (1997).

13. Ibid., p. 952 (footnote omitted).

14. Ibid., pp. 970, 971, 975.

15. New York v. United States, 505 U.S. 144 (1992).

16. 521 U.S. at 911–15 (emphasis in original).

17. Ibid., p. 972, n. 1.

18. Ibid., pp. 912, n. 5, 972, n. 1.

19. New York v. United States, 505 U.S. at 188 (emphasis added).

20. United States v. Morrison, 529 U.S. 598 (2000).

21. Ibid., pp. 607, 608, 609, 611, 612, 617–18.

22. Ibid., pp. 620, 626, 624; Civil Rights Cases, 109 U.S. 3 (1883).

23. Ibid., pp. 628, 634, 636; Heart of Atlanta Motel v. United States, 379 U.S. 241 (1964); Katzenbach v. McClung, 379 U.S. 294 (1964); Wickard v. Filburn, 317 U.S. 111 (1942).

24. 529 U.S. at 637, 646, 647.

25. Ibid., p. 654, quoting Robert H. Jackson, *The Struggle for Judicial Supremacy* (New York: Knopf, 1941), p. 160.

26. Ibid., pp. 654, 655, 627.

27. Seminole Tribe of Florida v. Florida, 517 U.S. 44 (1996): *Ex Parte* Young, 209 U.S. 123 (1908).

28. Hans v. Louisiana, 134 U.S. 1 (1890); Blatchford v. Native Village of Noatak, 501 U.S. 775, 779 (1991).

29. 517 U.S. at 74; Schweiker v. Chilicky, 487 U.S. 412, 423 (1988).

30. 517 U.S. at 78, 77, 99–100.

31. Ibid., pp. 127–28.

32. Ibid., pp. 166, 168; Lochner v. New York, 198 U.S. 45 (1905); Calder v. Bull, 3 Dall. 386 (1798).

33. 517 U.S. at 170, 184.

34. Alden v. Maine, 527 U.S. 706, 713 (1999).

35. Ibid., pp. 760–61; Chisholm v. Georgia, 2 Dall. 419 (1793).

36. 527 U.S. at 762, n. 1.

37. Ibid., pp. 763, 772, 773, 778, 781.

38. Ibid., pp. 795, 796, 801; Kawananakoa v. Polyblank, 205 U.S. 349 (1907).

39. Ibid., p. 811.

40. United States v. Causby, 328 U.S. 256 (1946); Batten v. United States, 371 U.S. 955 (1963); Pennsylvania Coal Co. v. Mahon, 260 U.S. 393, 415 (1922); Miller v. Schoene, 276 U.S. 272 (1928); Euclid v. Ambler Realty Co., 272 U.S. 365 (1926); Penn Central Transp. Co. v. New York City, 438 U.S. 104 (1978); Keystone Bituminous Coal Ass'n v. DeBenedictis, 480 U.S. 470 (1987).

41. Lucas v. South Carolina Coastal Council, 505 U.S. 647 (1992); Dolan v. City of Tigard, 512 U.S. 374 (1994).

42. Phillips v. Washington Legal Foundation, 524 U.S. 156 (1998).

43. 512 U.S. at 413; 524 U.S. at 172.

44. BMW v. Gore, 417 U.S. 559 (1996).

45. Ibid., p. 607.

46. Pacific Mutual Life Insurance Co. v. Haslip, 499 U.S. 1 (1991); TXO Production Corp. v. Alliance Resources Corp., 509 U.S. 443 (1993).

Chapter 6

1. *Wall Street Journal*, February 29, 2000; Rudman, *Combat*, p. 194.

2. *Union Leader*, March 2, 2000.

3. *Wall Street Journal*, May 16, 2000.

4. United States v. Morrison, 529 U.S. 598 (2000).

5. Books on the election and litigation include Alan M. Dershowitz, *Supreme Injustice: How the High Court Hijacked Election 2000* (New York: Oxford University Press, 2001); E. J. Dionne Jr. and William Kristol, eds., *Bush v. Gore: The Court Cases and Controversies* (Washington, D.C.: Brookings, 2001); David A. Kaplan, *The Accidental*

President (New York: HarperCollins, 2001); Larry J. Sabato, ed., *Overtime! The Election 2000 Thriller* (New York: Longman, 2002).

6. Bush v. Palm Beach County Canvassing Board, 531 U.S. 70 (2000).

7. Bush v. Gore, 531 U.S. 1046, 531 U.S. 98 (2000).

8. 531 U.S. 1046, 1047 (Stevens, J., dissenting); oral argument transcripts for Bush v. Palm Beach Canvassing Board and Bush v. Gore.

9. 531 U.S. at 112–13.

10. Ibid., pp. 134, 135.

11. Ibid., pp. 131, 132, 133.

12. Ibid., pp. 128–29, 158; *Boston Globe*, December 14, 2000; Charles Evans Hughes, *The Supreme Court of the United States* (Garden City, N.Y.: Garden City Publishing, 1928), p. 50.

13. 531 U.S. at 139, 140, 141.

14. Oral argument transcript, Bush v. Gore; *Pittsburgh Post-Gazette*, December 13, 2000.

15. *New York Times*, December 12, 2000.

16. New Hampshire v. Maine, 532 U.S. 742 (2001); *New York Times*, August 14, 2001; *Boston Globe*, August 18, 2001; Beazley v. Johnson, 533 U.S. 969 (2001); Beazley v. Cockrell, 534 U.S. 945 (2001); In Re Beazley, 122 S. Ct. 2322 (2002).

17. Evan Thomas and Michael Isikoff, "The Truth Behind the Pillars," *Newsweek*, December 25, 2000/January 1, 2001, pp. 46–47.

18. Kaplan, *The Accidental President*, pp. 291–93.

19. *Times-Picayune* (New Orleans), December 3, 2000.

20. Kaplan, *The Accidental President*, p. 284.

21. *Union Leader*, December 14, 2000.

22. Ibid.

23. *Union Leader*, December 2, 2000.

24. Crosby v. National Foreign Trade Council, 530 U.S. 363 (2000); American Insurance Association v. Garamendi, 123 S. Ct. 2374, 2393 (2003); Grier v. American Honda Motor Co., 529 U.S. 861, 894 (2000); Engine Mfgs. v. S. Coast Air Quality Manag., 124 S. Ct. 1756, 1765 (2004); Nixon v. Missouri Municipal League, 124 S. Ct. 1555 (2004); Tahoe-Sierra Preservation Council v. Tahoe Regional Planning Agency, 122 S. Ct. 1465 (2002); Florida Prepaid Postsecondary Education Expense Board v. College Savings Bank, 527 U.S. 627 (1999); Kimel v. Florida Board of Regents, 528 U.S. 62 (2000); Board of Trustees of the University of Alabama v. Garrett, 531 U.S. 356 (2001); Nevada Dept. of Human Resources v. Hibbs, 123 S. Ct. 1972 (2003); Tennessee v. Lane, 124 S. Ct. 1978, 1995 (2004).

25. Atwater v. City of Lago Vista, 532 U.S. 318 (2001).

26. Ibid., p. 344 (footnotes omitted).

27. Ibid., pp. 346 (footnote omitted), 347, 353 (footnote omitted), 354. In United

States v. Dominguez Benitez (2004) (slip opinion), Souter spoke for the Court in holding that in order to withdraw a guilty plea, a federal defendant who fails to make a timely challenge to a plea agreement must show a reasonable probability that, but for the claimed error, he would not have pleaded guilty in the first place.

28. 532 U.S. at 373, 372, 371, 354, n. 25.

29. County of Sacramento v. Lewis, 523 U.S. 833, 855 (1998).

30. Florida v. Bostick, 501 U.S. 429 (1991); United States v. Drayton, 122 S. Ct. 2105, 2116-118 (2002); Illinois v. Caballes, 125 S. Ct. 834, 839 (2005).

31. City of Indianapolis v. Edmond, 531 U.S. 32 (2000); Illinois v. Lidster, 124 S. Ct. 885 (2004); Veronia School District v. Acton, 515 U.S. 646 (1995); Board of Education v. Earls, 122 S. Ct. 2559 (2002).

32. Pennsylvania Board of Probation v. Scott, 524 U.S. 357, 370 (1998); Dickerson v. United States, 530 U.S. 428 (2000); Missouri v. Seibert, 124 S. Ct. 2601, 2610-11 (2004); United States v. Patane, 124 S. Ct. 2620, 2631 (2004).

33. Penry v. Lynaugh, 492 U.S. 302 (1989); Atkins v. Virginia, 536 U.S. 304 (2002); Roper v. Simmons (2005) (slip opinion).

34. Kansas v. Hendricks, 521 U.S. 346 (1997); Smith v. Doe, 123 S. Ct. 1140, 1155–56 (2003).

35. Rasul v. Bush, 124 S. Ct. 2686 (2004); Rumsfeld v. Padilla, 124 S. Ct. 2711, 2735 (2004) (footnote omitted).

36. Hamdi v. Rumsfeld, 124 S. Ct. 2633, 2659, 2660 (2004).

37. Poe v. Ullman, 367 U.S. 497 (1961); Washington v. Glucksberg, 521 U.S. 702, 767, 768, 761, 782, 789 (1997); Vacco v. Quill, 521 U.S. 793 (1997); Stenberg v. Carhart, 530 U.S. 914 (2000).

38. Bowers v. Hardwick, 478 U.S. 186 (1986); Romer v. Evans, 517 U.S. 620 (1996); Lawrence v. Texas, 123 S. Ct. 2472 (2003).

39. 367 U.S. at 552–53.

40. Troxel v. Granville, 530 U.S. 57, 75–76 (2000).

41. Elk Grove Unified School Dist. v. Newdow (2004) (slip opinion).

42. Santa Fe v. Doe, 530 U.S. 290 (2000); Good News Club v. Milford Central School, 533 U.S. 98, 138 (footnote omitted), 144–45 (2001); Lamb's Chapel v. Center Moriches School District, 508 U.S. 384 (1993).

43. Agostini v. Felton, 521 U.S. 203, 234 (1997); Aguilar v. Felton, 473 U.S. 402 (1985); School Dist. of Grand Rapids v. Ball, 473 U.S. 373 (1985).

44. 521 U.S. at 241, 242.

45. Mitchell v. Helms, 530 U.S. 793 (2000).

46. Ibid., pp. 912, 913.

47. Zelman v. Simmons-Harris, 122 S. Ct. 2460 (2002).

48. Ibid., p. 2485; 521 U.S. at 254.

49. 122 S. Ct. at 2486, 2491, 2497.

50. Ibid., pp. 2498, 2502.

51. Employment Division v. Smith, 494 U.S. 872 (1990); City of Boerne v. Flores, 521 U.S. 507, 565 (1997).

52. Boy Scouts of America v. Dale, 530 U.S. 640 (2000).

53. Ibid., pp. 701, 702.

54. National Endowment for the Arts v. Finley, 524 U.S. 569, 589 (1998).

55. Ibid., pp. 600–601, 603, 606, 608, 621.

56. United States v. American Library Ass'n, 123 S. Ct. 2297, 2319, 2320, 2321–22, 2324 (2000). In City of Littleton v. Z. J. Gifts (2004) (slip opinion), Souter filed a partial concurrence when the Court declined to subject a city adult business licensing ordinance to the strict procedural safeguards, including prompt final judicial review, required of motion picture censorship codes under Freedman v. Maryland, 380 U.S. 51 (1965). As the scheme at issue was "unlike full-blown censorship," he agreed that it did "not need a strict timetable of the kind required by *Freedman*." At the same time, he urged prompt disposition in the state courts of disputes arising out of the ordinance's enforcement. "Because the sellers may be unpopular with authorities, there is a risk of delay in the licensing and review process. If there is evidence of foot-dragging, immediate judicial intervention will be required, and judicial oversight or review at any stage of the proceedings must be expeditious."

57. Ashcroft v. ACLU (2004) (slip opinion). The case was previously before the Court in 2002, 534 U.S. 564.

58. City of Erie v. PAP's A.M., 529 U.S. 277, 316–17 (2000).

59. Grutter v. Bollinger, 123 S. Ct. 2325 (2003); Gratz v. Bollinger, 123 S. Ct. 2411 (2003).

60. Gratz v. Bollinger, 123 S. Ct. at 2440, 2441.

61. Ibid., p. 2442.

62. Shaw v. Reno, 509 U.S. 630 (1993); Miller v. Johnson, 515 U.S. 900 (1995); Shaw v. Hunt, 517 U.S. 899 (1996); Bush v. Vera, 517 U.S. 952, 1045 (1996); Easley v. Cromartie, 532 U.S. 234 (2001).

63. Vieth v. Jubelirer, 124 S. Ct. 1769 (2004); Davis v. Bandemer, 478 U.S. 109 (1986).

Epilogue

1. *News and Observer* (Raleigh, N.C.), June 5, 2003.

2. Snow interview.

3. *New York Times*, May 1, 3, 2004; *Washington Post*, May 2, 2004.

4. Glahn interview.

5. Ibid.

Index